Microsoft® Office PerformancePoint™ Server 2007

Microsoft® Office PerformancePoint™ Server 2007

Elaine Andersen
Bruno Aziza
Joey Fitts
Steve Hoberecht
Tim Kashani

WILEY

Wiley Publishing, Inc.

Microsoft® Office PerformancePoint™ Server 2007

Published by
Wiley Publishing, Inc.
10475 Crosspoint Boulevard
Indianapolis, IN 46256
www.wiley.com

Published simultaneously in Canada

ISBN: 978-0-470-22907-1

Manufactured in the United States of America

10 9 8 7 6 5 4 3 2 1

For general information on our other products and services or to obtain technical support, please contact our Customer Care Department within the U.S. at (800) 762-2974, outside the U.S. at (317) 572-3993, or fax (317) 572-4002.

Library of Congress Cataloging-in-Publication Data

Microsoft Office PerformancePoint server 2007 / Elaine Andersen . . . [et al.].
p. cm.
Includes index.
ISBN 978-0-470-22907-1 (paper/website)
1. Microsoft PerformancePoint server. 2. Performance — Management — Computer programs. 3. Business — Computer programs. I. Andersen, Elaine, 1971-
HF5548.4.M5257M53 2008
658.500285'55 — dc22

2008026306

Wiley also publishes its books in a variety of electronic formats. Some content that appears in print may not be available in electronic books.

To Mom and Dad, for your constant support and love. And to the rest of the gang: Camille, Darlene, Gary, Emily, Melissa, Jordan, Brandon, Frederic, Jodi, Greg, Emily, Aidan, and Mason. You're what makes it all worthwhile.

— Elaine Andersen

À Mamie, Papy Jo et Maman, à ma femme et mes enfants — merci de votre soutien constant et de votre amour inconditionnel.

— Bruno Aziza

First — to my wife Juliana and daughter Sophia, te amo muito! As always, to my family — Dad, Mom, Bob, and John — my love and deep appreciation for your continued support! I'd also like to thank my dear friends who have inspired me to take on bigger challenges and also to be a better person. Loke, Jake, Bruno, Ben, Eric, Brandy, John, Michele, Mikey, Paulo, Anderson, Maria Eliza, and the numerous friends who brighten my life — I have benefited from knowing such genuinely good-hearted and fun people. My time with close friends is precious, and I hope you know how much it means to me. Thank you!

— Joey Fitts

To my wife, Jannette, without whom I wouldn't have the support and foundation to challenge myself. To my wonderful children, Katie and Henry, who ensure there are never any dull moments. To my parents, Clint and Donna, sister, Lani, and brother, Randy, from whom I get nothing but support and encouragement. To all my colleagues on the PerformancePoint team who continue to inspire me by your passion and dedication to the product. I am grateful to work with such a talented team.

— Steve Hoberecht

To my loving wife Pamela and laughing son Timothy, who remind me daily that some things go way beyond anything we can plan, monitor, and analyze.

— Tim Kashani

About the Authors

Elaine Andersen is a senior program manager lead on the Microsoft Office PerformancePoint Server team at Microsoft. For the past two years, she has focused on the analytic and dashboard features of PerformancePoint, working with an experienced and talented team of program managers, developers, and test engineers.

Prior to joining Microsoft, Elaine was a program manager for ProClarity Corporation, a software company that developed business intelligence (BI) products for the Microsoft platform. During her 6 years at ProClarity, Elaine contributed to the ProClarity Desktop Professional, ProClarity Analytics Server, and ProClarity Live Server product lines as both a program manager and technical writer.

Elaine holds a master of arts degree in Technical Communication from Boise State University in Boise, Idaho, and a bachelor of arts degree in English from Brigham Young University in Provo, Utah.

Bruno Aziza has led marketing, sales, and operations teams at various technology firms, including Apple, Business Objects, and Decathlon. Bruno has worked and lived in France, the UK, Germany, and the United States, and holds a master's degree in business and economics from three European institutions.

He currently works on Microsoft's global business intelligence strategy and is the coauthor of *Drive Business Performance: Enabling a Culture of Intelligent Execution*.

Joey Fitts has consulted at over 25 of the Fortune 500 companies, guest lectured in Harvard's Executive Education programs, raised over $16 million in venture capital, and served on the board of advisors for InterVivos and the Computer Technology Industry Association (CompTIA).

He currently works on Microsoft's global business intelligence strategy and is the coauthor of *Drive Business Performance: Enabling a Culture of Intelligent Execution*.

Steve Hoberecht is a senior program manager lead on the Microsoft Office PerformancePoint Server team at Microsoft. He is responsible for the features and functionality of the application components targeted towards planning, reporting, and consolidation scenarios. Steve also supports the development and deployment activities of early adopter customers and partners.

Steve has been with Microsoft for 15 years and has occupied roles from finance to software quality to program management. Prior to his current role, he was test manager for data access components in Microsoft SQL Server. Steve began his career at Microsoft in the finance organization, where he occupied a variety of roles in accounting, operations, management reporting, and analysis.

Steve attended the University of Arizona and holds a bachelor of science degree in computer science from Seattle Pacific University.

Tim Kashani is the founder and CEO of IT Mentors, a Microsoft Gold Certified Partner. The company is a leading provider of technology consulting, custom training services, and learning content production. Tim and his team of technical professionals help organizations understand and apply Microsoft technology with the goal of increasing business productivity.

Tim was one of the first Microsoft Certified Trainers in the world. He also holds a bachelor of sciences degree in information and computer sciences and a master's degree in business administration from the University of California at Irvine. Tim's 22 years of experience in the training and consulting field have taken him to clients all over the world, including Asia, Europe, and many parts of the United States.

Tim has been involved in assessing the technical training needs of some of the country's major financial corporations and helping them implement corporate technology training universities. In addition to training, he has provided project coaching, architecture review, and project support to the chief information officers and senior engineers of these organizations. Tim's balanced blend of technical and business skills allows him to provide meaningful technology advice to CEOs, senior executives, and business leaders.

For the last five years, Tim has worked with Microsoft to develop and deploy their business intelligence offerings. He and his team created the official training material for Business Scorecard Manager 2005 and PerformancePoint Server 2007. They strive to educate the world on the value of the Microsoft BI platform.

Credits

Executive Editor
Bob Elliott

Development Editor
Kenyon Brown

Production Editor
Dassi Zeidel

Copy Editor
Foxxe Editorial Services

Editorial Manager
Mary Beth Wakefield

Production Manager
Tim Tate

Vice President and Executive Group Publisher
Richard Swadley

Vice President and Executive Publisher
Joseph B. Wikert

Project Coordinator, Cover
Lynsey Stanford

Proofreader
Kathryn Duggan

Indexer
Robert Swanson

Cover Image
© George Diebold/
Solus Photography/Veer

Acknowledgments

Many people contributed to the success of this product and this book. The PerformancePoint Server research and development, marketing, and sales teams combine great experience, unsurpassed passion, and amazing drive to do the right thing for customers.

To Rachel Vigier, without whom this book would never have been written.

To Ola Ekdahl for his deep technical experience and without whom IT Mentors would be far more boring (although we would have three more laptops and several more cell phones). Finally, to all the members of IT Mentors who helped (or were forced) to read draft after draft.

Steve Pontello and Alyson Powell Erwin are genuine experts in the world of analytics; they effortlessly blend the real world of business and decision making with the technical complexities of Multidimensional Expressions (MDX). Without their guidance, enthusiasm, and direction, we would all have had a much steeper mountain to climb. Many thanks to both of them for their always useful, always usable MDX samples and recommendations.

Much gratitude to Greg Bernhardt for his design expertise and tireless advocacy for elegant and usable designs. He inspires exceptional work and asks nothing less of himself.

Thanks to Josh Zimmerman, our security guru, for his patience with those of us who really have no clue how it works. And to Shannon House for her insight into how customers can be successful, and other valuable insights gained in the trenches. And to Rex Parker for his dashboard layout guidance and blog entries.

A special appreciation for the leadership and early vision of Lewis Levin, who began performance management efforts at Microsoft. To Peter Bull, who has continued to carry forward and develop the vision and ensures that the product delivers it. Peter has been instrumental in defining what is needed and why. To Oleg Ovanesyan for his counsel and help in relating core technical issues to business concepts and key stakeholders. Many insights and much inquiry into key aspects of a business application from a business user's perspective came from Eric Danas and Greg Parrott. To Mark Yang for the great partnership in delivering on the vision and the great debate and discussion of possible solutions.

Thanks for technical reviews from Patrick Baumgartner, Shelby Goerlitz, Nathan Halstead, Parul Manek, Srini Nallapareddy, Scott Sebelsky, Barry Tousley, and Roberta Vork. We sincerely appreciate all your help with content accuracy and guidance on communication.

To Michael Knightley, Elizabeth Smith, and Trevor Jones from Thorogood Associates for their contributions on how to effectively utilize partners and approach a performance management solution. We greatly appreciate the insights their over 20 years in the industry provided and are grateful for their contribution to this book.

Finally, thank you Bill Baker, Bob Lokken, Russ Whitney, Stephen Rauch, Kirk Haselden, Thierry D'Hers, Corey Hulen, Kevin Berens, Leif Brenne, Chen-I Lim, Melanie Swarner, Ramesh Arimilli, Carlos Veiga De Vincenzo, and, of course, Christine Bishop, Scott Allen, Ben Green, Tony Robinson, Tony Crowhurst, Nick Barclay, and Adrian Downes, and Guy Weismantel.

Contents at a Glance

Contents

Foreword

Writing a book is hard. That's why I write book Forewords. I do know that having passion is important to writing a good book. Passion carries you the distance, through the nights and weekends required to finish the book. Passion also drives the quality and depth of the book. Your authors have passion to spare. You'll see this and feel this as you read through *Microsoft Office PerformancePoint Server 2007*.

Performance management software is a relatively recent passion at Microsoft. We started our business intelligence journey with SQL Server Analysis Services (originally called SQL Server OLAP Services) and Microsoft Excel. We started there because we feel there is a logical evolution of BI in companies. That path starts with "sound data." If companies or organizations can't provide their employees and partners with data that is clean, integrated, consistent, and fresh, they are not able to provide the foundation for good decision making. At Microsoft, SQL Server is where structured data lives.

Once you believe you have sound data, the next step on our recommended path is to focus on personal and team insights. Your employees have the best sense of what is going on at "street level" in your organization. They frequently have hunches about the state of the business; more than upper management, they see daily what is working and what is not working. Insights come from hunches combined with data and experience. If your people can access the sound data you have built, using a tool they already know, they will form insights from their hunches and experience. If they can share those insights with others via a platform like SharePoint, your company will grow and improve.

All along, we wanted to grow the Microsoft BI stack into the performance management arena. Beyond insight comes decision making. Companies and organizations struggle to balance the agility and creativity a platform like

SQL Server, SharePoint, and Excel provides with accountability, alignment with strategy, and consistency with company processes and definitions. Once employees develop insights, companies want them to make sound business decisions that fit the company's strategy and processes. Performance management is the aspect of BI that records the company's business rules and definitions and relates business execution to the goals the company established.

We built PerformancePoint Server (PPS), the subject of this book, to provide critical performance management features in the Microsoft BI offering. PPS allows companies to manage the three key activities in performance management: plan the business, monitor the execution of the plan, and analyze variances from the plan. We call this Monitor, Analyze and Plan, or MAP. The order is explained well in *Drive Business Performance*: "This may seem backward, as it may seem logical that the first capability to be developed would be planning, since a plan is crafted before it is monitored and analyzed. However, the Monitor capability is listed first because most organizations are already in motion when they begin their performance management initiatives. They often first seek to have the ability to know 'what is happening.'"[1] MAP also happens to spell a word, PMA does not. . .and the key thing is to remember the three capabilities needed, not the order.

Bruno and Joey played key roles in the development and delivery of PerformancePoint. Bruno helped define the mission of the product and marketing strategy; Joey helped define the alliance and go-to-market strategy, recruiting a fine stable of global service partners to deliver successful customer deployments. I was lucky enough to collaborate with Joey and Bruno on this book as well as on *Drive Business Performance*. I have to say, I've not laughed so hard in a while. These guys had so much fun writing these books. Humor aside, they dedicated themselves to these two titles, and I think you'll agree that the high quality shows it.

Steve Hoberecht has been working on Microsoft BI for quite awhile, having helped us develop the SQL BI platform and then serving as a key leader in the development of PerformancePoint and aligning BI development efforts across the company. Elaine Andersen is one of our veterans from ProClarity who has driven the continued development of industry-leading analytics through PerformancePoint. She also played a key role in managing much of the manuscript development — and the authors. Tim Kashani and his company, IT Mentors, have helped to train the global Microsoft BI community on Microsoft's offerings, from SQL to Business Scorecard Manager to SharePoint and now PerformancePoint Server. His team has traveled the globe with us to ensure a readied ecosystem of customers and partners.

Numerous developers, testers, and program managers worked with the authors as they developed the chapters and then later did technical reviews. I will call your attention to two chapters in particular that illustrate the excellent collaboration between the product development team and your authors. In Chapter 19, the authors delve into best practices for implementing the monitoring and analysis phases of performance management. The vital tips and techniques come from our development team's knowledge of the product as well as the deep experience they attained while working with over 20 early PPS adopters. Chapter 20 is the analog for the planning phase of performance management.

I've often been amazed by the power of passion in any endeavor. The authors had the passion to create an excellent book on PerformancePoint Server 2007. They had the endorsement and the cooperation of the team that created PPS. And they had a great sense of humor throughout. It was my pleasure to help out in the small ways that I did. Enjoy this book, and profit from it.

Bill Baker
Distinguished Engineer
Microsoft Corporation, April 2008

Notes

1. Bruno Aziza and Joey Fitts, *Drive Business Performance: Enabling a Culture of Intelligent Execution* (Wiley, 2008).

Introduction

In late 2007, Bruno Aziza and Joey Fitts got together to write the book titled *Drive Business Performance: Enabling a Culture of Intelligent Execution* (Wiley, 2008). As they were completing their text, they saw an opportunity for a second book that directly applied the concepts presented in their book with the software capabilities in Microsoft Office PerformancePoint Server 2007. They envisioned this companion book as a unique bridge between business and technology, focusing on applying the principles of performance management through the framework of a software application. Subsequently, *Microsoft Office PerformancePoint Server 2007* was born.

Who Should Read This Book

Unlike many software books, *Microsoft Office PerformancePoint Server 2007* focuses on the business user, the person who needs to understand how a particular technology can help his or her organization succeed by adopting the principles of performance management. Although written for business users, the book doesn't focus exclusively on business concepts or theories. Instead, it presents the concepts needed to be successful with performance management as an integrated discussion with the capabilities of PerformancePoint Server.

Like the software itself, this approach bridges the technology and the business areas to ensure that organizations see the return on their investments in greater overall organizational accountability and alignment. We hope the benefits of this approach will be twofold: Readers will understand both the technology investments and the organizational investments they need to make to successfully implement performance management in their organization with PerformancePoint Server 2007.

To succeed in this goal, we brought together five authors who have been with the product from its early beginnings. Each author has in-depth experience with his or her area of the product, with customers, with performance management, and with enterprise-level businesses and organizations. They have seen all iterations of the product and understand the inspiration (and compromises) behind the concept, design, and implementation. They continually hear from those implementing the software about how to do it right and have consolidated all that shared learning to this book.

How This Book Is Organized

This book is organized into four sections. Part I, ''Performance Management and Microsoft PerformancePoint Server,'' answers the question ''Why should an organization invest in performance management with Microsoft Office PerformancePoint Server?'' Chapters 1–3 highlight the insights and recommendations of industry experts who recognize that effective performance management is pervasive performance management — reaching everyone from the individual contributor to the executive. It concludes by providing an overview of PerformancePoint Server and how it achieves this goal.

Part II, ''PerformancePoint Monitoring and Analytics,'' focuses on answering the questions ''How is my organization performing?'' and ''What are the driving forces behind this performance?'' These questions can be answered through the monitoring and analytics capabilities of PerformancePoint Server. Chapters 4–9 explain how to use performance dashboards to deliver actionable information to all users in the organization. The early chapters highlight the architecture of Monitoring Server as well as the components needed to deploy dashboards to Microsoft Office SharePoint Server. These chapters also go in-depth on building scorecards, analytic views, and dashboards. The later chapters highlight additional report types and security.

Part III, ''PerformancePoint Planning,'' focuses on answering the question ''How do I want my organization to perform?'' It explains how to use the planning capabilities of PerformancePoint Server to design and deploy planning and budgeting applications. Chapters 10–14 describe the overall system and how different users interact with the application at different times during the planning cycle. These chapters also explain how to write effective business rules and design effective forms and reports to enable all users to actively contribute to the planning process using Business Modeler and Microsoft Excel. Chapters 15–17 bring these concepts together by presenting an overall workflow and deployment strategy for planning applications.

The last section of the book, Part IV, ''Successfully Engaging Users in Monitoring, Analytics, and Planning,'' provides prescriptive guidance on how to be successful with PerformancePoint Server, using recommendations and tools from real-world customer deployments and experiences. The information presented in Chapters 18–20 is tailored to ensure that readers fully understand the key issues for achieving a successful performance management system in their organization.

Each part can be read independently of the other parts. For example, readers who are focused on planning and budgeting applications may want to spend their time primarily in Part III. Readers who want to gain a general understanding of performance management may start with Part I and then move to Part IV. Readers who are interested in a general overview of PerformancePoint Server may simply read the first couple of chapters in each part. Regardless, this book provides a comprehensive, business-oriented perspective of PerformancePoint Server and how it can be used to delivery accountability and alignment within organizations.

Microsoft® Office PerformancePoint™ Server 2007

Part I

Performance Management and Microsoft PerformancePoint Server

Microsoft Office PerformancePoint Server is a key component of the Microsoft performance management and business intelligence offering.

In the next two chapters, we describe how to think about Microsoft's business intelligence and how your company's considerations for performance can impact the type of solutions you might want to look for.

We expand on the concepts of personal, team, and corporate business intelligence and dive into the reasons that make Microsoft's approach so unique and different from the other options available.

We also look at the criterion that your end users are trying to address — the need for agility, flexibility, and productivity. Any business intelligence project should start with understanding what makes the end audience most efficient. Ultimately, your business intelligence solution is only going to be as effective as the people who use it. Is adoption an issue at your company? Did you start your project with the needs of the end users in mind? These first two chapters not only help you think about Microsoft's approach but also provide guidance for the types of scenarios in which your end users need to be able to perform. We provide you with a description of such a scenario with a before-and-after

PerformancePoint Server view, so you can truly envision what the solution can enable your organization to accomplish.

Additionally, we provide an overview of the key benefits that each end-user audience will get from performance management that is powered by PerformancePoint Server. We discuss flexibility, agility, and accountability — key concepts that are important to consider.

Chapter 2 also provides a quick view into the key capabilities provided by PerformancePoint Server — monitoring, analyzing, and planning. Why are they important? What should you consider when thinking about each of these? We provide a quick glance at some of the key functionalities provided by the solution. We hope that these first two chapters will act as a great introduction to the rest of the book.

Feel free to use some of the points made in these first two chapters with your colleagues on the business side, who might not know as much as you do about business intelligence and performance management. Then, expect to find much deeper descriptions, best practices, and details on how to use, deploy, and make the most of PerformancePoint Server starting in Chapter 3.

CHAPTER 1

Microsoft's Performance Management Strategy

There's no doubt that today's information era brings exciting opportunities to drive business performance. Information has never been more accessible, nor has it ever been less expensive. People need only do a quick Internet search to find pages and pages of Web sites, blogs, and documents that can provide them with all manner of information.

But as much as information has been a help in driving organizational performance, most of us today feel inundated by information. This situation directly affects how we make decisions. It drives our ability to achieve our own goals and objectives and affects how well we can execute them across teams inside and outside our organization. Ultimately, the way we use information has an impact on our organization's overall performance.

Only a few years back, the challenge was that people didn't have the capability to get to the information — the tools they had access to were rudimentary and limited; there were not enough data connections or network bandwidth, and often the information was locked behind firewalls. Today's challenge is the exact opposite. In fact, it has now become hard to corral the right information in time to help us do our jobs better.

The challenge for organizations, teams, and individuals today is to find a way to harness the power of information and make it work to their collective advantage.

Traditional Approaches to Business Intelligence

Business intelligence (BI) is not a new topic in the high-tech world. Since the first data warehouses and structured query languages were developed decades ago, people have been trying to find a way to make use of all the data and information they generate. As is the case with any immature technology, development and advancement has come in fits and starts. And as is usually the case, first came the general tools, such as SQL, to help access and aggregate the data. Then came the toolsets — specialized for industries and verticals, roles and functions, processes and certain-sized organizations — all to meet the same general need but focused on specific niches where the problem was most acute, and the market opportunity the greatest.

As is the case with most technologies, such as enterprise resource planning (ERP), when the software solutions became more advanced, it made more sense to start aggregating tasks again under one roof and one vendor. And one by one, the specialty vendors were bought, sold, and integrated into the larger BI vendors — let's call them pure plays. And while they too have now been bought, sold, and integrated, their legacy lives on and their approach has had a significant impact on how companies ultimately access, analyze, and share information.

For many years, these BI companies have talked a great deal about the overall market growth, penetration, and market opportunity they saw in front of them. Vendors rallied behind the idea that BI represents a lot of opportunity, that only about 20 percent of a typical organization uses BI, and that they were designing tools to access the other 80 percent. Then they'd release a new version of the product, and find themselves with the same users and the same penetration into a company. Why was this?

The problem with traditional BI approaches lies in the fact that they're ultimately able to access only a fraction of the information that people today need to become more productive and make better decisions. Traditional BI approaches are tied to the ERP system, the data warehouse, customer relationship management (CRM), and the many different transactional systems that they have all over the organization.

They're hard to use — and harder to maintain — and are often restricted to a few people or groups in the organization. Usage of the new system often peaks during the first few weeks after training, and eventually everyone drifts back to what they were using before, leaving the original 20 percent of the user population using a tool that was designed for 100 percent. Most often, the BI tools people are given don't reflect how they want to use information and make decisions.

Most BI tools make people conform to the tool's way of using information rather than the opposite, ultimately inhibiting productivity. Many people reading this book may have been to a BI training session in the past — and after a few weeks of trying to figure out how to go beyond the "basic" usage level of the system, have often gone back to their spreadsheets and "back of the napkin" calculations. Only the hard-core analysts — the people who are required to spend all their time with the data every day — are left. They're the ones who are willing to change the way *they* work since their jobs often depend on it. But analysts represent only a fraction of the total employee base in an organization. While analysts feel informed enough to make the right decisions, the rest of the organization often operates on hunches and gut feelings.

In *Drive Business Performance*, this dilemma is referred to as the ''Analytical Paradox'':

> *While analyts have the analytic capabilities to derive insights, they lack the ability to directly act upon these insights. Conversely, while employees have the ability to take action, they often lack the ability to derive insights by themselves. The result is that business analysts' request queues are overloaded on a daily basis, and employees end up making decisions which lack insight, timeliness, or both. This situation makes it impossible for organizations to quickly recognize and act upon changing market conditions — to be agile.*[1]

Business intelligence should reflect the way most employees use information — not the other way around. When it does, everyone in the organization can be empowered to make better business decisions. Putting BI capabilities in everyone's hands enables these critical decisions to be made locally, which makes them more relevant and immediate. It's this velocity of decision making that drives productivity and ultimately business performance.

A BI solution must have the flexibility to work the way that most employees do. And in looking at the way in which they do their jobs on a daily basis, we can categorize the use of BI into three main contexts: personal BI, team BI, and organizational BI.

Personal, Team, and Organizational BI

First, most often people use BI personally — just for themselves. This could be an Excel spreadsheet that they put together to see if a calculation still makes sense based on the ballpark numbers they received in an email. It could be a visual diagram that they created, a project plan that lets them know if they have the right resources to get the job done on time and under budget, an Outlook task list, a call sheet, a production report, and so forth. Whatever it is, it's not being shared with the board of directors, or maybe not even with their boss. It's for them, individually — and it's likely in the form of some sort of document or spreadsheet that they use to make themselves more productive.

Second, people work in teams. Employees can do all the individual analysis they want, but their own tasks should ensure that the team's goals and objectives are met as well. Even a sole proprietor has relationships with vendors, customers, and consultants — in most cases, individuals have to consider their impact on the rest of the team — whether they are part of a sales team in a retail store, a foreman on a factory line, and so on. The nature of team collaboration requires a business intelligence environment that allows individuals to work better within their group, or even across groups, to share information, and to ensure that everyone is on the same page. Team BI means that all individuals know where they stand with the most up-to-date information. They can make the right decision to help the team achieve its goals. More importantly, when we speak about teams, we mean to include the broadest possible definition of what constitutes a team. A team can range from the few colleagues who sit beside you in the row of offices on your floor or it can mean other people in the organization who do the same job that you do but whom you never have met. These people are not likely to ever be in the same place at the same time or even to know each other. But they're highly dependent on having the right information at the right time so that they make the right decision for the customer. Team BI means linking your teams together wherever they are, arming them with the right tools, and allowing them to share, collaborate, and manage information.

The last dimension is the corporate, or organizational, dimension of business intelligence. This represents the larger strategic goals and objectives set by the company, such as net profit, top-line revenue, and market share — the numbers that the entire organization is working to achieve. Teams may have different goals within this larger goal, but in this context, all teams are pushing towards the same objective. This type of BI is often developed and maintained centrally by the IT function so that everyone in the organization knows where they stand relative to their role in helping the company achieve its goals.

In order to support what people do on a regular basis — for themselves, their teams, and their companies — business intelligence needs to be thought of as a continuum of functionality required to help employees achieve their productivity and performance goals. The more formal part of BI — the corporate goals and objectives — influences what teams and individuals do. Personal and team BI are driven by the many knowledgeable workers across the organization and their needs for agility, speed, and empowerment.

In order for BI to reach its potential in organizations, it must have the flexibility and functionality to extend from the individual employee to the team and to the organizational level, while accommodating the different use cases and needs across the organization. Fundamentally, the ability to deliver on the promise of BI across the organization depends on three important factors: strong functionality, an integrated solution, and a scalable economic model.

Functionality

While far-reaching functionality is the most common item evaluated in a BI purchase decision, it is also critically important that a BI toolset provides tailored functionality for all the different users in the organization. If a BI suite offers so much functionality that it is too complicated for average users, or doesn't have enough horsepower for power users, the toolset will not be used. Further, the tool must be flexible enough to adapt to the needs of a diverse group of users. Flexibility and modularity are of paramount importance in selecting BI applications, as one size most definitely does not fit all when it comes to the needs and requirements of a diverse employee community for BI.

Aside from the analysts who work in different departments throughout the organization, most of employees don't spend their days inside a BI system — or an ERP, CRM, or supply chain management system. People work outside of the structured technology environment for much of the day — they meet customers, they respond to emails, they are out on the factory floor. But at those times when they need business intelligence, they need it immediately — they can't afford to interrupt the flow of their workday to learn a new tool or process. People need the BI system to adapt to what they are doing at the time and what they need the information for. That puts a huge emphasis on a full range of functionality that addresses both the power users — or employees who will spend most, if not all of their day in the BI environment — and those employees who will spend just a fraction of their time there. People don't want two different systems or two different interfaces or two different platforms to maintain for these user groups; they want one. And that's why an integrated BI solution is so critical.

An Integrated Solution

Achieving the promise of business intelligence requires the ability to pull data from virtually any data source, and the system must work well with line-of-business applications and desktop productivity tools, as well as email, portals, and document repositories.

Additionally, using the right tools and applications ensures that employees can use that data in the way they want to in order to make decisions rapidly and efficiently. They need applications and tools that range from personal to team, organizational, and corporate tools, with a familiar look and feel, integrated with elements of the employees' unstructured world such as email and documents.

Functionality and integration have quickly become the requirements for pervasive business intelligence and performance management. Many companies are now faced with the following dilemma: Now that the space has become consolidated and all vendors seem to have parity, why would I choose one over the other?

Microsoft's economic model is a strong differentiator because it helps companies move beyond their limitations. It is an asset that Microsoft has developed not only for business intelligence but also for just about anything the company sells.

The Economic Model

Microsoft was recently recognized as a leader in the BI space. While the recognition is recent, it rests on decades of work done on BI software as well as the BI model. From a software standpoint, the innovation in SQL Server and Office (Excel and SharePoint) as well as the recent release of PerformancePoint Server (PPS) point to this leadership.

In addition to software, Microsoft's unique approach can help companies reap the benefits of pervasive performance — improving performance throughout the organization. Microsoft's approach to BI and performance management can be summarized in a simple formula.

A Simple Formula

Here's a simple formula that illustrates the Microsoft value proposition:

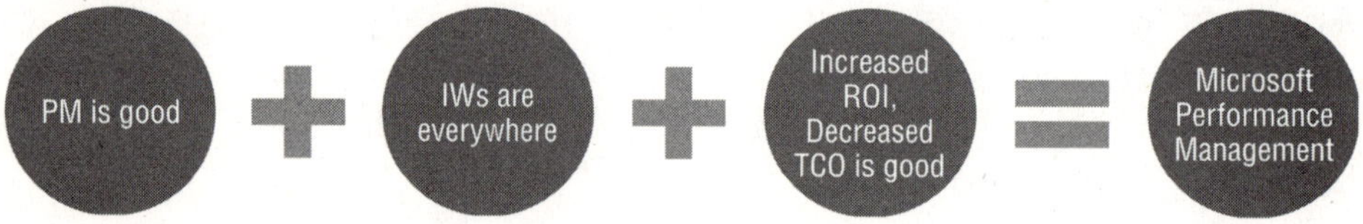

PM Is Good

The first premise of "why rely on Microsoft for performance management (PM)?" is that you believe that measuring what you manage, managing what you measure, and making data-driven decisions are all good things.

In an ever-increasing competitive, global economy, companies are tasked with continuing to compete at a world-class level — what got you here won't keep you there. Shareholders continually seek to see improved performance, and the competition continues to increase capabilities and value.

This is the starting point — these tenets are the foundation of the premise that Microsoft PM may be of value. Managing performance can only be of value if we value improving performance to begin with . . . hardly a controversial view.

IWs Are Everywhere

The difference with Microsoft's approach to PM is really in this component of the formula — the premise that people are making decisions throughout the entire organization, not just in the upper 1 to 5 percent of the organization where PM tools have historically been provided.

There are sometimes jokes about the lack of creativity in marketing from BI and PM software vendors — they all use the same language. "The right information, at the right time, in the right format'' is central to everyone's value proposition.

Two points that we think that are worth noting here are:

- ''Better information'' doesn't matter if results aren't improved — improved company performance is the whole reason for this entire endeavor of BI/PM.
- Empowering all employees requires a different approach, and this approach is what truly separates Microsoft from other vendors. Microsoft has always made the claim that information workers exist throughout the entire organization — and it is Microsoft's ability to serve this community that sets it apart.

Perhaps Randy Benz, CIO of Energizer Holdings, says it best in *Drive Business Performance*:

> *We used to have a view that only the top management members could deliver significant impact — we called these folks the ''difference makers'' and our IT efforts were geared toward getting information only to this select few. But not anymore. Now, we're aiming our efforts towards the hundreds of people across the organization who make the thousands of day to day decisions that really make the difference in business performance. We're getting new capabilities out to these ''difference makers'' across the enterprise — and recognizing wide scale increases in our effectiveness and impact.''*[2]

Increase ROI, Decrease TCO

This point seems self-evident ... and is also part of the standard marketing work of any vendor. Increasing the return on investment (ROI) for a customer of any technology is critical for any customer to be willing to make the investment ... and reducing a customer's total cost of ownership (TCO) is equally important.

Why would a customer lay out thousands or millions of dollars, pounds, euros, yen, or the like without knowing that they would get a greater return for the investment?

Changing the cost model is not new to Microsoft. In fact Bill Baker, Distinguished Engineer, Microsoft — the man who led Microsoft's entry into BI and the more recent PM push — continually makes this point:

> *Traditional inhibitors to the broad adoption of performance management have been high costs associated with implementations, complex tools and user interfaces that require costly and time-consuming training for employees, and confusion over disparate systems and tools for the various capabilities, including planning, budgeting, forecasting, analytics and scorecarding. Performance management tools and processes have also been siloed or stovepiped traditionally, meaning that they sit outside the day-to-day business processes of most employees.*

Office PerformancePoint Server 2007 was designed to address and wipe out these inhibitors, enabling performance management across the enterprise, not just for the CFO and financial analyst.

We plan to introduce Office PerformancePoint Server 2007 at an attractive per-user price point, pricing and licensing the performance management application for broad adoption. Probably the single most important differentiation from competitive offerings is that the complete capability set that includes scorecarding, analytics, planning, budgeting, forecasting, consolidation and financial reporting is delivered through Excel and other pervasive Microsoft Office products. These are the productivity tools that CFOs, financial analysts and information workers live in every single day. This limits or altogether eliminates the need for expensive training on complicated front-end business intelligence and performance management tools, and ensures that performance management is part of the rhythm of the business, not a process that lives outside it.''[3]

This approach has helped many companies think about their deployments differently. Although BI and PM could have been considered as departmental projects in the past, this new economic approach allows companies to expand the reach of their initiatives. This trend is particularly relevant to the ROI and TCO discussion.

As companies realize that all employees make decisions that have an impact on the company's bottom line, and that better results come from better information, the return on investment of empowering more employees grows. While in the past, companies might have empowered a few people — who, as discussed earlier, represent only a small fraction of the decisions made — these companies now have the opportunity to empower all.

This type of requirement calls for a different cost model and one that cannot be addressed by older and more traditional approaches to BI and PM. As Allen Emerick, Director of IT at Skanska, describes it:

We believe that business intelligence is for every individual in the organization because every individual needs to be able to make better, more informed decisions. . . . Microsoft business intelligence allows us to do that — and we have 2,000 employees using the solution. We expect to expand that to most of our 4,000 employees. We could never have done that with Hyperion.[4]

This model benefits companies, Microsoft, and its large ecosystem of partners. Phil Morris, CEO of Mariner, a Microsoft Gold partner summarized this best:

We are seeing a surge in deployments of Microsoft's BI solution from our customers. They are finding that they can enable BI throughout their organizations by expanding their Microsoft BI footprint only minimally, building on the investments in Microsoft that they've already made. We are also seeing our customers replace their BI pure-play solutions with Microsoft's solution, for no more cost than what they used to pay for the BI pure-play vendors' annual maintenance fees alone. With the Microsoft BI solution, they report overall cost savings and high user acceptance rates because employees are able to access, share and collaborate using the familiar interfaces of Word, Excel, SharePoint, and Outlook.[5]

Indeed, it is particularly true that Microsoft can meet the requirements of increasing the ROI and decreasing the TCO component of the equation based on their existing licensing model with customers.

And their customers have been looking to consume their BI/PM offerings in the same way. For the new PM offerings, Microsoft is taking a similar approach to what they did with the now large base of customers who are currently using their SQL BI platform. We will discuss Microsoft's pricing and licensing strategy for BI/PM in more detail later.

Beyond Microsoft's economic model and the benefits this brings to partners and companies alike, it is also important to note that Microsoft is in the business of information workers at its very core.

The Information Worker – The Core of Microsoft's Business

Peter Drucker coined the term ''knowledge worker'' in his book *Landmarks of Tomorrow*, published in 1959, to refer to the transition of the type of work that would be done by American laborers going forward within the century, moving from manual labor in factories to knowledge work.

Microsoft uses the term ''information worker'' to describe the large number of employees throughout an organization. It can be argued that there are more ''information workers'' than ''knowledge workers.''[6] However we will use these terms interchangeably throughout this book. Jeff Raikes, president of Microsoft's Business Division,[7] described an information worker as ''anybody who is an active participant in a business information flow or business information process.''

The Information Worker business unit delivers about $18 billion in revenue to Microsoft annually, or around one-third of its total revenue, and Microsoft's service and attention to this community are unparalleled. In addition to a development team that is focused on the user interface (UI) and that was responsible for developing the Office Fluent user interface, Microsoft's Office development organization has a dedicated user experience group called the Office Design Group, which focuses on the usability and design elements of the Office user interface.

The user experience research team conducts research to inform the design of the entire Office suite, and works with the Office development teams and UI designers to help create usable software that is designed to meet the needs of information workers. Over the years, the team has developed a deep and thorough understanding of the broad range of Office customers. The close connection between the usability research and design ensures that the UI design is tested and informed by customer research.

The team uses a variety of methods to test the user interface, including in-lab studies in which people are observed using Office to perform specific tasks, eye-tracking studies using equipment that actually lets the team see where people are looking on the screen as they use the programs, and workplace observation where the team watches people use Office and talks to them about their experience using Office. To gain deeper insight into people's levels of satisfaction with the Office Fluent user interface, the research team conducts focus groups and large-scale surveys. These types of research were extremely useful in helping the team develop a clear understanding of the sources of dissatisfaction that were most often expressed as ''bloat'' and address them in Office 2007.

The Customer Experience Improvement Program (CEIP) is a voluntary, opt-in program that collects anonymous information about errors, system performance, and frequency of command usage. The analysis of this broad, rich instrumentation data marked a significant advance in Microsoft's ability to understand and react to real-world use and scenarios.

As with most instrumentation systems, Microsoft has no insight into users' goals or the specific words, numbers, or objects that make up most of a user's content. But, looking across multitudes of users and analyzing how frequently commands are accessed and from where in the UI, they began to understand overall usage patterns. Microsoft used these general patterns to further inform their understanding of how commands were being used: how many people used a feature, how frequently it was used, and from where in the UI it was typically accessed. With observational and personal feedback data, Microsoft is able to begin to identify areas which, if improved, would have the greatest impact, plus it has gained insights into what those improvements might be.

The research is ongoing and continuous. For the launch of the 2007 Office system, this team conducted extensive research to continue to ensure a deep understanding of the information worker:

- Since Office 97, they have engaged 5000+ people in in-lab studies to evaluate the usability of Office.
- They have 26,000 hours of video-taped usage (Office 2000 to Office 2003). If you wanted to watch the tapes of every usability lab study they've done on Office 2000, XP, and 2003, it would take you over 3 years.
- For Office 2003 alone, they spent 3,500+ hours observing people use the software in their workplaces and in the teams' labs.

With this amount of customer feedback and involvement, the information worker community itself actually plays a key role in defining the very offerings Microsoft delivers and ultimately uses. Given the revenue impact of, deep relationship with, and size of this community of Microsoft users, it is clear that the information worker is core to Microsoft's business. In summary, when customers buy business intelligence and performance management from Microsoft, they benefit from the software, the unique economic model, and the unparalleled experience the company has in the information worker's world.

Regardless of which component of the equation you optimize for — whether you care more about "PM is good," optimizing for the total number of information workers you want to enable with PM capabilities, or the degree to which you want to increase ROI or decrease TCO — Microsoft's value becomes increasingly apparent.

Summary

In this chapter, we covered some of the key fundamentals of Microsoft's performance management and business intelligence capabilities.

We talked in detail about the traditional approaches to business intelligence and how Microsoft's unique approach to personal, team, and organizational BI can help your organization provide business intelligence for all types of uses.

Finally, we covered some of the key differentiators of the Microsoft value proposition and addressed what makes Microsoft a great source to help you address all your performance management and business intelligence needs, such as its economic model and its core knowledge of the information worker's world.

Notes

1. Bruno Aziza and Joey Fitts, *Drive Business Performance: Enabling a Culture of Intelligent Execution* (Wiley, 2008).
2. Ibid.
3. See `www.microsoft.com/presspass/features/2006/dec06/12-05performancepoint.mspx`.
4. See `www.microsoft.com/presspass/features/2007/may07/05-09BusinessIntelligence.mspx`.
5. See `www.microsoft.com/presspass/press/2006/sep06/09-22BIMomentumPR.mspx`.
6. See `www.directionsonmicrosoft.com/sample/DOMIS/update/2002/10oct/1002iwfonc.htm`.
7. See `www.microsoft.com/presspass/exec/jeff/default.mspx`.

CHAPTER

2

Microsoft PerformancePoint Server Fundamentals

As you saw in the last chapter, business intelligence takes many different forms, according to how people want to use information, how connected they need to be to what's going on above them, and what the information is going to be used for.

No single tool is meant to accommodate the infinite and changing ways in which we use data to make business decisions. To the contrary, companies need a flexible set of tools and applications that combine into a single solution.

Trusting Your Data — The Business Intelligence Platform

The bane of many business intelligence (BI) projects has been a lack of trust in the data we put in front of end users. They may use it once, and they may even use it a second time, but if they don't believe the numbers in front of them, if they don't get the numbers in time to use them, or if they can't make out what the data is trying to tell them, inevitably they'll drift back to what they were using before. This is why IT directors everywhere have spent a significant amount of time, budget, and resources on ensuring data integrity and integration across the entire enterprise.

Microsoft addresses this fundamental issue with its industry-leading data management and BI platform capabilities found in SQL Server. SQL Server provides a trusted data platform that integrates data from anywhere — be it structured sources like databases, ERP systems, general ledgers — wherever! And it does so in a fashion that gets the data where it needs to be, in a vast array of formats that fit the use case in mind — individuals, teams, or aligning the entire organization.

How SQL Server does this, in addition to its pure database management capabilities, is reflected in three key BI components within the product: integration, reporting, and analysis.

In SQL Server Integration Services, data from both structured and unstructured data sources is brought together seamlessly, finding its way to reports, dashboards, and metrics throughout the organization. And just as important as ensuring that data sources as disparate as spreadsheets and general ledgers are brought together is the timeliness with which this process takes place. After all, few people read yesterday's news (unless they're looking for something specific) — people want what's current, what's actionable. Effectively integrating data helps ensure that they achieve this goal.

Once the data is integrated, where does it all go? What form does it take in order to actually be actionable? For many people, it takes the shape of reports, which is where the second key business intelligence feature of SQL Server comes into play: SQL Server Reporting Services. Providing a range of documents from highly formatted and structured reports used for regulatory filings and financial statements, to ad hoc reports used by analysts and end users to find one number, the reporting capabilities within SQL Server have to be as flexible as the use cases for the information. With the 2008 version of the product now available, report authors, designers, and end users have a huge array options and alternatives to ensure that data gets to where it needs to go, in the right format for both the user and the occasion.

When people need to do more than just report on data and go beyond the surface-level information that a report can provide, they need to dig into the data and answer those pesky "why" questions: Why are sales going down? Why are lead times for this product taking longer than that one? Why aren't these budget figures adding up? All these questions require people to analyze data, ask questions of it, and root around to find connections and reasons. People need an efficient way to organize the data and facilitate this type of analysis.

The third component of SQL Server business intelligence includes analysis services, using the industry-leading (as rated by The OLAP Report[1]) SQL Server Analysis Services functionality. Built on top of the SQL Server database, Analysis Services allows users the ability to move around the data quickly and efficiently organize it so that employees can find the answers to their questions. In addition, SQL Server provides data-mining and other powerful capabilities that allow employees to take action far more quickly than conventional relational databases could ever hope to do.

Personal BI and Individual Productivity

Once the data is integrated, organized, and reportable, people can turn to how they want to use that data. Throughout the day, people need to work with BI as individuals, in a personal way; they need BI to help with personal tasks and projects.

There is no better product to accomplish this than Microsoft Excel, part of the Office family of products and applications. Excel is clearly the most frequently used personal BI tool on the market today — just look at the lengths to which other vendors go to connect to Excel. Most vendors today know that few employees actually spend time "inside" the BI tool — they want the data but in a tool that they know how to use and can manipulate to do their jobs.

Whether it's organizing table information or adding up sums and totals, Excel quickly and easily helps end users make sense of the information in front of them and get it into a format that allows them to move forward with their day. Advanced users can turn Excel into a highly sophisticated business intelligence tool as well. From its pivot table capabilities and charting options to its own slicing and dicing capabilities, the sky's the limit when it comes to using this most versatile of BI products.

Beyond powerful spreadsheet capabilities, the Office System of products provides other personal BI capabilities as well — from the data visualization capabilities within Visio to the flowcharting and resource intelligence gathering in Project to the mapping capabilities found in MapPoint.

All three products serve as a powerful supporting cast that helps individuals ensure that they are focused on utilizing information from reports and databases in the most efficient manner, which allows them to maximize their productivity and effectiveness within the organization.

Team BI Tools and Collaboration

People don't spend all their time on individual projects. Eventually, they must interact with the outside world — their teams, their vendors, and their customers — in some form or fashion.

We're all quite familiar with the challenge of integrating information from multiple spreadsheets and versions of reports. We never seem to get on the same page, and end up making wrong decisions, all because we don't all have the same information on which to base our decisions in the first place.

Microsoft SharePoint Server helps solve that problem. As one of the fastest-growing portal applications in the market today,[2] SharePoint brings individuals together and starts the flow of information sharing within the four walls of the organization, as well as with people outside.

Team BI requires that the team have a common starting point on which to base its analysis. Individuals may not end up with the same conclusion, but they need to have a common starting point if they are to live up to the ideal of having "one version of the truth." SharePoint allows teams and groups to share information, and increases the velocity of decision making inside and outside of the organization.

Using the Excel Services feature in SharePoint, employees can make changes and update information in their spreadsheets and change them from static documents to live reports, ensuring that they have the most up-to-date information on which everyone can base their decisions. In addition, SharePoint allows these individuals to connect their spreadsheets to multiple data sources more easily than ever before.

Collaboration is becoming increasingly critical to business success today. After all, it's not just the people in the next cubicle or office that we need to ensure are on the same page as us — it's the team across campus, across the country, and in many cases, across the world that needs to have the same information as we do.

SharePoint aligns teams of all shapes and sizes to ensure that they are all operating efficiently without more formal and structured corporate goals and metrics — think sales team targets as opposed to sales organization targets. SharePoint lets employees easily work together and speeds decision making in a team environment.

Corporate BI and Alignment

No matter what our individual and team goals are, they flow both up to and down from the corporate strategy goals set by the company.

This is where Microsoft PerformancePoint Server steps in, with its monitoring, analyzing, and planning capabilities that extend from individuals and teams through everyone in the company.

Increasingly, companies are adopting metrics en masse, as BI technology ensures that information is readily available. In most cases, these metrics — whether they're formally developed through management methodologies, such as the Balanced Scorecard, or they're informally developed within the organization — are viewed through the ubiquitous dashboard, which can ensure that the key performance indicators of the organization are visible to everyone.

Beyond just seeing how things are progressing, employees need to have the capability to take action. While that action may range from viewing a report to calling a coworker or boss, in many cases there's a need to go a bit deeper and analyze the reasons behind a red flashing light or an arrow that's pointed the wrong way.

The analysis capabilities of PerformancePoint Server allow people at all levels of the organization to utilize sophisticated techniques and models to perform causal analysis and develop trends that help predict future behavior, all with an eye on finding the answer quickly and taking action.

Much of the action that people would like to take is predicated on knowing where things stand. And knowing where things stand is largely a function of ensuring that you have a good plan in place. Whether it's for a sales plan, an operations plan, or the financial plan for a company, with PerformancePoint Server's planning capabilities, it's never been easier to assemble information and then compare it with the actual results as they come in, to determine if the alignment you need within your organization is actually being achieved.

With its easy-to-use Excel and SharePoint interface, combined with the back-end IT control and administration capabilities, PerformancePoint is being adopted by organizations around the world to quickly and effectively assemble plans and budgets, forecast results, and then, based on the monitoring and analysis capabilities in the product, take proactive action when it's needed to ensure that the company stays on track and achieves its goals and objectives.

How Does the PerformancePoint Server Story Come Together?

In this section, we explore performance management in detail. More specifically, we discuss the key imperatives that companies have when it comes to managing performance. The ability to monitor, analyze, and plan activities better drives business performance.

- **Monitoring** — The ability to understand what has happened and what is happening (typically addressed through reports and dashboards)
- **Analytics** — The ability to understand why things are happening (typically answered through analytics, data mining, and other means)
- **Planning** — The ability to understand what we want to happen next (often addressed through plans, forecasts, and budgets)

Very few organizations have an integrated solution that covers all three of these activities. Indeed, most companies have traditionally used a collection of vendors and applications to get to their answers. This approach not only creates multiple levels of integration across applications but also confuses end users by providing them with too many applications and interfaces.

According to the Hackett Group, organizations typically have an average of "10 general ledger systems, 12 different budgeting systems and 13 different reporting systems."[3]

In order to better elaborate on our points — let's take a look at what performance management typically looks like at any company. Notice that our description, which follows, does not focus on the technology involved but rather on the people empowered and the process they are involved in.

It's forecasting time at ABC company, and analysts, information workers, and company executives are looking forward to completing the forecasting process as soon as possible.

In the example that follows, the organization does *not* own PerformancePoint Server. What does this typical process looks like?

The Analysts

Analysts live and breathe by using Excel to model, analyze, and forecast business scenarios. Whether these individuals are in finance, in business units, or even in IT, they have a sense of where information is stored. They need to gather this information prior to starting the process of completing the forecast.

The information might be scattered across the organization, but business analysts typically work with IT to make sure that they get the right level of information from both a dimensionality and an aggregation standpoint. For instance, if information needs to go to a German employee, it needs to be data that is relevant and actionable for this individual in Germany (that is, the information that is intended for a German audience is in euros and so on). Once the business analysts have the information, they typically need to package it in a way that they can use to solicit contributions from others. They also need to aggregate the information (again, typically using Excel) at a level where they can consolidate, analyze, and ultimately load it back into the financial forecast system.

Our research and experience shows that, more often than not, the forecast process starts in Excel. It depends on hours of manual intervention — it is often slow, unreliable, and error-prone. In fact, a large portion of organizations follow the same process, and using Excel as just described, "between 50 percent and 60 percent of large enterprises still use Excel as their primary budgeting solution, while many also rely on Excel for financial consolidation."[4]

What happens next? Well, once the analysts have put the information they need into their spreadsheets, they have to send personalized spreadsheets to contributors across the organization and gather their forecast information.

The Contributors

Contributors typically work in the branch offices in the field, not in the corporate offices but closer to the operations of the business. These individuals may run a business in a local geography, but it is their input that is required in order to keep the forecast accurate and tied to day-to-day operational needs. Note that "contributor" here is not a full-time job. Contribution is just part of the individual's job.

These individuals are closer to the business than the analysts. They are in fact the best people to contribute the forecast numbers — often they are the ones being held responsible for the numbers. Unfortunately, the template sent by the corporate business analysts doesn't fit their local requirements, so the contributors make a few changes to the template, complete it, and send it back. Often, these contributors will have done some preparatory work and filled out the forecast sheets from corporate ahead of time. They might have their own databases outside the centralized data sources of IT.

When the business analysts receive the completed forecast sheets, they aggregate them across all business units so that they can analyze the numbers. In order to complete this consolidation, analysts might need to understand some of the changes that the contributors have made, so a back-and-forth exchange starts between contributors and analysts to try to stay synchronized. This back-and-forth process is exacerbated by the complexity of the business units — some might have multiple currencies or local data hierarchies that need to be matched with their corporate equivalent.

Often, this iterative process creates tension between corporate and the business units, which is only amplified by the pressure associated with completing the forecasting process — the original and ultimate goal of the entire exercise. Remember, that was what we were trying to get done.

The Executives

Executives might not be included in the process of consolidating the forecast. They might be C-level employees: They hold the ultimate profit and loss accountability for business groups, and they are interested in seeing the forecast completed as soon as possible, accurately.

The questions they ask relate to the overall health of the business. They might be less interested in the planning process and more interested in monitoring the progress of the business against the agreed-on plans and analyzing projections. They often ask for scorecards, dashboards, or even strategy maps to put the given forecast into the broader company context.

When a forecast process is as manually intensive as the one just described, it often becomes error-prone and slow. Additionally, the linked spreadsheets, manual consolidation, and large amount of moving parts make it virtually impossible for the analysts or the IT department to build a sustainable model to deliver high-quality monitoring and analytical capabilities to the executives. Frustration and disappointment can be high among executives.

Most executives seem to agree with Jack Welsh, former CEO of General Electric, who called forecasting, budgeting, and planning "the bane of corporate America."[5] Executives often question the value of the process and activity to which the organization dedicates such a large quantity of resources and time without achieving noticeable return on investment (ROI). Resolving these issues is not a trivial project. However, even before introducing the technology in this example, one has to think about the needs of each constituent. What do the analysts want? What do the contributors care about, and what do the executives expect from a complete performance management solution?

Executives care about better business performance. This translates into running their business with high agility, while driving accountability and alignment across the organization. They are conscious that changing business conditions may alter their ability to accelerate the decision-making process across their divisions, so they look for integrated and flexible applications. The length of processes such as forecasting exasperates them, and they have a hard time understanding why access to information isn't more fluid across the organization. They also witness business units working on various, sometimes conflicting, agendas and look for effective performance management to bring everyone together across divisional silos.

Contributors care about contributing to better performance by increasing their own productivity and their team's output. They currently spend too much time working for the data rather than working with information. Contributors look for a solution that is integrated with their daily routine so that, when forecasts are due, they don't have to stop everything to complete them.

Business analysts and the IT staff running the forecast process want to enable more information workers to contribute to performance by reducing the complexity of the process. While they have to reduce complexity, their imperatives are to maintain compliance, security, and audit ability. They need to make sure that the system enabling the process is flexible but also adheres to the company standards in terms of security and information access.

Sound familiar? Microsoft Business Intelligence and PerformancePoint Server in particular have been built in light of these requirements. In order to make it easy to comprehend the solution's benefits, let's see how this offering would address the issue of forecasting highlighted previously.

Each constituent of the forecast process will enjoy the following benefits:

- Technologists will benefit from the application's flexibility, security, and auditability capabilities.
- Analysts and contributors will particularly enjoy the product's collaborative, user-friendly, contextual advantages.
- Executives will be able to take advantage of the technology to drive better alignment and accountability throughout their organization.

Flexibility, Security, and Auditability

As described earlier in this chapter, Microsoft Performance Management enables analysts or IT staff to manage and build a system that will empower more employees to contribute to business performance while still adhering to the organization's security and audit standards.

In the specific forecast example chosen earlier — analysts have to extract information from source systems and dump it into Excel, where manual intervention is required. With PerformancePoint Server, these same analysts use the Modeler to build the attributes of a good forecast: dimensions, measures, hierarchies, scenarios security, and cycle management. The Modeler's functionality and benefits are reviewed in further detail throughout the book, particularly in Part III.

In a few words, the Modeler allows analysts to take the information that they would have previously put in a spreadsheet into a database. This new approach allows analysts to build a model that can scale better and remain secure and auditable (rather than manage their forecast in a spreadsheet, the forecast is managed in a database). Once the analysts are satisfied with their models, and they need the information workers to contribute to the forecast and submit their numbers, they will appreciate the application's usability advantages.

Collaborative, User-Friendly, and Contextual

Ease of use is one of the biggest hurdles for enterprise-wide adoption. In order to adopt a new technology, information workers need to be presented with that new technology within the applications they trust and that they already know how to use.

This is why PerformancePoint Server's end-user application is Excel, an application business that users already know and trust. Employees can work in Excel with the information that is the most relevant to them at the time of the forecast.

Additionally, instead of letting information workers create a multitude of spreadsheets, as they might otherwise do, the solution provides templates for worksheets according to the rights, roles, and security level of these contributors. For example, if a user is German, he or she should be able to forecast in euros. Ultimately, if the entire organization has standardized on reporting information in dollars, for example, the application will take care of consolidation into the appropriate currency, using the Modeler's rules and calculations.

The key difference to notice here is that PerformancePoint Server streamlines the interaction between analysts and contributors, removing the need for unproductive back-and-forth exchanges or the need to manually adjust spreadsheets because of requirement differences between corporate and local subsidiaries.

The application provides contributors with the most relevant information, in the format that is familiar to them. Then, if need be, the application translates the information back to the format that is most relevant to the corporate analyst. The server also manages the cycle of forecast submissions and approvals.

In the end, the application can help shorten the time to close and can make it easier for analysts to run the contribution process. It enables this while ensuring contributors' adoption, which will help ensure the accuracy of the numbers submitted. Once plan numbers are created, a good performance management system should allow managers to easily monitor and analyze the plan and the actual results. This is where the application's unique ability to use the information created comes into play.

Aligned, Actionable, and Accountable

Executives need to be able to monitor and analyze their business performance, which they often do through reports, dashboards, and scorecards. Most of their interaction occurs while working with their dashboards.

Confidence in the information presented from these dashboards is increased by the sheer fact that, with PerformancePoint Server, plans, dashboards, and analytics are integrated in the same product. This confidence allows executives and managers not only to take action based on the information but also to use the information to drive better alignment and accountability up, down, and across the organization.

Monitor, Analyze, and Plan

Monitor, analyze, and plan represent the key processes that organizations deploying and using performance management are involved in.

The premise behind PerformancePoint Server is that organizations will get the most value by deploying all three capabilities (monitor, analyze, and plan), but they can choose to deploy only the monitoring, analyzing, or planning capability, depending on where they are in terms of performance management needs and maturity.

Monitor

Monitor refers to the monitoring of performance across an organization. It answers the questions that individuals, groups, and organizations ask about performance, such as: "What is happening?" or "What has happened?"

Performance monitoring is best served by applications such as scorecards, reports, or dashboards.

Dashboards are named after car dashboards, which drivers glance at for key information on how their travel is going and things they need to know to operate the car: how fast they're going, how much gas they have, and alerts to potential problems (such as "oil change needed"). Similarly, a dashboard provides information on how the organization is performing.

While scorecards, dashboards, and reports might serve different audiences and purposes, the types of questions answered by monitoring applications are often about the past. They can sometimes display forecast information, but most end users think of monitoring applications as the entry point for answering their performance management questions: "How have I or we performed?" or "How has my company performed?"

End-User Experience and Information Portability

A key differentiator of the PerformancePoint Server application is that it utilizes performance management features and functionality within the familiar Office environment. When individuals need to know how their department is executing a plan, they open up their performance dashboard right from their internal portal site. There, along with information such as documents, PowerPoint presentations, and other relevant information (we call all these types of data "unstructured" data), they find a performance management page, which allows them to monitor the progress of their operation.

There are quite a few key benefits to providing simplified end-user adoption and utilization of these performance management features in an environment with which they are familiar. (For those interested in adding to your industry jargon, this is referred to as "consumption": the way information is consumed by end users. For example, "PerformancePoint Server provides a great consuming experience.")

- **People use a single application instead of swapping back and forth among multiple applications.** Employees do not need to navigate among a variety of systems and applications to find the information they need. Because PerformancePoint Server is integrated with SharePoint out of the box, people can find the information they need, structured and unstructured, right there in the applications they already know.
- **People can consume the information in the format they want.** PerformancePoint Server interfaces integrate with ASP.NET and Reporting Services out of the box. While many organizations have chosen to couple PerformancePoint Server with their SharePoint deployment, some organizations might want to deploy performance dashboards with non–Microsoft Web interfaces. They can do so by using the ASP.NET technology or even by deploying their scorecards to Reporting Services. This functionality is available out of the box, so it is very easy for IT departments to decide which delivery mechanism to use.
- **This solution provides flexibility in how performance management is delivered to employees.** The fact that PerformancePoint Server offers integration with ASP.NET, SharePoint, and Reporting Services provides great flexibility for end-user consumption scenarios. For instance, if end users need to see information in a connection environment over the Web, they can use SharePoint; if they need to see their scorecards in a disconnected environment (when Internet is not available), they

can export their scorecards from Reporting Services into formats other than HyperText Markup Language (HTML), such as PDF, GIF, and others. This provides a great deal of flexibility to end users and allows IT to cover the various needs of their diverse audience. This last point highlights a key benefit of this solution: portability.

Information Consistency

A key challenge of driving performance is the ability to deliver information consistently. We often talk about "one version of the truth" in the database — making sure that when we all see what the revenues are across different product groups, for example, we're all looking at the same numbers. The data is consistent.

However, information consistency is different from data consistency. Information consistency relies on the data being consistent but also provides additional context so that the information is relevant to and actionable by the end user.

For instance, a $6 million sales goal, a $1.5 million marketing budget, and a 13 percent profit margin are examples of numbers that we all may refer to in the database and need to work towards as common corporate objectives. However, the way that we work towards each of these goals may be different. Different people in the sales organization may want to monitor their performance towards their portion of the overall sales goal differently — some may choose to have red icons appear when they've attained $500,000 in sales or 50 percent of the goal, for instance. Some people in marketing may want to have red icons when they're below 25 percent of their marketing spending (too little) and also when they're at 90 percent of their marketing spending (too much) — or perhaps they want some type of icon that fills up to show the percentage of budgeted funds spent so that they can easily monitor the present status. An effective performance management solution allows employees to manage their business on their own terms.

In this specific example:

- *Data consistency* means that the numbers are valid. The $6 million sales goal is the real, actual, and valid number for the entire organization. If the organization wants to change this number to $8 million, that change will be reflected to all systems that report from that "one version of the truth" — the data warehouse.
- *Information consistency* relies not only on consistent data but also on two distinct attributes:
  - **Personalization.** An effective performance management solution allows people to monitor performance in their own way, choosing to monitor progress as different thresholds are met and with different iconography to indicate achievement in the end users' preferred

format and terms (at $500,000, when they're spending too little or too much, when the percentage is higher than 13 percent, and the like).

- **Consistency of data definitions.** Whenever the number changes in the data warehouse, the change needs to automatically occur in the performance management system, and the change should not disrupt the way that employees manage their business. For example, if the sales goal goes to $8 million and the sales manager is managing performance based on 25 percent, 50 percent, and 75 percent of that goal, the performance management system is automatically updated, and the percentages and visual displays of progress stay accurate. So, the information remains consistent with the consistent data.

In order to guarantee both data definition consistency and personalization, it is preferable to have a system between the database and the end user's preferred interfaces (the Web, other applications, and the like). While the data resides in the database, the information (the business logic for how managers want to run their business, the targets they want to monitor, and so on) is maintained in PerformancePoint Server. This allows end users to access and utilize their preferred performance management methods in the format they want.

Since PerformancePoint Server is a middle layer between an organization's databases and its end-user interfaces, the information logic ("25 percent of the $8 million sales goal") and result ("=$2M" and a red indicator) built into the server will be portable across multiple end-user interfaces (such as SharePoint and SQL Reporting Services in a Microsoft environment, as discussed earlier). So, if a scorecard built and managed by PerformancePoint Server can be integrated into various interfaces with little effort, IT can guarantee a better level of information consistency across the organization, regardless if end users are consuming the information in a connected (Internet, online) or disconnected (offline, no Internet) scenario.

This type of capability is key to guaranteeing that all employees work with consistent information (with the targets and business logic they prefer), regardless of the way they get to the information. In addition to integrating with ASP.NET, SharePoint, and Reporting Services, PerformancePoint Server offers further integration with Office applications. For instance, end users can export scorecards from their Internet Explorer browser into applications such as PowerPoint and Excel. This is quite powerful if they are trying to work with scorecard information inside the familiar environment of Office.

Collaboration and Unstructured Information

An effective performance management solution needs to enable employees to take action quickly. However, a large amount of the information that employees need to make decisions is unstructured. So, how can a scorecard, which by its very nature relies on structured data, provide employees with the information they need?

When an employee looks at a metric and wants to understand why it has become red, and when the explanation is not simply a number, what are the options? Often, they will instant message, email, or pick up the phone and call the owner of the metric. While this concept might be efficient in some companies, it delays the understanding of the issue and potentially invalidates the decision that this individual needs to make.

In PerformancePoint Server, annotations easily take care of this issue. Metric owners can write in plaintext the reason for the performance of a metric and address particular tasks to the person reading the annotation. These annotations are cell-dependent (not data-dependent) and are stored centrally. This means that when the numbers change, the information about this particular number will still be stored.

This will make it easier for reviewers to pull not only the numbers but also the justification added to the scorecards. Financial analysts using this feature find it very useful for financial book reviews, as it allows them to understand performance with a lot more context.

Another popular usage scenario of unstructured information is the ability to publish metrics definitions. For instance, if an end user is looking at a grow-margin metric, how does the organization make sure that he or she understands the definition of the metric (or even maybe the calculation or the data source behind that number)? Using annotations, employees can hover over a metric and get the metric definition as well as any other attribute that would have been configured in the solution.

The preceding text describes just a few of the benefits provided by the application.

CROSS-REFERENCE **We will expand further on this topic in Chapter 5.**

Analyze

The analysis capability of PerformancePoint Server refers to the ability of individuals, groups, and organizations to answer questions such as: "Why is this happening" or "Why did this happen?" (As opposed to the "what" questions answered by the monitoring capability.)

Analytical capabilities are enabled by applications that analysts use to learn more about an issue by slicing, dicing, drilling, and filtering data into thin charts and grids. Often people go into the analysis phase to investigate issues they were monitoring in a dashboard or scorecard, or observed in a report. The tight connection between the monitoring and analytical capabilities is a key benefit of the solution.

Analytical Paradox

In the past, analytical front ends have been deployed by a very limited number of people across the organization. This has primarily been because analytics have been seen as very complex and sophisticated. The training required to empower more users to use these applications was counterproductive to the job of most information workers. Indeed, we estimate that about 70 percent of employees use analytics less than 10 percent of their work time. Because of this, analytical front ends have been deployed mainly by business analysts, who live and breathe analytics on a daily basis. Business analysts are typically very tolerant of complex environments and applications, so they find the deployment of sophisticated and complex applications tolerable.

However, when an organization wants to empower more business users, the preceding model simply breaks. While most employees use analytics only a small percentage of the time, they crave valuable information and insight 100 percent of the time. In fact, it is precisely that need that overloads IT departments and business analysts on a daily basis. So, how can companies empower more users to do analysis efficiently and get the information to do their jobs more effectively?

Aligned and Thin Analytics

In the process of building complex analytical applications, vendors started out creating full-fledged desktop applications. Quickly, the need to deploy these applications to more users across the organization pushed them to create what are called thin client applications. The problem was that "fat" applications couldn't be easily deployed and updated on all client machines, while thin client applications provided too little functionality.

In addition, in the process of thinning their fat applications, many vendors failed to understand the needs of most information workers. Information workers rarely ask for the ability to do thinly all the complex functions and calculations that a desktop tool can.

Most employees are looking for analytics that they can jump to directly from their performance dashboard. Even though calculations and other complex features might sound appealing, most employeess need to quickly use analytics to answer the "why" of an issue they see on their dashboard — and they'd like to know this sooner rather than later. They might see, for example, that total backorders might be an issue, and they would like to quickly get access to the reasons why.

Employees analyze better if dashboards and analytics are tighly connected out of the box. Note that in PerformancePoint Server, scorecards, dashboards, and analytics are not only tightly connected visually but also tightly connected in the back — in fact, monitoring and analytical capabilities share the same Builder. The creation of monitoring applications is tightly linked to the creation of analytics and reports. Dashboards, scorecards, and analytics can easily share the same definitions, meta data, and security schemes. So, when end users use analytics, they are consuming the information in the analytics in the same context as the information they had in their scorecards. Analytics and scorecards keep the end users focused on the speficic area that they have access to look at and investigate.

Analytics also provide a set of robust features that enables employees to answer questions and resolve issues without having to install a client application or even know anything about the data structure of the database that they are about to query. Exploring the cross-drilling asset is a great example.

Analytics Made Easy: Cross-Drilling

A key differentiator for PerformancePoint Server analytics is the ability to drill into information at any level of the data hierachy. For example, a data hierarchy of geographic information may be composed of the following levels of information: Global, Country, State, County, City, Town, and so on. Naturally, PerformancePoint Server covers the typical drilling functions that users of analytic tools may have become accustomed to:

- Drilling up
- Drilling down

In addition to the typical drilling functions, PerformancePoint Server analytics enables users to perform cross-drilling. Cross-drilling refers to the ability to drill across data hierarchies to allow employees to answer a much wider variety of questions about the data.

Let's take a look at one scenario. Jack owns a bicycle retail chain. He notices that margins have been low but does not know what could be the cause of this. He opens his analytical application and loads the margin information across all his 150 retail stores. The dimensions of his analysis allow him to drill up and down margin dollars by country and product lines. He starts at the top line, which shows all products, all countries, and margin information. He drills down to Europe, where he can now see margin numbers for all products. He drills down from Europe and now can see the Germany, France, and UK margin information. At this point, he can compare the margin numbers from these countries against each other, and he can go up and down this path as much as needed. By drilling down, Jack is able to find out that France is losing money on all bikes.

While this analysis is useful, Jack really hasn't used his analytics as an interactive information tool. By strictly drilling down the data hierachy defined by his IT department, Jack hasn't been able to ask the data the questions that he really wants to answer. For instance: What products is Jack's company making money on? Where are these products primarily sold? Of these locations, when were the low-margin products in particular sold? What day of the week?. That's what cross-drilling is used for. As you can see, cross-drilling really is a different approach than just drilling up and down. It takes into account that a typical analytical path cannot be defined ahead of time. While drilling up and down a hierachy is useful in some cases, it rarely allows employees to use all the information available to fully answer their questions. With cross-drilling, end users enjoy the benefits of very flexible analytical paths. Because drilling is supersetted by cross-drilling in PerformancePoint Server, users can enjoy the benefits of both methodologies thinly and in one application.

Enabling navigation across multiple hierarchies in typical analytical tools would require significant IT and/or business analyst involment. By making this type of functionality available thinly and out of the box, PerformancePoint not only empowers more employees to take care of their own analytical needs but also frees up IT cycles otherwise used up providing the various data permutations that business users would like to see their data by.

Web and Office Integration

PerformancePoint Server analytics have been optimized for the thousands of employees who need quick access to their analytics in a browser across the organization.

With thin analytic functionality, employees perform analyses right from their Web browser. All they have to do is right-click on any analytical graph or grid and the answer to their question is a few clicks away.

This simplicity and functionality allow employees to:

- **Learn the details of the information being viewed.** For example, when the the user hovers over graphs and charts, underlined information about the data will appear (using SQL Server UDM [Unified Dimensional Model] definitions). The application also makes it very easy for any user to navigate through the analytics. Users can drill up, down, and across from virtually anywhere in the analytics — even right-click on legend items to drill from there.
- **Navigate easily in Internet Explorer.** The PerformancePoint Server analytics integration with Internet Explorer makes it very easy for end users to use the Back and Forward buttons in Internet Explorer to go back and forth throughout the entire analytical path. This feature provides flexibility for users who decide that they've gone down the wrong path in their analysis and want to backtrack or start a new navigation path.

- **Export and work offline in Excel.** In addition to strong thin interaction, end users can export their view into Excel. This scenario is quite useful for the folks who need to bring the analysis with them on trips where they might not have an Internet connection.
- **Export to Excel whenever you want during your analysis.** End users can simply export their analysis to Excel at any point during their analysis. They can extract the information at the beginning, the middle, or the end of their analysis cycle and anywhere between. In addition, when a PerformancePoint Server analytic view is pushed down to Excel, the application will show in the spreadsheet's data, accompanied by its meta data — for example, names and attributes of the query, as well as a link to the original analytics' views.

Planning

While monitoring answers the "what" (is happening or has happened) and analytics answer the "why" (is it happening or did it happen), planning answers the "how" (do I want it to happen or will it happen). Planning capabilities are provided by applications and tools that employees use to plan, budget, forecast, report, and perform financial consolidations. The business modeling functionality of the application is key to these processes, as its steps shape the way that the business operates, and it is the focus of the Business Modeler (thus the name).

The main organizational pain in the area of planning is the lack of integration across the applications that users need in order to properly drive the process of planning. According to the Hackett Group, only 26 percent of companies experience integration across reporting and planning.[6] The planning process is historically manual, slow, and error-prone.

The Modeler

Before an organization can plan on its business, it has to define what the levers of that business are. For instance, what drivers does this business react to? What are the important objectives and initiatives necessary to capture and take into account in the business performance planning exercise?

A model includes the set of data, calculations, and definitions that can bring together the historical, planned, budgeted, and forecasted views of that business.

Typically, users look for the most flexible application to build this model into. They also pick the application that they are the most familiar with: Excel. Organizations build fairly sophisticated Excel spreadsheets, including links across tabs and files as well as macros. While this solution might seem to be a great approach to getting started, many organizations quickly realize that change is particularly difficult to handle — changes can be lengthy, error-prone, and expensive. These spreadsheets often become a maintenance headache for the analysts who are tasked with maintaining them. They become inaccurate and inflexible, and they diminish the confidence the organization has in finding a correlation between these models and the way the business is run.

The PerformancePoint Server Modeler application allows business users to build and manage their models centrally. The Modeler is the place where business users set up their models, scenarios, dimensions, hierarchies, cycles, roles, and security. We will expand further on this topic in Part III of this book.

The key differentiator here is the application's ability to manage all aspects of planning in one place. The application has been designed to bring IT and the business together in order to streamline the performance management system and operations. When thinking about the Modeler, think about all the tasks that analysts try to accomplish throughout typical spreadsheets — with the Modeler, they can do more and do these things much more efficiently and effectively. A typical organization would use the Modeler to:

- Centralize all business logic required to run scenarios and their drivers.
- Administer security and cycles. This means that you need an engine that will run your performance management processes and help you streamline them. This includes not only the contribution aspect of the process but also the aggregation of the information received.
- Build a system that will scale for enterprise-wide complexity. The Modeler sits on top of SQL Server Analysis Services and, as Bill Baker often says, it is an application that allows an organization to build "better cubes." The consequences of "better cubes" is that organizations can not only manage performance management data and meta data centrally, but they can also scale it across the organization, taking advantage of the scalability enhancements built into SQL Server Analysis Services.

One of the functions that the Modeler does best is model-to-model mapping. While that functionality will be explored in further detail in Part III of this book, it is important to highlight this particular feature.

Let's take the following scenario: An organization has three business units, which all have different profit and loss (P&L) and models. However, the main organization wants to consolidate and aggregate the information of all three models into one corporate one. This task seems pretty daunting because the application not only needs to be very good at mapping all four models (three business units and one corporate one), but it also needs to account for all the changes that might occur to each model. A change might be a new piece of information introduced or maybe a new calculation. While a slight data change might seem fine, the repercussions could be felt all the way down the cycles in progress that input some of these models.

The Modeler is optimized to take care of this problem because it not only centralizes business logic, but it will also take care of roles, security, and the cycles impacted.

The End-User Experience

PerformancePoint Server users will quickly realize the amount of work that Microsoft has put into making the end-user experience intuitive, familiar, and user friendly. Office and Web integration is widely available through the monitoring and analysis experiences of the application. Planning is no exception to this rule. The main interaction interface for contributors to plans, forecasts, and budgets is Microsoft Office Excel.

Excel is a key application for driving adoption and participation across the organization, and PerformancePoint Server uses Excel as the main interface for deploying plans, forecasts, and budgets. In addition to the standard Excel functionality, end users benefit from some key performance management features worth noting.

"The right information, at the right time to the right people" is a common marketing promise for many performance management vendors. It is a common promise because it is a common organization problem. The process of acting on information or collaborating around a given task such as a forecast is extremely iterative and requires a lot of relevant information. Often employees find themselves overwhelmed by irrelevant information and half of the work they have to produce before they can even begin to participate in a forecast is about understanding the information they are looking at. For example: "What is this information?"; "How is it relevant to me?"; "Which are the drivers of this forecast?"

Ultimately, providing the right information to the right people at the right time requires an intimate knowledge of end-user roles, security, and relative position within a given process (sometimes approvers, sometimes contributors, and so on). In order to accomplish this, applications need to allow the customization of the information that is relevant to each individual and present it in a format that makes it easy for them to act on it. The best analogy for this mass-customization issue is probably to think about Starbucks and the company's ability to allow customers to customize a standard coffee order. When customers order their "tall, no whip, 360, no foam, soy milk, one pump, half-caf blended, white chocolate, nonfat latte," they have stretched the amount of customization required by the vendor to satisfy their requirement.

While performance management end-user needs rarely get as sophisticated as their latte order, performance management applications not only need to accommodate the needs of end users but also need to create a data set that meets the overall corporate needs. For example, if a forecast has to be run across units, the difficulties of running this forecast to close are numerous:

- First of all, the end-user application that users are providing their forecast numbers in needs to be user-friendly so that end users are not daunted by the thought of opening the file.
- Second, the information that the file will contain needs to be relevant to the end user.
- Third, the information in the file needs to be understood quickly by end users so that they can act on it.
- Finally, considering that a similar but personalized file has been sent around to many users across the company, an effective performance management application needs to be able to collect the information from end users and collect it in a straightforward fashion.

PerformancePoint Server is particularly optimized to resolve each of these issues. In addition to making contribution easy, the application manages security and roles centrally, automating a process that is typically done manually at most companies and that requires many hours to complete. The application also aggregates and consolidates all individual input from contributors so that the information makes sense at a corporate level.

CROSS-REFERENCE **The application handles consolidation of information across currencies and supports eliminations, reconciliation, and multiple allocations. We will expand on these functions in Chapter 12.**

Performance Management Is More Than Just Numbers

In addition to providing a very powerful end-user experience, PerformancePoint Server guides end users throughout the entire performance management process. For instance, if an employee needs to contribute to a forecast, the application will provide this individual with his or her personalized forecast sheet, specifically including the numbers that person needs to look at in the format he or she needs. For instance, it might be German forecast numbers in euros for the next four quarters.

Furthermore, the application colors the cells that this contributor needs to work with, such as the specific business drivers of the slice of the forecast owned by this individual. By doing this, the application makes it very easy for individuals to quickly understand the information and act on it in the context of their business. There are additional capabilities inside PerformancePoint Server spreadsheets that allow end users to use the centrally managed business logic to run calculations, consolidation jobs, and what-if scenarios. In addition, the application allows users to lock cells for particular values in the spreadsheet to isolate information but still run model assumptions with the rest of the spreadsheet.

In summary, PerformancePoint Server provides a good balance between supporting processes that a company might want to run centrally, such as business logic, and providing a large amount of end-user functionality to allow end users to become efficient quickly.

One of the features that best exemplifies this concept of productivity is spreading. Spreading is the ability of a spreadsheet to understand a top- or bottom-line number input by a contributor and spread values to its children based on the application's business logic. In order to best understand this functionality, imagine the following scenario. A contributor working for a hardware manufacturing plant has to input his numbers into a line item forecast for an entire product line of bolts. In this example, the contributor opens his forecast sheet and unfolds the bolt family. He can see that there are about 250 SKUs for bolts.

At this point, the contributor has multiple options to fill out his forecast:

- **Input data manually.** This would consist of inputting numbers line by line for each period. This is probably the slowest way to contribute to the forecast, but it might be the most accurate for the contributor.
- **Use Excel functions.** This could consist of using calculations across cells, dragging values across rows and columns. This method might be a little faster, although the end user has to remember how cells are connected to each other.
- **Use PerformancePoint Server functions.** By turning on the spreading function, the end user would essentially just enter the total number of bolts he wants to sell. PerformancePoint Server would run this number through the forecast model's centralized logic and fill out the numbers for the contributor inside the spreadsheet. This methodology might be the fastest and the one that is the most aligned to the corporate rules for this given forecast. Note that PerformancePoint Server can also seed a forecast for contributors, essentially prepopulating a forecast for a contributor to review. This seeding functionality would follow the same model as spreading — that is, relying on the application's centralized business logic.

When running numbers from the PerformancePoint business logic, end users can benefit from sophisticated algorithms that their business analysts have defined for them, based on seasonality, past information, or any level of sophistication. Also, remember that end users can lock certain cells when they feel strongly about particularly quantities for certain products. Even then, users can re-run spreading, which will apply to all cells except the locked ones.

Both the preceding methodologies are supported by PerformancePoint Server, truly highlighting the product's strong commitment to end-user choice, flexibility, and productivity.

Summary

In this chapter, we covered some of the key factors to consider in order to roll out a successful performance management initiative. Helping your employees develop trust in the data, and the information provided by any performance management system, is absolutely critical for the success and adoption of the system.

Focusing on what your analysts, managers, executives, and IT colleagues care about should be your second target. There is no cookie-cutter approach to performance management, but if you focus on the needs of your end users, you are on your way to better business performance.

Think about the role of each user served by your applications and what empowers them the best. Your analysts will need flexibility and agility for instance. Your managers and executives will need to align the organization and make everybody accountable by providing all employees with better, more actionable information.

Finally, we covered the basics of PerformancePoint Server — its capabilities and some of the most exciting functional areas.

It is now time to dive deeper into the technology. Let's go!

Notes

1. See `www.olapreport.com/market.htm`.
2. See `www.microsoft.com/presspass/press/2007/jul07/07-26SPPT800MPR.mspx`.
3. David A. J. Axson, "Best Practices in Planning and Management Reporting," *Best Practices in Planning and Performance Management: From Data to Decisions (Wiley Best Practices)* (Wiley, 2007).
4. "It's All About the Performance Management (Tools)," December 3, 2006, `http://esj.com/business_intelligence/article.aspx?EditorialsID = 8273`.
5. Jeremy Hope and Robin Fraser, "Beyond Budgeting," *Beyond Budgeting: How Managers Can Break Free from the Annual Performance Trap* (Harvard Business School Press, 2003).
6. "Best Practices in Planning and Management Reporting," p. 52.

CHAPTER 3

Setting Up and Configuring PerformancePoint Servers

This chapter provides an overview of the requirements and steps involved in setting up and configuring PerformancePoint Monitoring Server and PerformancePoint Planning Server. The chapter also includes best practices and troubleshooting information for installing and configuring PerformancePoint Servers.

Monitoring Server

Typically corporate organizations and other groups requiring large-scale distributions will choose to deploy a distributed topology in which PerformancePoint Monitoring Server is installed on multiple computers. Monitoring Server is made up of multiple components with specific requirements for installation and configuration. The following sections identify the hardware and software prerequisites and system requirements for these components in a distributed installation. Be sure to go through the prerequisites and requirements carefully to identify and remedy any gaps in your current environment to avoid costly surprises and delays during installation.

Hardware Prerequisites

Table 3-1 identifies the hardware prerequisites for Monitoring Server. Review the hardware prerequisites well ahead of your Monitoring Server installation to identify and remedy any gaps in your current hardware inventory.

Table 3-1 Hardware Prerequisites for Monitoring Server

ITEM	PERFORMANCEPOINT MONITORING COMPUTER	FILE SHARE SERVER FILE SHARE	PERFORMANCEPOINT DASHBOARD DESIGNER COMPUTER
Processor type	Minimum: 1x Pentium 4 Recommended: 2x dual-core 64-bit CPUs	Minimum: 1x Pentium 4 Recommended: 2x dual-core 64-bit CPUs	Minimum: 1x Pentium 3 Recommended: 1x dual-core 32-bit CPU (x86)
Processor speed	Minimum: 2.5 gigahertz (GHz) Recommended: 2.8 GHz	Minimum: 2.5 GHz Recommended: 2.8 GHz	Minimum: 1 GHz Recommended: 2.5 GHz
Available hard disk space	Minimum: 1 gigabyte (GB) Recommended: 5 GB + 7200 rpm hard disk drive	Minimum: 1 GB Recommended: 5 GB + 7200 rpm hard disk drive	Minimum: 512 megabytes (MB) Recommended: 2 GB
RAM	Minimum: 2 GB Recommended: 4 GB	Minimum: 2 GB Recommended: 4 GB	Minimum: 1.5 GB Recommended: 2 GB
Network interface	Minimum: 1000BASE-T	Minimum: 1000BASE-T	Minimum: 1000BASE-T

Software Prerequisites

Table 3-2 identifies the software prerequisites for Monitoring Server. These software applications must be installed before you start the Monitoring Server installation. For each software prerequisite, the table identifies the associated Monitoring Server component that requires the software for its installation.

NOTE **The support for Microsoft SQL Server 2008 begins with PerformancePoint Server 2007 Service Pack 2. Information on current and future service packs, including updated requirements, is found in the online Deployment Guide for PerformancePoint Server 2007. This guide is available at** `http://technet.microsoft.com/en-us/library/bb794637.aspx`**.**

System Requirements

Monitoring Server is made up of both server and client components. Tables 3-3 and 3-4 identify the system requirements for these server and client components, respectively. Review the system requirements prior to of your Monitoring Server installation to identify and remedy any gaps.

Table 3-2 Software Prerequisites for Monitoring Server

PREREQUISITE	REQUIRED FOR INSTALLATION
Microsoft SQL Server 2005 database software (Standard or Enterprise Edition)	Monitoring System Database
Internet Information Services (IIS) 6.0 Internet Information Services (IIS) 5.1 (for Windows XP) Microsoft ASP.NET 2.0 Microsoft .NET Framework version 2.0.50727 IIS 6.0 worker process isolation mode Microsoft ASP.NET 2.0 registration with IIS ASP.NET 2.0 Web Service Extension in IIS	Monitoring Server IIS component
Report Designer Plug-In for the Microsoft Visual Studio 2005 development system	Monitoring Plug-In for Report Designer
Windows SharePoint Services 3.0 Microsoft Office SharePoint Server 2007	Dashboard Viewer for SharePoint Services
Microsoft SQL Server 2005 Reporting Services	Scorecard Viewer for Reporting Services
SQL Server Native Client 9.0 SP2	Monitoring System Database Monitoring Server
ADOMD.NET 9.0 SP2	Monitoring Server This is required only if you want to monitor data from an Analysis Services back-end system.
ASP.NET AJAX 1.0	Dashboard Viewer for SharePoint Services

Table 3-3 Server Components for Monitoring Server

SERVER COMPONENTS	SUPPORTED OPERATING SYSTEMS	ADDITIONAL REQUIREMENTS	SUPPORTED BROWSERS
PerformancePoint Monitoring Server Configuration Manager	32-bit and 64-bit versions of Windows Server 2003 SP2 and Windows Server 2003 R2 32-bit and 64-bit versions of Windows Server 2008	Microsoft .NET Framework 2.0 Microsoft ASP.NET 2.0 SQL Native Client 9.0 SP2	
PerformancePoint Monitoring Server	32-bit and 64-bit versions of Windows Server 2003 SP2 and Windows Server 2003 R2 32-bit and 64-bit versions of Windows Server 2008 Windows XP SP2 (excluding Windows XP Embedded)	Microsoft Internet Information Services (IIS) 5.1 (Windows XP), IIS 6.0, or IIS 7.0 with IIS metabase and IIS 6 configuration compatibility, IIS 6.0 Isolation Mode Microsoft .NET Framework 2.0 Microsoft ASP.NET 2.0	Microsoft Internet Explorer 6.0 Microsoft Internet Explorer 7.0

(*continued*)

Table 3-3 *(continued)*

SERVER COMPONENTS	SUPPORTED OPERATING SYSTEMS	ADDITIONAL REQUIREMENTS	SUPPORTED BROWSERS
	32-bit and 64-bit versions of Windows Vista Business, Windows Vista Business N, and Windows Vista Enterprise	Microsoft ASP.NET AJAX 1.0	
		SQL Server 2005 Analysis Management Objects 9.0 SP2	
		SQL Server 2005 Native Client 9.0 SP2	
		SQL ADOMD.NET 9.0	
		MSXML 6.0	
		SQL Server 2005 SP2 Analysis Server OLEDB 9.0 Provider	
PerformancePoint Dashboard Viewer for SharePoint Services	32-bit and 64-bit versions of Windows Server 2003 SP2 and Windows Server 2003 R2	Microsoft Internet Information Services (IIS) 6.0, or IIS 7.0 with IIS metabase and IIS 6 configuration compatibility, IIS 6.0 Isolation Mode	Microsoft Internet Explorer 6.0
	32-bit and 64-bit versions of Windows Server 2008	Microsoft Office SharePoint Server 2007 or Windows SharePoint Services 3.0 SP1 (for Windows Server 2008)	Microsoft Internet Explorer 7.0
		Microsoft .NET Framework 2.0	
		Microsoft ASP.NET 2.0	
		Microsoft ASP.NET AJAX 1.0	
		SQL Server 2005 Analysis Management Objects 9.0 SP2	
		SQL Server 2005 Native Client 9.0 SP2	
		SQL ADOMD.NET 9.0	
		MSXML 6.0 + updates	
		SQL Server 2005 SP2 Analysis Server OLEDB 9.0 Provider	
PerformancePoint Scorecard Viewer for Reporting Services	32-bit and 64-bit versions of Windows Server 2003 SP2 and Windows Server 2003 R2	Microsoft Office PerformancePoint Monitoring Server 2007	
	32-bit and 64-bit versions of Windows Server 2008	Microsoft SQL Server 2005 SP2 Reporting Services server	
PerformancePoint Monitoring System Database	32-bit and 64-bit versions of Windows Server 2003 SP2 and Windows Server 2003 R2	Microsoft SQL Server 2005 SP2 Standard Edition	
	32-bit and 64-bit versions of Windows Server 2008		

Table 3-4 Client Components for Monitoring Server

CLIENT COMPONENTS	SUPPORTED OPERATING SYSTEMS	ADDITIONAL REQUIREMENTS	SUPPORTED BROWSERS
PerformancePoint Dashboard Designer	32-bit and 64-bit versions of Windows Server 2003 SP2 and Windows Server 2003 R2 32-bit and 64-bit versions of Windows Server 2008 Windows XP SP2 (excluding Windows XP Embedded) 32-bit and 64-bit versions of Windows Vista Business, Windows Vista Business N, and Windows Vista Enterprise	SQL ADOMD.NET 9.0 MSXML 6.0 + updates SQL Server 2005 SP2 Analysis Server OLEDB 9.0 Provider Microsoft .NET Framework 2.0	
PerformancePoint Scorecard Viewer for Reporting Services	32-bit and 64-bit versions of Windows Server 2003 SP2 and Windows Server 2003 R2 32-bit and 64-bit versions of Windows Server 2008 Windows XP SP2 (excluding Windows XP Embedded) 32-bit and 64-bit versions of Windows Vista Business, Windows Vista Business N, and Windows Vista Enterprise	Microsoft .NET Framework 2.0 Microsoft Visual Studio 2005 with SQL Server 2005 SP2 Report Designer	
PerformancePoint Dashboard client (Internet Explorer)			Microsoft Internet Explorer 6.0 Microsoft Internet Explorer 7.0

NOTE The support for Windows Server 2008 begins with PerformancePoint Server 2007 Service Pack 1. Information on current and future service packs, including updated requirements, is found in the online Deployment Guide for PerformancePoint Server 2007. This guide is available at `http://technet.microsoft.com/en-us/library/bb794637.aspx`.

Installing and Configuring Monitoring Server

The installation for Monitoring Server occurs in two parts. Part one runs the Windows installer package `PSCsrv.msi`. The installer package copies the necessary files to the local machine to prepare for server installation and initialize the Monitoring Server Configuration Manager. Part two launches the Monitoring Server Configuration Manager used to configure and install the selected Monitoring Server components.

During a typical installation, Monitoring Server installs the components listed below. You will learn more about the functionality of each of these components in the following chapters.

- **PerformancePoint Dashboard Designer.** A desktop application for developing dashboards.
- **PerformancePoint Monitoring System Database.** A SQL Server database that stores all Monitoring Server data and configuration settings.
- **PerformancePoint Monitoring Server.** Used by Dashboard Designer and Microsoft SQL Server databases that contain Monitoring Server meta data.
- **PerformancePoint Monitoring Server Web Service.** A collection of application programming interfaces (APIs) that provide the core functionality of PerformancePoint Monitoring Server.
- **PerformancePoint Dashboard Web Preview.** An ASP.NET Web site used for rendering dashboards for preview and development scenarios.
- **Monitoring Central.** A Web site from which users can install Dashboard Designer, view product documentation, and open the Dashboard Web Preview site.
- **SQL Server 2005 SP2 Reporting Services integration.** Reporting services that provide detailed information about Monitoring Server databases.
- **PerformancePoint Dashboard Viewer for SharePoint Services.** A Web Part used to render and display dashboards.
- **PerformancePoint Monitoring Plug-In for Report Designer (Visual Studio 2005).** An add-in to the Reporting Services Report Designer.

Monitoring Server Configuration Manager normally installs these components on the local machine. If you want to install the components in a distributed topology, you must run the Monitoring Server Installation and Monitoring Server Configuration Manager on each computer in the topology, and then select the component you want to configure on the local machine from Monitoring Server Configuration Manager.

NOTE **The Deployment Guide for PerformancePoint Server 2007 contains detailed instructions for configuring Monitoring Server. This guide is available for download from** `http://technet.microsoft.com/en-us/library/cc196370.aspx`.

Authentication Options

When configuring Monitoring Server, you can select one of the following authentication options to connect to SQL Server 2005 Analysis Services and other data sources. The option you select will depend on your environment, data sources, and security model.

Application Pool User Identity

With Application Pool Identity, the identity of the process is used for any connections to data sources. You can configure the Monitoring Server application pool identity account to use either of two account types — the Network Service account or Domain user accounts — depending on the needs of your domain and security model.

The Network Service account is a built-in account that has fewer access rights on the system than the Local System account but is still able to interact throughout the network by using the computer account credentials.

Domain user accounts include accounts that you create in the domain; for example, by using the Active Directory Users and Computers management console. Domain user accounts have limited access rights in the domain unless you specifically grant them access or add them to groups that already possess those access rights. Whenever possible, the preferred method is to run Monitoring Server with a Domain user account that has low privileges.

NOTE **When using Domain user accounts, the application pool identity that the SharePoint site runs under should be set up with the same account.**

Connection Per User

With the Connection per user option, the login user identity is used to connect to a data source. In this case, delegation is required for the process to connect on behalf of users.

Kerberos

In a typical distributed deployment, many client computers will access a Monitoring Server installed on one computer. In turn, Monitoring Server may connect to Analysis Services installed on a different computer. Security issues come up in this type of multi-server environment as user credentials must be passed from the client computer through the Monitoring Server computer on to the Analysis Services computer. By configuring delegation using Kerberos, user credentials can be passed through to Analysis Services while ensuring data and system security.

Custom Data

Some environments will not allow applications to configure delegation with Kerberos. If this is the case in your environment, you can use the Custom Data feature, which allows secure connections to be made to Analysis Services through shared Application Pool credentials. The Custom Data feature passes the user's login information directly to Analysis Services, and this login information can then be used to secure the cube dimensions. Since the application pool is used to connect to Analysis Services, credentials are not passed through multiple computers, so delegation is not required. To use the Custom Data feature, Monitoring Server must be configured to use a Domain user account.

NOTE **Custom Data applies to Analysis Services only.**

Secure Socket Layer

Monitoring Server uses the following security methods: Internet Information Services (IIS) security, file and folder security, and Secure Socket Layer (SSL) security. Of these security methods, SSL is the preferred method to secure the Monitoring Server deployment and all relevant Web sites.

TIP **When installing Dashboard Designer with SSL enabled, you will see the name of the computer that Dashboard Designer is being installed to in the installation address box. This might need to be changed if the SSL certificate address is that of a different computer.**

Microsoft SharePoint Server Settings

SharePoint sites are the primary means of consuming and presenting monitoring information, providing secure and easy access to business information. In order to use SharePoint with Monitoring Server, you must ensure that the following settings are applied to the SharePoint server.

Excel Services Settings

Excel Services is part of Microsoft Office SharePoint Server 2007 and is used to extend the capabilities of Microsoft Office Excel 2007 by allowing broad sharing of spreadsheets. With PerformancePoint and Excel Services, you can include references to existing spreadsheet reports on your deployed dashboard.

Excel Services must be enabled on the SharePoint instance in order to use this feature for reports in dashboards, and certain settings must be configured through the Shared Services Administration page from the SharePoint Central Administration site.

- **Unattended Service Account credentials.** You must enter the credentials for a default Windows Account that Excel Services will use for connecting to data sources that require username and password strings for authentication. If this account is not set, connections to these data sources will fail. You may want to set up a specific account with limited read access for use as this default account.
- **Set Trusted File Locations.** Every location used as a host or for storage of Excel files to be used by Monitoring Server must be entered in the list of Excel Services Trusted File Locations. Excel Services denies requests to open files that are not stored in one of the trusted locations.
- **Set Trusted Data Connection Libraries.** Every data connection library from which workbooks open in Excel Services are permitted to access data connection description files must be entered in the list of data connection library locations you consider to be trustworthy.
- **Set Trusted Data Providers.** Every data provider that can be used for external data sources in Excel workbooks (for example, OLE DB, ODBC, or ODBC DSN) must be entered in the list of trusted data providers.

Configure Root Site

Monitoring Server assumes that a top-level Web site or root site is defined for the SharePoint Server site collection. If a top-level Web site is not defined, Excel Services reports may not render in published dashboards. To avoid this issue, you may either create a top-level Web site for the SharePoint site collection or edit the `web.config` file for the SharePoint site collection to include the path for the subsite of the SharePoint installation.

Reporting Services Settings

With PerformancePoint, you can include references to existing SQL Server 2005 Reporting Services (SSRS) reports on your deployed dashboard. To use this report option, Reporting Services must be installed in the background with the following settings.

Reporting Services can be installed either in standalone or SharePoint integrated mode. The difference is how SSRS reports are accessed when adding them to a PerformancePoint Dashboard. When adding a SSRS report, you must specify which SSRS installation mode is being used.

When using standalone mode, you must specify the URL that is being used by the report server. When using integrated mode you must specify the location of the SharePoint document library that is storing the report and the URL for the report server.

ProClarity Analytics Server Settings

With Monitoring Server you can include existing ProClarity Analytic Server (PAS) views in dashboards. In order to use PAS views in Monitoring Server, you must ensure that the hotfix has been applied to PAS.

Apply the PAS Hotfix

To enable ProClarity Analytic Server (PAS) views in Monitoring Server dashboards, you must install the PAS hotfix on your PAS server. Without the hotfix, you will receive errors when viewing PAS pages in Monitoring Server dashboards. The PAS hotfix is available from `http://support.microsoft.com/kb/942523`.

NOTE **For additional information on how to resolve problems with Monitoring Server and its associated components, refer to "Troubleshoot PerformancePoint Monitoring Server," available from `http://technet.microsoft.com/en-us/library/bb660558.aspx`.**

Best Practice Monitoring Server Installation

- Review all hardware and software prerequisites and system requirements before installation. Identify and remedy any gaps well before installation.
- Identify the various data sources that you will be using with Monitoring Server and grant appropriate login and read permissions to the various data sources.
- Install the most recent version of Internet Explorer with all current updates.
- Use Secure Sockets Layer security to secure your Monitoring Server deployment.
- When running multiple Monitoring Server application pools on a single server, limit the ASP.NET cache to prevent performance degradation.
- Use the Monitoring Server installation log files to troubleshoot issues during installation. These files are called `MonitoringStatus%date%.log` and `MonitoringVerbose%date%.log`. They are created in a directory called `%temp%`.

Planning Server

PerformancePoint Planning Server is composed of two server components: a front-end server (Web Service) based on Internet Services and a back-end process service layer interacting directly with a SQL Database server. Two additional installations support the Business Modeler and Excel Add-In. The subsequent sections outline the requirements and installation processes for these components.

Hardware Prerequisites

Table 3-5 identifies the hardware requirements for the Planning components of PerformancePoint Server.

Table 3-5 Hardware Prerequisites for Planning Server

ITEM	PLANNING WEB SERVICE COMPUTER	PLANNING PROCESS SERVICE COMPUTER	BUSINESS MODELER COMPUTER	EXCEL ADD-IN COMPUTER
Processor type	Minimum: 1x Pentium 4 Recommended: 2x dual-core 64-bit CPUs	Minimum: 1x Pentium 4 Recommended: 2x dual-core 64-bit CPUs	Minimum: 1x Pentium 3 Recommended: 1x dual-core 32-bit CPU	Minimum: 1x Pentium 3 Recommended: 1x dual-core 32-bit CPU
Processor speed	Minimum: 2.5 gigahertz (GHz) Recommended: 2.8 GHz	Minimum: 2.5 gigahertz (GHz) Recommended: 2.8 GHz	Minimum: 1 GHz Recommended: 2.5 GHz	Minimum: 1 GHz Recommended: 2.5 GHz
Available hard disk space	Minimum: 1 gigabyte (GB) Recommended: 5 GB + 7200 rpm hard disk drive	Minimum: 1 gigabyte (GB) Recommended: 5 GB + 7200 rpm hard disk drive	Minimum: 512 megabytes (MB) Recommended: 2 GB	Minimum: 512 megabytes (MB) Recommended: 2 GB
RAM	Minimum: 2 GB Recommended: 4 GB	Minimum: 2 GB Recommended: 4 GB	Minimum: 1.5 GB Recommended: 2 GB	Minimum: 1.5 GB Recommended: 2 GB
Network interface	Minimum: 1000BASE-T	Minimum: 1000BASE-T	Minimum: 1000BASE-T	Minimum: 1000BASE-T

Software Prerequisites

Table 3-6 specifies the software prerequisites for Planning Server components, both clients and servers. The required applications must be installed prior to installing PerformancePoint. The installation of the specified PerformancePoint software component will check for the existence of the required software.

Table 3-6 Software Prerequisites for Planning Server

PREREQUISITE	REQUIRED FOR INSTALLATION
Microsoft SQL Server 2005 database software (Standard or Enterprise Edition) Service Pack 2	Planning System Database
Microsoft SQL Server Analysis Services 2005 (Enterprise Edition) Service Pack 2	Planning Analysis Services Server
Internet Information Services (IIS) 6.0 Internet Information Services (IIS) 7.0 with IIS metabase and IIS 6 configuration compatibility Microsoft ASP.NET 2.0 Microsoft .NET Framework version 2.0.50727 IIS 6.0 worker process isolation mode Microsoft ASP.NET 2.0 registration with IIS ASP.NET 2.0 Web Service Extension in IIS 6.0	Planning Server Web Service Planning Administration Console Server
SQL Server Native Client 9.0 SP2	Planning System Database Planning Server Web Service Planning Server Process Service Planning Administration Console Server Planning Configuration Wizard Planning Business Modeler Planning Add-In for Excel
ADOMD.NET 9.0 SP2	Planning System Database Planning Server Web Service Planning Server Process Service Planning Administration Console Server Planning Configuration Wizard Planning Business Modeler Planning Add-In for Excel
MSXML 6.0 + updates	Dashboard Viewer for SharePoint Services
SQL Server 2000 Analysis Services Service Pack 4 - Build 2174 for Client Systems (to use SQL Server 2000 Analysis Services as a data source)	Planning Add-In for Excel
Excel 2003 SP2 Excel 2007 Excel .NET Programmability Support	Planning Add-In for Excel
Windows SharePoint Services 3.0 Microsoft Office SharePoint Server 2007	(Optional) Form and Report storage for
Microsoft SQL Server 2005 Reporting Services	(Optional) Report publishing from Excel Add-In

System Requirements

Planning Server delivers separate installations for server and client components. Tables 3-7 and 3-8 list the system requirements for both server and client components, respectively.

Table 3-7 Server Components for Planning Server

SERVER COMPONENTS	SUPPORTED OPERATING SYSTEMS	ADDITIONAL REQUIREMENTS	SUPPORTED BROWSERS
PerformancePoint Planning Server Configuration Manager	32-bit and 64-bit versions of Windows Server 2003 SP2 and Windows Server 2003 R2 32-bit and 64-bit versions of Windows Server 2008	Microsoft .NET Framework 2.0 Microsoft ASP.NET 2.0 SQL Native Client 9.0 SP2	
PerformancePoint Planning Server Web Service	32-bit and 64-bit versions of Windows Server 2003 SP2 and Windows Server 2003 R2 32-bit and 64-bit versions of Windows Server 2008	Microsoft Internet Information Services IIS 6.0, or IIS 7.0 with IIS metabase and IIS 6 configuration compatibility, IIS 6.0 Isolation Mode Microsoft .NET Framework 2.0 Microsoft ASP.NET 2.0 SQL Server 2005 Analysis Management Objects 9.0 SP2 SQL Server 2005 Native Client 9.0 SP2	
PerformancePoint Planning Server Process Service	32-bit and 64-bit versions of Windows Server 2003 SP2 and Windows Server 2003 R2 32-bit and 64-bit versions of Windows Server 2008	Microsoft Internet Information Services (IIS) 6.0, or IIS 7.0 with IIS metabase and IIS 6 configuration compatibility, IIS 6.0 Isolation Mode Microsoft .NET Framework 2.0 Microsoft ASP.NET 2.0 SQL Server 2005 Analysis Management Objects 9.0 SP2 SQL Server 2005 Native Client 9.0 SP2	

(*continued*)

Table 3-7 *(continued)*

SERVER COMPONENTS	SUPPORTED OPERATING SYSTEMS	ADDITIONAL REQUIREMENTS	SUPPORTED BROWSERS
PerformancePoint Planning Administration Console Server	32-bit and 64-bit versions of Windows Server 2003 SP2 and Windows Server 2003 R2 32-bit and 64-bit versions of Windows Server 2008	Microsoft Internet Information Services (IIS) 6.0, or IIS 7.0 with IIS metabase and IIS 6 configuration compatibility, IIS 6.0 Isolation Mode Microsoft .NET Framework 2.0 Microsoft ASP.NET 2.0 SQL Server 2005 Analysis Management Objects 9.0 SP2 SQL Server 2005 Native Client 9.0 SP2	Microsoft Internet Explorer 6.0 Microsoft Internet Explorer 7.0
PerformancePoint Planning System Database	32-bit and 64-bit versions of Windows Server 2003 SP2 and Windows Server 2003 R2 32-bit and 64-bit versions of Windows Server 2008	Microsoft SQL Server 2005 SP2 Standard Edition (Optional) SQL Server 2005 SP2 Reporting Services	
PerformancePoint Planning Analysis Services Server	32-bit and 64-bit versions of Windows Server 2003 SP2 and Windows Server 2003 R2 32-bit and 64-bit versions of Windows Server 2008	Microsoft SQL Server Analysis Services 2005 Enterprise Edition SP2	

NOTE **The support for Windows Server 2008 begins with PerformancePoint Server 2007 Service Pack 1. Information on current and future service packs, including updated requirements, is found in the online Deployment Guide for PerformancePoint Server 2007. This guide is available at** `http://technet.microsoft.com/en-us/library/bb794637.aspx`.

Table 3-8 Client components for Planning Server

CLIENT COMPONENTS	SUPPORTED OPERATING SYSTEMS	ADDITIONAL REQUIREMENTS	SUPPORTED BROWSERS
PerformancePoint Planning Business Modeler	Windows XP SP2 (excluding Windows XP Embedded) 32-bit and 64-bit versions of Windows Vista Business, Windows Vista Business N, and Windows Vista Enterprise	SQL ADOMD.NET 9.0 MSXML 6.0 + updates SQL Server 2005 SP2 Analysis Server OLEDB 9.0 Provider SQL Server 2000 Analysis Services Service Pack 4 - Build 2174 for Client Systems (to use SQL Server 2000 Analysis Services as a data source) Microsoft .NET Framework 2.0	
PerformancePoint Planning Add-In for Excel	32-bit and 64-bit versions of Windows Server 2003 SP2 and Windows Server 2003 R2 32-bit and 64-bit versions of Windows Server 2008 Windows XP SP2 (excluding Windows XP Embedded) 32-bit and 64-bit versions of Windows Vista Business, Windows Vista Business N, and Windows Vista Enterprise	Excel 2003 SP2 Excel 2007 Excel .NET Programmability Support SQL ADOMD.NET 9.0 MSXML 6.0 + updates SQL Server 2005 SP2 Analysis Server OLEDB 9.0 Provider SQL Server 2000 Analysis Services Service Pack 4 - Build 2174 for Client Systems (to use SQL Server 2000 Analysis Services as a data source) Microsoft .NET Framework 2.0	

(*continued*)

Table 3-8 *(continued)*

CLIENT COMPONENTS	SUPPORTED OPERATING SYSTEMS	ADDITIONAL REQUIREMENTS	SUPPORTED BROWSERS
PerformancePoint Planning Administration console (Internet Explorer)	32-bit and 64-bit versions of Windows Server 2003 SP2 and Windows Server 2003 R2 32-bit and 64-bit versions of Windows Server 2008 Windows XP SP2 (excluding Windows XP Embedded) 32-bit and 64-bit versions of Windows Vista Business, Windows Vista Business N, and Windows Vista Enterprise		Microsoft Internet Explorer 6.0 Microsoft Internet Explorer 7.0

Installing and Configuring Planning Server

The installation for Planning Server contains two distinct component setups: one that installs the Web Service and one that installs the Process Service. Both servers are included in the Windows installer package `PPLSrv.msi`. Installing the server components can be done in a standalone configuration, where all components are installed on a single server computer, or in a distributed configuration, where components are spread across multiple server computers. Once the installer package executes to extract and install the software components, the Planning Server Configuration Manager launches and is used to configure and install the selected Planning Server components.

The following components are described in more detail later in the book:

- **PerformancePoint Planning Web Service.** A set of Web Service interfaces that provides the core functionality of PerformancePoint Planning Server.
- **PerformancePoint Planning System Database.** A SQL Server database that stores all Planning Server system data, service queues, and configuration settings.

- **PerformancePoint Planning Process Service.** A Windows service that processes data and actions against the Microsoft SQL Server databases that contain Planning Server meta data, reference data, and value data.
- **PerformancePoint Administration Console Server.** A set of Web Service interfaces to configure and administer system and application settings.

When running in a standalone configuration, the Planning Server Configuration Manager installs all components on the local machine. When running in a distributed configuration, the Planning Server Installation and Planning Server Configuration Manager must be run on each computer in the distributed topology, with each component selected and configured on the local machine from Planning Server Configuration Manager.

NOTE **The Deployment Guide for PerformancePoint Server 2007 contains detailed instructions for configuring Planning Server. This guide is available for download from** `http://technet.microsoft.com/en-us/library/cc196370.aspx`.

Authentication Options

When configuring Planning Server, two security accounts are specified. First is the global administrator account to set up with the server. Second is the service identity account to run the services.

Global Administrator

The global administrator is the system-level administrator role in Planning Server. When performing the installation, the default global administrator account is specified. Subsequent to the server's being set up, this global administrator can assign other users to the system and specify other security roles (described in Chapter 15).

Service Identity

The service identity account is the machine or network account with which the Planning Server Web Service and process service execute. For better segmentation of security responsibilities and access, it is recommended that these Windows accounts be a true "Service Account" (i.e., not the domain account of any real individual), which is created for the sole purpose of Planning Server usage.

Kerberos

In a typical distributed deployment, many client computers will access a Planning Server installed across multiple servers. Kerberos authentication and delegation allows the caller's identity to be the account under which server services are executed. If the Planning Administration Console Service is installed on a separate computer from the other Planning Web Service, Kerberos delegation must be used to access the Administration Console from any client machine. Kerberos enables the passing of the client user's credentials from the Administration Console Service to the Web Service for authorization.

Secure Socket Layer

Planning Server uses the following security methods for the Web Service Server: Internet Information Services (IIS) security, file and folder security, and Secure Socket Layer (SSL) security. Of these security methods, SSL is the preferred method for securing the Planning Server deployment.

Installing the Planning Clients

PerformancePoint Planning has two separate client installations to allow for distinct usage of the clients; each has a very different purpose. The Excel Add-In will be installed by business users needing to work as an end user of an application to interact with its data and processes, and as a contributor of data or viewer data. The Business Modeler client is installed by business users or developers who will work on creating application objects such as models or business rules.

Excel Add-In Client

The Excel Add-In client setup is available in the Windows Installer package `PPLXCli.msi`. This package extracts and installs the Add-In for Excel to the default location, `C:%Program Files%\Microsoft Office PerformancePoint Server\3.0\Excel Client`. The installation supports both Excel 2003 and Excel 2007. In addition to the Add-In itself, there are two utilities available once the installation is complete:

- **PerformancePoint Add-In for Excel Configuration Settings.** A diagnostic tool that checks environment settings in order to assist with troubleshooting Add-In failures.
- **PerformancePoint Server Protocol Handler.** A protocol registration that enables launching of PerformancePoint assignments through hyperlinks.

Business Modeler Client

The Business Modeler client setup is available in the Windows Installer package `PBMCli.msi`. This package extracts and installs the Business Modeler to the default location: `C:\%Program Files%\Microsoft Office PerformancePoint Server\3.0\BizModeler`. In addition to the Modeler client, there is a command-line client tool installed as well:

- **PPSCmd.exe.** A command-line tool for executing modeler functionality via scripts or other processes commonly involved in production environment batch processing.

Best Practice Planning Server Installation

- Review all hardware and software prerequisites and system requirements before installation. Identify and remedy any gaps well before installation.
- Use Secure Sockets Layer security to secure your Planning Server Web Service deployment.
- Use the Planning Server installation log files to troubleshoot issues during installation. These files are called `MonitoringStatus%date%.log` and `MonitoringVerbose%date%.log`. They are created in a directory called `%temp%`.

Summary

This chapter provided an overview of the requirements and steps involved in setting up and configuring PerformancePoint Monitoring Server and PerformancePoint Planning Server. Typically, corporate organizations and other groups requiring large-scale distributions will choose to deploy a distributed topology in which Monitoring Server is installed on multiple computers. PerformancePoint Monitoring Server is made up of multiple components with specific requirements for installation and configuration. PerformancePoint Planning Server is composed of two server components: a front-end server (Web Service) based on Internet Services and a back-end process service layer interacting directly with a SQL Database server. Best practices and troubleshooting information for installing and configuring PerformancePoint Servers were also discussed.

Part

II

PerformancePoint Monitoring and Analytics

PerformancePoint Monitoring and Analytics helps you quickly and effectively gain deep understanding and insight about your organization's performance through interactive performance dashboards. For example, you can answer such questions as these: "What are the key indicators of performance in my organization?"; "How well is my team performing with respect to those indicators?"; and "Why didn't we achieve our revenue targets last quarter?"

PerformancePoint Monitoring and Analytics provides a flexible environment for creating and deploying performance dashboards that contain the right visualizations for conveying the right information to the right users at the right time. What this means is that an organization can make strategic, operational, and tactical decisions that are aligned to team or company goals and current status, with minimal overhead and maintenance.

The next several chapters describe the broad set of PerformancePoint Server Monitoring and Analytics features and how they support relevant, usable, and effective performance dashboards. In Chapter 4, you will learn about the components of PerformancePoint Monitoring and Analytics, including Dashboard Designer and Monitoring Server. You will also learn about dashboard concepts such as reports, filters, and data sources and how they come together for optimal dashboard solutions.

Chapter 5 provides a detailed look at key performance indicators (KPIs) and scorecards and how they can be used to provide an at-a-glance view of performance status. It also discusses how KPIs and scorecards can be aligned to a specific performance methodology, such as the balanced scorecard or Six Sigma.

Chapter 6 describes the analytics features of PerformancePoint, focusing on analytic visualizations and navigation. It also discusses Online Analytic Processing (OLAP) and how analytics can be used to understand the driving forces behind the numbers.

Chapter 7 brings together scorecards and analytics into performance dashboards, where performance can be monitored and managed. It explains filters, sizing, and conditional display options and provides guidance on how to ensure dashboard content is relevant for all users.

Chapters 8 and 9 complete the detailed view of PerformancePoint Monitoring and Analytics by highlighting additional report types (such as Strategy Maps and Excel Services) and security controls.

CHAPTER

4

PerformancePoint Monitoring and Analytics Architecture: Overview

This chapter provides an overview of PerformancePoint architecture for monitoring and analytics.

The first section, "Product Overview," explains the concepts and features of monitoring and analytics and how the different concepts and features are related and support each other in the implementation of a business intelligence solution.

The second section, "System Architecture," provides an overview of the different components that make up the PerformancePoint Monitoring and Analytics environment, including a discussion of a deployment topology in a distributed installation.

The third section, "Application Concepts," describes the PerformancePoint Monitoring and Analytics application concepts through the use of business examples that illustrate key concepts such as dashboards, scorecards, reports, and data sources and how they can be implemented.

The final section, "Workflow Concepts," provides information and instructions on creating, deploying, and consuming content.

Product Overview

Organizations often respond to the need for data-driven decisions by generating reports — predefined, highly formatted data sets with standard calculations delivered at regular intervals. Reports are efficient tools for revealing answers to explicit questions: What was last year's revenue? What is the highest selling product? Which region had the highest sales? However, reports are less effective at addressing the inevitable follow-up questions: Why was revenue so low last year? Why did one product sell better than another? Why did sales drop in the Southeast region?

In attempting to respond to follow-up questions, organizations generate more reports. The new reports lead to more questions, and the cycle — or reporting treadmill, as it's often called — continues. And while reports are being generated, business goes on, opportunities come and go, crises are managed when they might have been averted, and so on.

The tools and features introduced in PerformancePoint Server do more than replace the reporting treadmill. They enable managers and individual contributors at every level to continuously monitor their progress and perform their own analysis, quickly and effectively. Moreover, these tools promote accountability, consistency, and alignment throughout the organization by delivering a cohesive strategy backed by actionable metrics and informative reports.

Collaborative Performance Management

The architecture and design of PerformancePoint Server and the Microsoft BI stack acknowledge that effective performance management isn't something that can be packaged into a standard report and delivered to users once a month. Rather, it is an iterative and interactive process of monitoring status, identifying exceptions, finding cause-and-effect relationships, and validating assumptions. For example, a regional sales manager sees that a particular product line has unexpectedly declined in sales for the past 2 months. The regional manager works with her business analyst to understand the cause, and they discover that the decline in sales is localized to two stores. They then find that both stores receive inventory from the same distribution center, and both stores have recently hired new managers.

The regional manager meets with the store managers to discuss the trend in product sales. In one store, she discovers that the store has incorrectly coded the product family for that particular product line. She works with IT to correct the problem and update the sales data for the past 2 months. In the other store, she discovers that the store has received the wrong inventory for the past 4 months, and the new store manager wasn't aware of the problem. She reviews inventory processes with the new manager to ensure that the problem is resolved. She also recommends that the analyst create a new view in the sales dashboard showing expected-to-actual inventory metrics.

The multi-tiered architecture of SQL Server 2005 Analysis Services, Microsoft PerformancePoint Server 2007 Dashboard Designer, and Windows SharePoint Services supports this ongoing, collaborative effort among IT, analysts, and business users to gather and organize the data, gain insight, and take action — all within the enterprise environment, as shown in Figure 4-1.

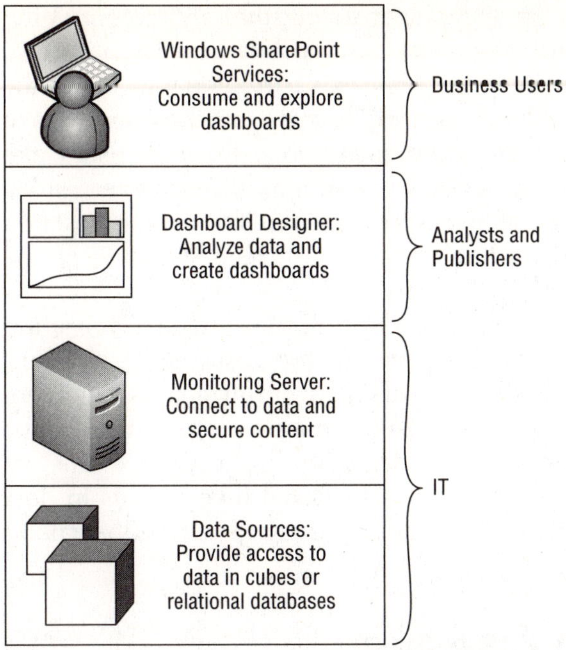

Figure 4-1 Tiered architecture of PerformancePoint Server

Through collaboration, all stakeholders contribute their expertise: IT centrally manages the data, analysts discover and communicate relevant and compelling relationships within the data, and business users apply that insight to their decisions and actions. All three roles work together to continually improve the data, content, and outcomes. The result of this collaboration is an organization that can effectively align its day-to-day activities and decisions to its business strategies.

Figure 4-2 illustrates this collaboration among roles within an organization.

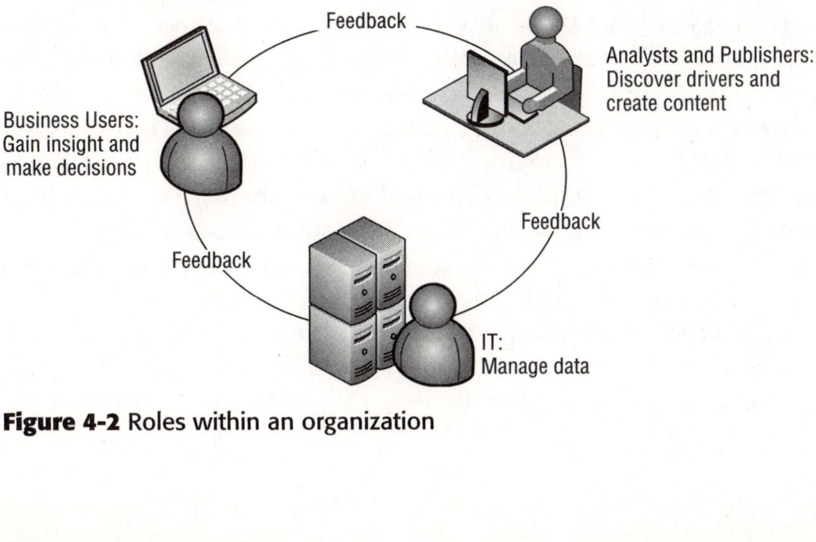

Figure 4-2 Roles within an organization

IT centrally manages the data warehouse, ensuring that security, quality, and compliance standards are met. They make this data available to analysts in the form of relational or multidimensional databases. Analysts work with the data to find answers and draw conclusions, and they present these findings to business users in reports, spreadsheets, and presentations. Business users take this information and apply it to the decisions they make to achieve results. The process doubles back as business users provide feedback to analysts on the type of information they need, and analysts provide feedback to IT on the type and form of data they need.

With PerformancePoint Server and the Microsoft BI stack, this collaboration is managed holistically, with a single architecture for all three roles. Thus, PerformancePoint brings together the benefits of centralized management and control with the power and flexibility of continuous monitoring, ad hoc exploration, and analysis. It gives users full flexibility and control to answer their own questions, while ensuring that organizational investments in data quality, control, and management are maintained through the decision-making cycle.

Pervasive Performance Management

Pervasive performance management means that all decision makers in an organization are aligned, accountable, and empowered. Users have relevant, personalized, and current dashboards available to them at all times. They have guidance on what views are meaningful and how they should be used. And they don't have to install specialized software or endure lengthy training classes on how to use the software. They begin by monitoring their business performance using intuitive, Web-based scorecards and dashboards and then move to analytics to better understand the driving factors behind unexpected results.

When performance management is applied pervasively throughout an organization, data becomes insight and insight becomes a strategic, competitive advantage. Regardless of where they are within the organization, individuals can make timely decisions that align with corporate strategy and their own personal organizational commitments. For example, a quality control officer discovers a correlation between product failures and overtime. By adjusting resource utilization rates on his team, he is able to reduce product failures to achieve his quality goals. And his improvements then influence higher corporative objectives of on-time delivery and customer satisfaction.

For performance management to become pervasive within an organization, it must be accessible and tailored to the individual business user. The most accessible of applications is often a Web browser: users simply open it, click a link, and begin working. To go one step further with pervasive performance management, users will respond with even greater enthusiasm if the information has a personal connection. Consider how much more interesting stock prices are when you have invested money in a company. Or how much more exciting sports scores are when your alma mater plays a crosstown rival. Personalized information is what drives people to pay attention, go a bit deeper, and encourage change.

This personalized experienced is achieved through context and relevance:

- **Context.** The information is presented with the appropriate scope for the user. For example, executives see aggregated performance data, and information workers see data for their specific areas.
- **Relevance.** The analysis directly relates to users and their tasks. For example, executives see how the entire organization is performing compared to corporate strategy, and information workers see how they are performing against others in their group or their previous performance.

When deployed successfully in an organization, PerformancePoint Server can help ensure that the goals of alignment, accountability, and consistency are achieved through collaboration and the continual evolution of content for optimal context and relevance. As the specific features and capabilities of PerformancePoint Server are discussed in the coming sections, you will find practical, concrete ways to help ensure that these goals are met in your organization.

System Architecture

Performance management solutions allow for continuous business improvement through planning, monitoring, and analyzing information within an organization. The monitoring and analytics aspect of a performance management solution with PerformancePoint Server is made up of the following components:

- **Dashboard Designer** — Client application used to create and manage dashboards, scorecards, reports, filters, and data sources.
- **Consumer** — Methods for displaying business information and allowing business analysts and others in an organization to consume and present information.
- **Monitoring Server** — Computer or group of computers set up to host the Monitoring System Database and Monitoring Server Web Service.
- **Dashboards** — Scorecards and report views that are organized together in a single SharePoint site and that provide organizations with a view into performance in key business areas.

- **Scorecards** — A collection of KPIs and objectives that together provide a comprehensive view of the organization's objectives for monitoring and analyzing business performance and strategy.
- **Reports** — Dynamic displays of business information for monitoring and analyzing business performance and strategy. Examples include detailed charts, pivot tables, spreadsheets, and SQL Server reports that are based on dashboard data as well as strategy maps created with Microsoft Visio 2007.
- **Data Sources** — Sources of business data that provide the raw data for PerformancePoint Server applications. Examples include SQL Server, Analysis Services, Excel, SharePoint lists, and ODBC connections.

Figure 4-3 illustrates the relationship between these components; additional information about each is provided in the following sections of this chapter.

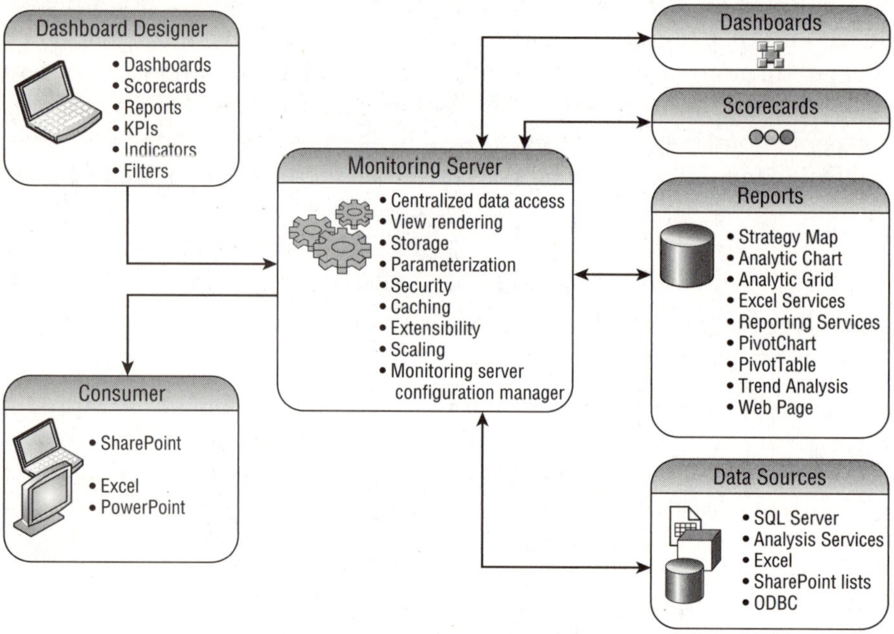

Figure 4-3 PerformancePoint Monitoring Server system architecture

Dashboard Designer

Dashboard Designer is the client application for creating and managing the elements of a performance management solution, including dashboards, scorecards, reports, KPIs, filters, and data sources.

PerformancePoint Monitoring and Analytics is a *visual* decision-making application. This visual quality applies at the design level as well as at the business level with the Dashboard Designer tool, as shown in Figure 4-4. With Dashboard Designer, you build monitoring and analytic decision-making dashboards using a graphical interface that is visual, intuitive, and interactive.

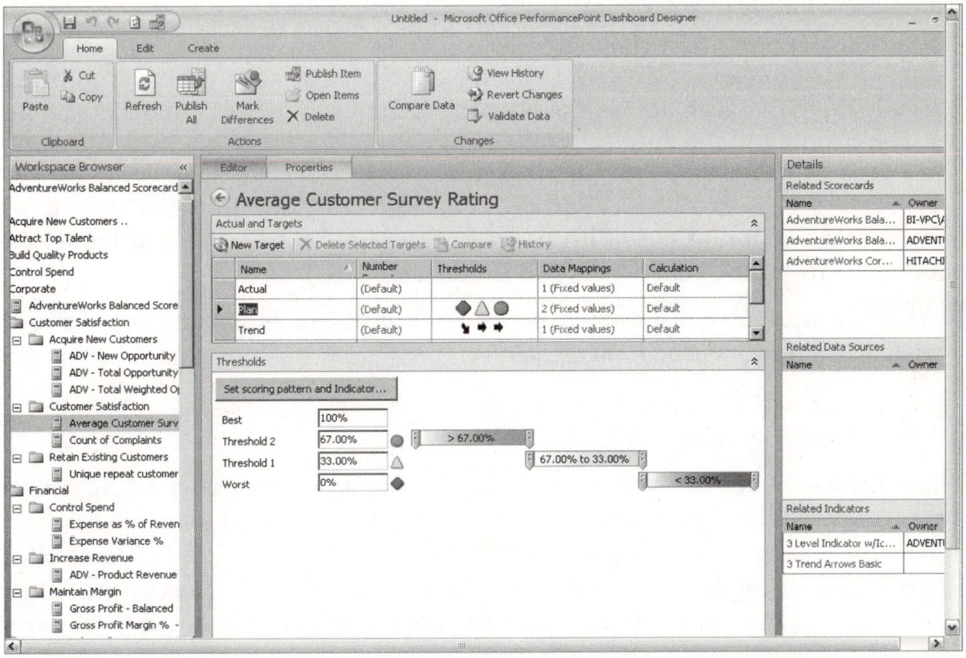

Figure 4-4 The Dashboard Designer interface is visual, intuitive, and interactive.

The Dashboard Designer interface is based on Office 2007 and makes use of workspace panes and the Ribbon interface which can be customized by adding extensions such as tabs, panels, and buttons. Use Dashboard Designer to:

- Connect to different types of data sources
- Create dashboards and scorecards
- Modify and adjust individual dashboard and scorecard elements, including KPIs
- Publish dashboards and dashboard elements to Monitoring Server
- Create reports to publish to Monitoring Server
- Publish dashboards and scorecards to a SharePoint site or an ASP.NET Web site for business analysts and others to view
- Import scorecards, analytic charts, or analytic grids into a Microsoft Excel spreadsheet or Microsoft PowerPoint presentation

Dashboard Designer includes wizards and templates to step through the most frequently used operations. It also includes a preview capability for viewing dashboards and scorecards on ASP.NET pages prior to deployment.

The Dashboard Designer installation includes an IIS Web site called Monitoring Central and accessed from this link once the application is installed:

```
http:// <Monitoring_server_name> : <Port_number> /Central
```

Once the Monitoring Server setup is complete, users connect to Monitoring Central where they can access Dashboard Designer. In a Secure Sockets Layer (SSL) environment, this link is:

```
https:// <Monitoring_server_name> : <Port_number> /Central
```

Note that a separate server license is not required for Dashboard Designer, but the appropriate client access licenses are required.

TIP In a distributed deployment, define scorecards and dashboards in the client while being disconnected from the server.

Consumer

SharePoint sites are the primary means of consuming and presenting monitoring and analytics business information. Create dashboards, scorecards, and reports in Dashboard Designer, and then publish these to SharePoint sites where business analysts and others in the organization can access the information. Figure 4-5 illustrates an example of a dashboard published to a SharePoint site.

Dashboards, scorecards, and reports can be deployed to either Microsoft Office SharePoint Server 2007 or Windows SharePoint Services 3.0 sites. When using Microsoft Office SharePoint Server with PerformancePoint, you will need a separate SharePoint license. You can deploy dashboards, scorecards, and reports to either a full SharePoint Server or Windows SharePoint Services but it's important to know that if you deploy to SharePoint Services you will not have the ability to use Excel Services for reports or as a data source. Also important to note is the requirement of a SharePoint external connector license if you are exposing to the Internet. The rule of thumb is: two separate products, two separate licenses.

PerformancePoint makes use of ASP.NET Web pages but only for a very specific preview function and only in Dashboard Designer. While working in Dashboard Designer, developers and designers can choose to preview their work before publishing it to test or production SharePoint sites. This function makes use of ASP.NET Web pages.

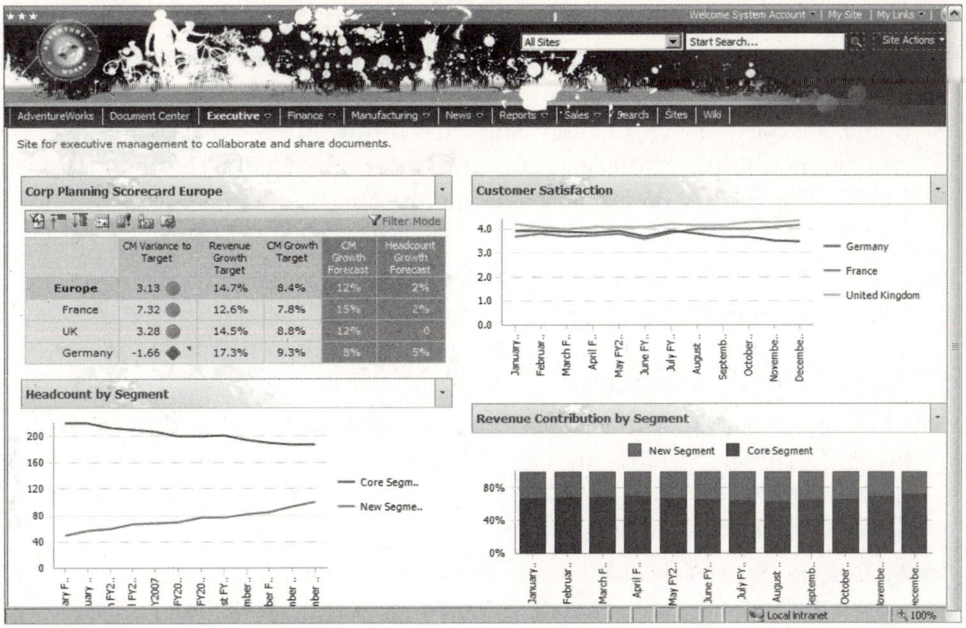

Figure 4-5 Dashboard with scorecard and reports available from a SharePoint site

On the client side, business analysts and others in the organization who view dashboards, scorecards, and reports from SharePoint sites can export the information to Excel or PowerPoint. When exporting data or data views from dashboards into a Microsoft Excel spreadsheet, Monitoring Server generates an Excel .xlsx file in open XML format stored on the client. Use this option to view the information in Excel or work with the data for further analysis. When exporting data or data views from dashboards into a Microsoft PowerPoint presentation, Monitoring Server generates a PowerPoint .pptx file in open XML format stored on the client. Use this option to include the data or data views in a presentation.

NOTE **To export data or data views from dashboards to Excel or PowerPoint, .NET Framework 3.0 must be installed on the computer running Monitoring Server.**

Monitoring Server

PerformancePoint Monitoring Server is made up of server components and a system database. You may recall from Chapter 3 that the components and system database are installed and configured during deployment. The server components and system database each provide specific capabilities:

- The *Monitoring Server Web Service* facilitates communication between the Dashboard Designer client and the Monitoring Server database. The collection of application programming interfaces (APIs) that make up Monitoring Server Web Service define the core functionality of Monitoring Server.
- *Dashboard Web Preview* is an Internet Information Services (IIS) Web site that provides the capability to preview and deploy dashboards as ASP.NET Web pages. Dashboard Web Preview can reside on one or more Windows computers.
- *Monitoring Central* is an IIS Web site central download location for Dashboard Designer. Monitoring Central allows users to download and work with Dashboard Designer, view product documentation, and open the Dashboard Web Preview site.
- *Monitoring System database* is a SQL Server application database that stores the meta data information for Monitoring Server, including reports, data sources, dashboards, and supporting meta data for dashboard elements. When you create and save dashboards and dashboard elements, Dashboard Designer publishes and stores element definitions to this database using a role-based security model, which is also stored in the database. Monitoring Server then retrieves dashboards and dashboard element definitions as required from the database.

NOTE Monitoring Server databases must run on SQL Server 2005 with the most recent service pack.

Deployment Topology

Corporate organizations and other groups requiring large-scale distributions will choose to deploy a distributed topology in which Monitoring Server is installed on multiple computers. In a series of scalability and performance tests Microsoft concluded that "For the test scenario, a single Monitoring Server computer can serve up to 5,700 user sessions per hour without delays. To serve larger loads, the system can be scaled out by adding more SharePoint Server Web server computers. A three-server configuration served 17,700 user sessions per hour."[1] Security configurations may have an impact on scalability and performance, but there is plenty of room to scale up if your organization has modest requirements now but is considering a future large-scale distribution. Even in these enterprise settings, a standalone topology in which all Monitoring Server components are installed on a single computer may be useful for testing and evaluation.

Application Concepts

The best way to explain key monitoring and analytics application concepts is by example. This section provides examples of dashboards, scorecards, report views, filters, custom properties, and data sources.

Dashboards

Dashboards are made up of scorecards and report views that are organized together in a single SharePoint site, providing organizations with a unified view into performance in key business areas. Dashboards are the essence of analytics. Dashboards can be complex or simple. They can contain a single scorecard, or they can contain multiple scorecards and report views made up of charts, tables, and graphs, as shown in Figure 4-6, which is a dashboard that tracks Gross Profit and Loss for a fictitious sports sales company.

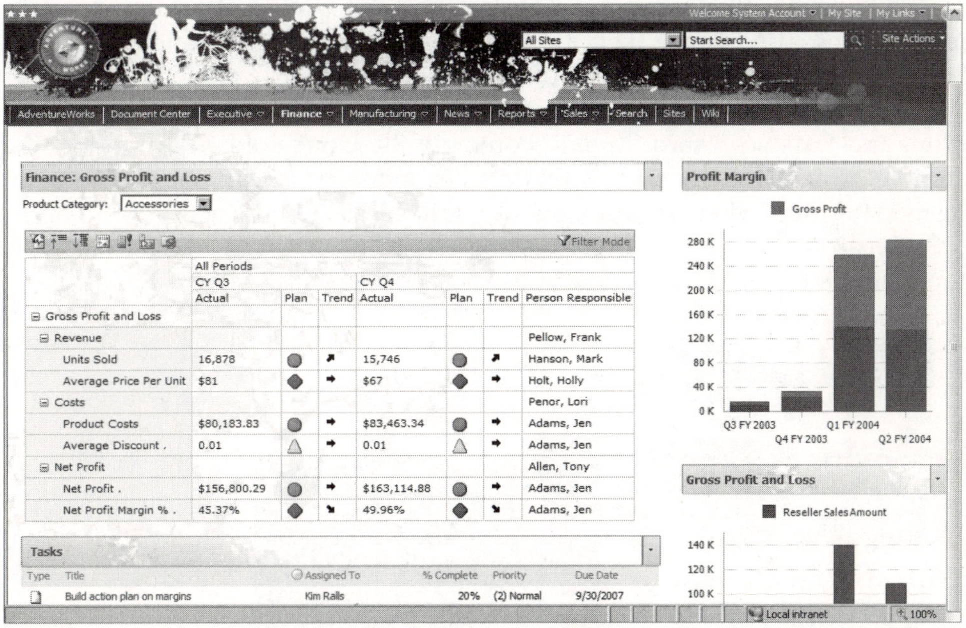

Figure 4-6 Dashboard with scorecard and report views

Dashboards unify structured and unstructured data to facilitate analysis. Structured data refers to data that can be structured in rows and columns in spreadsheets or databases. The Finance: Gross Profit and Loss Scorecard shown in Figure 4-6 is an example of structured data. Unstructured data refers to data that provides context and supporting information rather than data in a structured format, such as a database. A list of documents is an example of unstructured data.

In a dashboard, structured data provides a current and easily understandable snapshot of performance in key areas, while unstructured data enables business analysts and others to drill down and understand more deeply these performance results. The relationship or link between unstructured and structured data enables business decision makers to drill down and analyze the results as seen through the structured data. In Chapter 6, you will examine different tools and methods for making and analyzing decisions, and Chapter 7 steps through the process of designing and building effective dashboards.

Scorecards

Scorecards are a collection of KPIs and objectives that together provide a comprehensive view of the health of an organization's business and strategy. Scorecards are the essence of monitoring. Scorecards make use of KPIs to measure performance in specific areas. Comparison and evaluation are at the core of KPIs. A KPI always compares and evaluates a target or desired value set by business decision makers against an explicit and measurable value taken directly from an objective source of business data.

The dashboard example shown previously contains a scorecard called Gross Profit and Loss Scorecard. In this scorecard, the Units Sold KPI monitors the number of actual units sold so that a sales manager looking at this KPI can easily determine whether or not overall unit sales are on target.

Scorecards are based on three concepts — objectives, KPIs, and targets — as shown in Figure 4-7.

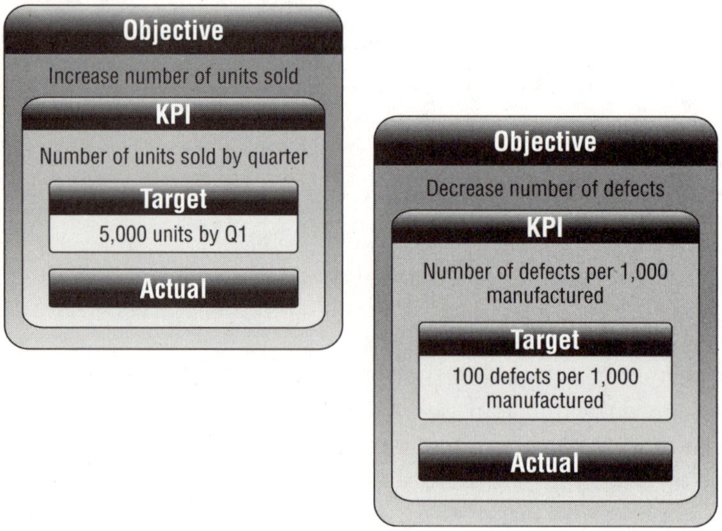

Figure 4-7 Key scorecard concepts

Objectives refer to statements of goals for your organization — for example increase the number of units sold or decrease the number of defects in products. Scorecards can contain one or more objectives, and these objectives can roll up to higher-level objectives.

Each objective in a scorecard is measured by a KPI, with KPIs tracking performance. Examples of KPIs for the objectives stated previously are number of units sold per quarter and number of defects per 1,000 manufactured.

Targets are the numeric goals for a KPI. For example, how many units does the organization want to sell in Q1? In Q4? How many defects per 1,000 are acceptable for Q1? For Q4?

Scorecards can be based on performance management methodologies, which provide a framework or perspective and identify areas for monitoring and analysis. Examples of performance management methodologies include the Balanced Scorecard, Six Sigma, Capability Maturity Model Integration (CMMI), Agile, or customer relationship management (CRM). Organizations can create scorecards from any performance management methodology as long as they follow performance management principles and understand the relationship between the performance measurement areas and their KPIs. Figure 4-8 is an example of a Balanced Scorecard, which is based on a complete FOSH (Finance, Operations, Sales, Human Resources) metric set.

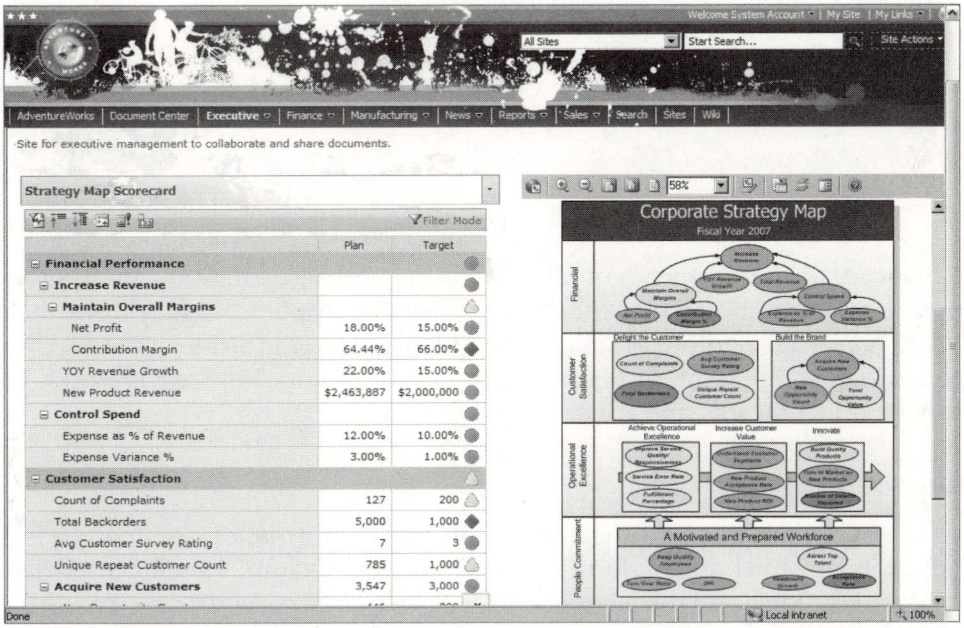

Figure 4-8 Balanced Scorecard with a strategy map

In this Strategy Map Scorecard, Increase Revenue is an example of an overall financial performance objective. This objective is supported by two related objectives — Maintain Overall Margins and Control Spend — each with its KPIs set. Together, the objectives and KPIs measure the organization's performance with regard to the overall Finance objective of increasing revenue.

Scorecards can have a completely different look and feel. Compare the previous top-level Strategy Map Scorecard with the Finance: Gross Profit and Loss Scorecard shown in Figure 4-9.

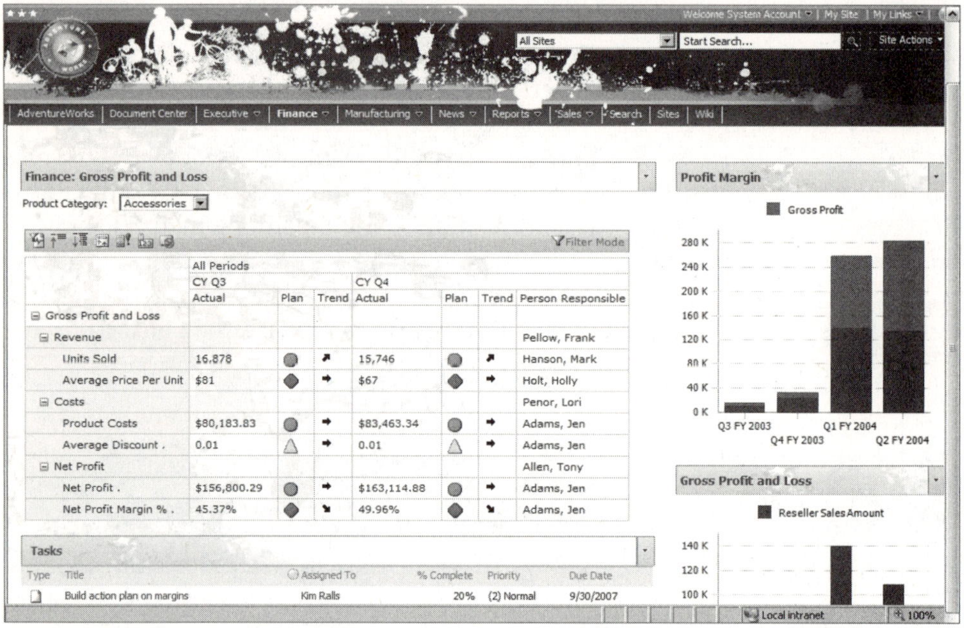

Figure 4-9 Scorecards can have a completely different look and feel.

Notice that the Finance scorecard includes Actual, Plan, and Trend information by Quarter as well as the names of those responsible for the various objectives — detail information that is not required in the Strategy Map Scorecard. Chapter 5 explores different types of scorecards and covers how to implement scorecards and KPIs.

Report Views

Reports provide dynamic displays of business information for monitoring and analyzing business performance and strategy. Examples include detailed charts, pivot tables, spreadsheets, and SQL Server reports that are based on dashboard data as well as strategy maps created with Microsoft Visio 2007.

Figure 4-10 illustrates different report types available within a single dashboard.

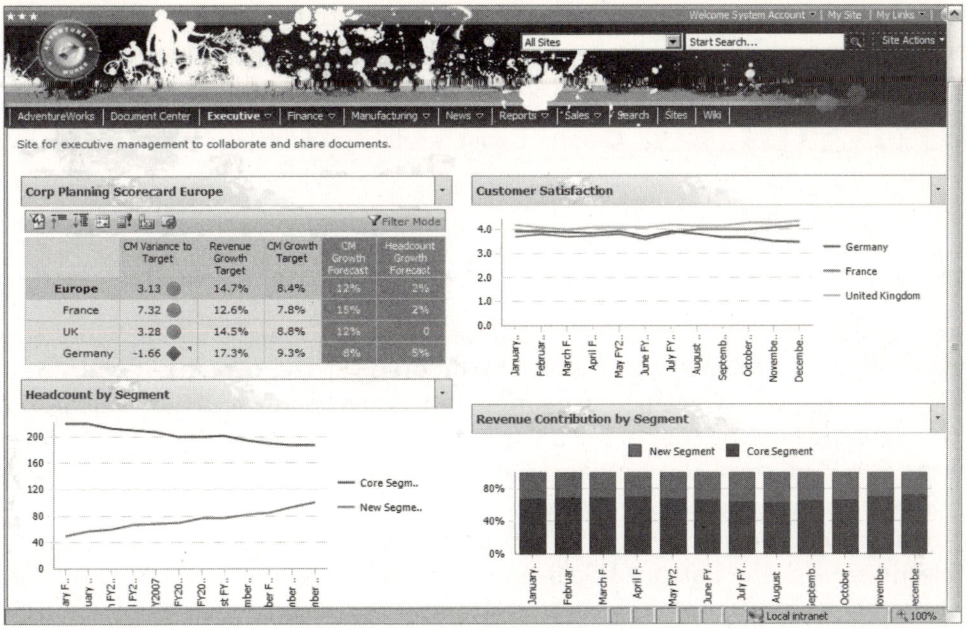

Figure 4-10 Scorecard with different report views

The following section briefly describes the different report types. Chapter 8 explores in detail these different report types and how to build reports.

Scorecards

Typically, scorecards provide the focus of a dashboard with the report view made up of charts, tables, spreadsheets, and documents providing supporting information for further analysis. A scorecard will provide a quick view of performance with indicators that show at a glance how well the organization is doing in key performance areas, but it's important to note that the data from the scorecard can be used to build report views as well.

In Dashboard Designer, you will see that scorecards have available fields that can be passed to report views, including, for example, the Display Value of selected KPIs, the Name, ID, and Description of selected KPIs or the Display Value of cells and dimensions. In practice, this means that you can build highly relevant and targeted reports from a consistent data set.

Analytic Charts and Analytic Grids

Analytic Charts and Analytic Grids are reports based on SQL Server 2005 Analysis Services data sources published to the server. Create the basic structure for the Analytic Chart in Dashboard Designer using the Analytic View Designer, which allows you to arrange measures, dimensions, and named sets on a graphical chart workspace. You can then adjust report properties and permissions as required. The Analytic View Designer also allows you to create analytic grids through a drag-and-drop interface.

CROSS-REFERENCE **Chapter 6 covers Analytic Charts and Analytic Grids in detail.**

Strategy Maps

Strategy maps were developed by Robert Kaplan and David Norton, the creators of the Balanced Scorecard methodology. These maps illustrate in one consolidated diagram the relationship between the four key balanced scorecard areas at the core of the Balanced Scorecard methodology and known as the FOSH metrics. These areas are F (Financial), O (Operational Excellence), S (Sales), and H (Human Resources).

Strategy maps connect stated business objectives with four overall business objectives from the Balanced Scorecard methodology into a visual representation that shows cause-and-effect relationships between the objectives. The strategy map shown previously in Figure 4-8 illustrates each area of the FOSH metrics. Arrows connect and define cause-and-effect relationships between the objectives identified in each layer. Although the strategy map concept is based on the Balanced Scorecard methodology, you are not required to implement this methodology in PerformancePoint scorecards to use the Strategy Map report type.

To create strategy maps, you will use Dashboard Designer with Microsoft Office Visio 2007 templates and data-driven shapes linked directly to PerformancePoint KPI values and targets. You must use Microsoft Office Visio 2007 for this feature. You will need a license for Microsoft Office Visio 2007 to build strategy maps with Dashboard Designer, but licenses may not be required for all those in your organization who may need to view the maps. Chapter 8 covers creating strategy maps in detail.

Excel Services

Dashboard Designer allows you to create a report using Excel Services. Excel Services is part of Microsoft Office SharePoint Server 2007 and is used to extend the capabilities of Microsoft Office Excel 2007 by allowing a broad sharing of spreadsheets.

When using Excel Services for a report, you can publish an Excel workbook to a dashboard in a SharePoint site. Chapter 8 covers using Excel Services to include spreadsheet reports in dashboards.

Reporting Services

With Dashboard Designer, you can include a reference to an existing SQL Server 2005 Reporting Services report on your deployed dashboard. Optionally, you can include the SQL Server toolbar, parameters, and a documentation map. This also is covered in Chapter 8.

Trend Analysis

Create trend charts to predict future growth based on the key performance indicators you are tracking in your scorecard. For example, a sales organization might create a scorecard to track unit sales by quarter and then create a trend chart to predict unit sales for Q1 2009 based on unit sales for each quarter in 2008.

Trend charts make use of the scorecard KPIs. In fact, in Dashboard Designer you must connect the scorecard to the trend chart. These KPIs provide historical data to the Time Series Data Mining algorithm in SQL Server Analysis Services 2005 (SSAS 2005), which then creates predictions and forecasts. Since trend charts use this algorithm, an SSAS 2005 server must be available. Chapter 8 covers how to create trend charts in detail.

Filters

Dashboard Designer allows the creation of filters on dashboard elements to help organizations manage large amounts of data on a deployed dashboard. The use of filters results in highly targeted and relevant scorecards and report views. For example, in a global sales organization, it's typical to want to view data by region or by product. A sales manager in Europe does not have the same concerns or responsibilities as his or her counterpart in North America. With filters, you can create targeted views for these managers to reflect their areas of responsibility and the specifics of their sales activities. By using a Geography filter, you can ensure that the manager in Germany will see sales information for his region only and will not have to spend time searching through unnecessary data from North America.

Dashboard Designer provides a Dashboard Filter Template that allows you to select from the following types of filters:

- Multidimensional or tabular
- MDX Query
- Time Intelligence

CROSS-REFERENCE **Chapter 7 covers the use of these different filter types in detail.**

Custom MDX

Filter MDX Query is an advanced method of creating filters using multidimensional expressions to build a query for the filter list. The filter list is then created from the results of the MDX query. When using MDX Query to create filters, it's important to ensure that the MDX statement matches the chosen data source.

TIP **Test your MDX externally before entering it as a filter.**

Time Intelligence

Using Time Intelligence, you can build filters to create scorecards and report views that allow business analysts and others in your organization to answer time-related performance questions. How many units did we sell in Q1 compared to Q2? What do our sales for the last 6 months look like? As of today, what do sales look like for the past 3 years?

Dashboard Designer provides two Time Intelligence filters templates. Use the Time Intelligence Members and Formulas template to build filters based on the following formulas:

- Year, Quarter-1, Month:
- Month+6, Day+1, Day+2
- Year.FirstQuarter:Quarter

These filters can appear as a list, a tree, or a multi-tree format.

Use the Time Intelligence Post Formula template to define the current time period, mapping the data source to a reference date and building time dynamic filters from the current date to create report views. This option creates a filter that prompts users to select the current time from a calendar, and then builds scorecards and report views based on the date selected.

Custom Properties

Use custom properties to associate additional meta data to elements on the scorecard. Meta data refers to descriptions that provide further insight into elements displayed on the scorecard. Every KPI on a scorecard has built-in properties available from the Properties section in the Details pane of Dashboard Designer. These built-in properties include Name, Description, and Person Responsible. With custom properties, you can add to this list of properties. For example, do you want to add a comment to the Sales Amount KPI on a scorecard? Would you like to display a date to indicate when the Sales Amount KPI value was last modified? Or do you need to create a link to a document explaining how the Sales Amount KPI value is derived?

Properties are associated to individual elements on the scorecard, so you must first select the element to add the custom property — in this case, the KPI called Sales Amount. Then create custom properties on the Properties tab for the selected element, as shown in Figure 4-11.

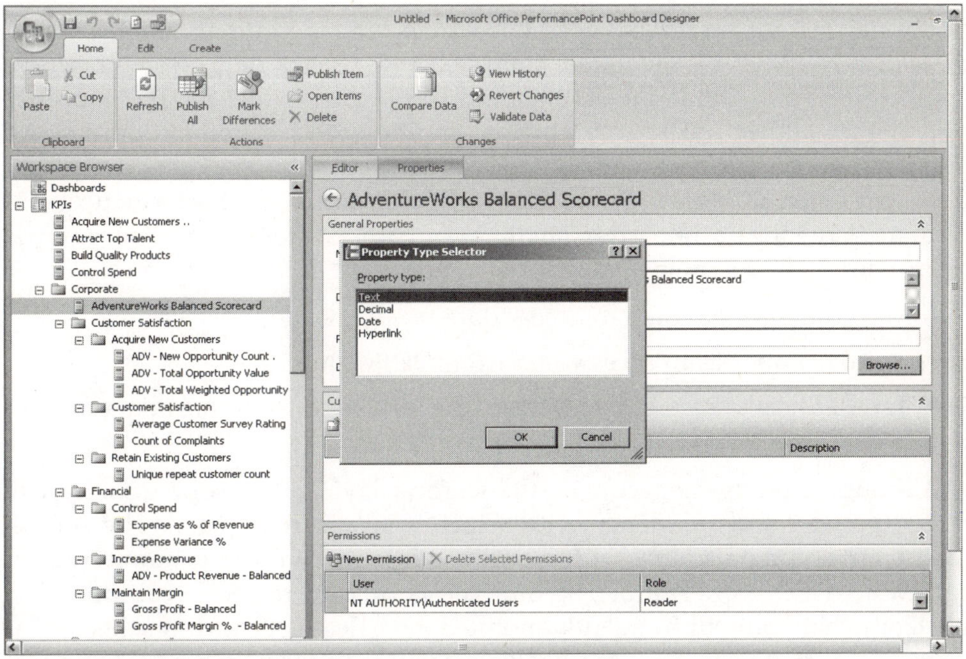

Figure 4-11 Set Custom Properties for a specific element.

The Property Type Selector allows you to pick one of the following property types:

- Text
- Decimal
- Date
- Hyperlink

After you create the custom property, Dashboard Designer adds it to the Properties list on the Details pane. From there, you then drag and drop the custom property into its position on the scorecard.

The custom property displays only for the element it is associated to. So if you add a comment to the Sales Amount KPI, the comment will show only for the Sales Amount KPI and not for any other KPI in the scorecard.

When creating custom properties, stay away as much as possible from creating manual values, and always use a dimension value if possible.

TIP **Before creating a custom property, study your data source. Can you use a dimension to display the information you want?**

Data Sources

PerformancePoint Server allows you to connect to many types of data sources to take advantage of the often complex and varied data systems where organizations store their data. Dashboard Designer provides a Data Mappings option that allows the specification of multiple and different sources. An organization may store its data in Analysis Services cubes, in Excel, or in other back-end Open Database Connectivity (ODBC) solutions. PerformancePoint facilitates creating dashboards from these and other different data source types by providing the following categories of supported data source types:

- Multidimensional data to access data from Analysis Services
- Standard queries to access data from ODBC queries
- Tabular lists to access data from Excel Services or to import data from Excel, SharePoint lists, or SQL Server tables

Although monitoring occurs on the scorecard, your data source choice will affect the way and frequency with which a scorecard is used. The refresh frequency of a data source will impact the frequency of your monitoring or review activities. For example, if your Sales scorecard receives real-time data, it's likely that you will frequently monitor the Sales scorecard. If sales data is refreshed on a weekly basis, it's likely you will monitor it on a weekly basis.

The following sections describe the actual data sources you can connect to.

Analysis Server Data Sources

Create a data source connecting to data from SQL Server Analysis Services. First, set up the basic structure for the data source and configure it, and then adjust the properties and define Time Intelligence if required. This is the most flexible type of data source because data is stored in multidimensional cubes.

SharePoint List

Create a data source connection to a Window SharePoint Services 3.0 list or Microsoft Office SharePoint Server 2007 list. First, set up the basic structure for the data source and configure it, and then adjust the properties and define Time Intelligence if required.

TIP **OLAP data sources should be used for scalability. Tabular data sources have a 25,000-row limit.**

SQL Server Table

Use a table from a SQL Server database as a data source for your dashboard elements. First, set up the basic structure for the data source and configure it, and then adjust the properties and define Time Intelligence if required.

Excel 2007

When creating a data source using an Excel data source, PerformancePoint Server imports and saves the data to the PerformancePoint Server database. You can then set a column as a key, choose to aggregate data in a number of ways, and even choose to ignore a column.

TIP Use an Excel 2007 workbook for a data source when you do not want to share the Excel data with users via Excel Services. The Excel workbook will be stored and hosted within the Dashboard Designer database, and it can only be edited and updated from within Dashboard Designer.

Excel Services

With Dashboard Designer, you can create a data source using Excel Services, which is part of Microsoft Office SharePoint Server 2007. Excel Services extends the capabilities of Microsoft Office Excel 2007 by allowing a broad sharing of spreadsheets, in addition to providing improved manageability and security.

When using Excel Services as a data source, you can publish an Excel workbook to a dashboard in SharePoint and refer to Named Objects (Table, Named Range, and Pivot Table) within the workbook, using this data as a data source. When updating the workbook within Excel, any changes to the data will automatically be reflected in the data source. To create an Excel Services data source, you must have Microsoft Office SharePoint Server 2007 Enterprise Edition installed.

ODBC Connections

Dashboard Designer provides the ability to use an Excel ODBC connection to connect to external Excel workbook files located on the PerformancePoint Server. This solution allows organizations that do not have SharePoint the ability to update Excel files outside of Dashboard Designer. For this usage, Dashboard Designer supports Excel 97 through Excel 2007.

Fixed Values

Value can be realized from visualizing business information even without automated data sources. Organizations that do not have existing data sources to draw on can start the monitoring process by creating and specifying fixed values as the data source. Using Blank and Fixed scorecards, organizations can manually update data on a schedule — monthly or weekly for example. It is not an ideal solution, but in cases where data is not available, it can be a practical solution and a first step toward a fully supported monitoring solution.

TIP **At the design stage, fixed values can be used to create mock up screens for dashboards and scorecards.**

Workflow Concepts

Here is a checklist of questions for you to ask and answer before beginning to create content:

- Who are your key business users? Do they belong to a single department or to several departments with different roles and responsibilities? Are they located in one region or in several regions around the globe? This will help you understand whether or not you need to build one or several dashboards, and what filters you will need to apply.
- Have you defined performance management objectives? Will you be using a performance management methodology?
- Do you have one set of objectives for the organization, or do you have objectives for different areas? Do the objectives roll up into an overall set of objectives for the organization?
- Have you defined KPIs for each objective? How will you measure each objective?
- Have you defined targets for each KPI?
- Have you identified data sources for the KPIs? Will you be using existing data sources or do you need to build new data sources? Will you be using documents as well as databases and spreadsheets? Where are these data sources located? Are they located in a centralized repository or are they scattered around the globe?
- Have you defined the reports your business users will need? What types of reports will you need to build? Do you need strategy maps? Do you need spreadsheets, pivot tables, and/or charts?
- Have you designed the structure for your dashboards? For example, do you need one dashboard or several?
- Have you identified the different views your business users will need on each dashboard?
- Who in IT will develop the dashboards, scorecards, KPIs, and reports?

Now that you've answered these questions and you've got a list of users, dashboards, scorecards, reports, KPIs, and data sources, you're ready to create content.

Creating Content — Dashboard Designer

Dashboard Designer is the client application that you will use to create and control the elements of a performance management solution, including dashboards, scorecards, reports, KPIs, filters, and data sources. Figure 4-12 illustrates the steps for creating content using Dashboard Designer.

Figure 4-12 Creating content workflow

Step 1: Create a Workspace

First create a workspace, which is a type of file that stores information, called elements, on which dashboards are based. The elements are KPIs, scorecards, data sources, reports, and indicators. After you create a workspace, you can create multiple scorecard elements within that workspace.

Step 2: Create Elements

Next, create the elements for your workspace. These elements are KPIs, scorecards, reports, data sources, and indicators. You can create the elements in any order, but some dependencies apply. For example, except for fixed data KPIs, you will need to create the data source before creating KPIs.

Step 3: Configure Elements

Next, configure elements in Dashboard Designer by adding data sources and indicators to KPIs. You may build new KPIs or use KPIs that already exist and are stored on the server.

Step 4: Configure Scorecard

Now configure the scorecard by selecting a data source, and adding KPIs and filters. In this step, you also arrange the hierarchy of objectives in the scorecard, aligning the objectives with your business goals and strategy.

Step 5: Configure Dashboard

Take the elements you've created and design the dashboard with scorecards, reports, and filters. Create relationships and interactions of elements on the dashboard. For example, add filters to provide data by region or by quarter, as required by your key business users.

Step 6: Deploy Dashboard

Finally, deploy the dashboards so that users can begin monitoring and analyzing business performance and strategy.

TIP **When you're designing elements, think of how you can create elements for reuse.**

Data Sources

Dashboard Designer provides a data source template that allows the selection of the three available types of data sources:

- Multidimensional
- Standard Queries
- Tabular List

As mentioned previously, data sources include OLAP cubes, relational databases, or any other ODBC or ADOMD.NET data source.

Once you select the data source template based on your data source type, you specify the data source name and select to grant read permission to all users who are authenticated to PerformancePoint Monitoring Server. You then specify Connection and Cache settings, specifying the length of time to wait before refreshing data. Dashboard Designer provides an option to test the connection.

Reports

Dashboard Designer provides a report template that allows the selection of report types: Analytic Chart, Analytic Grid, Excel Services, PivotChart, PivotTable, ProClarity Analytics, Spreadsheet, SQL Server Report, Strategy Map, Trend Analysis Chart, and Web Page.

Once you select the report template based on the type of report you need, you specify the report name, and select the option to grant read permission to all users who are authenticated. Next, select the data source from the list of data sources previously created. After confirming the template and data source, Dashboard Designer provides a blank report in the design area. Fill in details for your report by dragging and dropping Measures and Dimensions from the Details list in the Dashboard Designer workspace. Another way to create a report is by entering an MDX Query through the Query tab in the Report Design workspace, although it's important to note that you may lose some interactivity with the use of custom MDX.

Dashboards

Dashboard Designer allows you to select from various Dashboard Page templates. Each template provides a unique layout. Examples include 1 zone, 2 or 3 Columns, 2 or 3 Rows, Column with Split Column, and Header with 2 Columns. A dashboard can contain a relationship of one to many pages, and each page can contain its own format. When publishing to SharePoint Services or ASP.NET, one dashboard page equals one Web Part page.

Once you select the dashboard page template, you specify the dashboard page name and select the option to grant read permission to all users who are authenticated. Then on the Dashboard screen, from the Details pane select the scorecards and reports to be displayed, and configure the appropriate filters.

TIP Create your own dashboard templates using the SDK provided with PerformancePoint Monitoring Server. Dashboard templates are stored as assemblies in the file system.

Deploying Content — Dashboard Designer

After creating content, you're ready to deploy the dashboard to a SharePoint site. There are a few items you need to take care of before you can use the Dashboard Designer Wizard to step through the final export process.

Update

For each of the elements — Data source, KPIs, Scorecard, Reports, Indicator, and Dashboard — select the Properties tab and update the Person Responsible field and the Permissions field by entering the appropriate domain\alias.

Refresh

In your dashboard you may have used elements from the centralized repository (for example, shared KPIs) so you want to make sure to deploy the most current version of any elements from the centralized repository. Refresh all the elements with the most current versions from the centralized repository by selecting the single-click Refresh option. This will refresh data as well as any other elements that you've used from the centralized repository.

Publish

Before content can be ported to other containers, it must be synchronized with the Monitoring server. The Publish All single-click option accomplishes this synchronization.

Deploy

Use Deploy a Dashboard to a SharePoint site to select the dashboard to deploy, and specify the SharePoint Site URL. You will also need to specify the document library for the dashboard. The deployed dashboard will be displayed in the SharePoint site and available for monitoring and analyzing business performance and strategy.

Consuming Content — SharePoint

As mentioned earlier, for performance management to become pervasive within an organization, it must be accessible. SharePoint sites are the primary means of consuming and presenting monitoring and analytics business information, providing easy access to business information and meeting the condition of accessibility with ease (see Figure 4-13).

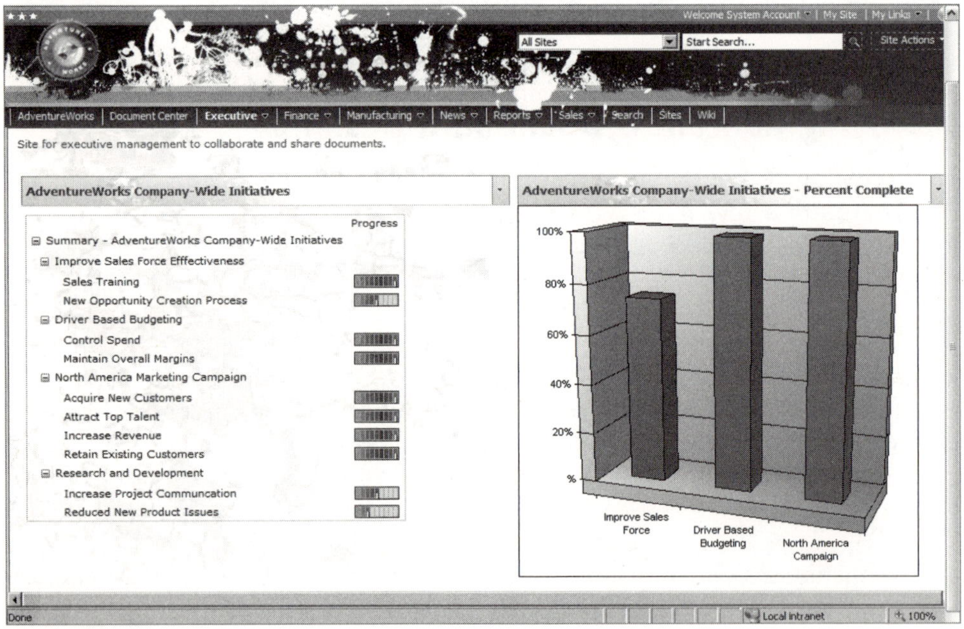

Figure 4-13 SharePoint sites provide easy access to dashboards.

Once a performance management system is deployed to a SharePoint site, business users simply open it, click a link, and begin working.

Viewing

As a second condition for performance management to become pervasive within an organization, it also must be tailored to the individual business user. As mentioned earlier, to go one step further with pervasive performance management, users will respond with even greater enthusiasm if the information has a personal connection. You've seen how to provide targeted and personalized business information while designing and building dashboards, scorecards, and report views. The ability to view targeted and personalized information does not stop once the dashboard is deployed through the SharePoint site to individual business users.

For example, once a business analyst from a sales organization accesses the performance management system from the SharePoint site, she will be viewing information targeted to her region. This has been built into the design of the dashboard, but she can further apply filters when viewing information to display it by quarter, by geography, or by product line, for example. When she applies filters, the data specific to the filter she selected is reflected in both the scorecards and the report views. Does she want to see how many units were sold in Q1 2008? She would select the Quarter filter and see the results appear in both the scorecard and the associated report views. Does she want to see a different distribution? She would select the average weighted rollup that reflects overall performance or select the worst child rollup to view performance by the lowest-performing KPI. These are all options available for the business user at the point of viewing business information.

Analyzing

Dashboards containing analytic views allow the user to perform analysis on the data, to reveal the most relevant information behind the values. With analytic grids and charts, users can drill down to find more detailed information about a particular data point. For example, a user can discover which individual products contributed the most revenue to a product family by drilling down on the product family. A user can also see summarized information by drilling up — for example, seeing the overall contribution of the product family to revenue, rather than an individual product's contribution.

Another key analytic technique is cross-drilling (or drilling down to). This feature allows users to answer questions regarding how one aspect (or dimension) of the organization influences another. For example, a user can answer such questions as "how do my product sales break down across geographies?" or "what products are my most valuable customers buying?" With cross-drilling, the relationships among the various aspects of an organization are revealed, leading to a much greater understanding of the overall dynamics of the organization.

Users can also sort and filter their data to uncover other important trends or issues. For example, sorting a product family based on sales immediately reveals top and bottom performers. Filtering can remove irrelevant items from the view, allowing the user to focus on only those items that have a negative or positive impact on the organization's performance.

By providing these analytic capabilities to business users, PerformancePoint enables them to answer their own questions, discover their own opportunities, and draw their own data-supported conclusions. With a fully empowered user base, organizations can maximize the impact of their performance management investments.

Summary

In review, we've provided information on the architecture and capabilities of PerformancePoint Monitoring Server along with a discussion of the factors that promote successful collaborative and pervasive performance management in an organization.

The architecture and design of PerformancePoint Monitoring Server acknowledge that effective performance management is an iterative and interactive process and that it is most successful when users feel a personal connection to data. Using examples, we've shown how it's possible to design and build dashboards, scorecards, and report views that provide this kind of targeted and personalized information to business users. We've also explained how it is possible to connect to multiple types of data sources to take advantage of varied data systems where organizations store their data.

Finally, we've provided an overview of the workflow for creating, deploying, and consuming targeted, personalized, and effective dashboards.

Notes

1. From "Performance Tuning and Capacity Planning for PerformancePoint Monitoring Server" scalability whitepaper from Microsoft (September 2007).

CHAPTER

5

Implementing Scorecards and KPIs

This chapter explores concepts and features of scorecards and key performance indicators (KPIs) in PerformancePoint Monitoring and Analytics. It explains how to implement scorecards and KPIs to build business performance monitoring and analytics solutions that fit with your organization's plans and environment.

The first section, "Scorecards: Distributing Metrics to the Masses," explores concepts and features of scorecards in a performance monitoring solution through the examination of various scorecard examples, including an example of a Balanced Scorecard based on the Balanced Scorecard methodology developed by Robert S. Kaplan and David P. Norton.

The second section, "Scorecard Key Performance Indicators," provides detailed information on implementing KPIs, including details about KPI banding, modifying and adding indicators, scorecard KPI weighting, and adding additional actual and target values. The goal of this section is to provide you with the knowledge you need to design and create KPIs that track the performance of goals, objectives, plans, initiatives, and/or processes in your organization.

Scorecards: Distributing Metrics to the Masses

In the past, it was not uncommon for an organization to view itself as a pyramid and to centralize its decision-making process at the top of the pyramid at the senior executive level. Consequently, decision making and decision support systems channeled information to the highest level of the pyramid only.

What's different today is that many organizations are operating under a less-hierarchal model, and they are looking at empowering, as much as possible, people at all levels of the pyramid, from the top level to the middle and bottom levels. This is aptly described by the phrase "metrics to the masses" and raises the question of how organizations can help their people at all levels make better decisions. This chapter discusses how PerformancePoint scorecards and monitoring through scorecards fits into this scheme and focuses on how to define appropriate monitoring indicators to track and evaluate decisions made at all levels of an organization.

In any type of organization, knowing what happened and what is happening can alert decision makers to potential issues and drive informed business decisions. For example, for an online travel company, measuring customer satisfaction is critical. What is the purchase fulfillment percentage? What is the count of complaints? What is the average customer survey rating? These are only a few examples of the types of measures that can be used to monitor results in the area of customer satisfaction. If the fulfillment percentage is consistently low, the organization may decide to change the online experience to make it easier for customers to purchase flight and hotel reservations. Continuous monitoring will let this online travel company measure the impact of changes to the online experience. An increase in the fulfillment percentage signifies a successful change. However, if the fulfillment percentage remains the same or drops even lower, the company must reevaluate its strategy.

In another example, a call center functioning as a customer help desk for a large technology company measures and monitors the average call wait time. Knowing that the average call wait time for customers is unacceptably long allows a manager to take actions to align the call wait time to an acceptable level perhaps by adding agents, changing the agent schedule to accommodate call volume at peak times, or providing agent training to speed call completion time. Regardless of the action taken, continuous monitoring on scorecards will let this manager measure results to determine the success of his business decision.

What Is a Scorecard?

You'll remember that Chapter 4 defined scorecards as a collection of KPIs and objectives that together provide a comprehensive view of the health of an organization's business and strategy (see Figure 5-1).

To briefly review, scorecards are based on three concepts:

- **Objectives.** Objectives refer to statements of goals for your organization.
- **KPIs.** Each objective in a scorecard is measured by a KPI, with KPIs tracking performance.
- **Targets.**Targets are the numeric goals for a KPI.

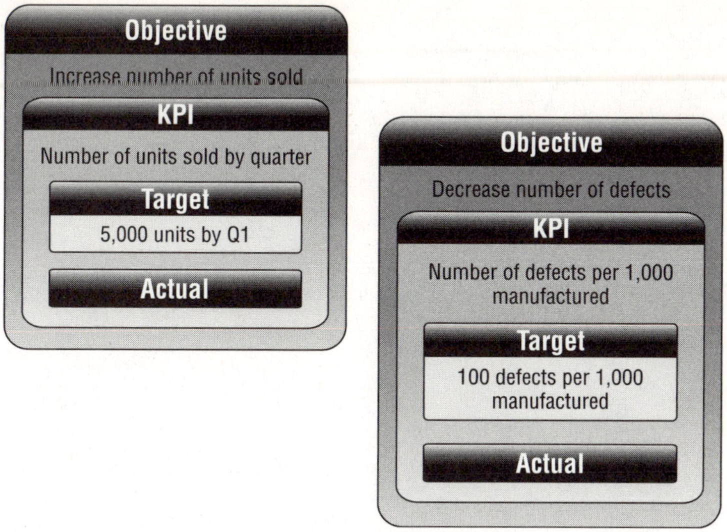

Figure 5-1 Key scorecard concepts

Figure 5-2 displays a finished dashboard with a Sales Scorecard and shows how these three concepts work together to measure performance in specific areas. With PerformancePoint, monitoring is done through a dashboard and through the KPIs available from the scorecards on the dashboard. A later section in this chapter examines KPIs in depth. Briefly, KPIs are the metrics that help an organization monitor performance and assist in making business decisions. In the example of the Summary dashboard shown in Figure 5-2, the KPIs are the traffic icons in the Sales Scorecard table on the top left.

On the Sales Scorecard, there are KPIs for Revenue items such as Sales Amount and Units. For Margins, the KPIs measure Gross Margin % and Gross Profit %, while Costs has one KPI to measure Cost. A sales manager looking at this scorecard can tell at a glance that Revenue Sales Amounts from Q1 to Q4 are consistently below target levels, while Cost from Q1 to Q4 is consistently on target (see Figure 5-2).

As you can see from this example, scorecards can contain both KPIs and objectives. An objective is a collection of related KPIs or subobjectives and is created by logically grouping KPIs or creating subsets under larger objectives. Notice that in this scorecard, KPIs are organized hierarchically, with the lower-level KPIs rolling up to the higher-level categories — Revenues, Margins, and Costs — which also have KPIs assigned. Notice also that these higher-level categories in turn roll up to an overall Financial Objectives level, which has its own KPI. In this case, a sales manager can look at the KPIs for Q1 and Q2 and quickly determine that for these quarters, the Sales Amount is below the projected target but that the overall Financial Objectives are on target.

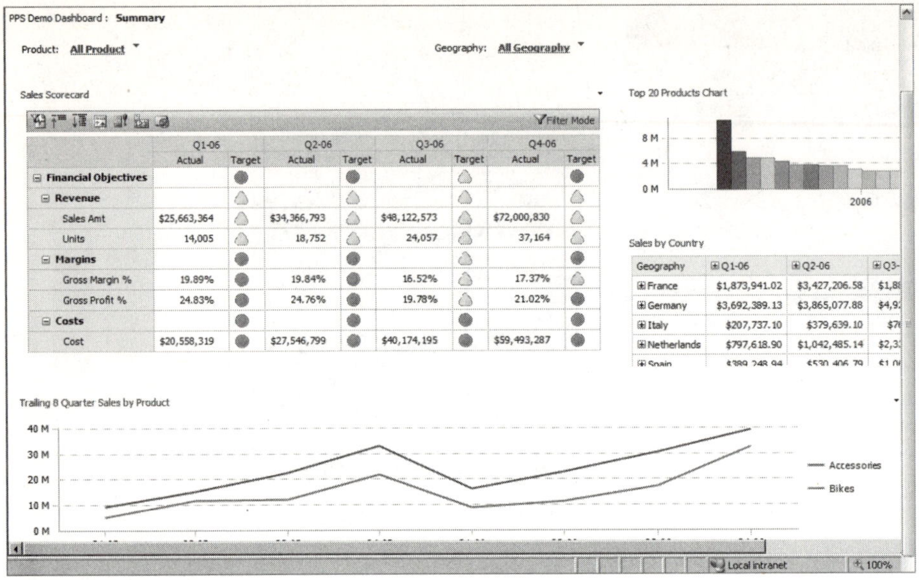

Figure 5-2 Sales Scorecard

Looking further at the Sales Amount KPI, you can see how this KPI has an actual value and a target value and how the scorecard displays a number for the Actual value, while the Target appears as an indicator that ranks the performance of the organization in this area. As you will see later in this chapter, comparison and evaluation are at the core of KPIs, with KPIs always comparing and evaluating a target or desired value set by business decision makers against an explicit and measurable value taken directly from an objective source of business data.

Notice also that the dashboard presents additional information. There is a Top 20 Products Chart, a Sales by Country table that presents sales information by country and by quarter, and at the bottom of the dashboard, a line chart that tracks Trailing 8 Quarter Sales by Product. These additional elements clarify and deepen the information available from the KPIs in the Sales Scorecard. You will learn more about using these additional elements with scorecards to create a rich view of information in Chapters 7 and 8.

Figure 5-3 displays a dashboard with another example of a sales scorecard, called Finance: Gross Profit and Loss. In this scorecard, the Units Sold KPI monitors the number of actual units sold so that a sales manager looking at this KPI can also easily determine whether or not overall unit sales are on target. The KPIs in this example use the popular traffic colors — red, green, and yellow — which are meant to monitor performance and prompt action when things have gone poorly (red), provide an alert when performance is deteriorating (yellow), and motivate the user when everything is going well (green).

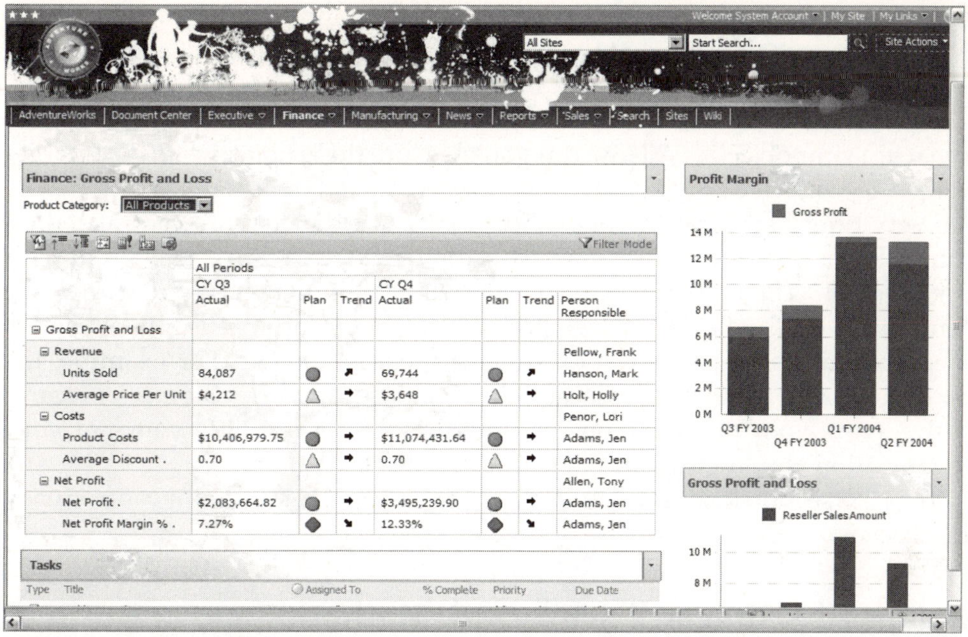

Figure 5-3 Finance: Gross Profit and Loss

Scorecards can each have a completely different look and feel. Comparing these two sales scorecards notice that the Finance: Gross Profit and Loss scorecard in Figure 5-3 includes Actual, Plan, and Trend information by quarter as well as the names of those responsible for the various objectives — detailed information that is not included in the first example of a sales scorecard.

Scorecards and Performance Management Methodologies

Scorecards can be based on a performance management methodology that provides a framework or perspective and identifies areas for monitoring and analysis. There are several types of performance management methodologies, including, for example, the Balanced Scorecard, Six Sigma, Capability Maturity Model Integration (CMMI), Agile, and customer relationship management (CRM).

The choice to use a performance management methodology with a scorecard to create a performance management solution is a business decision and not a PerformancePoint technical or application requirement. Selecting a performance management methodology can provide a framework for performance management that may make good business sense for your organization. You can create scorecards from any performance management methodology as long as you follow performance management principles and understand the relationship between the performance measurement areas and your KPIs.

Regardless of whether or not you select a performance management methodology, and regardless of what type of performance management methodology you select, your organization still must formulate its own performance measures. What are your current business challenges? What are your priorities? What are your objectives? How can you measure these objectives? What target values do you need?

Every time a scorecard is published, its KPIs indicators are centralized on the PerformancePoint server. In a sense, these KPIs are really the DNA of your organization. They are rich with business information, and because they are centralized on the PerformancePoint Server, they can be reused as business measures in scorecards based on different methodologies. For example, the KPIs used in a Balanced Scorecard can be reused in a Six Sigma scorecard, truly giving your organization the option to create multiple views of your organization with metrics and data you can trust.

The next section focuses on the Balanced Scorecard methodology introduced in Chapter 4.

Balanced Scorecard: Scorecard, Methodology, or Both?

> *. . . a properly constructed Balanced Scorecard should tell the story of the business unit's strategy. It should identify and make explicit the sequence of hypotheses about the cause-and-effect relationships between outcome measures and the performance drivers of those outcomes. Every measure selected for a Balanced Scorecard should be an element in a chain of cause-and-effect relationships that communicates the meaning of the business unit's strategy to the organization.*
>
> Robert S. Kaplan and David P. Norton, *The Balanced Scorecard* (p. 31)

As mentioned earlier, the Balanced Scorecard is a scorecard based on the performance management methodology developed by Robert Kaplan and David Norton. Kaplan and Norton's comprehensive approach analyzes an organization's performance in four areas (see Figure 5-4):

- Financial performance
- Customer satisfaction
- Operational excellence
- People commitment

Collectively, these areas are called the FOSH metrics.

Figure 5-5 provides an example of a Balanced Scorecard with a complete FOSH (Finance, Operations, Sales, Human Resources) metric set. Notice how the KPI categories reflect the FOSH metrics.

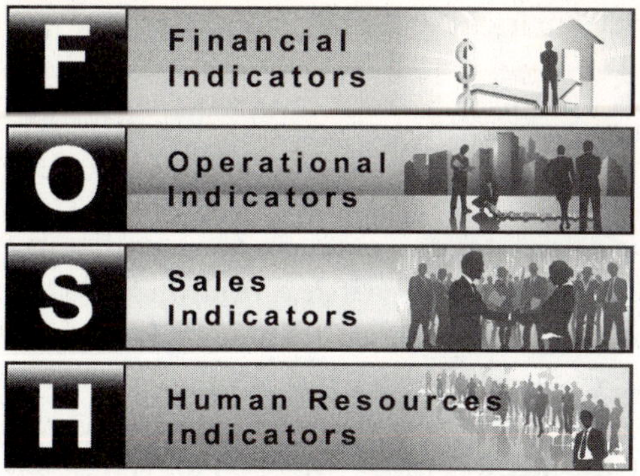

Figure 5-4 The FOSH metrics from the Balanced Scorecard methodology

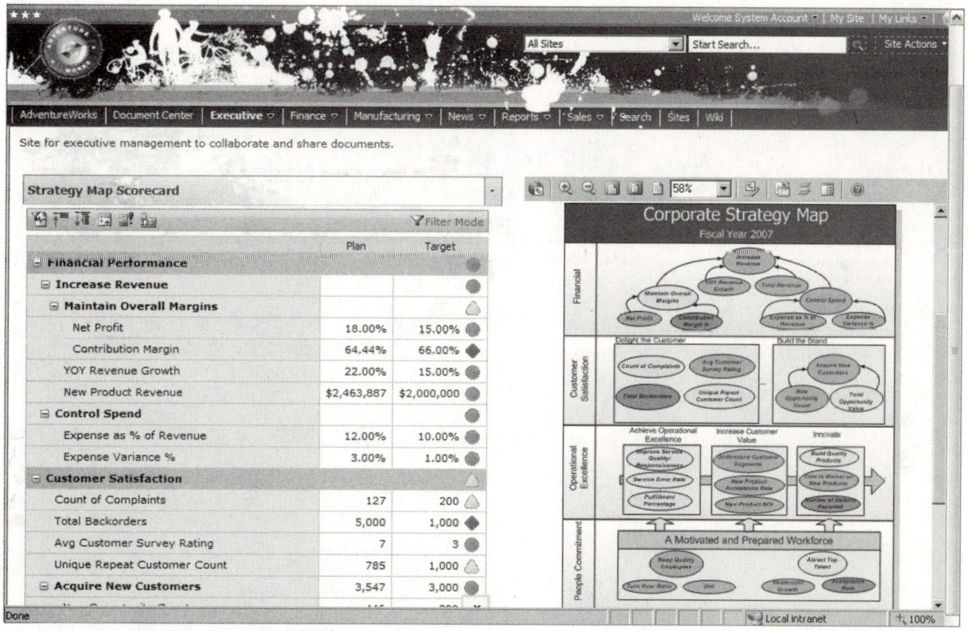

Figure 5-5 Balanced Scorecard

In this Strategy Map Scorecard, there are four primary KPI objectives, which map to the areas identified by the Balanced Scorecard methodology. These objectives in turn contain a set of KPIs to track performance in each of the different areas:

- Financial Performance with financial indicators to monitor finance
- Customer Satisfaction monitors sales and customer indicators to monitor sales

- Operational Excellence with internal business indicators to monitor operations
- People Commitment with innovation and learning indicators to monitor human resources

Each area of the Balanced Scorecard provides a framework for identifying underlying objectives and KPIs. Together, these objectives and related KPIs tell a story about the overall health, performance, and strategy of this organization. Let's look at the different views offered by this Strategy Map Scorecard.

The CEO, looking at this scorecard, may want to look only at the overall objectives. Is her company on target in the four critical areas? The Balanced Scorecard tells her that in the areas of finance, operations, and human resources, the company is on target. Customer Satisfaction displays a yellow alert, so she may call the VP of sales to analyze the situation and determine what action needs to be taken to align the sales strategy with its target (see Figure 5-6).

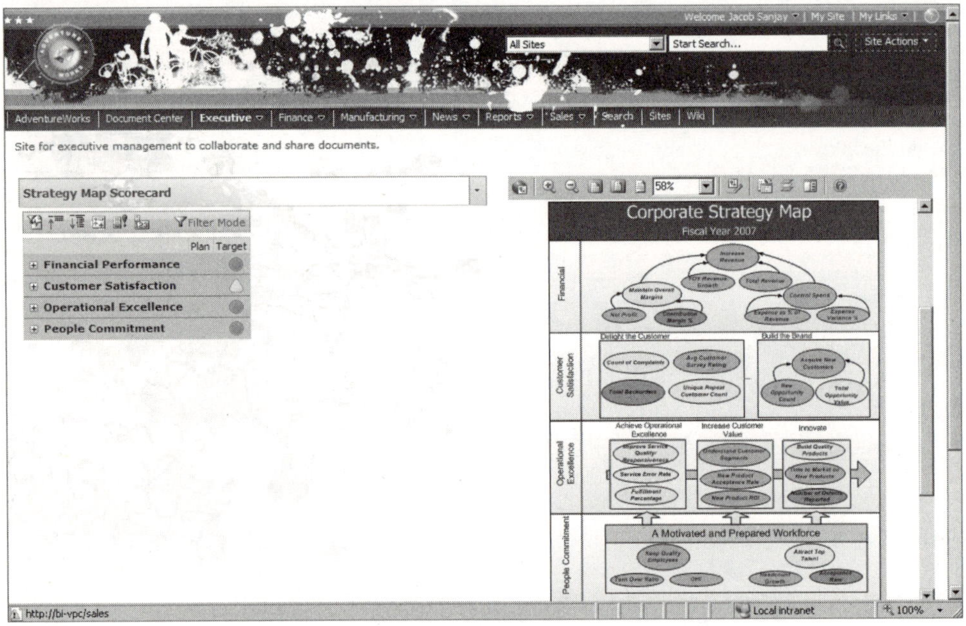

Figure 5-6 Balanced Scorecard with four key areas

The VP of sales receives the call from the CEO and expands the Customer Satisfaction objective to examine the associated KPIs. In this case, the Customer Satisfaction objective is measured by the following KPIs: Count of Complaints, Total Backorders, Avg Customer Survey Rating, and Unique Repeat Customer Count. A second objective, Acquire New Customers, is measured by two KPIs: New Opportunity Count and Total Opportunity Value. On examination, the

VP of sales sees that the measure for Total Backorders displays a red indicator (see Figure 5-7).

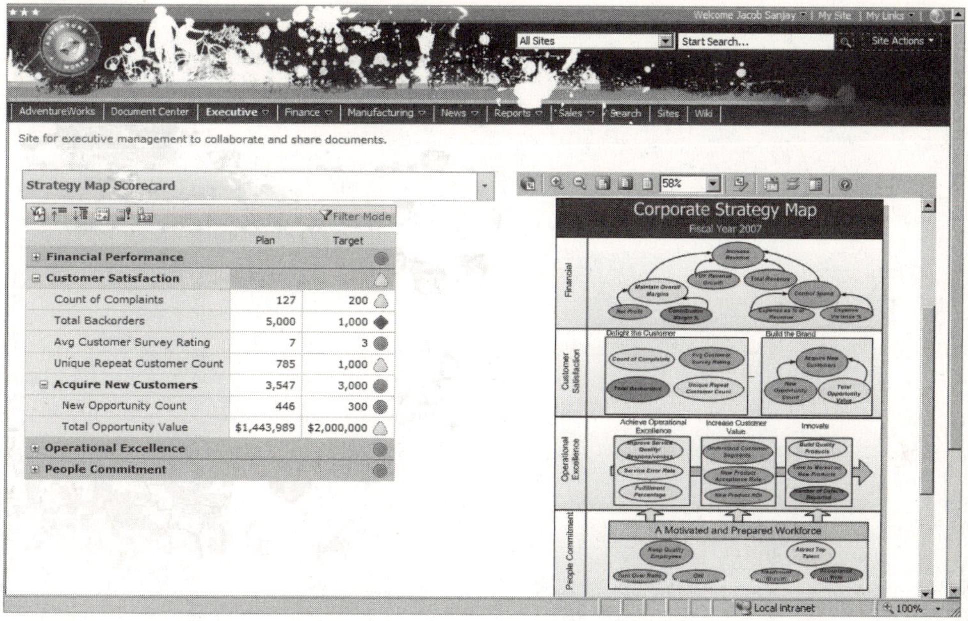

Figure 5-7 Customer Satisfaction KPIs

While the CEO may want to view performance for key areas only, the VP of sales will be most interested in the details of the metric found under Customer Satisfaction. This information alerts the VP to the fact that action must be taken to change the unacceptably high number of backorders. He may ask if the high number of backorders is related to the high complaint count and if this in turn is affecting the repeat customer count as well. The VP of sales now has valuable information that can help him determine the appropriate actions to take to align Customer Satisfaction with corporate strategy.

Even a Simple Scorecard Provides Value

A scorecard can be a very complex picture of an organization's business information or it can be as simple as a list of KPIs. Even a simple scorecard, such as the one shown in Figure 5-8, provides value.

This scorecard was created using a Fixed Value scorecard and is an example of a simple scorecard with Cost and Profit KPIs that will be updated manually. The scorecard was created in a few steps and is available immediately for deployment or for additional design in Dashboard Designer. Value can be realized from visualizing business information even without the benefit of automated data sources or performance management systems. If your organization is new to monitoring, a simple scorecard like this can be used to introduce the concept and habit of monitoring performance.

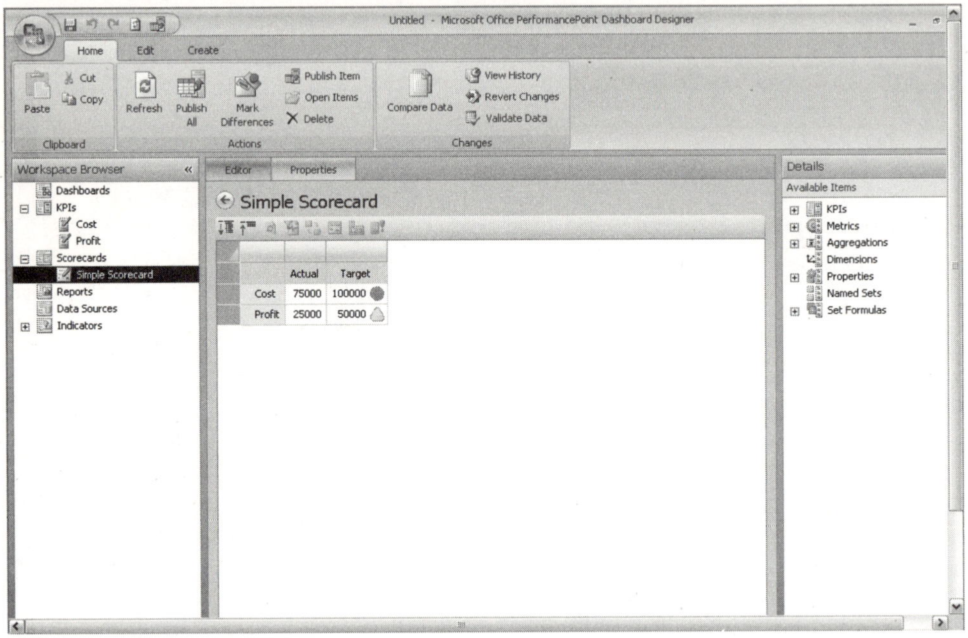

Figure 5-8 Simple fixed value scorecard

Scorecard Key Performance Indicators

Key performance indicators (KPIs), are predefined measures that are used to track the performance of goals, objectives, plans, initiatives, and/or processes. In their book *Drive Business Performance: Enabling a Culture of Intelligent Execution* (Wiley, 2008), Bruno Aziza and Joey Fitts define KPIs as the way organizations can do the following:

- **Express strategy and objectives.** A KPI can describe a particular metric (such as revenue or margin) or describe an initiative (such as create a great customer experience).
- **Define success.** KPIs are matched with a target or goal measure symbolizing what failure (red), average results (yellow), and success (green) look like.

- **Hold individuals and teams accountable.** KPIs are created for a reason — to drive results. KPIs don't drive results by themselves — people do! Therefore, KPIs need to be associated with an owner — an individual who is responsible for the performance of that metric.[1]

In the following sections, you will learn how to design and implement KPIs, converting these business concepts into actual measures for tracking performance.

What Are Key Performance Indicators?

Key performance indicators (KPIs) are business metrics that help decision makers at all levels of the organization monitor progress toward meeting organizational performance goals. KPIs are among the core scorecard elements that you create using the Scorecard Builder in Dashboard Designer. When organizational stakeholders carefully plan what KPIs to use in their scorecards, KPIs provide a logical and comprehensive way of describing and tracking organizational strategy.

All KPIs in a scorecard must be associated with an actual value and one or more target values. To determine how much progress has been made toward the organization's performance goal, PerformancePoint compares the actual value and the target values of the KPI in the business scorecard. KPIs can be compared against multiple targets. This is useful if you want to track 1-year targets against 3-year and 5-year targets, for example. The section called "Creating Additional Actual and Target Values" later in this chapter shows how you can define multiple target values for a single KPI.

Each key performance indicator should be closely aligned with a specific organizational, departmental, or functional unit or with a specific business strategy or goal. This alignment makes it possible for individual employees in an organization to monitor the KPIs that apply to their areas of responsibility and for the organization to ensure that business actions align with defined goals and strategies.

KPIs are differentiated by the presence of two critical values, which together enable the assignment of meaningful interpretation to data. These values are:

- **Actual value.** The actual value is the value for any KPI at a specific point in real time.
- **Target value.** The target value or values represent the desired level of performance as measured by the KPI with respect to a business goal or strategy.

In a KPI, the actual value is the number a business user wants to look at. For example, in the Operational Excellence section of the Strategy Map Balanced

Scorecard, the manager wants to see KPIs that indicate the percentage of service errors and the fulfillment percentage. Together, these KPIs roll up to measure the objective of improving service quality and responsiveness. In this case, the actual value of the Service Error Rate is 3.00% compared to the target value of 6.00%, indicating an area that requires attention and possible action (see Figure 5-9).

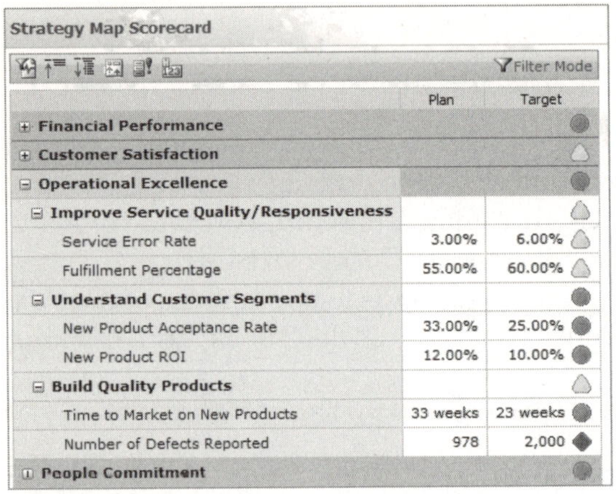

Figure 5-9 Operational excellence KPIs

Compare these KPIs to the ones in the area of People Commitment. Of course, the KPIs in People Commitment are different and designed to reflect the responsibility and commitment of human resources. Here, KPIs measure Turn Over Ratio, OHI, Acceptance Rate, and Headcount Growth (see Figure 5-10).

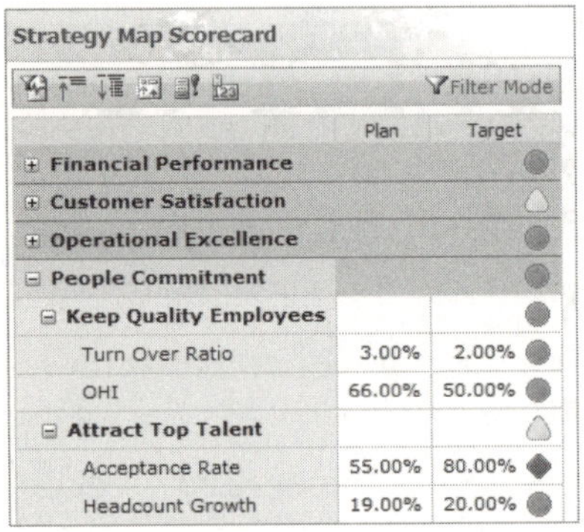

Figure 5-10 People commitment KPIs

In each of these examples, the data collected to support the indicator is the actual value. The target value is different but is related to the actual value. Basically, the target value is determined by answering the following question: What do you want to achieve? For example, how many employees do you want to retain? How many employees do you want to hire? How quickly do you want to build and send your products to market? How many defects do you want to report?

Dashboard Designer, used to create KPIs, breaks down each KPI into an actual value and a target value, as shown in these sample KPIs. Setting these values is the starting point for any KPI at the business level as well as the design level.

Key Performance Indicator Components

A common misconception is that KPIs are an all-in-one package. In fact, this is not the case. KPIs are one part of a set of three components, which together work to provide performance monitoring capabilities in key business areas. These components are:

- Data elements
- Measures
- Indicators

Fundamentally, KPIs rely on data elements. These data elements must be converted into measures, which are then used as the building blocks for KPIs. In the course of this process, raw data elements are converted into meaningful business information displayed through KPIs.

To better understand the relationships among these three components, consider a transactional sales system that tracks and stores sales quantities and orders as they are entered. These data elements are stored in a relational database. The transactional sales system captures and stores valuable information that a manager may very well want to use when making daily or long-term decisions or when generating reports. The challenge is to extract the information that is most valuable and to transform it into a usable form for monitoring.

In order to use the data for analysis, the data elements must be converted into measures. This is done by associating data elements with a dimension. Raw data elements are considered facts, and dimensions group these facts by Time or Geography, for example. Associating a fact with a dimension enhances its informational value. In this case, it is a fact that the sales organization sold 10,000 bicycles. It is important to know that 5,000 of these bicycles were sold in Quarter 4. It is also important to know that of these 5,000 bicycles 3,000 were sold in Europe. The measure that surrounds the fact communicates a dimension. In this case, Quarter is an example of the Time dimension, whereas Europe is an example of the Geography dimension (see Figure 5-11).

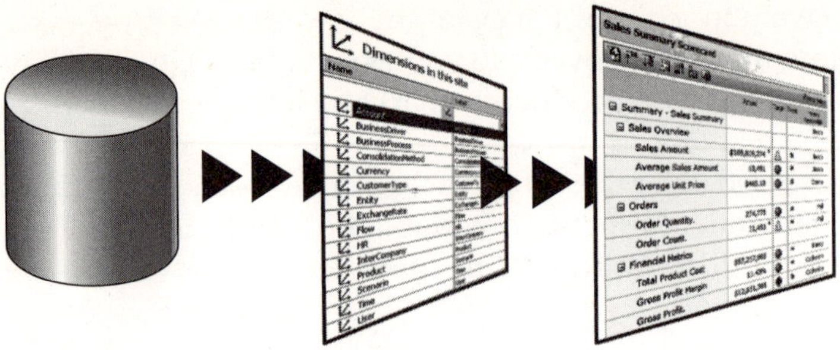

Figure 5-11 KPIs are one part of a set of three components.

In other words, dimensions allow you to measure facts in different ways that communicate valuable business information. These measures can then be used in the final step in this process, which occurs in PerformancePoint where KPIs are built on available measures and presented in scorecards. So in this example, KPIs might appear as sales by Quarter and by Region. This information is populated dynamically from the underlying transactional database, reflecting at all times a current view of the organization's sales performance.

Key Performance Indicators and Data Sources

A key point to remember is that multiple data sources can define actual and target values, and that actual and target values do not need to be fixed values, nor do they need to originate from the same source.

The actual value may be derived from a queue, while the target value may come from a completely different system. PerformancePoint Server allows you to connect to many types of data sources to take advantage of the often complex and varied data systems where organizations store their data. Dashboard Designer provides a Data Mappings option that allows you to specify multiple and different types of data, including Analysis Server Data Sources, SharePoint List, SQL Server Table, Excel 2007, Excel Services, and ODBC Connections.

Centralizing data sources facilitates data sharing across multiple dashboards and scorecards and promotes consistency throughout an organization. When business analysts or designers create a scorecard, they simply need to point to an existing data source with its security settings already defined. Using centralized data sources minimizes the risk of pointing to the wrong data and ensures consistent and appropriate security settings for valuable business information. As shown later in this chapter, the Server tab lists the data sources available on the server. By double-clicking an available data source, business analysts or designers can select a data source for use in the local Workspace tab, where the actual design work occurs. In effect, the data source becomes a reusable component in the design framework.

Centralizing data sources is similar to implementing content and style rules for a Web site. When organizations first started setting up Web sites, there was little consistency or unity. It was not uncommon to see a wide range of functionality and styles across departments in the same organization, from exploding poodles to blinking text. Now, master pages and style sheets have allowed organizations to impart a consistent look and feel to their Web sites. Centralized data sources share the same intent. The Workspace tab is like an artist's palette, where an analyst or designer can build individualized scorecards, while the Server tab with the defined data sources ensures that the design will be based on the organization's informational structure.

Storing Key Performance Indicators

KPIs themselves can also be centralized on the server and be made available for reuse. In fact, this is another best practice: Create categories for KPIs and centralize KPIs on the server.

Again, this promotes consistency in information sharing and reduces the risk of error with regard to data and security. When a designer or analyst selects a KPI from the list of KPIs available on the server, the KPI along with its supporting information, including data source settings, is brought into the local workspace. Using the KPI from the Server tab ensures that the design will be based on the organization's informational structure and performance measures.

Microsoft SQL Server 2005 Analysis Services also provides the ability to create and store KPIs, through the KPI tab in Business Intelligence Development Studio. This choice brings with it a question: Is it better to store KPIs in SQL Server or in PerformancePoint? The answer is: It depends on your overall environment. Organizations with back-end data solutions in SQL Server 2005 should look seriously at storing KPIs in SQL Server 2005. An environment centralized on SQL Server 2005, with KPI solutions stored at this level, has the additional advantage of being able to share KPI solutions across applications, including PerformancePoint, SharePoint Server, and Excel. For organizations with back-end data solutions in a SQL Server 2000 environment or with data solutions built on other products, it may be better to build and store KPIs in PerformancePoint.

Considering the development environment is also important when making a choice between SQL Server 2005 and PerformancePoint. Dashboard Designer provides a graphical environment for building KPIs, whereas the KPI tab in SQL Server 2005 provides a programmatic interface with deep programmatic control but few graphical interface options.

Best Practices KPIs

Agree on what counts in your organization and how best to count it. If an organization understands what it wants to measure, 70 percent of the work has already been done toward defining meaningful KPIs. In fact, often the primary challenge is to agree on a methodology; that is, to agree on what counts in your organization and how best to count it. PerformancePoint monitoring simplifies the creation and centralization of the KPIs. The difficult questions have to do with setting business goals and objectives and determining how best to view results. For example, in a sales organization with offices in Europe, Latin America, Asia-Pacific, and North America, one person may prefer to roll up sales amounts for all geographical regions into one KPI called Sales and parse the data by geographical region in other parts of the scorecard or dashboard. Another person may want to view the information at its most elemental level and have a KPI for each geographical region. PerformancePoint monitoring can accommodate both scenarios, but these are business questions that must be resolved outside of the application itself.

Make sure you have the data to support your organization's chosen methodology and KPIs. Having the data sources to support the methodology and the resulting KPIs is another issue that can present significant challenges. At the design stage, fixed values can be used to create mockup screens, but most businesses operate dynamically with dynamic data. Available data sources need to adequately reflect this quality. Additionally, an organization may require not only actual and target values but also trending values. Again, the underlying data must be able to support the business trends embedded in the KPIs.

Centralize data sources. This facilitates data sharing across multiple KPIs and scorecards, promoting consistency throughout an organization.

Centralize KPIs. Create categories for KPIs and centralize storage of KPIs on the server.

Creating KPIs

KPIs must be defined before they can be used in a scorecard. Creating a KPI in Dashboard Designer is a multi-step process:

1. Select the KPI type (blank KPI or objective).
2. Name the KPI.
3. Set permissions.
4. Create and define the actual and target values for each KPI. It is possible to set multiple actual and target values for a KPI.
5. Set the scoring patterns (banding) methods.

You will learn more about KPI types, creating actual and target values, and setting scoring patterns in the following sections.

KPI Types and Calculations

There are three types of KPIs, and each KPI type has calculation settings that can affect the final scoring result displayed in the scorecard. Figure 5-12 illustrates the three different KPI types:

- Standard KPI (leaf level)
- Standard KPI (non-leaf-level)
- Objective KPI

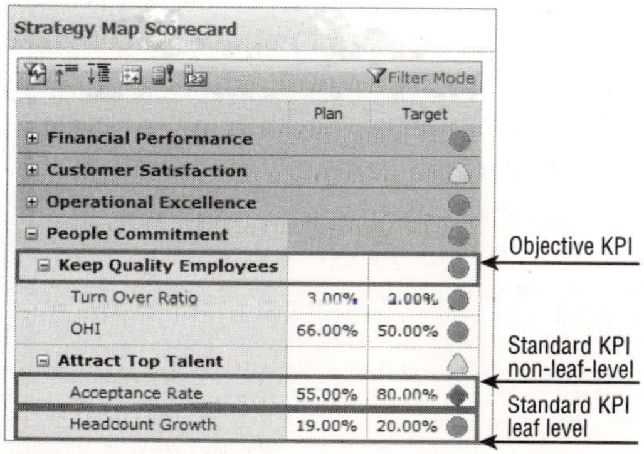

Figure 5-12 There are three different KPI types

Each KPI has a value and a score, with the scores appearing on the scorecard. KPI scores are based on calculation settings, which are applied differently, depending on the type of KPI you've chosen to create. For standard KPIs, the value is a number that comes directly from a data source or is calculated based on child KPIs. Values are not used with objective KPIs.

For standard KPIs, the score is a percentage that compares the KPI's actual value to its target value. This percentage can be a raw score or normalized score, based on its thresholds. For objective KPIs, the score is the weighted average of the scores of the child KPI. The score determines which indicator is shown.

Standard KPIs (Leaf Level)

Standard KPIs (leaf level) do not have child KPIs underneath them in the scorecard hierarchy. Leaf-level KPIs, are shown as a value in the scorecard.

This value can be explicit or it may originate in a cube, where it may be the result of a calculation. This value is never the result of a scorecard calculation. For standard leaf-level KPIs, select the Use calculated values of actual and target to compute score option in the Calculation dialog box.

Standard KPIs (Non-Leaf-Level)

Standard KPIs (non-leaf-level) have one or more KPIs underneath them in the scorecard hierarchy. In other words, these KPIs have child KPIs. This is the only type of KPI that should be used in a scorecard calculation. For standard non-leaf-level KPIs, select the Use calculated values of actual and target to compute score option in the Calculation dialog box.

Objective KPIs

Objective KPIs are non-leaf-level KPIs or KPIs that have one or more KPIs underneath them in the scorecard hierarchy. In other words, they are like non-leaf-level standard KPIs with child KPIs. Objective KPI types are always shown as an indicator on the scorecard, never as a value. An objective KPI is an averaged rollup of all children of the objective KPI. To define a KPI as an objective, clear the Use calculated values of actual and target to compute score option in the Calculation dialog box. It is possible to override the score by selecting Band by Stated Score in the Edit Bandings dialog box. You will learn more about KPI banding later in this chapter.

Best Practices Calculations

- Use calculations only with standard KPIs (non-leaf-level).
- Accept the default values for standard KPIs (leaf level).
- Accept the default values for objective KPIs.

KPI Banding

KPI banding refers to the use of bands to represent ranges of performance. These ranges are based on thresholds, which define the boundaries between changes in the status of an indicator. The KPI banding method is determined by the combination of the scoring pattern and the selection of a banding method. There are three types of banding methods:

- Band by Normalized Value of Actual/Target
- Band by Numeric Value of Actual
- Band by Stated Score

For each KPI on a scorecard, you may see three elements: actual value, target value, and status indicator. The status indicator, often displayed in the familiar traffic light icon pattern, is determined by the KPI score, which is a normalized score based on the KPI settings. This score allows the KPI to be properly compared with other KPIs and aggregated into an objective KPI (see Figure 5-13).

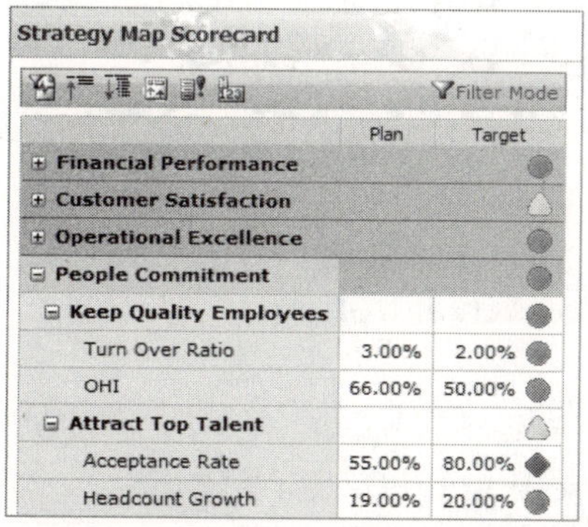

Strategy Map Scorecard

Filter Mode

	Plan	Target
Financial Performance		
Customer Satisfaction		
Operational Excellence		
People Commitment		
Keep Quality Employees		
Turn Over Ratio	3.00%	2.00%
OHI	66.00%	50.00%
Attract Top Talent		
Acceptance Rate	55.00%	80.00%
Headcount Growth	19.00%	20.00%

Figure 5-13 The status indicator is determined by the KPI score

For example, in the People Commitment section of the Strategy Map Scorecard shown in Figure 5-13, two KPIs — Turn Over Ratio and OHI — roll up to the Keep Quality Employees objective. The score for Keep Quality Employees is determined by the scores of these two KPIs. Two other KPIs — Acceptance Rate and Headcount Growth — roll up to a second objective, Attract Top Talent. The score for Attract Top Talent is determined by the score of these two KPIs. The overall People Commitment score is determined by the aggregated scores of the Keep Quality Employees and Attract Top Talent objectives.

The steps for calculating the KPI score are described next.

Step 1: Calculate the Band by Value (BBV)

The Band by Value (BBV) is the value that will ultimately map into the threshold ranges of the KPI to determine a score. The BBV is calculated differently, depending on the banding method and scoring pattern chosen.

Case 1

Scoring Pattern: Increasing Is Better, Decreasing Is Better, Closer to Target Is Better

Banding Method: Band by Numeric Value of Actual

```
BBV = Value of the actual
```

Case 2

Scoring Pattern: Increasing Is Better, Decreasing Is Better, Closer to Target Is Better
Banding Method: Band by Stated Score

```
BBV = Query Result
```

Query Result is the result of the MDX expression entered when you set up the threshold. This is also the point where you select the banding method and scoring pattern.

Case 3

Scoring Pattern: Increasing Is Better, Closer to Target Is Better
Banding Method: Band by Normalized Value of Actual to Target

```
BBV = (Actual Value - Worst) / (Target Value - Worst)
```

The Worst value is a value you enter when setting up the threshold.

Step 2: Identify the In-Band Value (IBV)

The In-Band Value (IBV) is a 1-based value that determines in which threshold range the BBV lies. Range 1 is always the bottom range in the threshold settings, range 2 is the range immediately above the bottom range, and so on. A three-state indicator has three ranges; a four-state indicator has four ranges.

Step 3: Calculate the Normalized Band by Value (NBV)

The Normalized Band by Value (NBV) is the normalized score displayed in the scorecard. This value is calculated to equalize KPI scores so that the scores can be accurately aggregated for objective KPIs.

Although the NBV calculation for Decreasing Is Better KPIs is identical to the NBV calculation for Increasing Is Better KPIs, the BBV is calculated differently.

The NBV calculation for Closer to Target KPIs is identical to the NBV for Increasing Is Better KPIs, with one exception. The NBV from the preceding Increasing Is Better calculation makes the following adjustment:

```
If In-Band < (# of Bands/2) then
NBV = NBV * 2
Otherwise
NBV = 2 * (1 - NBV)
```

Scoring Rollup to Objectives

The score for objectives is calculated when each KPI score has been determined. The score for objectives is the calculated average of the KPIs below the objective, unless weighting has been applied to one or more of the KPIs. If weighting has been applied to one or more of the KPIs, the weighting is factored into the calculated average. You will learn more about scorecard KPI weighting later in this chapter.

Fine-Tuning Rollup Types

In scorecards where KPIs roll up to higher-level objectives, you can select rollup types to visualize specific business objectives based on select calculations. For example, in a Sales Scorecard where Revenue, Margins, and Costs roll up to overall Financial Objectives do you want to know which regions are operating below the sales revenue target? Using the Worst Child score rollup type will display this informational view in your scorecard.

KPI Weighting on the Scorecard

You can further refine KPIs and scoring on scorecards by changing the Score rollup weight of a KPI in a scorecard. Weighting KPIs gives importance to the measures that are critical to your organization, with their criticality reflected in the scores that appear on the scorecard. When you change the Score rollup weight on a KPI, PerformancePoint multiplies the number you enter by 10 in the scorecard calculation. For example, if you enter 5 as the value for a KPI Score rollup weight, PerformancePoint makes that KPI 50 times (5 * 10 = 50) more important than other KPIs in the scorecard. The weighting value for a KPI is stored with the scorecard and not with the KPI. It applies at the KPI view level with the scorecard so if you reuse the KPI in another scorecard, the weighting value will not automatically apply or be carried over into another scorecard. Use the Properties option in Dashboard Designer to set the KPI view options for the scorecard.

Sometimes the result of a calculation with a weighted KPI may generate a confusing display of indicators. In a scorecard with no weighting applied, a business analyst may see a KPI with a green indicator and a red indicator, and expect to see these results roll up to a yellow indicator for the objective KPI. This is the case if KPI weighting is not applied, as shown in Figure 5-14.

But if greater weight is applied to the Cost KPI — for example, if 10 is entered as the KPI Score rollup weight — the result for the Financial Health Objective KPI will appear as a red indicator, as shown in Figure 5-15.

To clarify the result and avoid confusion, you may want to use Custom Properties to add a note describing the weighting applied to the KPI score.

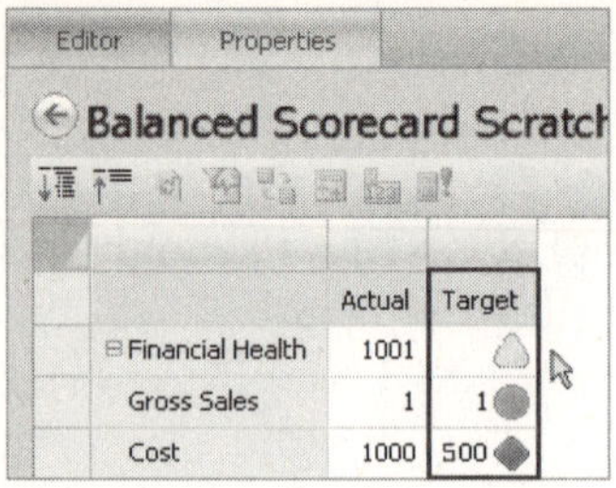

Figure 5-14 Scorecard with no KPI weighting applied

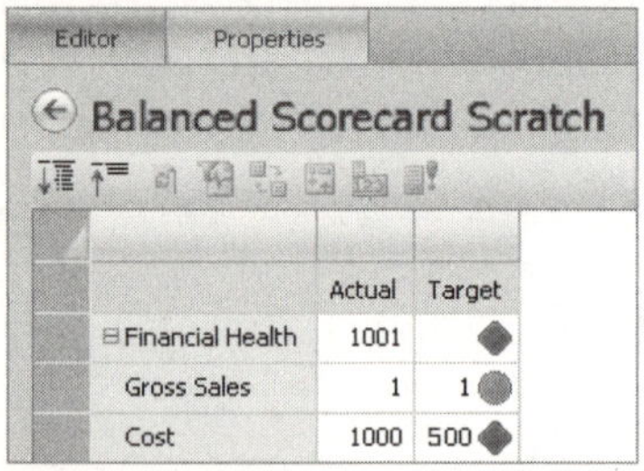

Figure 5-15 Same scorecard with KPI weighting applied

What Are Indicators?

Indicators refer to graphical, textual, and color representations of the status of KPIs and scorecards. Indicators translate numerical KPI values into colors, icons, and text to emphasize and clarify the status of values on the scorecard. There are two categories of indicators:

- *Standard indicators* use a pattern that is linearly increasing or decreasing. For example, as revenue increases, the status of the KPI changes as you get closer to your target revenue. Standard indicators may also indicate decreasing values. Decreasing values are not always negative. For example, as manufacturing defects decrease, you get closer to your target level of acceptable defects. This target is set at a low level, so a decrease in actual value indicates a positive result.
- *Centered indicators* use a different pattern where the target is a specific value. For example, an IT department has an annual budget that needs to remain on target. If they spend less, they are under-utilizing their resources and are likely to receive fewer resources for the next fiscal year, but if they spend more, it creates problems for IT management, with the CIO likely to receive inquiring phone calls from the CFO and CEO. The closer the IT budget is to the target value, the better the score. Moving further away from the target value, either above or below it, decreases the score.

Creating Indicators

You have the choice of creating either a standard or centered indicator type. Standard indicators use a pattern that increases or decreases linearly. For example, as revenue increases and you get closer to the target revenue, the status of the KPI changes from red to green as the values increase.

Centered indicators use a different pattern, because the target is a specific value. The closer you get to this target, the better the score. With a centered indicator, you can define status bands both above and below the value of your target.

Use the Indicator Template Wizard in Dashboard Designer to select the type of indicator you want. The indicator will appear in the Workspace Browser under the Indicator list.

Fine-Tuning KPIs with Thresholds

The indicators measure the score visually and reflect the business logic built into the measures by analysts and designers. Typically, actual and target values are either fixed values or dynamic values supplied by a database and differentiated by dimension. With the Thresholds option, you set the relationship between indicators to demarcate good, acceptable, and bad performance (see Figure 5-16).

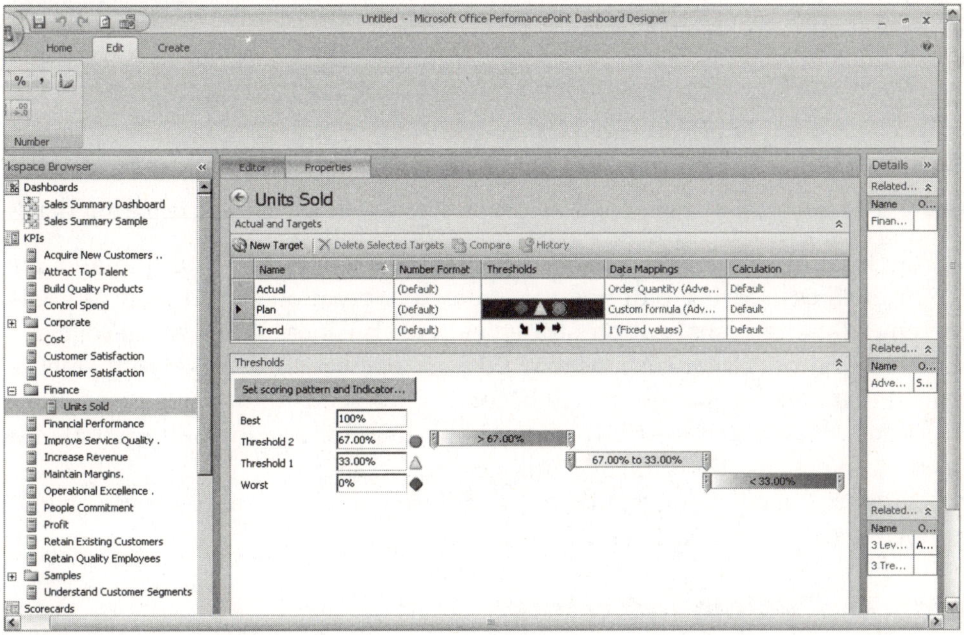

Figure 5-16 Use thresholds to set the relationship between indicators.

In this example, a score greater than 67% indicates a good performance visualized by a green traffic light indicator, a score between 67% and 33% is acceptable, and a score less than 33% indicates danger visualized by a red stoplight indicator.

The more ranges your organization specifies in its indicators, the more specific the indicators can be in measuring performance objectives. Thresholds can be further refined by setting scoring patterns and banding methods for each range (see Figure 5-17).

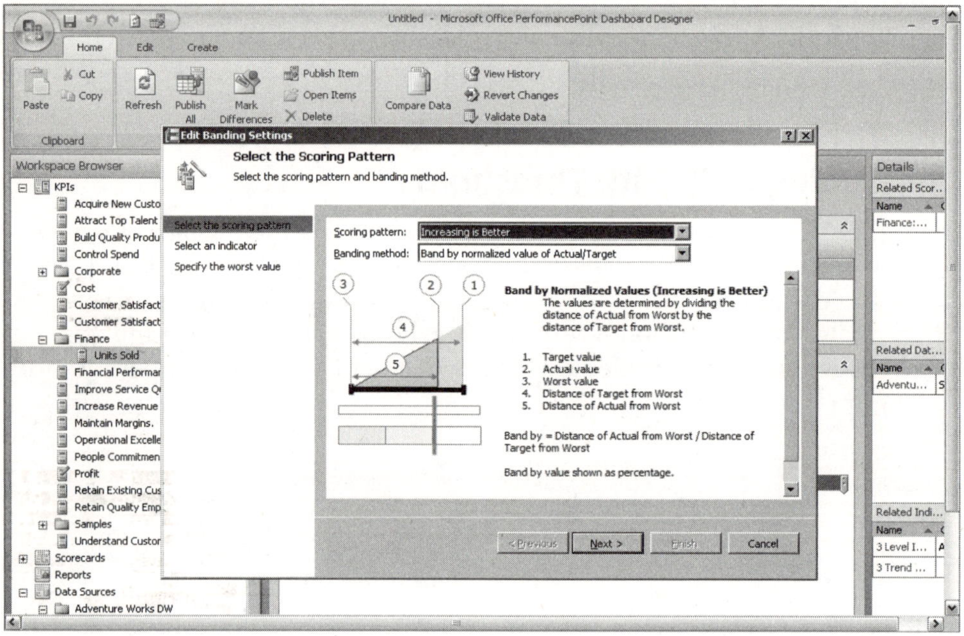

Figure 5-17 Set scoring patterns and banding methods for each range to refine thresholds.

This kind of refinement allows organizations to specify multiple and different business scoring patterns for strategic, operational, and tactical goals, thereby aligning visualization strategies with business goals at all levels of the organization. Organizations may be wary of creating detailed refinements, fearful that making changes might become a time-consuming and painstaking process. What if you have 15 KPIs based on a detailed scoring pattern that now needs to be changed? With the bulk editing capability, you can easily select the KPIs that need changes, make the required edit once, and see the change applied across all the KPIs you've selected.

Creating Custom Indicators

Indicators translate numerical values into colors, icons, and text to emphasize and clarify the status of KPIs. The classic stoplight indicator types work well because they are so familiar to us from other contexts. We know that red means "stop, danger"; green means "good, proceed"; and yellow means "proceed with caution."

It is possible to create and use indicator types customized to your industry — for example, people icons for customer-related KPIs or building icons for real estate–related KPIs. While it can be fun, at least in the prototype phase, to let people know that they have control over indicator types, it's also important not to go overboard and overwhelm the display with jumping frogs and leaping lizards. Best practice is to pick a uniform set of indicator types for all your KPIs and to rely on your designer to help align the visual presentation of the KPIs to your organization.

TIP With indicators, shape is as important as color. For a color-blind employee, a red stop light indicator will appear as different shades of brown.

Create a custom indicator for a scorecard by using the Create Indicator Wizard. When you create a custom indicator, you have the choice of defining its properties, including the image, text, and background color, and number of levels (see Figure 5-18).

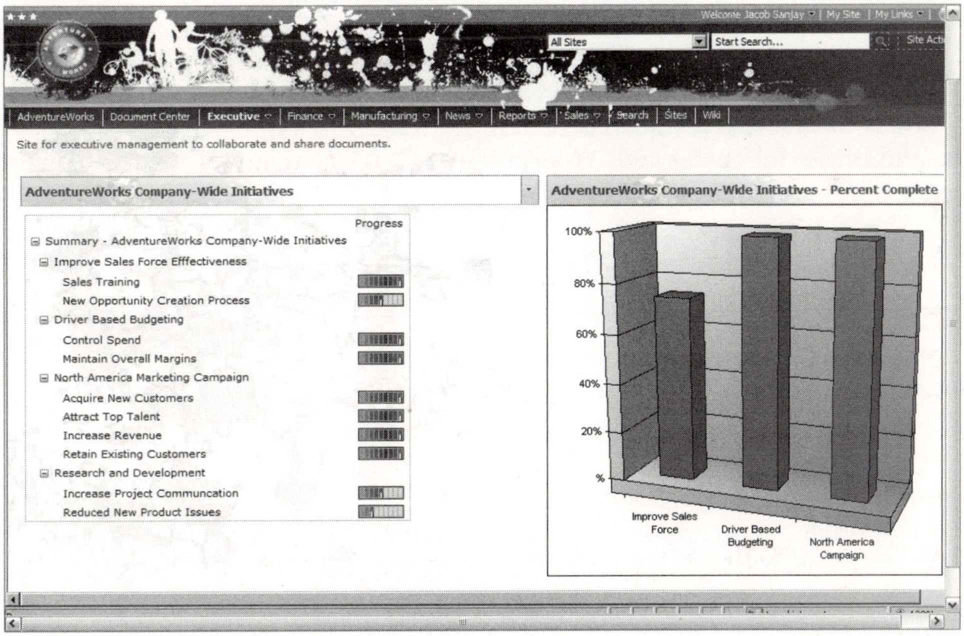

Figure 5-18 Example of a custom indicator

To create a custom indicator, use the Indicator Template Wizard in Dashboard Designer and select Blank Indicator, which allows you to select custom images and colors.

A large set of indicator images is provided in Dashboard Designer for each indicator band. Dashboard Designer provides the ability to customize the indicator image by changing the text color or the background. You can also change the indicator image entirely (see Figure 5-19).

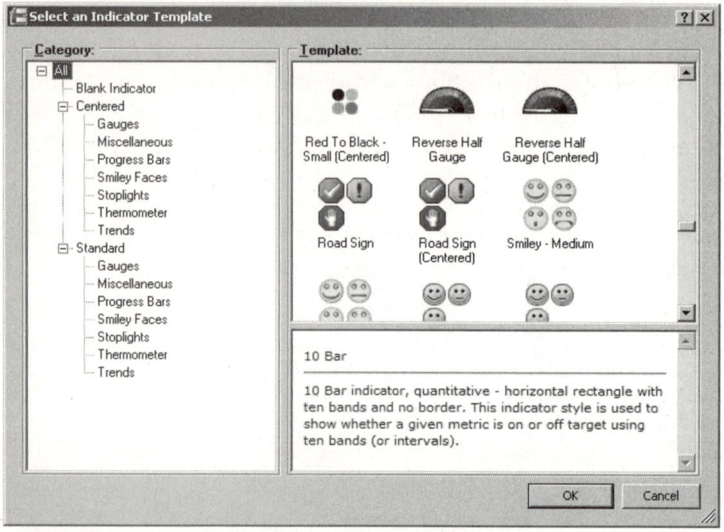

Figure 5-19 Indicator images from Dashboard Designer

When adding a new indicator to a target value, you must create a .gif, .jpg, or .png image for each band. You can create images in any of the three sizes: small, medium, or large.

It is recommended that you use the following indicator image sizes in Dashboard Designer when you create new indicators:

- **Small:** 80 × 22 pixels
- **Medium:** 65 × 124 pixels
- **Large:** 87 × 175 pixels

Best Practices Indicators

- Use thresholds to fine-tune indicators.
- Use scoring patterns and banding methods to fine-tune thresholds.
- Pick a uniform set of indicator types for all your KPIs.
- Rely on your designer to help align the visual presentation of the KPIs to your organization.
- Use the recommended image sizes when creating custom indicators.

Creating Additional Actual and Target Values

What if your organization needs to monitor both gross actual and net actual results on a scorecard? Or what if your organization needs to add a secondary target, for example a stretch target, to a scorecard? PerformancePoint provides default out-of-the-box actual and target values as well as an option to create additional actual and target values on a scorecard for cases like the ones mentioned previously.

Creating additional actual and target values is a multi-step process, and the same process applies whether you are creating an additional actual or additional target value.

Use the New Target option and give the new target a name. (Remember this can refer to an actual or a target Value.) Set the Number Format, Thresholds, and Data Mappings as required for the new value. The secondary Actual or Target appears in the list of Metrics as an available item, which you can then drag to any position on the scorecard. Once the secondary Actual or Target item appears in the scorecard, use the Target Settings option to choose values, scoring, and indicators to display for the item. It's important to know that calculations for additional actual and target values automatically refer to the default out-of-the-box actual value in the different equations.

Creating Trend Values

Trends display patterns over a period of time, providing valuable business information. In the example shown in Figure 5-20, you can see that it's important to recognize the downward trend shown in the Sales Amount KPI. This is the kind of business information a sales executive wants to know about sooner rather than later.

In Dashboard Designer, a trend is simply another target value created on the scorecard. Create trends on a scorecard by adding a new target. Best practice is to indicate on the scorecard the time period of the trend data, because trends display a pattern over a period of time you specify.

A common misconception about trends is that the trend indicator is derived by comparing the actual value against the target value. In fact, trend indicators are associated with thresholds defined in the scoring pattern set on each KPI. This explains why in the example shown in Figure 5-20, a yellow target indicator for the Target value on the Sales Amount KPI displays a downward trend indicator, while a yellow indicator on the Target value on the Order Count KPI displays a flat trend indicator. It also explains why a green indicator for the Target value of Gross Profit Margin also displays a flat trend indicator.

Looking at the Gross Profit Margin KPI in Dashboard Designer, you can see that the trend is added to the KPI where the thresholds and scoring pattern are set (see Figure 5-21).

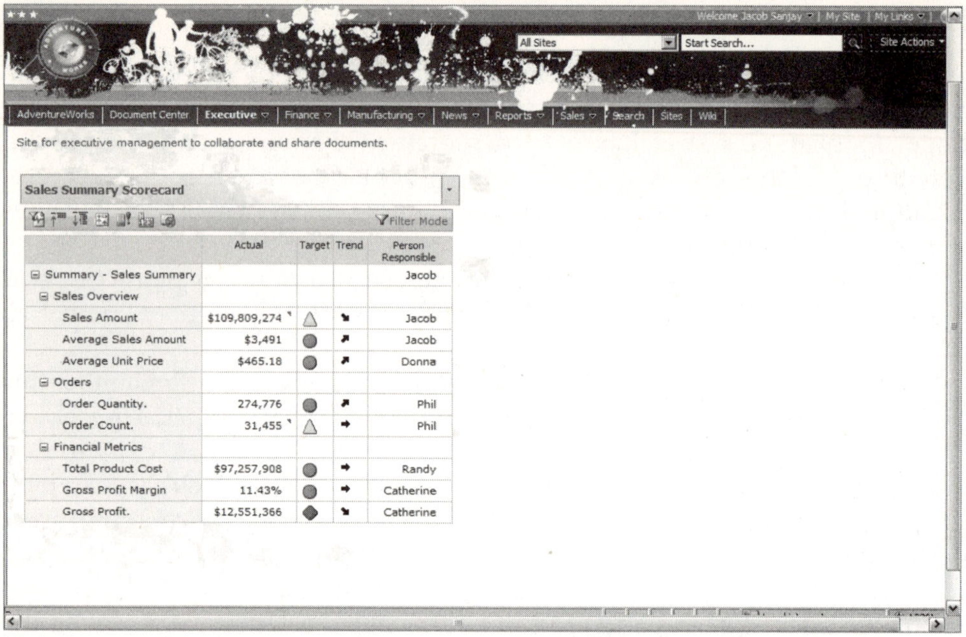

Figure 5-20 Sales Summary Scorecard with a Trend display

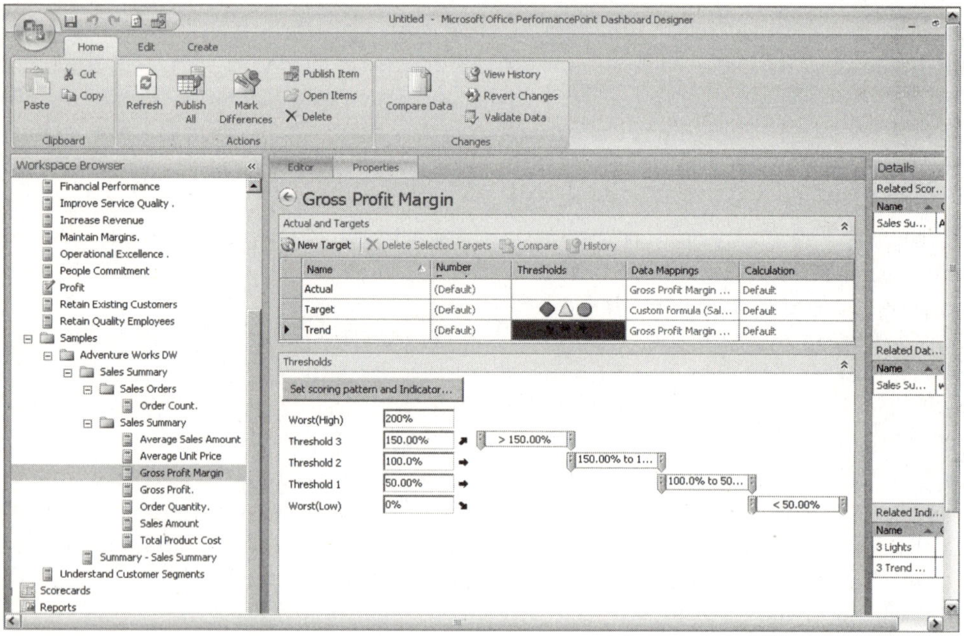

Figure 5-21 Trend values appear on each KPI in the scorecard.

In the example shown in Figure 5-21, percentages specify ranges for the direction of the trend arrows. In other words, the trend indicator is determined by the Threshold settings. A value above 150 percent will display an upward arrow in the scorecard. A value below 50 percent will display a downward arrow. Values in between will display a flat arrow. Remember that these values apply only to the Gross Profit Margin KPI and not to any other KPI on the scorecard.

Best Practices Trends

- On the scorecard, indicate the time period for the trend data.
- In Target Settings, choose to show only the trend indicator.

Summary

This chapter covered the concepts and features of scorecards and KPIs in PerformancePoint Monitoring and Analytics. It explored various scorecard examples, including scorecards based on the Balanced Scorecard methodology, and explained how to build scorecards and KPIs that fit your organization's plans and environment.

The chapter provided detailed information on implementing KPIs, including information on KPI banding, modifying and adding indicators, scorecard KPI weighting, and adding additional actual and target values.

This general overview of scorecards and KPIs supplemented with best practices information will allow you to begin working with Dashboard Designer to create scorecards with KPIs that effectively track the performance of goals and of your organization.

Notes

1. Bruno Aziza and Joey Fitts, *Drive Business Performance: Enabling a Culture of Intelligent Execution* (Wiley, 2008).

CHAPTER

6

Developing Effective Analytic Views

Organizations are dynamic and fluid — with new people, opportunities, trends, and roadblocks that constantly evolve and change. For some, this evolution is a frustration, a never-ending struggle to align people and goals with a moving, undefined target. For others, this constant change is key to a significant competitive advantage. Consider the organization that recognizes a new market trend before its competitors — it has the advantage of defining the rules and capturing an early lead. Or consider the organization that notices a small but unexpected drop in revenue — it has the advantage of taking corrective action quickly, before the small drop becomes a serious revenue shortage. Or consider the organization that can identify emerging markets for products early enough to make a well-planned entry. In each case, the organization that has substantial, timely insight into changing conditions has the advantage for sustained success.

Scorecards are the first step to gain this insight into the organization, as shown in the previous chapter. They clearly declare and align the most important objectives for an organization's success and provide up-to-date status information for those objectives. The next step to gain this insight is analysis: drilling into data (up, down, and across), sorting and filtering data to uncover pertinent information, and synthesizing the results into meaningful information upon which good business decisions can be made. Analysis is an iterative process in which data is continually examined and questioned in search of the patterns and anomalies that reveal the underlying health of an organization.

Analysis is dynamic and fluid — it helps you answer questions you haven't been asked before, find problems you haven't had before, and spot opportunities you haven't seen before. Done right, analysis is pervasive throughout the organization, allowing each person to ask questions, find answers, and identify problems and opportunities within his or her individual job scope. With the right guidance and tools, a store manager can analyze her store's inventory to determine the right product mix for her customer's demographics and buying patterns. A marketing executive can identify which marketing campaigns have most successfully expanded the sales pipeline and plan similar campaigns in the coming months. And a university registrar can identify at-risk students early enough in the semester to ensure that they have the proper support to achieve their goals.

This chapter highlights the analytic capabilities of PerformancePoint Server and shows how you can make analysis an integrated part of your organization's performance strategy. It begins by discussing the general concepts behind Online Analytical Processing (OLAP), the key technology for making analysis available to any user within your organization. It then explains the analytic capabilities available in Dashboard Designer and how to create relevant views that provide the right context for users. It concludes by explaining the navigation capabilities available in published dashboards and the insights that can be gained by navigating through the data.

Understanding OLAP

OLAP structures data into dimensions, hierarchies, lists, and calculations that correspond directly to tangible entities and performance indicators within an organization. By structuring raw data into cubes that can be easily queried, organizations enable information workers to take control of analysis and answer their own questions. They no longer need an expert to write scripts or generate reports because they know what relationships are significant and what questions they want answered, and they have intuitive, visual tools that help them explore the data themselves.

Because it relies on OLAP technology — specifically, Microsoft SQL Server 2005 Analysis Services — PerformancePoint Server can support pervasive analytics, a situation in which every information worker has the power to find root causes, discover driving factors, and gain insight to make better decisions. To better understand how OLAP achieves this lofty goal, let's look more closely at the fundamental structures of OLAP: dimensions, hierarchies, sets, and calculations.

Dimensions

Organizations are complex and multidimensional. They comprise internal organizations such as human resources, information technology, research and development, manufacturing, and marketing; and external groups such as customers, vendors, and partners. Organizations conduct business across multiple geographies, and they support countless products or services. Thus, no single dimension can capture all aspects of an organization, nor can one dimension solely define an organization's successes or challenges.

For example, a book retailer gathers data for the following business dimensions: buyers, customers, distribution centers, items, stores, and time. Each dimension can influence the other dimensions: Items are ordered by buyers for stores at regular time intervals. Items are purchased by customers, and store inventory is controlled by distribution centers. To understand the overall performance of the book retailer, analysts must be able to explore one dimension within the context of another dimension: How does a buyer's product mix affect what customers buy? How does the inventory at a distribution center affect the availability of items for a store? How do inventory needs change over time?

Because an OLAP cube organizes data using dimensional structures, it models the way that organizations are structured. Users have immediate context for their analysis because the data is shown in the same way that they experience it in the organization itself. They don't have to learn how one part of their business maps to the data, nor do they have to learn a new way to interact with the data, such as writing SQL scripts.

Hierarchies

Within a particular dimension, organizations are naturally structured in hierarchies: through organizational charts (CEO, directors, managers, and individual contributors), geographies (countries, regions, states, and cities), and product families (categories and subcategories). Hierarchies define a natural scoping within the organization, and individuals typically manage one or more levels within those hierarchies. For example, a store manager is primarily concerned with his direct reports, his product inventory, and his annual sales. On the other hand, an executive is concerned with the total revenue of all business units in all geographies. Figure 6-1 shows a product hierarchy represented in PerformancePoint Dashboard Designer.

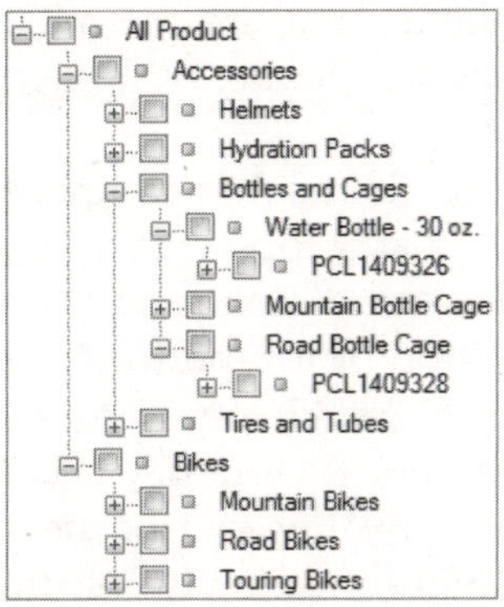

Figure 6-1 A product hierarchy in a dimension

In this example, All Product is the top of the hierarchy and is broken down into two product categories: Accessories and Bikes. Below each of those categories are additional categories, each with a smaller scope than its parent. In this company, the scope of a regional sales manager is at the product category level. He is responsible for ensuring that overall sales of these categories improve year-over-year. He doesn't spend much time looking at the items below this level in the hierarchy because he is most concerned with aggregated sales numbers. However, his store managers are interested in the individual items in the hierarchy because they monitor inventory turns to ensure the right buying patterns for their stores. Because data is represented in a flexible hierarchical tree, users can work with the data at the right level for their role.

Like dimensions, hierarchies represent how users see their organization. Users can ask questions (or analyze the data) using the same terminology they use to conduct business: products, customer, claims, plants, or projects. They can target those questions to the level that matches their scope, making their analysis personally relevant. And they are shielded from the complexities of databases, keys, and tables, encouraging meaningful interactions with the data without extensive, specialized training.

Lists and Sets

OLAP also fosters an extensive use of lists (or sets). Lists are simply items that share one or more common attributes that can be grouped together into a meaningful unit. Although ostensibly mundane, lists are surprisingly powerful analytic tools. At the simplest level, a list can be the projects you are working on, the clients you represent, or the investments you have in your portfolio. However, with a small amount of logic applied, lists can produce considerable meaning within your data. For example, a list can contain the customers that contributed 80 percent of your revenue over the past 3 years. Based on the characteristics of the customers in that list, you can determine how to restructure your sales organization or expand your customer base to maximize future revenue. Or a list can contain the items that are the most expensive to manufacture but generate the least amount of revenue. With such a list, you can easily identify which products to retire.

Some of the most useful lists are dynamic. That is, the items that compose the list change based on specified criteria. For example, a list of top-performing regions may include the Western and Southern regions one month and the Southern and Eastern regions the next. The list definition of top-performing regions remains constant, but the criterion applied to the list changes: in this case, a time period. By extending lists with any number of criteria, users can quickly gain significant insight into their business by uncovering new relationships and driving factors among the items. Figure 6-2 includes the named sets available for the AdventureWorks data source, as displayed in the PerformancePoint Dashboard Designer (AdventureWorks is the sample database provided with Microsoft SQL Server 2005 Analysis Services).

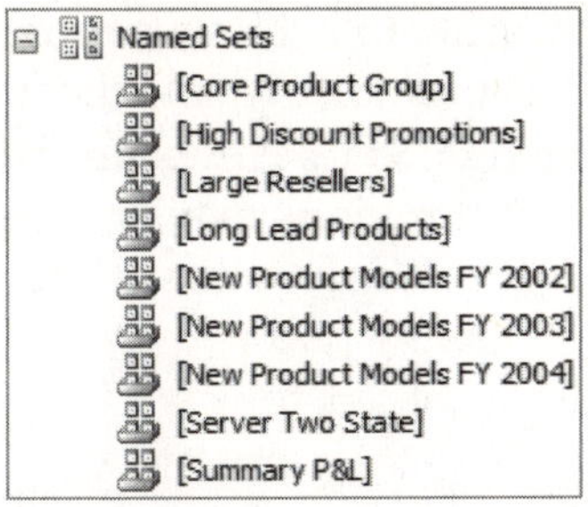

Figure 6-2 Named sets within AdventureWorks

As you can see by the names beside each icon, these sets include logic that makes them valuable for the business user. Rather than each user in the organization individually deciding what defines Large Resellers or High Discount Promotions (and determining how to create a list based on those criteria), the definitions are provided for them within the cube. Users simply select the named set and perform their analysis. The list is consistent for all users for all analyses because it comes from the same source, which is defined and maintained centrally.

Calculations

Like named sets, calculations are valuable components of business logic that are managed centrally. They provide the values and measurements behind the data, completing the basic OLAP story. Calculations, such as average sale price or cost to manufacture, provide fundamental, objective guidance on business performance. They are created through OLAP's Multidimensional Expressions (MDX) language and can be as simple or complex as needed to accurately capture the key measurements that drive performance.

For example, a simple growth calculation can show improvement from year to year. A more complex standard deviation calculation can be used to assess risk within a portfolio by determining which investments have performed consistently well over time. A rank calculation can determine the top-selling products in a particular geography, relative to all products in all geographies, while a scoring calculation can produce a normalized percent that considers weighted values of sales, profit margin, and cost to determine overall value. By identifying which measurements are relevant for improving performance and providing those measurements in the cube, an organization can essentially guide users on how to conduct effective analysis for their business.

Three types of calculations exist in OLAP databases: measures, calculated measures, and calculated members. Measures are basic calculations that can be derived from values within the source data itself, such as Sales Amount, Number of Product Sold, and Average Call Wait Time. Calculated measures combine one or more measures in a mathematical formula to achieve a more meaningful metric, such Growth, Profit Margin, or Cost of Sale. A calculated member is a group of items that are aggregated into a single item. For example, an All Regions calculated member may be the sum of all regions available in the data source. Figure 6-3 shows some of the AdventureWorks calculations, or measures, as shown in Dashboard Designer.

Figure 6-3 Measures available in AdventureWorks

Although this has been a very brief introduction to a complex technology, it has highlighted why OLAP is so key to timely, productive analysis: The data is modeled to match the way that users see their organization. Users don't need to know how to generate a specific query from a SQL Server table; instead, they simply need to know what dimensions of their business are relevant to them, what levels within the hierarchy are relevant to their job scope, how items should be grouped together, and what calculations drive the success of their business. Users are empowered to answer their own questions, making OLAP a technology that can be deployed successfully throughout an organization.

Discover, Create, and Deploy

As an organization develops and refines OLAP cubes, analysts begin working with the cubes to uncover key relationships and driving factors to improve the performance of their organization. In the following section, we will focus on the role of analysts in collaborative, pervasive analytics: specifically, conducting ad hoc and directed analysis and creating content for business users. We will also show how PerformancePoint can help analysts achieve their business performance goals.

Translating Data into Insight

Analysts within an organization are responsible for providing decision makers with the information and data they need to make decisions. Some people may have "analyst" in their job title, but often analysis is simply part of an employee's extended job responsibilities. Employees, typically managers, deliver information in formal reports and presentations or informal spreadsheets or lists. They are often required to do analysis of raw data from multiple data sources and draw conclusions or explain the results. And they usually understand their industries very well and can make recommendations based on their experience.

Analysts, by profession or by the nature of their job, play a key role in ensuring that decision makers, from executives to individual contributors, have the data and data analysis results to effectively do their jobs. With limited time and unlimited tasks, analysts must empower users to answer their own questions, draw their own conclusions, and make their own effective decisions. This means that analysts must understand how to deliver analytic content to users in such a way that they encourage further ad hoc and personal analysis. This involves not only creating the right views for the right type of analysis but also providing context and showing relevance.

Creating Successful Views

Designing the right type of view for the right analysis means understanding how best to visualize the answers to common questions. For example, questions about peer relationships, such as Top 10 Products by Sales or Highest Ranked Stores for Customer Service, are best displayed in a sorted grid or chart. In the following example, both PerformancePoint grids display the same list of members. Notice how much faster you can identify the top-selling product in the grid on the right (see Figure 6-4).

By sorting items in a relevant order (in this case, from highest to lowest sales), analysts can help their users draw quick conclusions: "Silver mountain bikes are my top-selling product line." They eliminate the burden of requiring their users to mentally sort the list themselves to find high and low performers.

Another useful view type is a line chart, used to assess performance over time. Again, notice how much easier it is to draw a conclusion from the chart than the grid (see Figure 6-5).

Product	⊞ 2006
⊞ Sport-200 Helmet, Ye..	$8,122,321.59
⊞ Sport-200 Helmet, Wh..	$4,967,692.10
⊞ Sport-300 Helmet, Red	$6,266,295.20
⊞ Sport-300 Helmet, Bl..	$6,611,209.41
⊞ Sport-100 Helmet, Bl..	$7,504,759.73
⊞ Mountain Bottle Cage	$7,940,092.31
⊞ Mountain-100 Silver,..	$7,915,559.28
⊞ Mountain-100 Silver,..	$18,332,990.19
⊞ Mountain-200 Black,..	$6,632,460.13
⊞ Mountain-200 Black,..	$8,763,657.51

Product	⊞ 2006 ↓
⊞ Mountain-100 Silver,..	$18,332,990.19
⊞ Mountain-200 Black,..	$8,763,657.51
⊞ Sport-200 Helmet, Ye..	$8,122,321.59
⊞ Mountain Bottle Cage	$7,940,092.31
⊞ Mountain-100 Silver,..	$7,915,559.28
⊞ Sport-100 Helmet, Bl..	$7,504,759.73
⊞ Mountain-200 Black,..	$6,632,460.13
⊞ Sport-300 Helmet, Bl..	$6,611,209.41
⊞ Sport-300 Helmet, Red	$6,266,295.20
⊞ Sport-200 Helmet, Wh..	$4,967,692.10

Figure 6-4 Comparing unsorted (left) and sorted (right) grid views

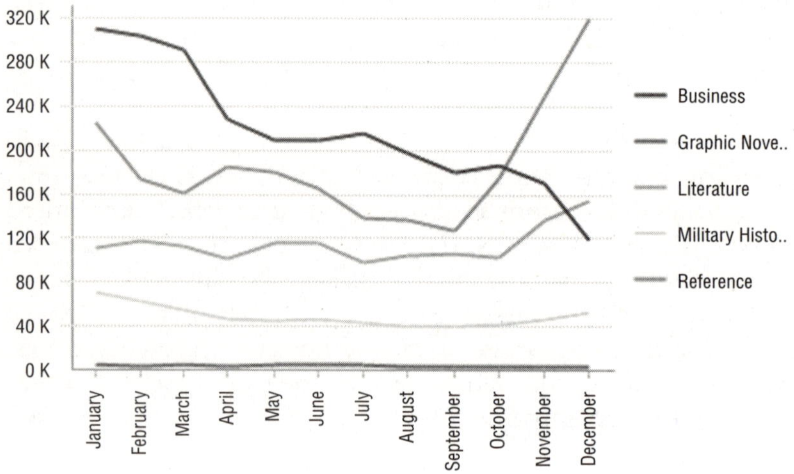

Figure 6-5 Analytic chart comparing performance over time

Unlike the grid view, the chart view easily shows which book categories had a growth in sales, a decline in sales, or flat sales. Users will naturally ask follow-up questions after looking at the chart view: "Why did Reference books spike in December and why did Business books decline throughout the year?" By asking these questions, users engage with the data and take ownership of understanding driving factors. With this understanding, they are well equipped to make the right decisions to improve performance. It is unlikely a simple grid view would encourage users to engage the same way (see Figure 6-6).

A third view type that can be used to communicate large amounts of information quickly is the stacked bar chart or 100% stacked bar chart. A stacked bar chart shows contributions within a category; a 100% stacked bar chart shows relative contributions within a category. For example, in Figure 6-7, the stacked bar chart shows the contribution made by each product category to overall sales.

Item By Category	⊞ January	⊞ February	⊞ March	⊞ April	⊞ May
⊞ Business	$310,575.59	$304,412.76	$291,066.65	$229,297.08	$209,812.01
⊞ Graphic Novels	$4,228.40	$3,865.46	$4,273.55	$3,717.60	$4,596.43
⊞ Literature	$110,729.17	$117,196.90	$111,901.44	$100,820.88	$115,332.33
⊞ Military History	$71,114.83	$62,689.33	$55,404.27	$46,434.01	$44,621.09
⊞ Reference	$224,846.49	$173,318.92	$160,729.49	$185,479.26	$180,889.83

Figure 6-6 Analytic grid view comparing performance over time

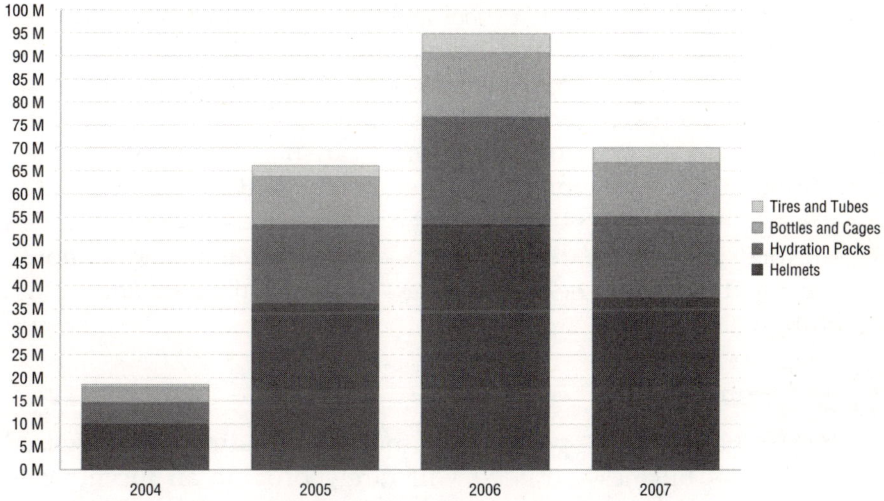

Figure 6-7 Chart view showing contributions over time

From this chart, users can quickly identify that helmets contribute the greatest amount of sales and tires contribute the least. They can also see that the percent contribution of each product to overall sales has remained relatively consistent for the past 4 years, and that sales declined considerably from 2006 to 2007. The follow-up questions that may come from this view include the following: "What caused the drop in sales in 2007?" "Which products had a decline in sales?" "What products grew in sales during 2007?" "Did the sales decline across all regions or just one or two?"

PerformancePoint provides numerous report and view types to ensure the right view is available for the right type of analysis. Combined with navigation capabilities, such as drilling down, drilling down to (cross-drilling), and show details, PerformancePoint views help enable users to effectively manage their own performance and performance improvements. By providing users with the right views in their dashboards, analysts can help ensure that users are empowered to answer their own questions, whenever they need to do so.

Providing Context

In addition to designing the right type of views, analysts must create content with the right context. As mentioned earlier in this book, context means the views and data are aligned to the job scope of the person or team. For example, a sales representative sees the sales breakdown within her region, not all regions. A plant manager monitors plant downtime for his plant, not all plants. And a project manager see the status for his projects, not all active projects.

Meaningful comparisons are key to the context. For example: "How am I doing compared to my peers?"; "How am I doing compared to the organization as a whole?"; "Am I doing better today than I was doing last year?" Through comparisons such as these, a person has context to assess his or his performance: "I missed by goal by 10 percent, but others in the company missed their goal by 50 percent. This probably means I'm doing fairly well considering the economic conditions of the past year." Or, "My team's claim-processing time went down from last year, which means our process changes are making a difference." Or, "Our room occupancy numbers are higher than other hotels in this area, but they are lower than hotels outside this area. We may want to look at a more aggressive marketing campaign to drive those numbers up."

Analysts responsible for creating effective content for their users should consider the context needed to help those users engage in the data and design views accordingly.

Ensuring Relevance

Relevance means that views are personal for the user. Building views focused only on a high-level business strategy will rarely provide an incentive to individual contributors to improve their performance. On the other hand, building views that directly relate to a person's bonus potential, commission, or professional recognition will immediately engage him personally in the data and results. Given the right tools and incentives, users will seek to understand the driving factors behind results and actively address issues.

For example, an accounts receivable clerk may ignore a strategic objective to increase corporate net profit by 10 percent because she is not directly involved in the sales aspects of the business. However, the number of outstanding invoices that remained unpaid for over 90 days does have a measurable impact on the corporation's profitability. Providing views that have the right context for the accounts receivable clerk, such as a trend chart showing unpaid invoices over time, will allow her to respond appropriately to positively affect the company's strategic objective.

Further, giving the clerk the analytic tools to quickly identify which specific invoices have not be paid, which customers have a pattern of not paying invoices on time, and the total amount of interest lost or paid because of delinquent invoices empowers her to act. She can not only aggressively pursue unpaid invoices, but also recommend delaying future purchases by at-risk customers until current invoices are paid. She can track the financial impact of her efforts over time and have concrete and compelling evidence of her contribution for her next performance review. She is no longer simply responsible for doing paperwork; she is responsible for the financial well-being of the company.

Using PerformancePoint to Create Analytic Views

The primary tool for creating analytic content in PerformancePoint is the Analytic View Designer, available in Dashboard Designer. This application enables analysts to explore Analysis Services 2005 cubes and create interactive analytic views for dashboards. The Analytic View Designer is opened by creating an analytic chart or analytic grid report view type, as shown in Figure 6-8.

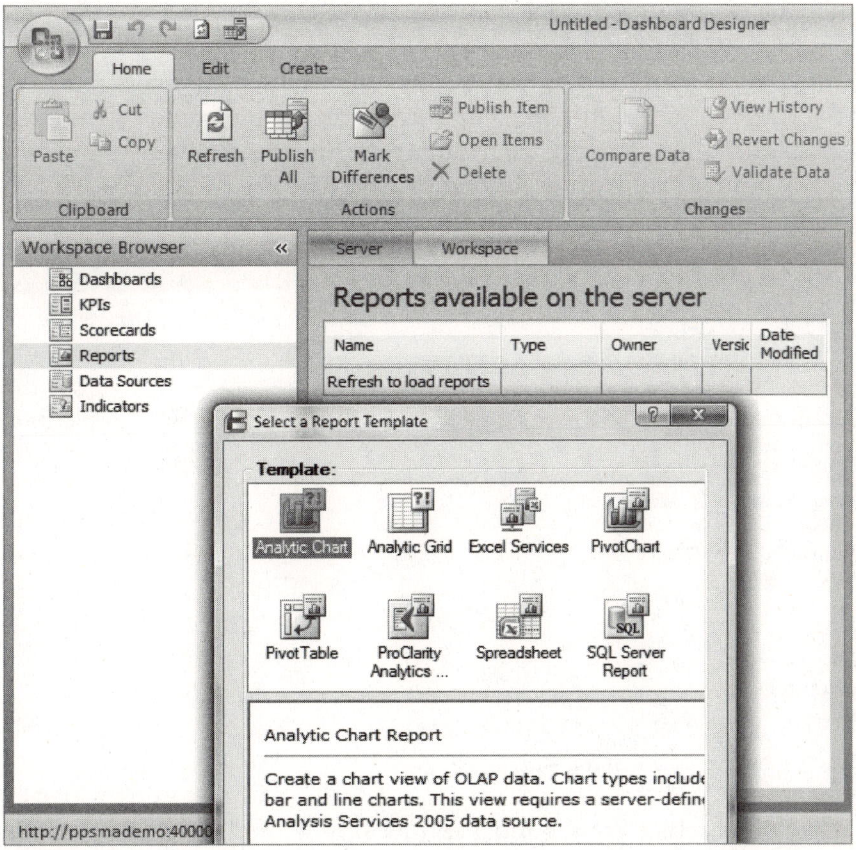

Figure 6-8 PerformancePoint Server Dashboard Designer

(Note that prior to using the Dashboard Designer to create analytic views, the analyst must define an Analysis Services 2005 data source.)

Placing Items in the View

The Analytic View Designer opens with a blank analytic workspace. On the right side of the analytic workspace is the Details pane (see Figure 6-9), which contains the dimension, measures, and sets that you can use in the view.

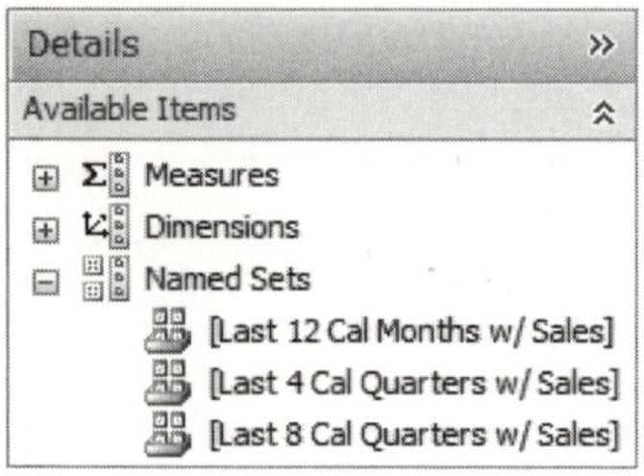

Figure 6-9 Dashboard Designer Details pane

Within the Details pane is the dimensions tree, which displays icons to represent the different types of hierarchies available. The pyramid icon indicates a user-defined hierarchy. This means that the hierarchy is organized into logic levels representing an organizational structure. In Figure 6-10, two user-defined hierarchies are shown: Geography and Product.

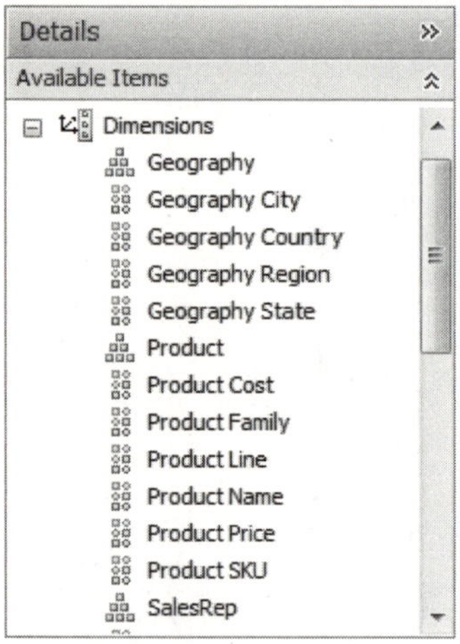

Figure 6-10 Hierarchies shown in the Details pane

User-defined hierarchies are the most common type of hierarchies used for analysis because they support vertical navigation, which is moving from one level within a hierarchy to another level. For example, an analyst wants to see how product sales break down across geographies. To do this, she navigates from the Product hierarchy to the Geography hierarchy. If she wants to then see how products break down from the state level to the city level, she can move from the State level to the City level within the Geography hierarchy.

Two other types of hierarchies are also shown in the Dimensions tree: attribute hierarchies and time hierarchies. An attribute hierarchy is a flat list of items that can be used to add relevant information to the items in the view, such as product IDs or contact information. In Figure 6-11, the user-defined hierarchy SalesRep and the attribute hierarchy SalesRep Email are added to an analytic grid view.

SalesRep	SalesRep Email	Sales Amt
Corets, Eva	rep013@contoso.com	$10,666,360.87
Duffy, Terri Lee	rep014@contoso.com	$15,733,665.06
Giorgi, Adriana	rep019@contoso.com	$74,860,915.67
Wallace, Anne	rep017@contoso.com	$23,176,211.36

Figure 6-11 An attribute hierarchy placed in a grid view

Note that the grid view in Figure 6-11 is shown in tabular format, which means that the attribute hierarchies are on the same row as the related member in the user-defined hierarchy. An alternative display is the compact format, where the attribute hierarchies are shown below the related member in the user-defined hierarchy. To change the grid format, select Report Layout from the Edit tab of Dashboard Designer (see Figure 6-12).

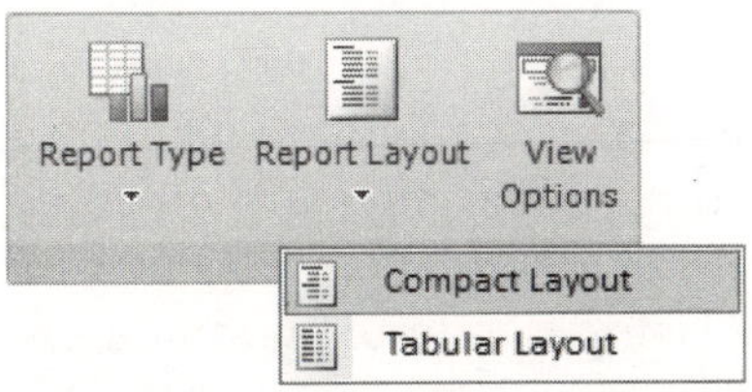

Figure 6-12 Grid format options from the Edit tab

In analytic charts, attribute hierarchy values are displayed in flyovers, as shown in Figure 6-13.

Although users can't navigate vertically on the SalesRep hierarchy (because it doesn't have multiple levels), it does add valuable information to the view. In our example, users can quickly email a sales rep to clarify concerns about an unexpected Sale Amount value.

Because time is considered a unique dimension in cubes, time hierarchies are designated with a special icon in the Dimensions tree as well (see Figure 6-14).

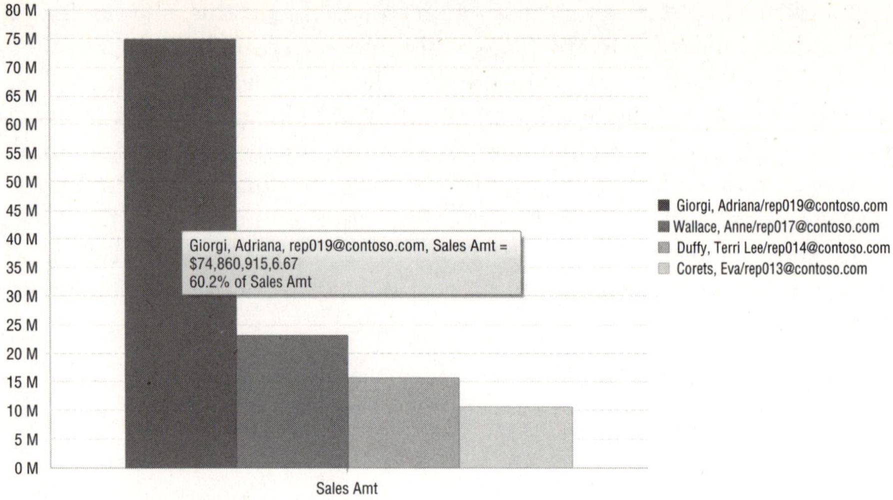

Figure 6-13 Attribute hierarchy values shown in chart flyovers

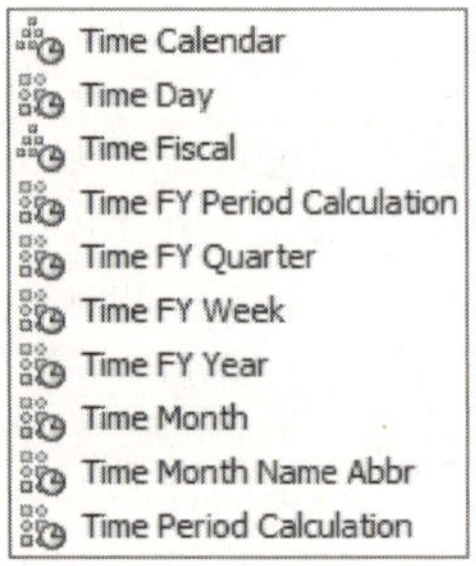

Figure 6-14 Time hierarchies shown in the Details pane

In this example, two user-defined hierarchies are available: a standard calendar and a fiscal calendar. The remaining time hierarchies are attribute hierarchies. Time hierarchies are generally mutually exclusive. That is, you can use one type of time hierarchy in your view. Using two time hierarchies in the view simultaneously will nearly always result in an empty data set. One exception to this is a time-folded analysis, whereby time hierarchies appear on both foreground dimensions. For example, Figure 6-15 compares monthly product sales across 3 years, showing common peaks and valleys within the sales cycle.

The first step to create an analytic chart or grid in the Analytic View Designer is to drag items from the Details pane to the Series (or Rows), Bottom Axis (or Columns), or Background box in the workspace. This will establish the basic configuration of your analytic view, as shown in Figure 6-16.

To create a view displaying sales performance over time, we place the user-defined hierarchy SalesRep on Series, the named set Last 4 Cal Quarters w/Sales on the bottom axis, and the Product hierarchy on the background. We also include the attribute hierarchy SalesRep Email on the same axis as its related user-defined hierarchy. Though not shown in the view itself, items placed on the background filter the results in the view. In this example, the values shown include only the product category Bikes, not all products.

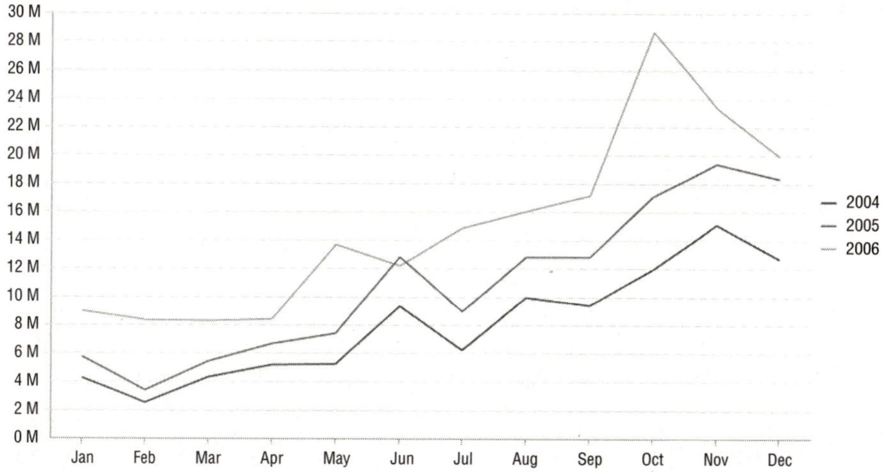

Figure 6-15 Time-folded analysis

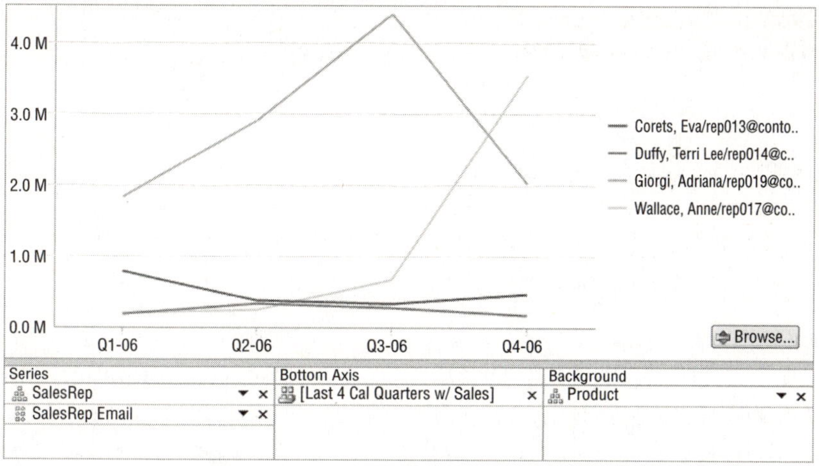

Figure 6-16 Basic analytic chart view layout

If multiple dimensions are placed on a single axis, the dimensions will be joined, resulting in a type of query called a cross join: Each member of the first dimension will be combined with every member in the second dimension. Figure 6-17 shows a cross join of Store Geography and Item by Category on Rows.

Store Geography, Ite..	Sale Amt
Central	
Book	$9,890,023.21
Pre-Pack	$175,255.65
West	
Book	$3,419,008.10
Pre-Pack	$49,120.73

Figure 6-17 A cross join of Geography and Item

In this example, the sales amount of each geographic area is shown, broken down by product categories. This type of query is especially important in analytic views because it allows you to explore relevant relationships among dimensions that may not be immediately apparent from the source data.

Note that filters can be created from any hierarchy that is placed on an axis in the view. Hierarchies that are not placed on an axis are not available for filters. If no selection is made for a hierarchy, the default value designated in the cube is used in the query. Filters are discussed in greater detail in Chapter 7.

Selecting Items for the View

In addition to the layout capabilities of the Analytic View Designer, you can select the specific items to include in the view using the Member Selector. The Member Selector is opened by clicking the drop-down menu next to a hierarchy, as highlighted in Figure 6-18.

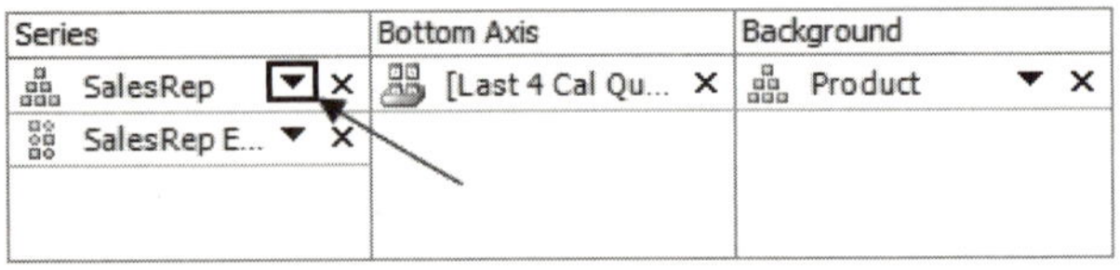

Figure 6-18 Opening the Member Selector

The Member Selector supports both dynamic and static selections. With dynamic selections, such as Children or Descendants, views will automatically change based on the data within the cube. If a new item is added to a hierarchy in the cube, the item will appear as part of the query results when that hierarchy is used. If explicit member selections are made, the items in the query remain constant, regardless of any additions to the cube.

Dynamic selections are made using the Autoselect Members option, available on the right-click menu (see Figure 6-19).

The Select Children operation selects all items immediately below the selected member. The Select Leaves option selects all items at the leaf-level (or bottom) of the hierarchy. The Select All Descendants option selects all items below the selected member in the hierarchy. You can also select items at a specified level.

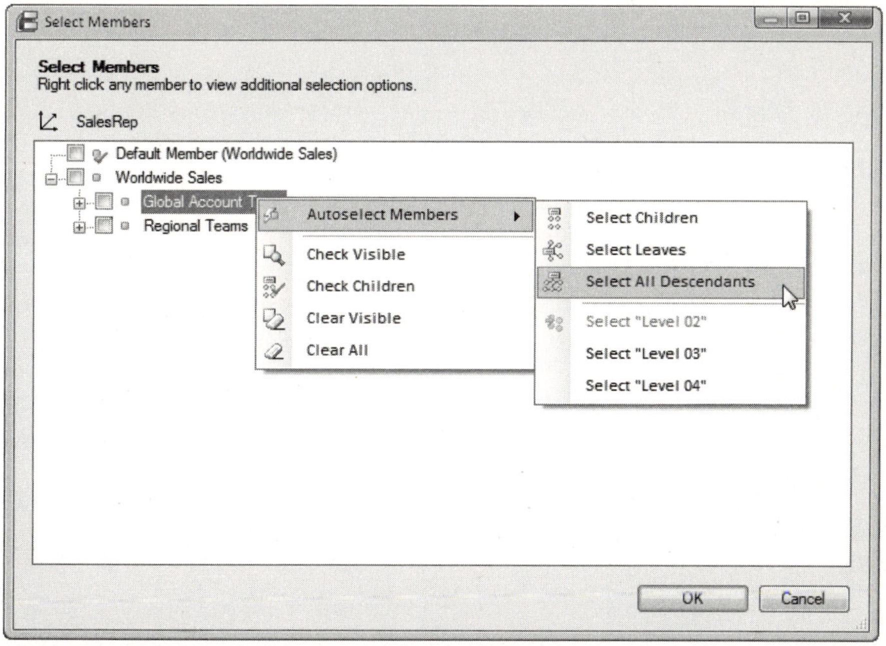

Figure 6-19 Making dynamic member selections

Static selections are made by checking the boxes next to the items in the hierarchy, as shown in Figure 6-20.

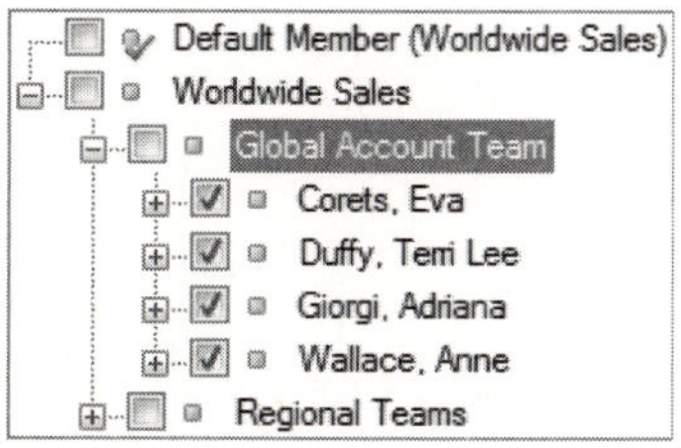

Figure 6-20 Making static member selections

Selecting the View Type

The Analytic View Designer supports numerous view types, so you can present the results in the format that is most conducive to gaining insight. As you design analytic content for users, it's important to recognize which visualizations to use for each type of analysis. You select the report type from the Edit tab of the Analytic View Designer ribbon bar, as shown in Figure 6-21.

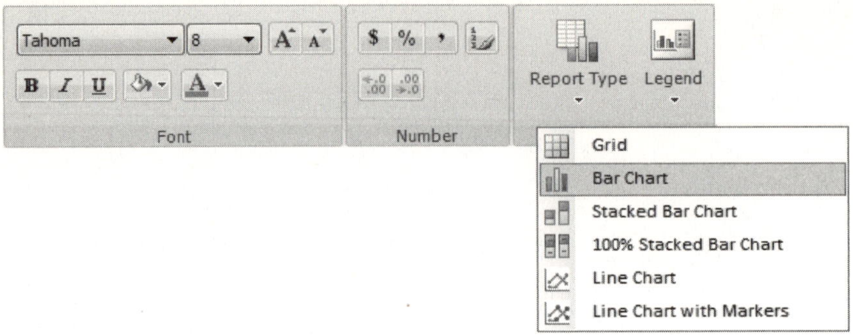

Figure 6-21 Selecting the view type

As previously discussed, line charts are most useful to show trends, momentum, or growth over time. You can show multiple metrics together to identify cause and effect or related shifts in momentum. Figure 6-22 compares two metrics (markdown and sales) across two product lines (art books and business books).

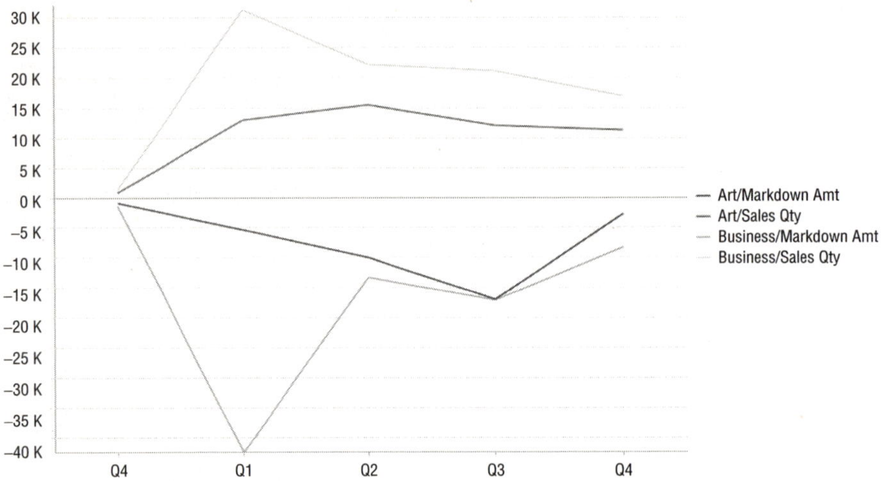

Figure 6-22 Comparing two metrics with a line chart

As expected, greater discounts lead to greater sales, at least for business books. Note the increased discount amount and corresponding rise in sales in Q1. For art books, the conclusion is a little less clear. Even when discounts increased significantly in Q3, art books did not see a corresponding increase in sales. And when discounts decreased for art books in Q4, they didn't see a corresponding drop in sales. One conclusion that could be validated with further analysis is that discounts do not have a significant impact on art book sales.

Bar charts show comparisons across categories. Figure 6-23 compares the profit margin percent achieved by each state.

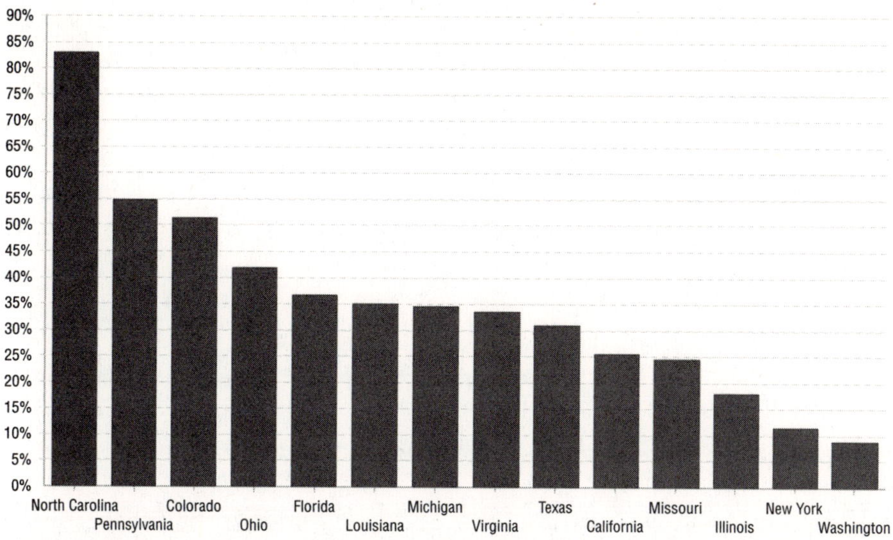

Figure 6-23 Comparing performance across states

With this type of view, a user can quickly see that Washington and New York may have significant performance deficiencies, especially when compared to the highest performing states of North Carolina and Pennsylvania.

Mixed bar and line charts compare two metrics that are based on different units (a value and a percent), as shown in Figure 6-24.

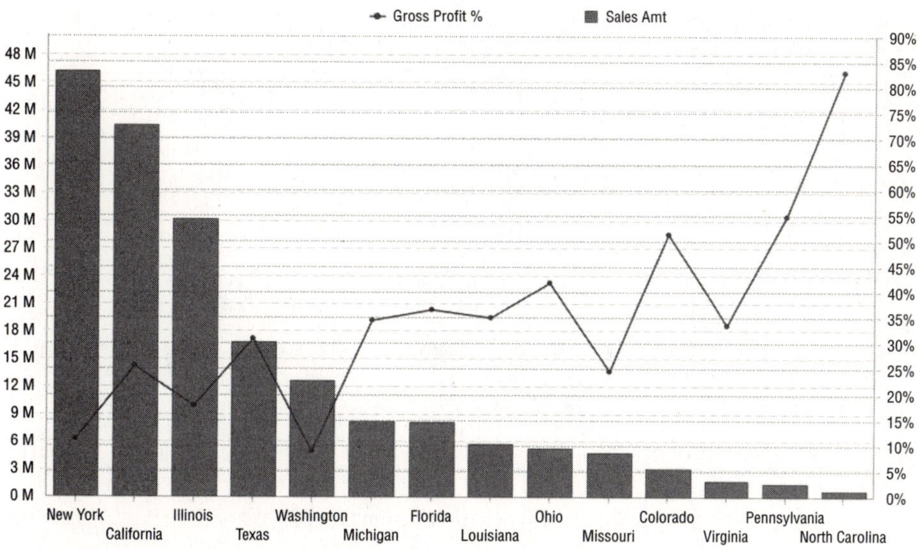

Figure 6-24 Comparing performance across states by comparing two metrics

This view provides additional insight into the sales performance of New York and North Carolina. Although New York had the lowest profit margin, it had the highest sales amount. Conversely, North Carolina had the highest profit margin but had the lowest sales. Likely, the low sales numbers in North Carolina distorted the relevance of the profit margin percent in comparing its performance to the other states in the first view. The best performing states in this example may be California or Texas, since both have higher profit margins and sales amounts.

In Analytic View Designer, mixed bar and line charts are created automatically when a non-percentage measure and a percentage measure are placed on the Series axis together, as shown in Figure 6-25.

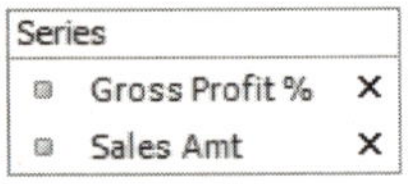

Figure 6-25 Measure on Series to create a mixed bar and line chart

Stacked bar charts show contributions, and 100% stacked bar charts show relative contributions. For example, Figure 6-26 shows the relative contribution of book categories in stores across three geographies.

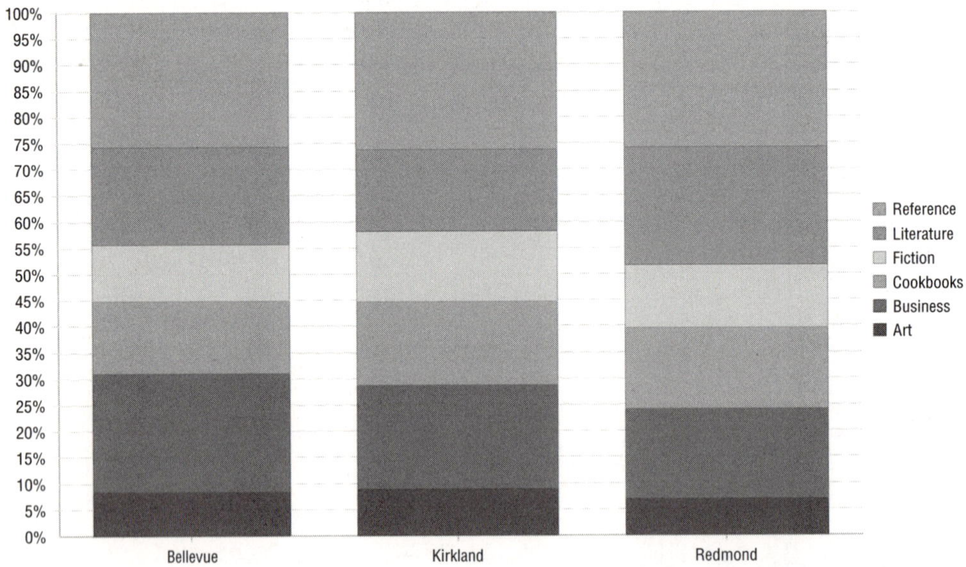

Figure 6-26 Comparing the relative contribution of products across geography

From this chart, you can see that Redmond stores sell more Literature books than Kirkland or Bellevue, as a percent of overall sales. And Bellevue stores sell more Business books, as a percent of overall sales. Although PerformancePoint does not provide pie charts in this version, 100% stacked bar charts are an excellent alternative to pie charts.

Grid views are useful for small sets of numbers where exact values are important for context. Grid views are also good complements to chart views, where the chart views quickly show comparisons and grid views show the values.

Using Advanced Visualizations

Discovering meaningful information that can truly improve performance sometimes requires a specialized way of displaying and navigating the data. In the classic board game Scrabble, players will often rearrange their letters or turn the board to gain a new perspective on the game. They find new words that were invisible to them before, even though the game itself hasn't changed. Analyzing data is the same: Changing the way that data is presented can often reveal opportunities or problems you didn't see before.

In PerformancePoint, two unique visualizations are available to help reveal these hidden relationships: the performance map and the decomposition tree. (These visualizations are available in ProClarity, an OLAP analysis tool available to licensed users of PerformancePoint. This report type is discussed in Chapter 8.) The performance map is derived from the tree map conceived by Ben Shneiderman, a computer scientist and professor at the University of Maryland, College Park. It allows you to see data patterns among a group of items using the size and color of boxes arranged together in a small space. In Figure 6-27, the performance map compares sales and percent markdown among History books.

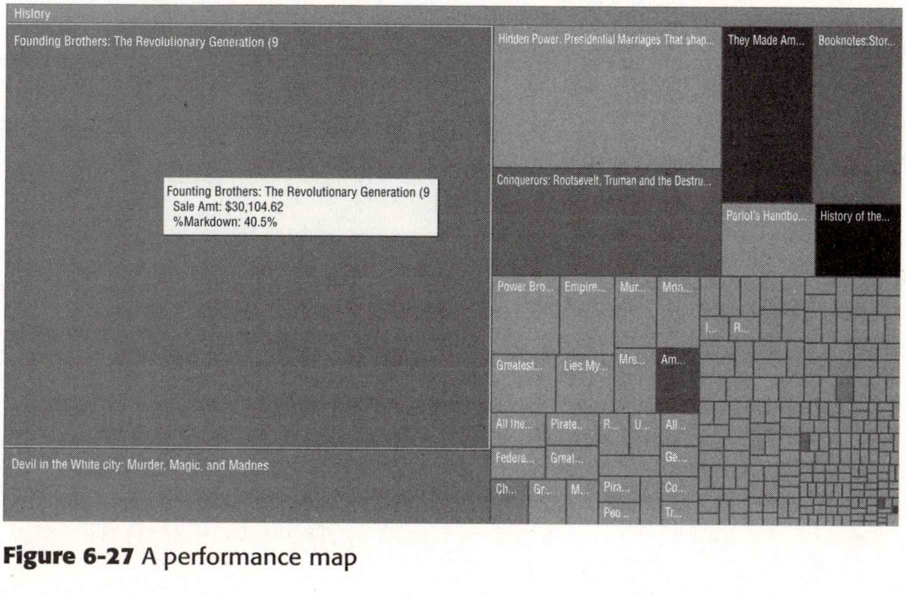

Figure 6-27 A performance map

The size of the box represents the gross sales for the book (bigger is better), and the color of the box represents how much the book price has been marked down (greener is better). Ideally, books with the highest sales would have the lowest percent markdown; that is, the largest boxes would be the brightest green. This view indicates a serious problem in the top-selling book *Founding Brothers* because it has the highest markdown percent of all books in this category. Reducing the markdown on this book may improve overall revenue for the company.

Another unique way of uncovering insight within data is the decomposition tree. The decomposition tree is a graphical, intuitive way of finding the root cause of issues. Each level of the decomposition tree shows a sorted list of items filtered by the items selected in the levels above it. You can break down any value based on any hierarchy in the cube or compare items at the same cube level.

For example, in Figure 6-28, the decomposition tree shows the highest contributors to the overall sales amount: Accessories make up 61 percent of the total product sales, North America makes up 54 percent of all Accessories sales, and the Global Accounts Team makes up 60 percent of Accessories sales in North America.

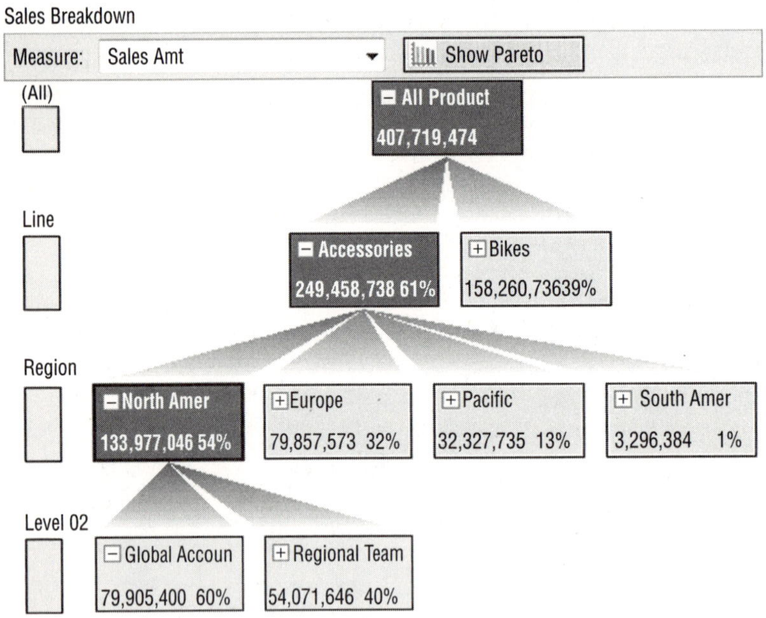

Figure 6-28 A decomposition tree

The decomposition tree is a unique way of navigating through the data, providing rapid visibility and understanding of the driving factors behind a number.

Over time, the capabilities of ProClarity will be moved into PerformancePoint, but until that migration is complete, Dashboard Designer allows you to integrate ProClarity views directly into your dashboards, using the ProClarity Analytics Server report type.

Using MDX Mode

The Analytic View Designer includes a Query mode where you can provide valid MDX to generate views that are not possible through the drag-and-drop interface of the Design mode. This mode requires a complete, valid MDX query. Although advanced users may be comfortable writing MDX, other users may feel more comfortable creating queries in a more visual tool such as ProClarity and then copying and pasting the query into Dashboard Designer. Although you can't navigate on views created in Query mode, you can create advanced analytic views for your users.

For example, a user wants to show how stores in a region are performing compared to all stores in all regions. One way to accomplish this is by displaying a store's numeric rank next to its sales amount. One store may rank sixteenth in overall sales but first in its particular region. Another store may rank first in its region but ninth in overall sales. Because both ranks are relevant to understanding how well this store is performing, the analyst wants to create a view that displays both values. When they receive the view, regional managers select their region to see the breakdown of their stores — sorted by the sales amount within their region and their rank in overall sales, as shown in Figure 6-29.

Store Geography	Sale Amt	Rank(Total)
Seattle	$131,644.76	1
Tacoma	$94,197.09	6
Bellevue	$62,993.55	11
Portland	$50,627.25	21
Everett	$47,507.47	26
Hillsboro	$38,469.66	36
Salem	$38,416.80	37
Federal Way	$38,161.32	38
Yakima	$32,248.12	44
Kennewick	$31,064.83	47
Gresham	$30,334.21	48
Lakewood	$26,967.13	52
Kirkland	$25,982.22	54
Corvallis	$25,782.28	55
Vancouver	$24,181.46	59

Figure 6-29 Grid view showing sales and rank, sorted by sales

As this example shows, Tacoma has the second-highest sales in Washington but is ranked sixth in sales overall. Because this view applies a rank calculation, it is not supported through the drag-and-drop interface of the Dashboard Designer. To create this view, an analyst uses the following MDX:

```
With Member [Measures].[Rank(Total)] as ' iif(IsEmpty([Measures].[Sale
Amt]), NULL,Rank([Store].[Geography].CurrentMember,
Order([Store].[Geography].CurrentMember.Level.Members,([Measures].[Sale
Amt]), BDESC))) '
SELECT { [Measures].[Sale Amt], [Measures].[Rank(Total)] } ON COLUMNS ,
NON EMPTY { ORDER( { DESCENDANTS( [Store].[Geography].[All],
[Store].[Geography].[City] ) }, ( [Measures].[Rank(Total)] ), BASC ) } ON
ROWS
FROM [REAL Warehouse]
WHERE ( [Store].[Region].&[3], [Time].[Calendar].[Calendar
Qtr].&[4]&[2004] )
CELL PROPERTIES VALUE, FORMATTED_VALUE, CELL_ORDINAL
```

Next, a user wants to display a view that includes a grand total of sales for selected items, so the business user can see not only the breakdown of sales across the items but also a sum of the sales of all those items, as shown in Figure 6-30.

Item By Category	2004
Art	$900,710.47
Beginning Readers	$201,967.69
Business	$2,625,210.78
Cookbooks	$1,306,337.52
Education	$1,076.50
Fiction	$722,304.33
Gardening	$176.75
Graphic Novels	$46,508.21
History	$557,163.44
Literature	$1,375,166.52
Military History	$593,978.81
Organizers And Dateb..	$2,254,779.88
Reference	$2,240,331.88
Romance Series	$517.71
Study Aids	$286,135.87
Transportation	$99.23
Westerns	$2,525.10
Grand Total	$13,114,990.69

Figure 6-30 Items with a grand total

With this type of view, the user is able to see the sales amount for each category and the grand total of all categories. The MDX to create this grid view is:

```
WITH MEMBER [Item].[By Category].[All].[ Grand Total] AS 'AGGREGATE(
EXISTING INTERSECT( { { EXTRACT( { DESCENDANTS( [Item].[By
Category].[Product].&[B], [Item].[By Category].[Subject] ) }, [Item].[By
Category] ) } }, { DESCENDANTS( [Item].[By Category].[Product].&[B],
[Item].[By Category].[Subject] ) } ) )', SOLVE_ORDER = 1000
SELECT {( [Time].[Calendar].[Calendar Year].&[2004)} ON COLUMNS ,
{ { DESCENDANTS( [Item].[By Category].[Product].&[B], [Item].[By
Category].[Subject] ) }, ( [Item].[By Category].[All].[ Grand Total] ) }
ON ROWS
FROM [REAL Warehouse]
WHERE ( [Measures].[Sale Amt] )
CELL PROPERTIES VALUE, FORMATTED_VALUE, CELL_ORDINAL
```

In our next example, a user wants to show which cities are generating the most sales, an important consideration for his board of directors as they decide where to expand their business. The view he creates is similar to Figure 6-31.

Store Geography	2004
Seattle	$531,587.31
Minneapolis	$458,715.30
Oshkosh	$420,405.39
Moorhead	$399,561.05
Tacoma	$394,832.74
Woodbury	$386,631.31
Arlington Heights	$360,480.91
Edina	$351,568.60
Eagan	$341,866.00
Bellevue	$277,976.66
Coon Rapids	$260,132.30
Rock Island	$258,905.10
Cicero	$249,049.64
Portland	$244,804.90
Rockford	$238,342.22
St. Louis Park	$237,273.01
Duluth	$233,333.28
Eden Prairie	$225,104.47

Figure 6-31 Top cities by sales amount

The MDX used to create this view is:

```
SELECT { [Time].[Calendar].[Calendar Year].&[2004] } ON COLUMNS ,
{ ORDER( { TOPCOUNT( { DESCENDANTS( [Store].[Geography].[All],
[Store].[Geography].[City] ) }, 20, ( [Time].[Calendar].[Calendar
Year].&[2004], [Measures].[Sale Amt] ) ) }, ( [Time].[Calendar].[Calendar
Year].&[2004] ), BDESC ) } ON ROWS
FROM [REAL Warehouse]
WHERE ( [Measures].[Sale Amt] )
CELL PROPERTIES VALUE, FORMATTED_VALUE, CELL_ORDINAL
```

In the next example, an analyst wants to show the top five items for each city, so business users can compare which products are succeeding in which areas. With this information, they can create specialized marketing campaigns to boost sales even further. The view created is similar to Figure 6-32.

Store Geography, Ite..	2004
Bellevue	
Bird by Bird: Some I..	$2,072.25
All the Best Pasta S..	$1,366.53
Family Tree Guide Bo..	$805.75
Celebrating the Fami..	$699.19
Sleuth Book for Gene..	$633.33
Bellingham	
Letters to a Young C..	$29.25
Getting Business to..	$20.22
Insight Compact Guid..	$17.99
Wolfgang Puck's Pizz..	$17.94
DK Eyewitness Travel..	$13.47
Edmonds	
All the Best Pasta S..	$752.64
Bird by Bird: Some I..	$625.79
Celebrating the Fami..	$326.28
Family Tree Guide Bo..	$230.66
18 Month, 2001-2002..	$224.04

Figure 6-32 Top five items by geography

The MDX used to create this view is:

```
SELECT { [Time].[Calendar].[Calendar Year].&[2004] } ON COLUMNS ,
{Generate( {existing [Store].[Geography].[District].&[56].children},
 exists ([Store].[Geography].CurrentMember ,,"Store Sales") *
{TopCount([Item].[By Category].[Item].Members, 5,
( [Time].[Calendar].[Calendar Year].&[2004], [Sale Amt]))})}
ON ROWS
FROM [REAL Warehouse]
WHERE ( [Measures].[Sale Amt] )
CELL PROPERTIES VALUE, FORMATTED_VALUE, CELL_ORDINAL
```

In the last example, a user wants to create a control or target line within an analytic chart. This will set the context for users by establishing what they should consider "good" and what they should consider "bad" with respect to their profit margins (see Figure 6-33).

Figure 6-33 Target line shown in a chart

As shown, the target percentage for Reseller Gross Profit Margin is 4 percent, which was achieved in 10 of the last 12 months. To create this view, you add a calculated measure to the query, using `WITH MEMBER`. The MDX for this view is:

```
WITH MEMBER [Measures].[Target] As 0.04, FORMAT_STRING="0.0%"
SELECT {DESCENDANTS([Date].[Fiscal].[FY 2003],
[Date].[Fiscal].[Month] ) }
ON COLUMNS,
{ [Measures].[Reseller Gross Profit Margin], [Measures].[Target] }
ON ROWS
FROM [Adventure Works]
```

Although Query mode is typically something that would be used by advanced users of Dashboard Designer, it does provide great flexibility and power in building your analytic views.

As discussed in this section, PerformancePoint provides the framework for analysts to develop insight into data that can be used to improve business performance at a tactical, operational, or strategic level. It allows analysts to deliver information to business users in a way that ensures both context and relevance, and it provides flexibility through its view types, advanced visualizations, and Query mode. In the next section, we discuss how this insight is transferred from the analyst to the business user, distributing the benefits of analytics throughout the organization.

Business Users: Gaining Insight

Pervasive analytics is achieved when decision makers are empowered to navigate the data themselves to understand driving factors and root causes. They don't have to wait for reports or recommendations from analysts or managers; they simply need to engage with the data to answer their own questions. For example, project managers within a company need to know what issues are affecting the success of their projects. Each project has different characteristics that may influence how well the project is progressing, including people, raw materials, milestones, dependencies, and approvals or permits. A project analyst can't produce reports to cover every possible combination of projects and characteristics for the project managers. However, the analyst can create an interactive dashboard that is delivered to the project managers through the Web.

When project managers have questions about the progress of their projects, they can conduct the analysis that is relevant to them. For one project manager, this may be comparing resource utilization rates for the past 3 months to determine why expenses are higher than expected. For another project manager, this may mean identifying the average time needed to complete inspections, based on similar projects completed in the same city last year. With this information, the project manager can adjust her milestones accordingly. The project analyst has empowered the project managers to gain their own insight into the performance of their individual projects, making them more accountable and capable of responding to problems and taking corrective action early.

This section shows how business users can use the dashboards provided to them by analysts to conduct their own analysis and gain insight into the data by filtering the data, drilling down, drilling down to, sorting, and exporting to Excel.

Use Filters

Dashboard filters provide a simple way to update all views within a dashboard to show only information for a specific item. For example, selecting North America will update all views to show only information for North America. Filters can also contain additional logic that can drive more compelling views, such as the top 10 products for a selected region or performance over the past year for a selected manager. By simply applying a filter to a view, a business user can make the view relevant and personal to him or her. In Chapter 7, filters are discussed in detail, including tips on creating tailored filters for a custom analytics experience.

Drill Down and Drill Up

Drilling down returns the next level of detail within the view. This is useful when summarized data may indicate a problem or opportunity that merits further investigation. In PerformancePoint dashboards, you can drill down on both analytic grid and analytic chart views by double-clicking an item or data point. The following scenario illustrates how drilling down can be used to gain new understanding of the data.

The published view indicates a sharp upward trend in product sales during the last four quarters (see Figure 6-34).

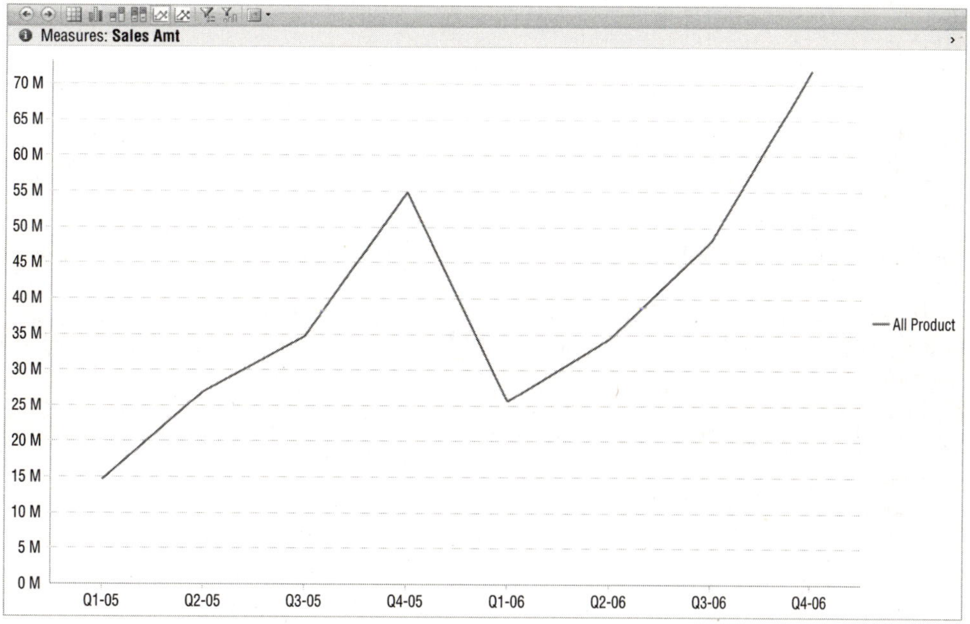

Figure 6-34 An aggregated view

By drilling down on All Product, you can see that both product categories (Bikes and Accessories) saw similar increases in these quarters (see Figure 6-35).

Drilling down on Accessories shows that Helmets greatly contributed to the spike in accessory sales (see Figure 6-36).

Drilling down on Helmets shows that it was primarily the blue and yellow Sport-100 Helmets that contributed to the increased sales (see Figure 6-37).

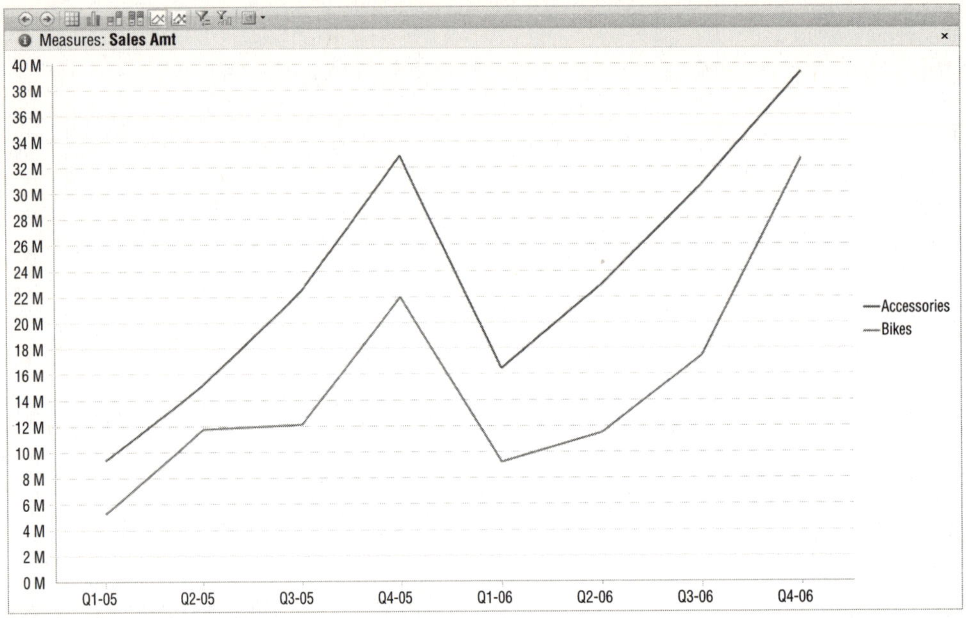

Figure 6-35 A view following a drill-down operation

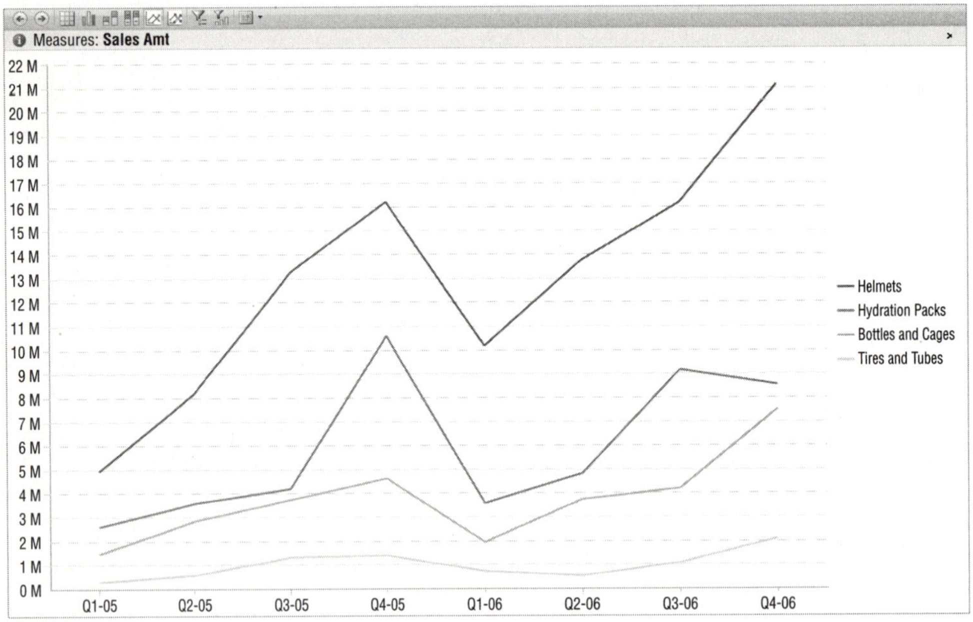

Figure 6-36 A view following a second drill-down operation

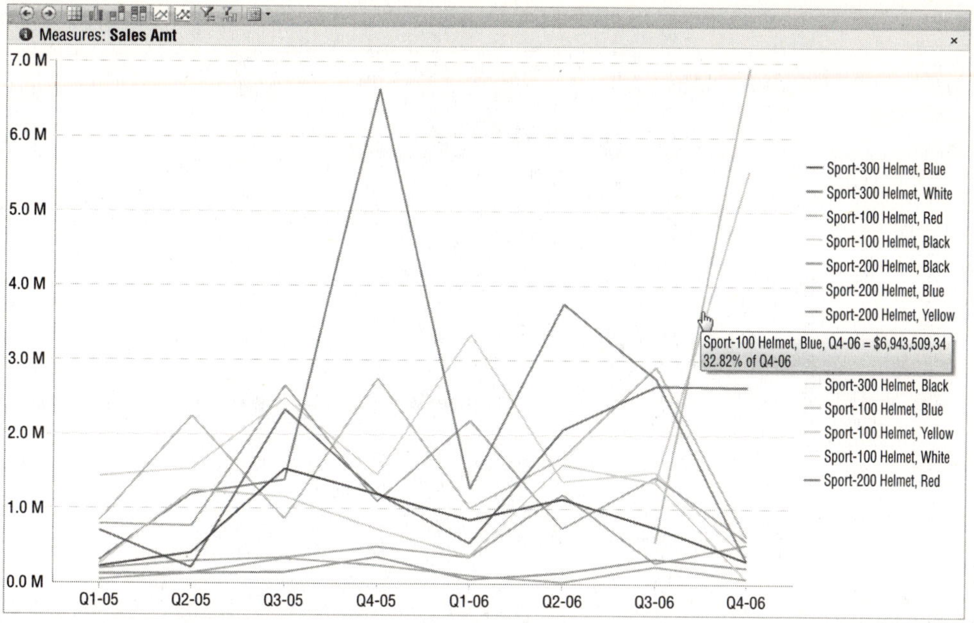

Figure 6-37 A view following the last drill-down operation

This view also indicates that while two types of helmets increased in sales, the remaining helmets were either flat or decreased in sales. Drilling up on a view allows users to retrace their steps to follow another path of investigation. In this example, a user may drill up to the category level to do a similar investigation on Bikes.

Drill Down To (Cross-Drilling)

While drilling down allows you to explore relationships within a single dimension, Drill Down To (or cross-drilling) allows you to uncover relationships among all dimensions within your data. Available from the right-click menu on an analytic chart or grid, Drill Down To places a new hierarchy on the foreground and filters the entire view with the originally selected member. The following scenario illustrates how Drill Down To can be used to gain new understanding of the data.

Figure 6-38 shows sales of all products.

To see the breakdown of these sales across the geographic regions, you can perform a Drill Down To action by selecting the Region level within the Geography hierarchy, as shown in Figure 6-39.

The result in Figure 6-40 shows that the greatest product sales are in the North America region.

Figure 6-38 A view showing aggregated data

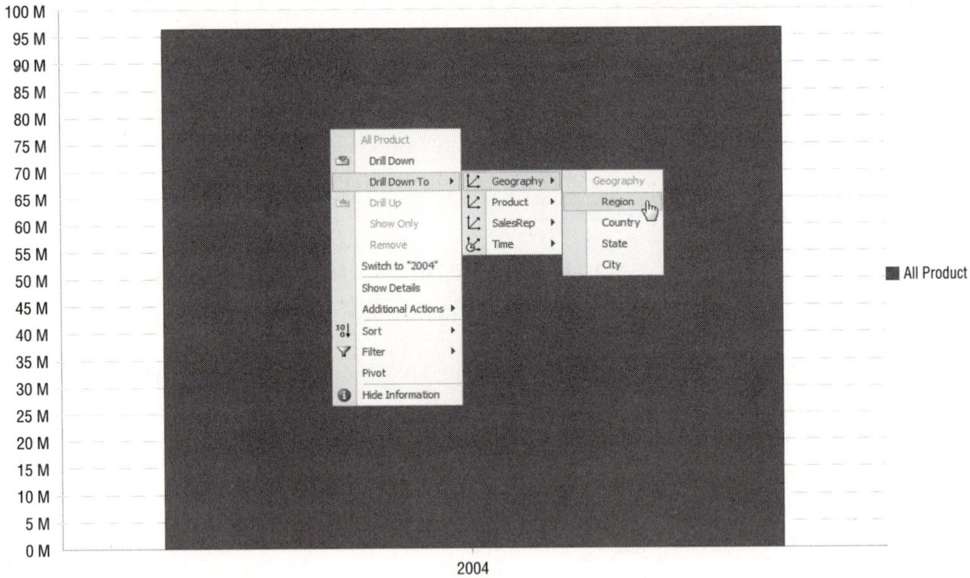

Figure 6-39 The menu options for a Drill Down To operation

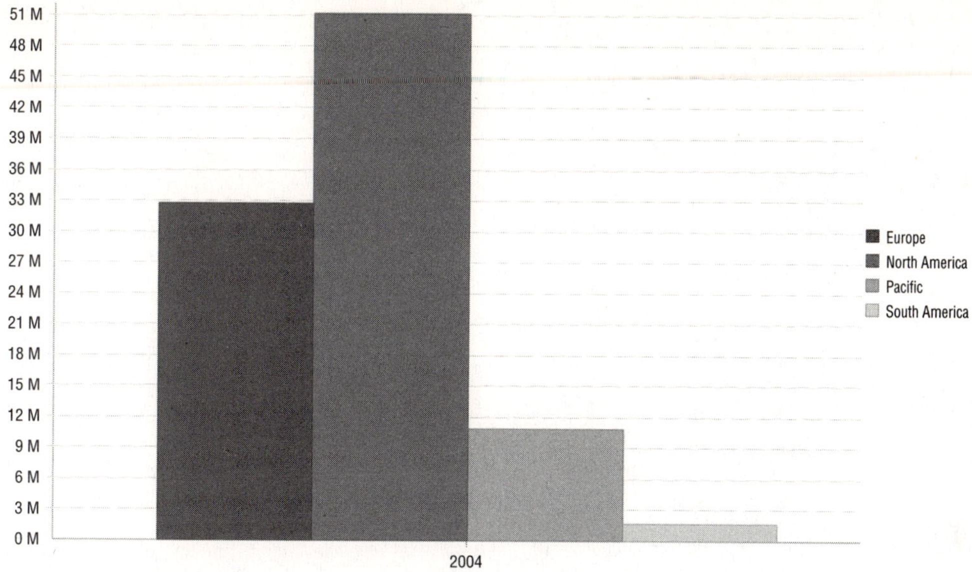

Figure 6-40 The results of a Drill Down To operation

You can sort the view from highest to lowest, and then use Drill Down To again to discover that Adriana Giorgi is the most successful North America sales representative, with the highest product sales (see Figure 6-41).

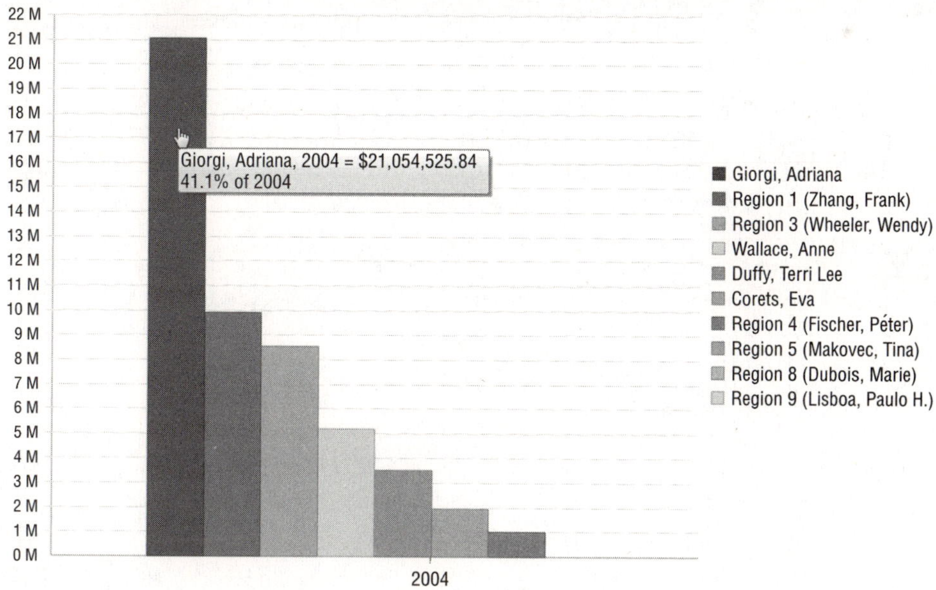

Figure 6-41 A sorted view following a Drill Down To operation

And finally, you can drill down to products to see Adriana's highest selling products (see Figure 6-42).

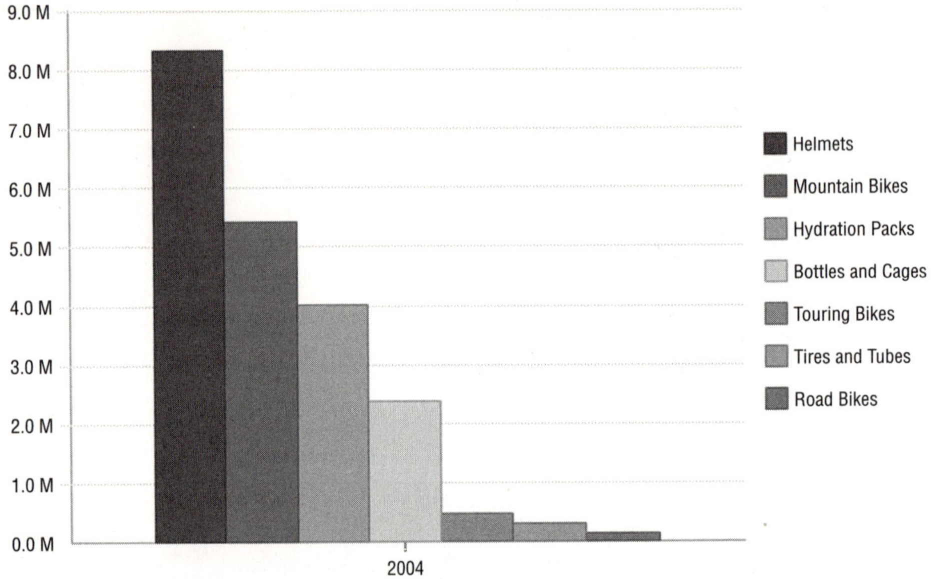

Figure 6-42 The final view of a Drill Down To operation

In this example, Adriana has had her greatest sales success with Helmets and Mountain Bikes. As shown in this example, Drill Down To allows users to ask how one dimension of their business affects another: How does geography influence sales? How do products break down over geography? How do products breakdown for a particular sales representative? This exploratory process allows users to gain a much deeper understanding of the driving forces behind the data — and more importantly, the business — than they would by simply knowing the discrete sales figures for a product family.

NOTE **To return to the original view after navigating through the data, select Reset View from the View drop-down menu, as shown in Figure 6-43.**

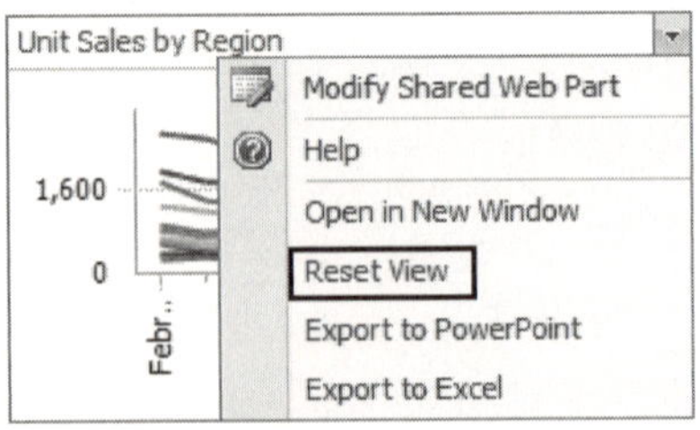

Figure 6-43 Reset the view to the original view.

Show Details

Show Details allows you to display the individual transactions behind a summarized value. This can provide an additional level of detail that can be used to further analyze unexpected results or validate assumptions. For example, a call center has logged seven customer complaints in the past month. This is unusually high compared to past months. Using Show Details, a manager can display the individual calls logged and study the specific information about each call to determine if there are common issues among them that should be addressed. The manager may find that one customer service representative received the majority of the complaints or that several complaints were filed by the same customer. In either situation, the manager now has actionable information to improve customer satisfaction going forward: Coach the service representative or contact the customer to identify their specific concerns.

Show Details is available from analytic grids and charts and from scorecard values that are created using Analysis Services 2005 cubes. (In addition, the Analysis Services property for drill through must be enabled on the cube.) To see the details contributing to a value, right-click a data point in a visualization and select Show Details (see Figure 6-44).

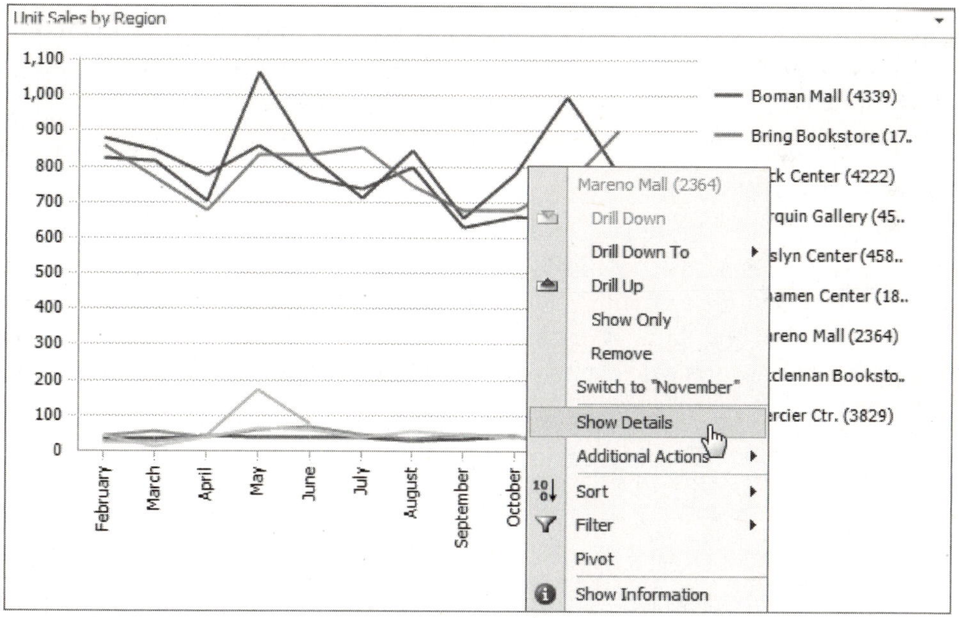

Figure 6-44 Show Details menu option from an analytic chart

The transactions are shown in a new window, with the ability to page through the results by clicking the arrows in the upper-right corner (see

Figure 6-45). The transactions can also be exported to Excel for further reporting or formatting.

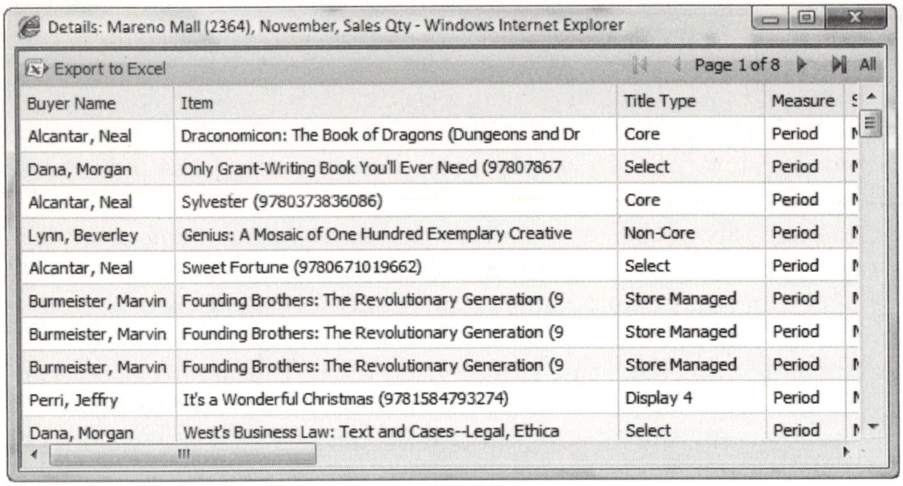

Figure 6-45 Detailed transactions displayed in a new window

NOTE **To use Show Details on a scorecard value, the Calculation column for the KPI must be set to Source Data and "Allow show details" must be checked under View Options.**

Sort

As discussed earlier, sorting allows you to more easily compare performance across multiple items. Sorting shortens the time needed to make a quick assessment about the data: What are the most profitable products? Who had the greatest increase in sales last year? Which region saw the greatest decline in revenue?

To sort within a dashboard view, right-click a row, column, or series and select Sort, as shown in Figure 6-46.

Export to Excel

Export to Excel enables users to bring their performance data into Excel to add calculations, apply formatting, and use other Excel features. To export a view to Excel, click the menu button on the view and select Export to Excel, as shown in Figure 6-47.

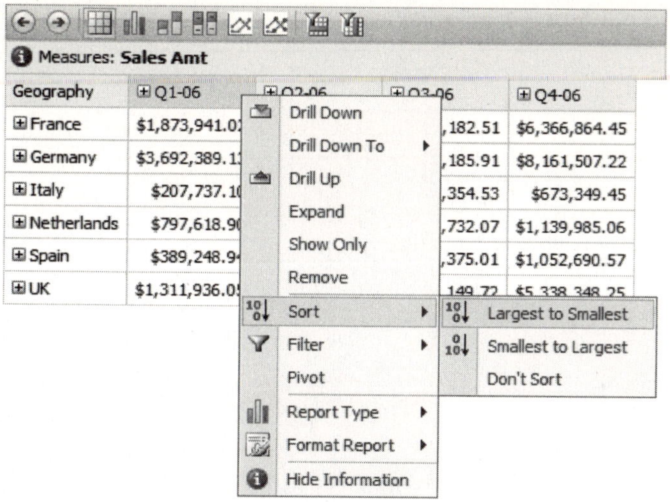

Figure 6-46 Sorting an analytic grid view

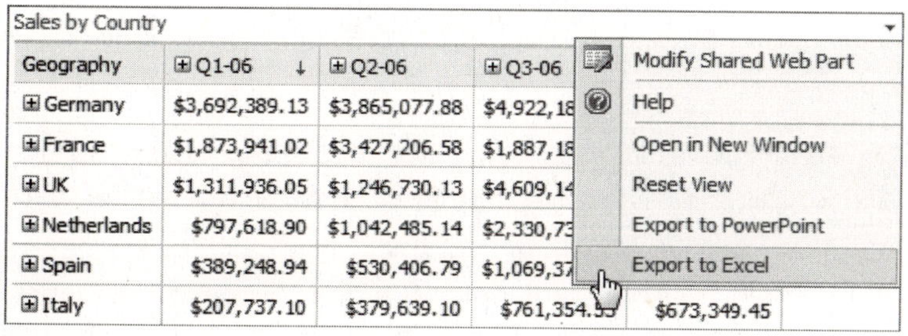

Figure 6-47 Export to Excel from an analytic grid.

Summary

As business users work with the views within the dashboard, they will gain their own insights into the data. They will become more comfortable with using the analytic tools within PerformancePoint dashboards to drive decisions based on data, not on assumptions or guesses. In turn, these good decisions will help align all business users with the overall corporate strategy and drive improved performance, from the individual worker to the CEO.

CHAPTER 7

Creating Effective Dashboards

Dashboards bring together scorecards and reports in a cohesive, interactive display of performance information. Because they present consistent views of overall performance, dashboards can foster alignment and accountability among the team and organization. All users have the same information, presented in the same way, and based on the same data. Dashboards also allow users to interact with the data, providing them with flexibility to investigate, understand, and act according to their own scope, role, and goals. And because they are deployed through Web browsers, dashboards allow users to be in an environment they know and understand.

This chapter describes how to design and deploy effective dashboards using PerformancePoint Server and Dashboard Designer. It begins by highlighting considerations for creating effective dashboards, such as audience, interactivity, and feedback. It then reviews the process of creating dashboards in Dashboard Designer, including adding content, sizing reports, creating and adding filters, setting conditional visibility, previewing them, and deploying them to SharePoint Server. Throughout the chapter, recommendations are made on how to create effective and useful performance dashboards.

Successful Dashboards

In his book *Information Dashboard Design: The Effective Visual Communication of Data* (O'Reilly Media, Inc., 2006), Stephen Few, a recognized expert in dashboard design, defines dashboards as "a visual display of the most important information needed to achieve one or more objectives; consolidated and arranged on a single screen so the information can be monitored at a glance."

This definition provides several useful guidelines on how to design effective dashboards. First, Few suggests dashboards should be limited to a single visual field. Although this may not be possible in all circumstances, limiting a dashboard to a single screen has some clear benefits: minimal or no interaction is required for users to quickly identify performance status and any actionable events. Users don't have to scroll down or hunt through numerous links to find the information that is important to them.

Limiting the content to a single screen also requires the dashboard's author to be disciplined in identifying the most important and relevant content for users. Rather than putting every possible KPI or report in the dashboard, the author must carefully craft and design a screen where every pixel conveys meaning to the user. This discipline will help ensure that the dashboard is ultimately successful because all content will be focused and relevant, with minimal distractions to users.

Few also suggests that the information be visual. As discussed in earlier chapters, PerformancePoint Server enables you to create visual displays in scorecards and charts that convey much more meaning than simple tables of numbers or paragraphs of text. Because dashboards are meant to be consumed "at a glance," they should present information in the format that is most appropriate for gaining quick insight and understanding. Dashboards' authors should take care to understand which visualizations are most effective in communicating different types of information, such as presenting time-based views as line charts and status as indicators.

Earlier chapters highlighted the principle of relevance and ensuring that reports have focus and meaning to both the organization and users. This concept applies equally to dashboards. Relevant dashboards are those in which all information is timely, of value, and essential for the user to understand, base decisions on, and act on. They provide a personalized view for individual users and deliver information based on the organizational perspective, not the data perspective.

For example, data for an organization's key performance indicators may come from multiple sources. Past sales data may be organized and consolidated into an Analysis Services cube. Current sales goals may be stored in an Excel spreadsheet that is updated quarterly. And detailed sales transactions may be available from a relational system. Although this accurately describes the data, it's likely not that meaningful to a sales manager. What is meaningful to the sales manager is to see her current sales performance and goals in a scorecard, with indicators showing red, green, or yellow; her past sales performance in an interactive analytic chart that she can drill down into to see the performance of individual product lines over time; and a detailed, highly formatted report view that allows her to filter individual transactions to better identify the specific details contributing to significant sales in her organization. Her dashboard should be updated based on the current sales quarter automatically, so she doesn't have to worry about tracking down the right report for the right quarter. And her dashboard should be filtered to show her sales regions and her direct reports, which is much more relevant to her than a general dashboard showing all sales numbers for all regions.

Successful dashboards are also dashboards that remain fresh and focused. Organizations change, market conditions change, technology changes, and users change. What may have been extremely useful for making good business decisions last year may no longer be the best way to track business performance today. Having a simple and effective feedback and change management process in place for dashboards is one way to ensure continued success. As users gain more confidence with the data and begin analyzing it in earnest, the dashboard should evolve. New reports with better visualizations and interactivity should replace dated reports that have less visual information and no interactivity. Reports that offer little value to users should be removed from the dashboard, eliminating unnecessary noise and distraction. KPIs should continually be revisited to ensure that they offer the most precise and updated view of where the organization wants to be. In short, creating a performance management dashboard that offers a real competitive advantage to an organization is a process, not a task.

Creating and Deploying Dashboards

Creating dashboards in Dashboard Designer is a straightforward process. First, you choose a basic layout for your dashboard using a wizard. Second, you place reports on the dashboard by dragging and dropping them into the design workspace. Third, you create filters for your dashboard content and connect the filters to the reports. And fourth, you publish and deploy your dashboard to SharePoint Server. Although creating a basic dashboard is a simple task, Dashboard Designer provides many features and tools to help you create more customized and tailored dashboards, providing, for example, the ability to create dynamic filters. These features and tools are discussed in detail in the following sections.

Creating a New Dashboard

In Dashboard Designer, you create a new dashboard by right-clicking Dashboards in the workspace browser and selecting New Dashboard. You can also click the Dashboard icon on the Edit tab of the ribbon (see Figure 7-1).

You are then presented with seven default dashboard templates. These templates provide you with a shortcut layout. They do not prevent you from adding columns or rows once you have started designing your dashboard.

Also note that these templates can be extended through the PerformancePoint Server Software Development Kit. If you have a particular dashboard layout that you commonly use in your organization, you can add it to this wizard screen.

Figure 7-1 Creating a new dashboard in Dashboard Designer

After you have selected and named your dashboard layout, you are presented with the dashboard workspace, a canvas for creating your dashboard content. The workspace has three tabs: Editor, Properties, and Filters. The Editor tab is the area where you will add, size, and configure your dashboard layout. The Properties tab allows you to change the name, display folder, description, and person responsible for the dashboard. The Properties tab also lets you set permissions on the dashboard. These permissions are described in detail in Chapter 9.

NOTE The Properties tab also lets you set custom properties for the dashboard; however, these properties are not used in the dashboard nor do they appear to users. Custom properties are primarily useful when set on KPIs.

The Filters tab is used to create filters, which are described in detail in a later section. For the remainder of this section, we will focus on the Editor tab of the dashboard workspace.

Managing Pages

The Editor tab is split into two sections: Pages and Dashboard Content. The Pages section allows you to manage the pages in your dashboard. These pages are shown in a published dashboard as a breadcrumb trail at the top of your dashboard, as shown in Figure 7-2.

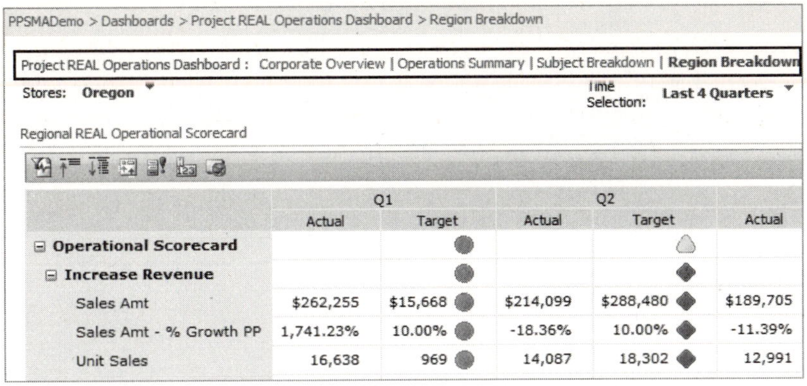

Figure 7-2 Pages in a published dashboard

These pages are represented in Dashboard Designer as shown in Figure 7-3.

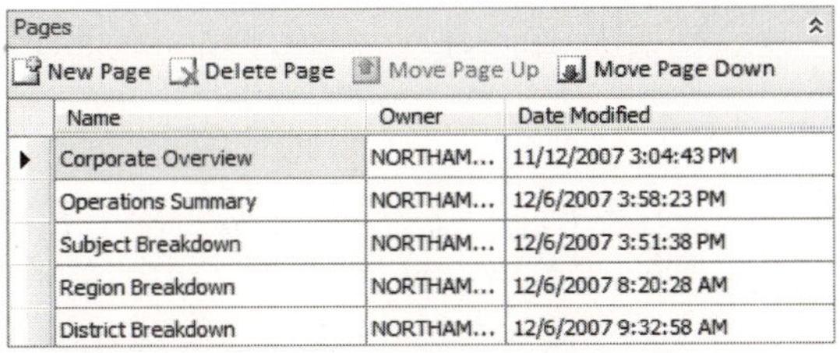

Figure 7-3 Pages in Dashboard Designer

NOTE By default, pages are shown in a hyperlinked breadcrumb trail at the top of the published dashboard page. You can also display these links as tabs in your SharePoint site. For instructions on how to do this, see Greg Bernhardt's blog posting "How do I make a dashboard show up in the tabs in SharePoint" on the Microsoft PerformancePoint Team Blog (`http://blogs.msdn.com/performancepoint`).

In the Pages section, you can add, delete, and organize the pages in your dashboard. When deployed to SharePoint, each page is saved as a separate ASPX file in the SharePoint document library, within a folder named for the dashboard (see Figure 7-4).

Each individual page is accessible by users through the document library. However, to construct a more guided and tailored experience with the dashboard, you may prefer to create a single link from a portal page, Web site, or email to the first page of the dashboard. This will enable users to simply open and see the dashboard as you've designed it (see Figure 7-5).

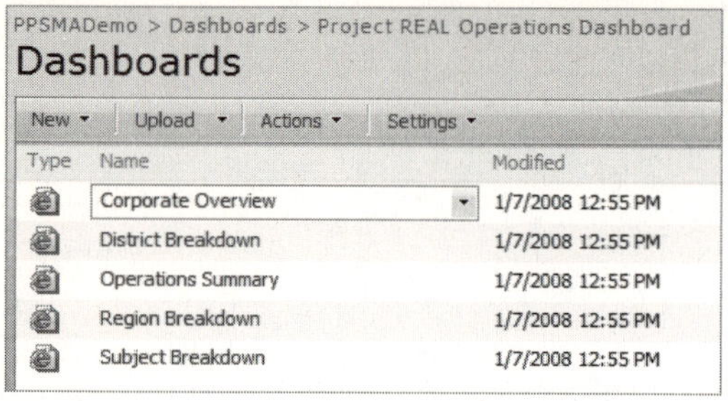

Figure 7-4 Dashboard pages saved within a SharePoint document library

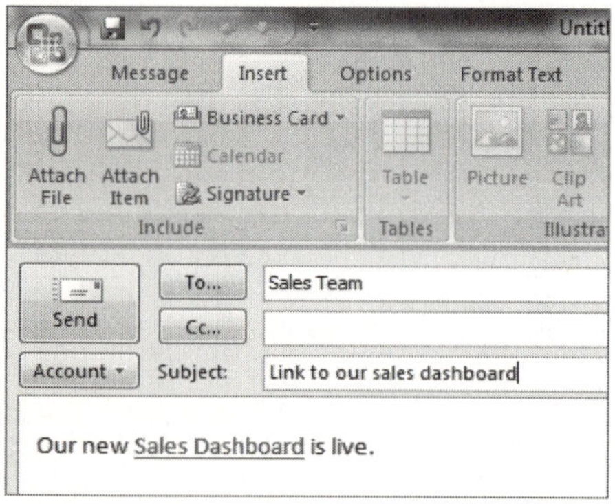

Figure 7-5 An email link to a dashboard page

Configuring Zone Layout and Size

When first opened, the Dashboard Content area contains wireframe zones based on the layout chosen when you created the dashboard. Each zone is sized based on a percentage of the overall dashboard page size. For example, Figure 7-6 shows a layout containing three zones: Header, Left Column, and Right Column.

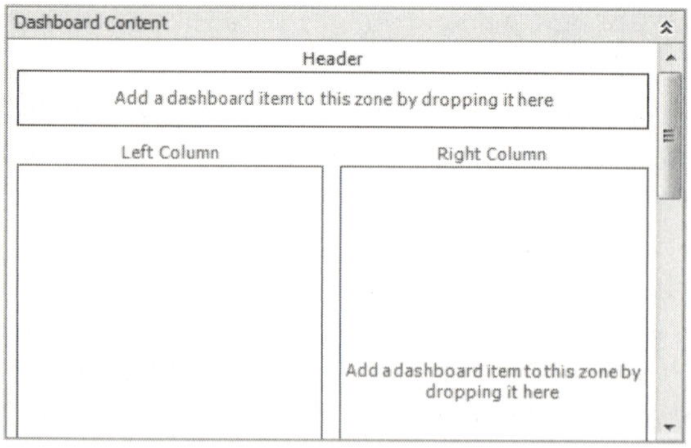

Figure 7-6 A three-zone layout in Dashboard Designer

The Header zone is 100 percent of the dashboard page width, since it extends across the entire page, and 9 percent of the dashboard page height, since it takes up only a small portion of the vertical space. The Left Column and Right Column zones are each 50 percent of the dashboard page width, since they share equally the horizontal space. They are 91 percent of the dashboard page height, the portion not used by the Header zone. These sizes can be changed by right-clicking a zone and selecting Zone Settings. In the Zone Settings dialog box, select the Size tab (see Figure 7-7).

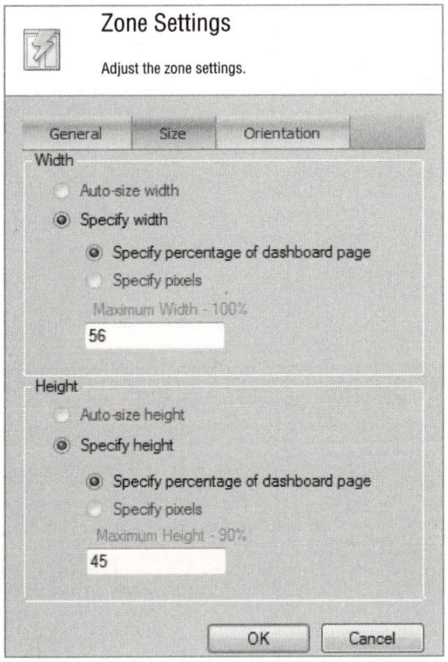

Figure 7-7 The size tab of the Zone Settings dialog box

You can also add or remove existing zones by right-clicking the zone and selecting from one of the available options. For example, if you want to add a third column to the dashboard layout, right-click the Right Column zone and select Add Left (see Figure 7-8).

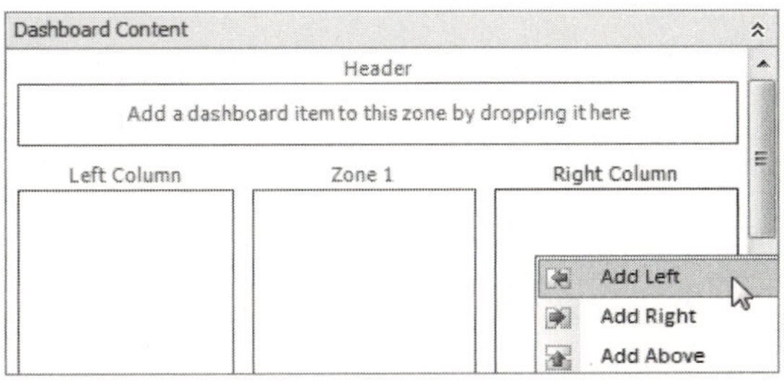

Figure 7-8 Zone 1 is added to the dashboard layout.

Split a zone by right-clicking the zone and selecting Split Zone. Note that the orientation of the zone will determine whether the zone is split horizontally or vertically. (To set the zone orientation, right-click the zone and select Zone Settings. Then, select the Orientation tab.) For example, to split the rightmost column into two stacked boxes, the Zone Orientation should be set to Vertical prior to selecting Split Zone (see Figure 7-9).

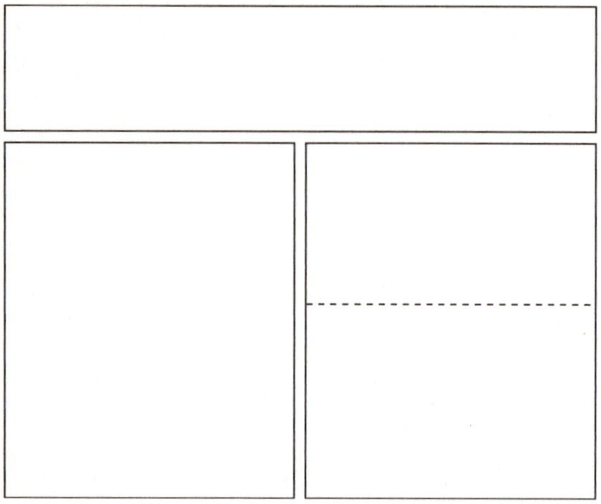

Figure 7-9 Splitting a vertical zone

The size is adjusted automatically based on the new configuration. In this example, the rightmost boxes now share 91 percent of the vertical space, so each box is allocated approximately 45 percent of the total vertical space.

To split the rightmost column into two columns, the Zone Orientation should be set to Horizontal prior to selecting Split Zone (see Figure 7-10).

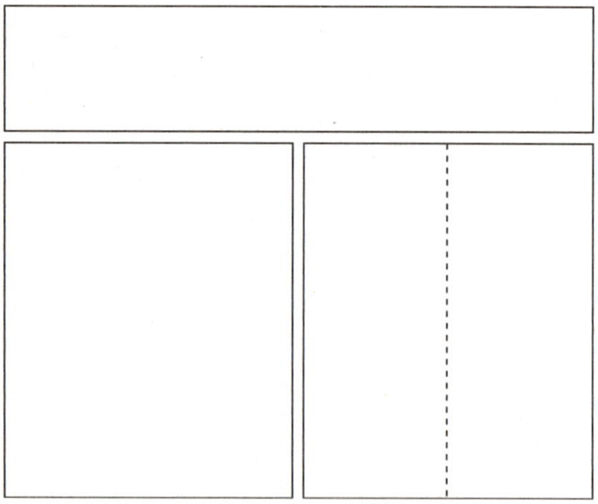

Figure 7-10 Splitting a horizontal zone

The size is adjusted automatically, so now each column is allocated approximately 33 percent of the horizontal space. You can change these sizes using the Zone Settings dialog box from the right-click menu.

NOTE Stacked orientation is commonly used with display conditions, described later in this chapter. This orientation enables users to display a single report when a scorecard KPI or filter item is clicked, rather than showing reports together, all the time.

After you have created the zone layout for your dashboard, you can drag items from the Available Items tree to the right of the workspace browser and drop them onto a zone. As you place items into zones, you have several layout and size options for these items as well. To configure item sizes, right-click the drop-down menu in the upper-right corner of the item and select Edit Item (see Figure 7-11).

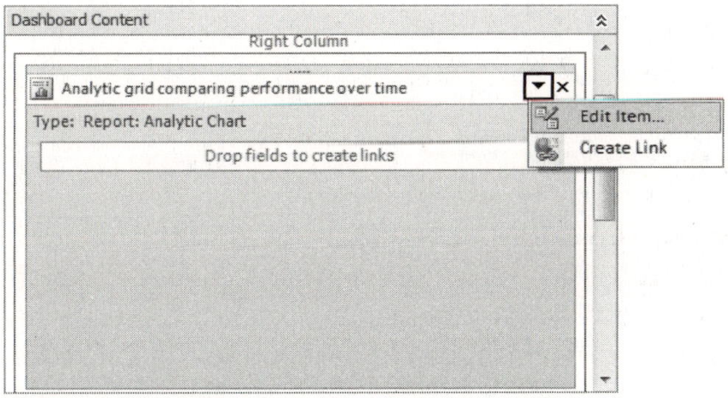

Figure 7-11 Editing the sizes of dashboard items

Each item's height and width can be configured three ways: auto-sized, as a percentage of the dashboard page, and by pixel. Auto-sizing will use a pixel-based default size for each item. The default pixel size varies based on the report type. For example, the default size for an analytic chart is 450 (height) x 800 (width). Auto-sized reports are not resized when the browser window is resized, making this setting less preferable than other options.

The percentage of dashboard page option sizes reports based on the percent of page occupied by its zone. For example, if a zone occupies 50 percent of the dashboard page, any item that occupies that zone will take up a maximum of 50 percent of the dashboard page as well. If more than one item is added to a zone, all items share the parent's percent of the page. That is, two items in a zone that occupies 50 percent of the dashboard page will each occupy 25 percent of the dashboard (half of the zone's space). This option is useful when the dashboard author wants reports to resize content based on the size of the browser window.

NOTE **Reports have different resizing behavior. Depending on the report type, scroll bars may be shown instead of the report resizing to fit the available space.**

The final option, Specify Pixels, allows the dashboard author a high degree of control over how items appear in the dashboard. Specifying pixels is also useful when you have a stacked zone and conditionally displayed reports. This allows you to ensure that each report, when visible, occupies the entire available space within a zone. Also note that specifying pixels for an item may override its parent zone's size.

TIP **See Rex Parker's blog post titled "PerformancePoint Dashboard Sizing Explained" (`http://blogs.msdn.com/performancepoint`) for a more detailed explanation of how to size dashboard items.**

Now that you have a general understanding of how to lay out and size dashboard items, we will next explore the other capabilities of dashboards, including filters, conditional display, and deployment to SharePoint Server.

Creating Interactive Dashboards Using Filters

Filters are a primary means of providing interactivity to dashboard users. They allow the user to make simple selections to gain further, personal insight into the data. For example, a regional sales manager may select her region to see how it's performing, narrowing the dashboard views to the content that is most relevant to her. Filters can be applied to most report types, and a filter can be applied to a single report or multiple reports within a dashboard page.

NOTE **Filters cannot be applied to PivotTable and PivotChart report types. These report types are supported only for backward capability with Business Scorecard Manager and should not be used as a primary report type in PerformancePoint dashboards.**

At the most basic level, filters pass a selected value to a query that contains a placeholder. The query placeholder is replaced with the selected value, the query is run, and the results are returned and displayed in the dashboard. When the selected item is being passed to a report with an OLAP data source, the passed value must be properly formatted as an MDX member with a unique name. When the selected item is being passed to a report with a non-OLAP data source, the value must be properly formatted for the receiving query and data source. In most cases, this will be the display value of the selected member, but this may also be a custom value determined by an expression or a custom property. This process is managed for you by Monitoring Server, as long as you configure your filters properly.

When you create a filter, you define the list of items to be presented to users as a drop-down box or tree control in the dashboard. Filter lists can be defined several ways, including as an MDX query or a named set. To create a filter, select the Filter tab from the dashboard workspace and click New Filter (see Figure 7-12).

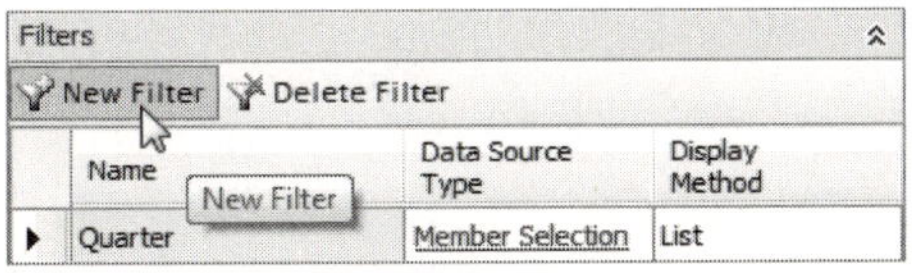

Figure 7-12 Create a new filter for a dashboard.

You are presented with six filter templates, described briefly as follows:

- **MDX Query.** Provides a custom MDX query that defines the memberset. This filter type is used with OLAP data sources and can contain MDX logic, such as descendants or children.
- **Member Selection.** Allows the dashboard author to explicitly select the members to show in the filter. This filter type is used with OLAP data sources and does not allow dynamic member selections, such as descendants or children.
- **Named Sets.** Defines the filter list using an Analysis Services named set. This filter type is used with OLAP data sources and is dynamic, updating as the named set itself is updated in the cube.
- **Tabular Values.** Allows the dashboard author to explicitly select members from relational data sources, such as Excel or SQL Server.
- **Time Intelligence.** Defines a time-dynamic filter set based on the current date and a time intelligence expression. These filters can be used for both OLAP and relational data sources.
- **Time Intelligence Post Formula.** Defines a time-dynamic filter set based on selections from a calendar control. These filters can be used for both OLAP and relational data sources.

After you select the filter type, you are presented with the steps for creating that type of filter. For example, if you choose MDX Query, you are given a text box for providing a valid MDX member expression (see Figure 7-13).

If you choose Member Selection, you are given options for selecting the hierarchy and members, as shown in Figure 7-14.

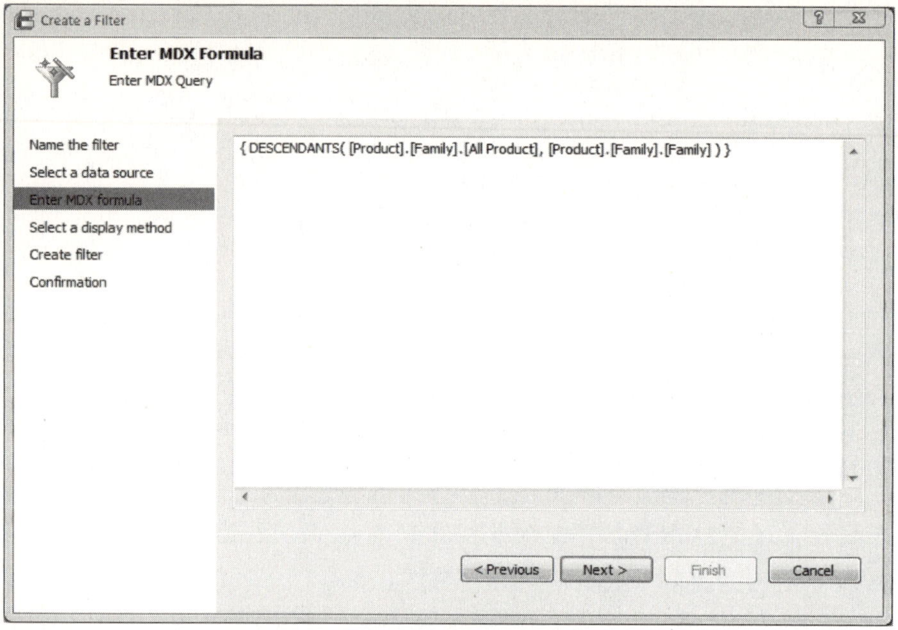

Figure 7-13 Using an MDX Query to define a filter list

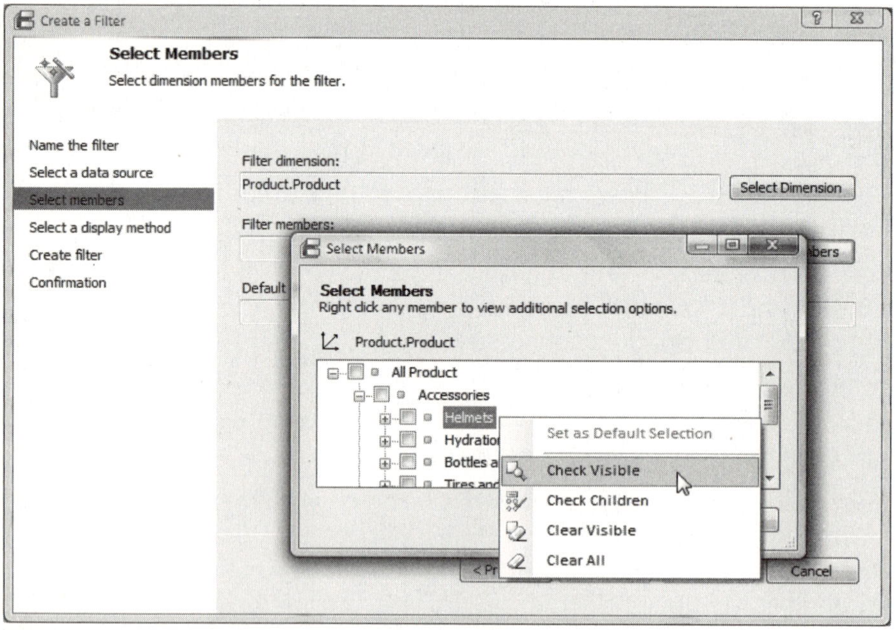

Figure 7-14 Using Member Selection to define a filter list

As you create filters, note that the name of the filter is displayed next to the filter in the dashboard (see Figure 7-15).

Figure 7-15 The filter name shown next to the filter list in a dashboard

For all filter types, you have the option of selecting from three display types: list, tree, and multi-select tree (see Figure 7-16).

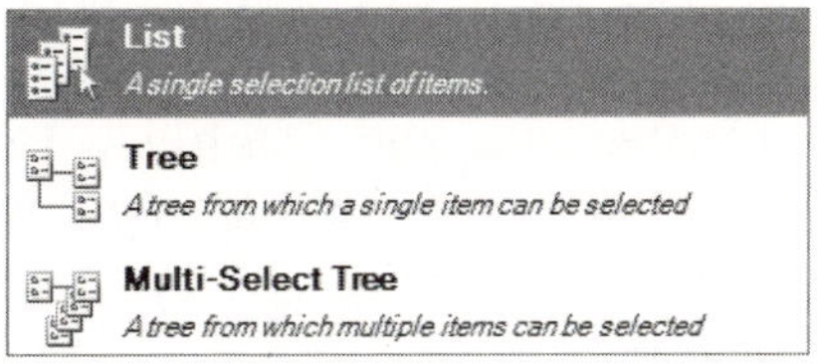

Figure 7-16 Filter display types

Filters are limited to 500 members, and the 500 members are counted from the first parent down through all its descendants, and then to the next parent and all it descendants. This means that you may have a filter that contains the first two top-level items in a hierarchy and all their descendants, rather than all members at each level until you reach 500 members.

In some cases, the 500-member limit may be too prohibitive for the dashboard design you want to create. You can change the limit by adding a `Bpm.TreeViewControlMaxNumRecordsToRender` property and value to three `web.config` files, located on the computer where the PerformancePoint Monitoring Server is installed. By default, these files are installed in the following directories:

```
C:\Inetpub\wwwroot\wss\VirtualDirectories\80\web.config

C:\Program Files\Microsoft Office PerformancePoint Server\3.0\
  Monitoring\PPSMonitoring_1\Preview

C:\Program Files\Microsoft Office PerformancePoint Server\3.0\
  Monitoring\PPSMonitoring_1\WebService
```

Simply add the key and value to the `appSettings` element in each file, as shown in Figure 7-17. In this example, we've changed the server setting to support 600 members, rather than the default 500 members.

NOTE **Changing the maximum number of filter members may have significant performance implications. To ensure optimal performance, you should create your filter list to be within the default 500 members, if possible.**

```
<appSettings>
  <add key="FeedCacheTime" value="300" />
  <add key="FeedPageUrl" value="/_layouts/feed.aspx?" />
  <add key="FeedXsl1" value="/Style Library/Xsl Style Sheets/Rss.xsl" />
  <add key="ReportViewerMessages" value="Microsoft.SharePoint.Portal.Analytics.UI
  <add key="Bpm.TreeViewControlMaxNumRecordsToRender" value="600" />
  <add key="Bpm.MonitoringConnectionString" value="Data Source=localhost;Initial
```

Figure 7-17 Changing web.config files to support 600 filter members

Creating MDX Query Filters

MDX Query filters allow you to provide a valid MDX set expression for the filter list. This is most useful when you want your filters to be dynamic — continually updating content based on the current members in the cube. For example, your organization frequently adds new products to its product line. Each time this happens, your cube is updated to include the new products in its Product hierarchy. As a dashboard author, you want these products to be included in the filter list, but you don't want to manually redefine the filter and publish the dashboard each time this occurs. You can achieve this by creating a named set in your cube or by providing dynamic MDX. The following MDX creates a dynamic filter list that includes descendants of the Family level in the Product hierarchy:

```
{ DESCENDANTS( [Product].[Product].[All Product], [Product].
  [Product].[Family] ) }
```

When used as the MDX Query filter definition, it generates the list shown in Figure 7-18 in the dashboard.

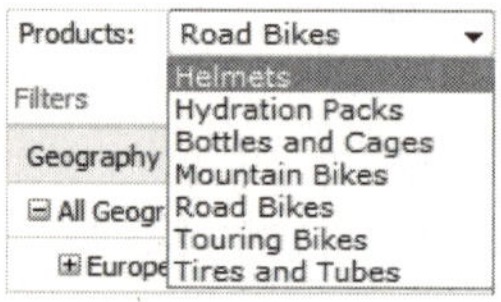

Figure 7-18 Filter list generated from a dynamic MDX expression

You can make a simple modification to the MDX expression, as follows:

```
{ DESCENDANTS( [Product].[Product].[All Product], [Product].
  [Product].[(All)], AFTER ) }
```

This expression will generate the tree view shown in Figure 7-19.

In the first example, we selected the List display method when defining the filter; in the second, we selected Tree. Any valid MDX memberset expression is supported by the MDX Query filter type.

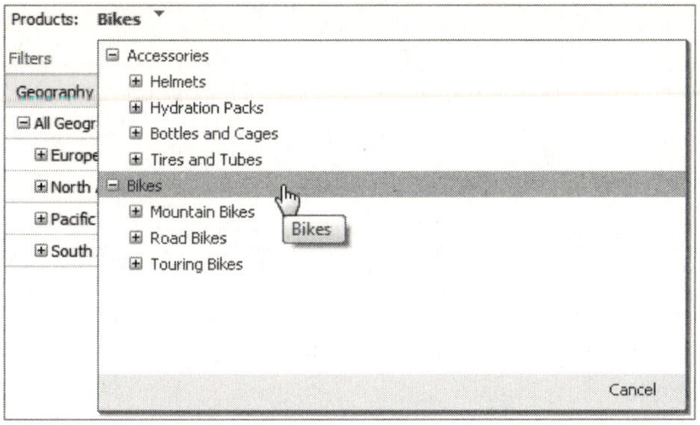

Figure 7-19 Filter tree generated from a dynamic MDX expression

Using Filter Link Formulas

Filter link formulas allow you to apply MDX logic after a filter item has been selected by the user but before it is sent to the server with the query. For example, in Figure 7-20 a user selects a Product Line from the drop-down filter in a dashboard.

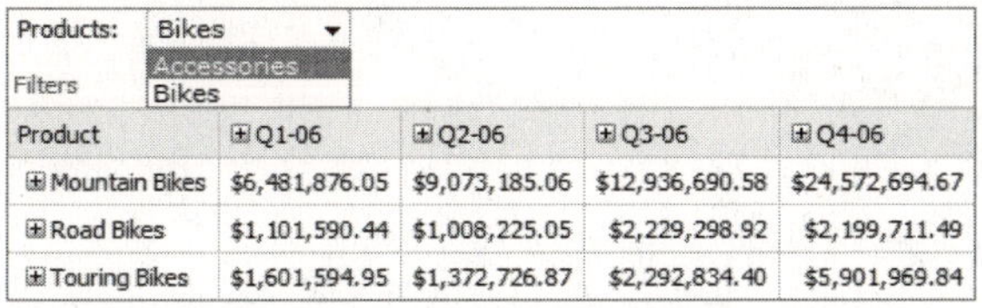

Product	Q1-06	Q2-06	Q3-06	Q4-06
Mountain Bikes	$6,481,876.05	$9,073,185.06	$12,936,690.58	$24,572,694.67
Road Bikes	$1,101,590.44	$1,008,225.05	$2,229,298.92	$2,199,711.49
Touring Bikes	$1,601,594.95	$1,372,726.87	$2,292,834.40	$5,901,969.84

Figure 7-20 Selecting a product line in a dashboard

A filter link formula has been applied to this filter to return the children of the selected item. In this case, the product families for the product line are shown in the analytic chart, not the selected item (see Figure 7-21).

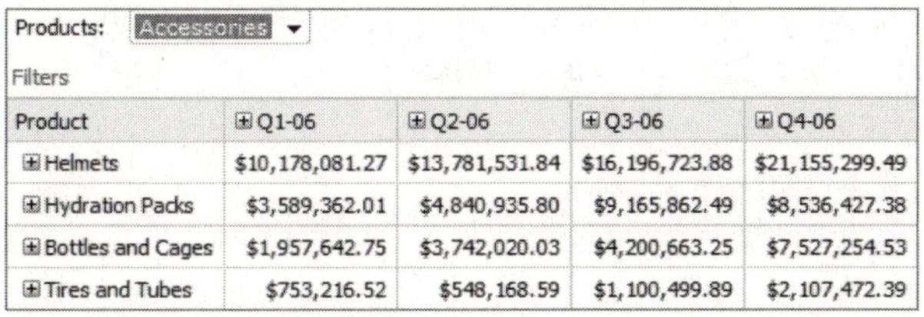

Product	Q1-06	Q2-06	Q3-06	Q4-06
Helmets	$10,178,081.27	$13,781,531.84	$16,196,723.88	$21,155,299.49
Hydration Packs	$3,589,362.01	$4,840,935.80	$9,165,862.49	$8,536,427.38
Bottles and Cages	$1,957,642.75	$3,742,020.03	$4,200,663.25	$7,527,254.53
Tires and Tubes	$753,216.52	$548,168.59	$1,100,499.89	$2,107,472.39

Figure 7-21 The children of the selected item shown in the analytic grid

Filter link formulas are written using `<<UniqueName>>` as the placeholder for the selected filter item within the query. The filter link formula shown in Figure 7-22 is the simple syntax for the example presented in this section.

Figure 7-22 The filter link formula for returning the children of the selected item

The Formula Editor shown in Figure 7-23 is available when you link a filter to a report type, which is discussed later in this chapter.

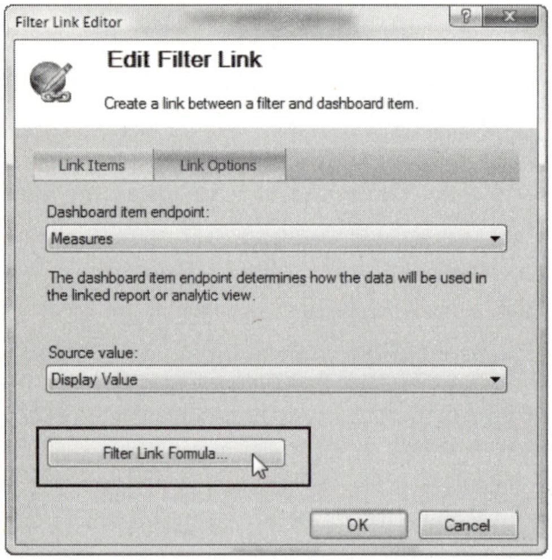

Figure 7-23 The Formula Editor dialog box with the Filter Link option

Filter link formulas can be used with much more complex MDX, providing greater flexibility in the interactivity you provide in your dashboard. For example, filter link formulas can be used to display the top 10 products based on sales for the selected product in an analytic chart or to display aggregated values in a scorecard for the past 6 months, based on the current day.

NOTE **Filter link formulas work only with the filter List or Tree display method. They do not work with the Multi-Select Tree display method.**

Creating Time Intelligence Filters

How many units did you sell in Q1 compared to Q2? What do your sales for the last 6 months look like? As of today, what do sales look like for the past 3 years? These are the kinds of performance-related questions that provide valuable business insight but have in the past been a challenge to answer. In previous performance monitoring or reporting solutions, providing the tools for business users to answer these questions involved a multi-step and complex development process. The business user identifies a need for information, contacts IT, and describes the filter she needs. Development then begins with a programmer writing MDX against the cube and demonstrating the result to the user for feedback. After the required test and revision cycles, the filter is moved into production. By the time the filter is developed and implemented, the original critical need for information may well have passed.

PerformancePoint Monitoring provides Time Intelligence capabilities that allow organizations to add filters to the dashboard, enabling business analysts and others in the organization to answer time-related performance questions in a timely manner. The process of creating these filters is simple, effectively bypassing a potentially costly and lengthy development cycle and freeing up IT resources for other projects.

Simple Time Period Specification

Time Intelligence filters in PerformancePoint Monitoring and Analytics are based on an expression language called Simple Time Period Specification, or STPS. STPS introduces formulas for creating filters that work with multiple types of standard time periods such as month, date, and quarter. Once a Time Intelligence filter is implemented in a performance management solution, a sales executive wanting to compare sales of units for the quarter or sales year-to-date compared to last year now has the tools to autonomously generate the required information from the data.

Dashboard Designer provides two Time Intelligence filter templates for this purpose. These templates are called Time Intelligence and Time Intelligence Post Formula. Use the Time Intelligence template to build filters based on single-member formulas or formulas that return a range of time dimension members. This filter is used to answer the following types of business questions: How many units did we sell this month? This quarter? This year? Use the Time Intelligence Post Formula template to define the current time period, mapping the data source to a reference date and building time dynamic filters from the current date to create report views. This filter is used to answer the following types of business questions: As of today, how many units did we sell month? As of today, how many units have we sold this year? As of today, how many units have we sold this quarter? The next two sections outline the steps for using these templates to create Time Intelligence filters.

Creating Time Intelligence Filters

The Time Intelligence template is used to build filters based on single-member formulas or formulas that return a range. Examples of single-member formulas include:

- Month returns data for the Current Month
- Year returns data for the Current Year

- Month - 1 returns data from the Prior Month
- Quarter - 2 returns data from the Prior Two Quarters

Examples of formulas with ranges include:

- `{Month-6:Month-1}` returns data from Prior 6 Whole Months
- `{Year.FirstMonth:Month}` returns data on Year-To-Date
- `{Month:Year.LastMonth}` returns data on Current Month to Current Year End (This is an example of a forecasting range.)

Creating the Time Intelligence filter is a multi-step process done in Dashboard Designer.

Step 1: Configure Mapping for the Data Source

First, select the data source for the scorecard, and using the Time tab set the reference data mapping for the Time Intelligence filter (see Figure 7-24).

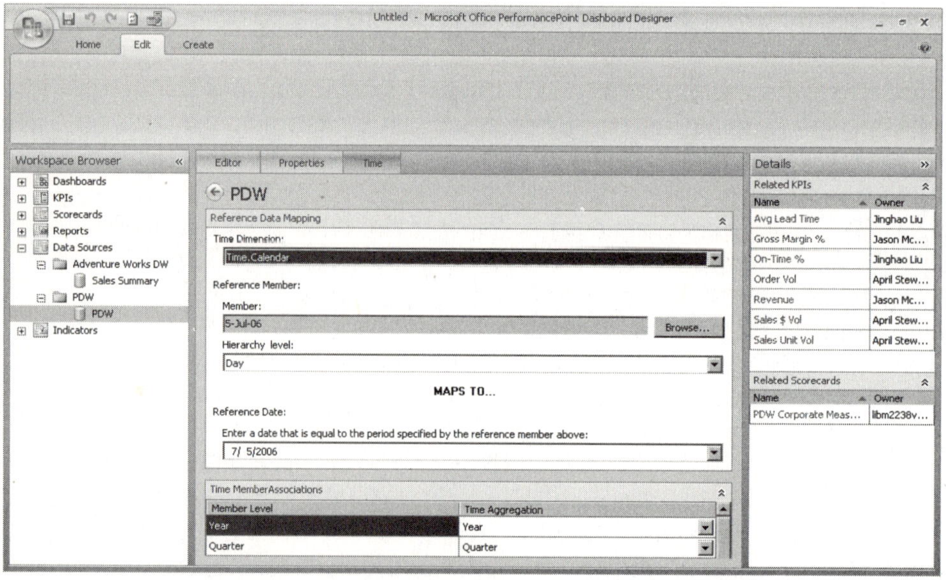

Figure 7-24 Use the Time tab for reference data mapping.

In a cube, there are different ways of looking at a time period. A time period may be viewed as a Calendar dimension, as a hierarchy, or as a fiscal time hierarchy, for example. To use the expression language correctly, PerformancePoint Monitoring must understand during runtime how a period in the filter maps to the dimension in Analysis Services.

The Time dimension offers several types of mapping options, such as Time.Day, Time.Month, and Time.Fiscal. Select the hierarchy in the Time dimension to define Year, Quarter, or Month as required. Then specify the hierarchy in the reference member by picking the member and hierarchy level. When selecting the hierarchy level, be sure to specify the lowest member or the finest granularity of the data you want. For example, if you want to view data by month, select Month. If you want the option to view data by day, select Day as the hierarchy level.

After specifying the reference member, you must specify the reference date that the reference member maps to. The reference date will be the date that is equal to the period you specify in the reference member. It is possible to pick a future reference date, but you may want to alert users that data may not appear for the future time period, since the data source may not yet contain data for a future date. For example, if a sales organization specifies a reference date in 2020, it's likely that the data source will not contains orders for that period. Consequently, filter results will appear blank.

Finally, in Time Member Associations, map the internal dimensions by mapping Member Level to Time Aggregation.

TIP Make sure that these mappings are correct and consistent; otherwise, unpredictable results will occur when using the Time Intelligence filters.

Specify the levels and aggregation only for the external dimension members you want to include. The levels that appear here are based on the hierarchy level you select. For example, if you select Day, you will see Month, Quarter, and Year member levels as choices to include in the time aggregation (see Figure 7-25).

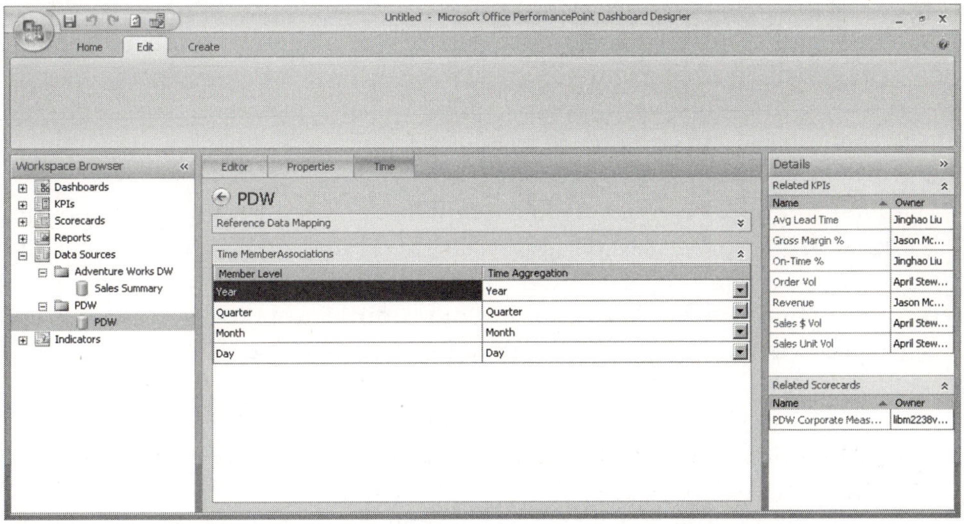

Figure 7-25 The levels that appear are based on the hierarchy level selected.

Step 2: Apply Filters

Once the mapping is complete, you are ready to apply the filters. From the Dashboard Designer view, click the Filter tab, where you can select from the two available Time Intelligence filter templates: Time Intelligence and Time Intelligence Post Formula. Once you name the formula and select the data source, you are ready to enter the time formula. For example, Year - 2 returns data for 2008 – 2 = 2006 and Year.FirstMonth:Month returns data for Year-To-Date. Use the Preview option to view the range of dimension members that will be returned as a result of the formula. To finish, select the display method — Tree, for example.

NOTE All formulas are based on the current date. Entering Quarter returns data for the current quarter based on the current date. Entering Month returns data for the current month based on the current date.

Step 3: Add the Filter to the Dashboard

Time Intelligence filters that you create appear in the Filter list on the Workspace list of items available for use in the dashboard. Place the filter on the scorecard zone of the dashboard and when you publish the dashboard, the Time Intelligence filter will appear in the dashboard as an item for the user to select. You will learn more about adding filters to dashboard zones later in this chapter.

Creating Time Intelligence Post Formulas

Time Intelligence Post Formulas are also based on the PerformancePoint Monitoring and Analytics Simple Time Period Specification (STPS) expression language. The difference is that these filters use the current date or a date selected by the user as a reference or starting point to return results. There is also a slight difference in how you enter the formula.

The Time Intelligence Post Formula template defines the current time period, mapping the data source to a reference date and building time dynamic filters from the current date to create scorecard and report views. From the client's perspective, this option creates a filter that prompts users to select the current time from a calendar, and then builds scorecards and report views based on the date selected.

When creating a Time Intelligence Post Formula, the first step, in which you configure mapping for the data source, is the same as described previously for a Time Intelligence formula. Differences begin in Step 2 in the choice of the filter template. In this case, select Time Intelligence Post Formula as the filter template. Enter the filter name and description. (The name is required; the description is optional.) Add the data source from the list of data sources on the server or workspace tab, and then enter the time formula and caption. Finally, choose how you want the filter to appear on the dashboard from the Time Intelligence Calendar. Another difference here is that the Time Intelligence Post Formula always sets the display method to Time Intelligence Calendar. At this point, the formula itself has not been defined. Defining the formula comes later in the process after the filter has been added to the dashboard zone.

Like other filters you create, Time Intelligence Post Formula filters appear in the Filter list on the Workspace list of items available for use in the dashboard. Place the filter on the scorecard zone of the dashboard, where you will be prompted to edit the filter link. Use the Filter Link Formula button to call up the Formula Editor where you actually enter the formula for the link (see Figure 7-26).

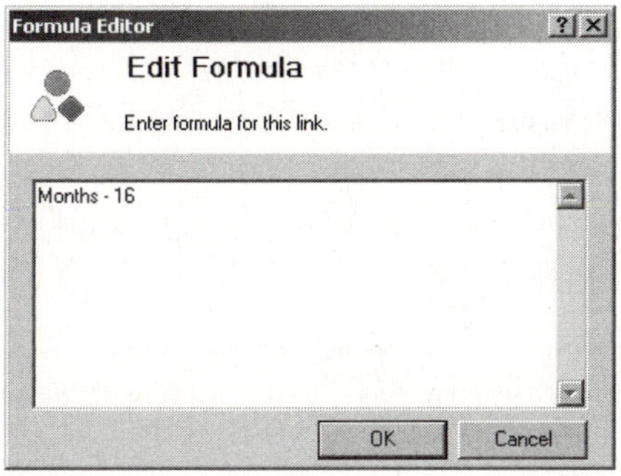

Figure 7-26 Use the Formula Editor to enter Time Intelligence Post formulas.

When you publish the dashboard, the Time Intelligence Post Formula filter will appear in the dashboard as an item for the user to select. As mentioned previously, this filter first prompts users to select the current time from a calendar, and then builds scorecards and report views based on the date selected.

Adding Reports

Reports provide dynamic displays of business information for monitoring and analyzing business performance and strategy. A single dashboard may contain multiple report types, as illustrated in Figure 7-27.

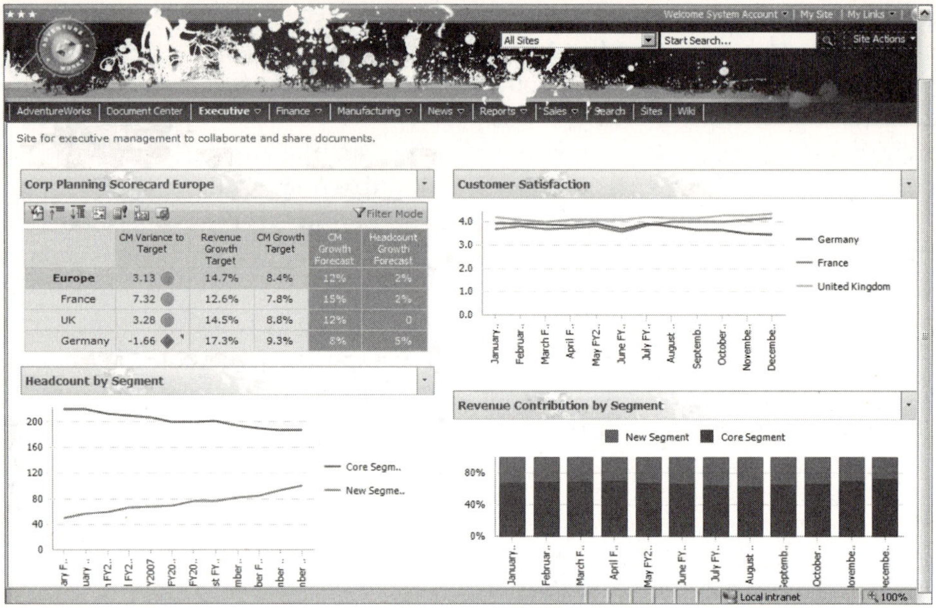

Figure 7-27 Dashboard with several different report types

Chapter 4 covered the different report types you can create and add to dashboards. These report types are:

- **Scorecards.** Provide a quick view of performance with indicators that show at a glance how well the organization is doing in key performance areas.
- **Analytic Charts and Analytic Grids.** Reports based on SQL Server 2005 Analysis Services data sources published to the server.
- **Strategy Maps.** Illustrate in one consolidated diagram the relationship between the four key balanced scorecard areas at the core of the Balanced Scorecard methodology.
- **Excel Services Reports.** Reports based on an Excel Services data source. Excel Services is part of Microsoft Office SharePoint Server 2007 and is used to extend the capabilities of Microsoft Office Excel 2007 by allowing broad sharing of spreadsheets.
- **SQL Server 2005 Reports.** Reports based on references to existing SQL Server 2005 Reporting Services.
- **Trend Charts.** Predict future growth or historical trends based on the key performance indicators tracked in the scorecard.

Adding reports to dashboard zones is a straightforward process in Dashboard Designer. Reports you create appear in the Details pane in the Reports list. From the Reports list, grab the report you want to add, and drag and drop the report on the dashboard. Drop the report in the zone where you want the report to appear in the deployed dashboard. You can connect filters to reports views (see Figure 7-28). This process is described later in this chapter.

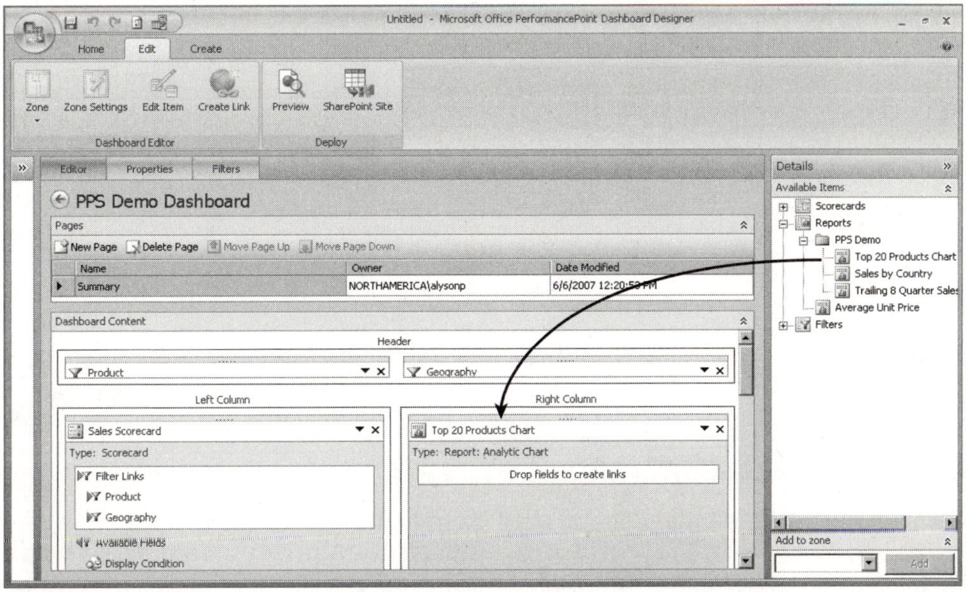

Figure 7-28 Drag and drop reports into position on the dashboard.

Best Practice Reports

Thinking about sharing data sources early in the design process allows you to build dashboard components that deliver reliable and consistent data with flexible uses. This concept applies to reports as well as KPIs and other dashboard elements.

Best practice is to build universal reports and report components by creating reports as separate element types. This allows you to drag and drop reports into different dashboards or to link them specifically to objectives or KPIs from Dashboard Designer.

Adding Filters to Dashboard Zones

Like adding reports, adding filters to dashboard zones is a straightforward process in Dashboard Designer. Filters you create appear in the Details pane in the Filters list. From the Filters list, grab the filter you want to add, and drag and drop the filter onto the dashboard (see Figure 7-29).

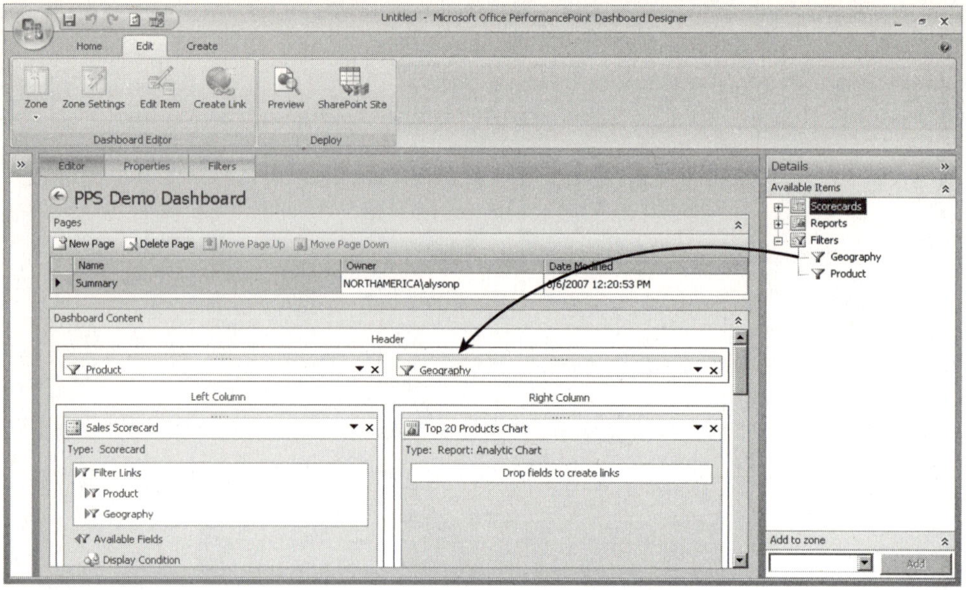

Figure 7-29 Drag and drop filters into position on the dashboard.

Drop the filter in the zone where you want the filter to appear in the deployed dashboard. In the example shown in Figure 7-29, the Product and Geography filters have been added to the Sales scorecard. These same filters can be added to a report, as shown in Figure 7-30.

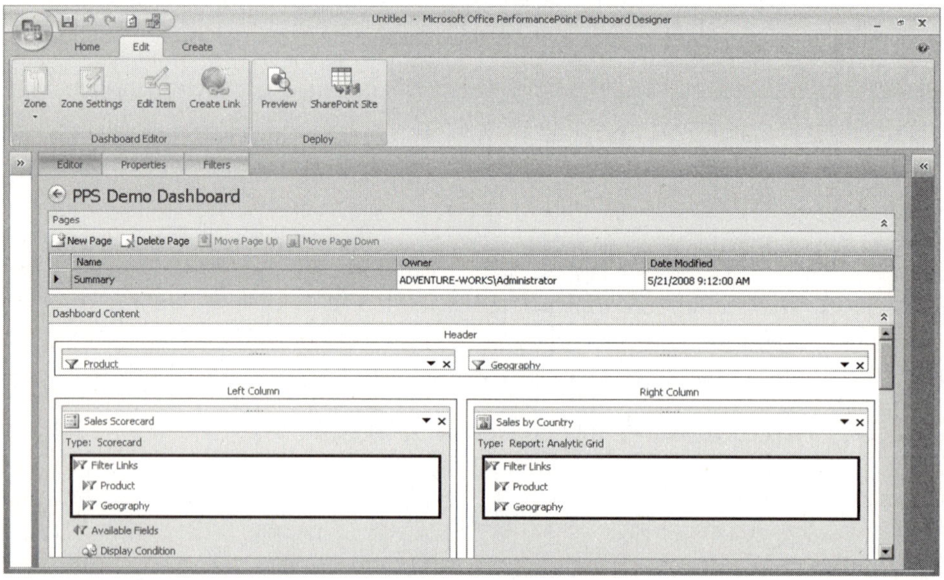

Figure 7-30 Linked views and reports are updated together.

Implementing filters between scorecard and report views provides highly targeted information to business analysts and others viewing the scorecard. When multiple dashboard elements are connected to a single filter, the linked views and reports are updated together, thereby providing analytics capabilities at the level of the dashboard itself. The following section explains how you can further use filters to connect scorecard and report views.

Enabling Filters for Analytic Grids and Charts

You have two options for enabling filters for analytic grids and charts. The first option occurs when you design a report using the Design tab of the report workspace. This is the drag-and-drop method of creating analytic reports. To enable filters in this environment, place the hierarchy you want to filter on an axis (Rows, Columns, Background, or Series) within the report. If your hierarchy isn't shown in the report, place the hierarchy on the Background or Series axis (see Figure 7-31).

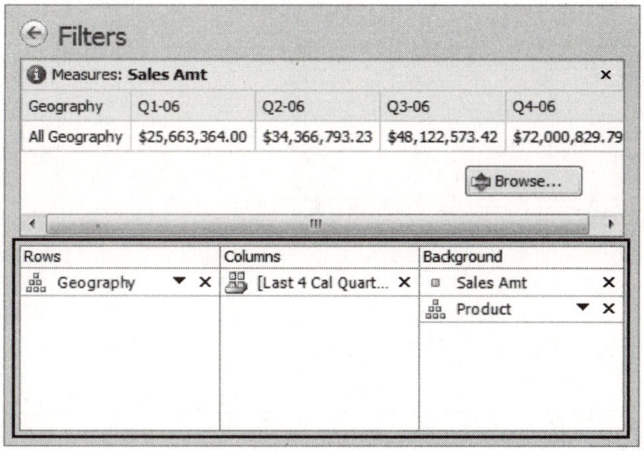

Figure 7-31 The axes of an analytic grid

Hierarchies that are explicitly placed within one of these boxes are shown as options for Dashboard item endpoints (see Figure 7-32).

The second option for enabling filters for analytic grids and charts occurs when you have designed the report using the Query tab of the report workspace. (This is the mode that allows you to write a custom MDX query for the report view.) To enable filters when using this mode, enclose the MDX expression to be replaced by the unique name for the selected filter item with angle brackets: << and >>. Figure 7-33 shows a query where the row member is defined using this syntax.

In this example, `<<Product>>` will be replaced in the MDX query by the unique name of the selected filter item. When the dashboard is first opened, the default value, Bikes, will be used (see Figure 7-34).

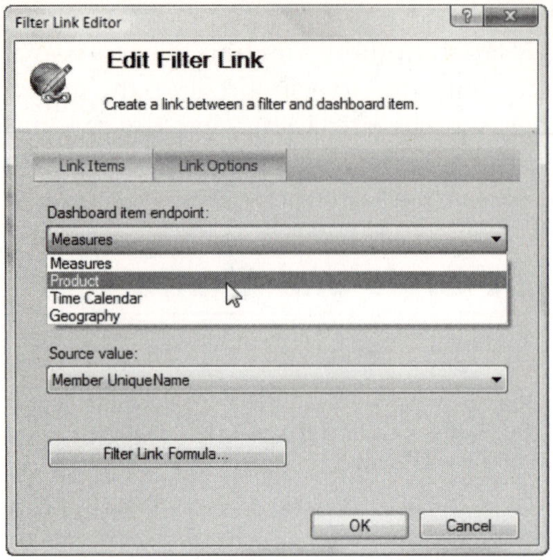

Figure 7-32 Available hierarchies for linking filters to analytic reports

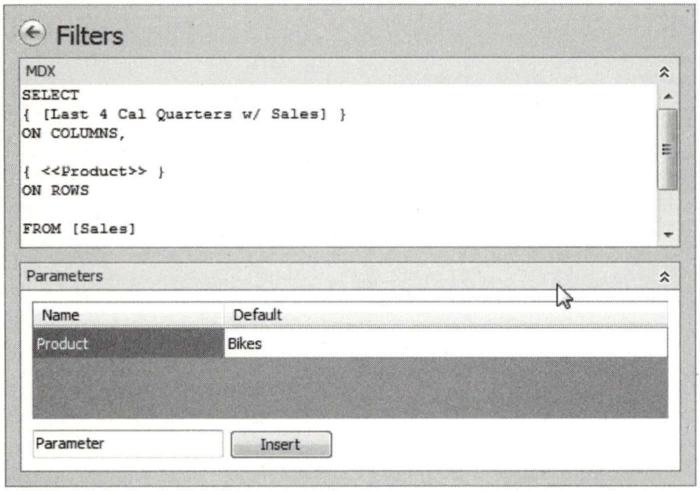

Figure 7-33 A filter endpoint defined for a custom MDX view

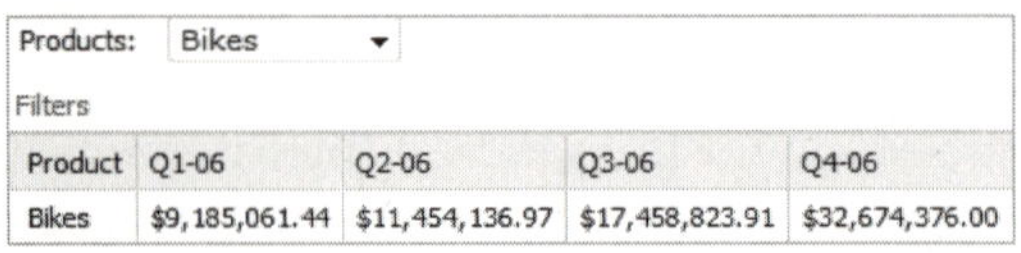

Figure 7-34 A custom MDX view with Bikes selected as the default filter item

Connecting Filters to Scorecard and Reports Views

After placing the filter for display in the dashboard, you're ready to connect the filter to scorecard and report views. Filters can be connected to a single dashboard element such as a scorecard, or to multiple dashboard elements such as scorecards and reports. To connect the filter to the scorecard or report, simply drag and drop the filter onto the scorecard or the report. There are differences in the options you can select when connecting filters based on a dimension as opposed to filters based on Time Intelligence. These differences are explained next.

The example in Figure 7-35 displays the Acme Sales dashboard with the Sales scorecard, Sales report, and two filters: Country and YTD. The Country filter is a dimension filter in which the dimension is Country and the member is every country that exists in the dimension. YTD filter is a Time Intelligence filter with two members: Year-To-Date and Quarter-To-Date.

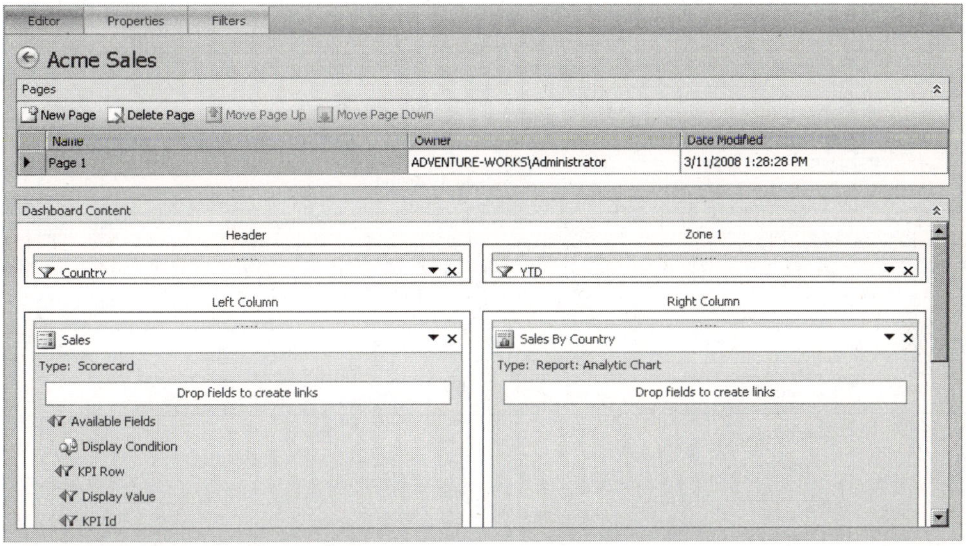

Figure 7-35 Acme Sales dashboard

Compare the illustrations shown in Figure 7-36 and Figure 7-37. Notice that the options for the dimension-based filter are different from the options available on the Time Intelligence filter.

Dimension filters are based on named sets, dimension members, and MDX or tabular values. These filters can use only one data source, whereas Time Intelligence filters can use multiple data sources, which appear as options on the filter. In the Time Intelligence filter example in Figure 7-37, PDW and PDW FY appear as the data sources available on the filter.

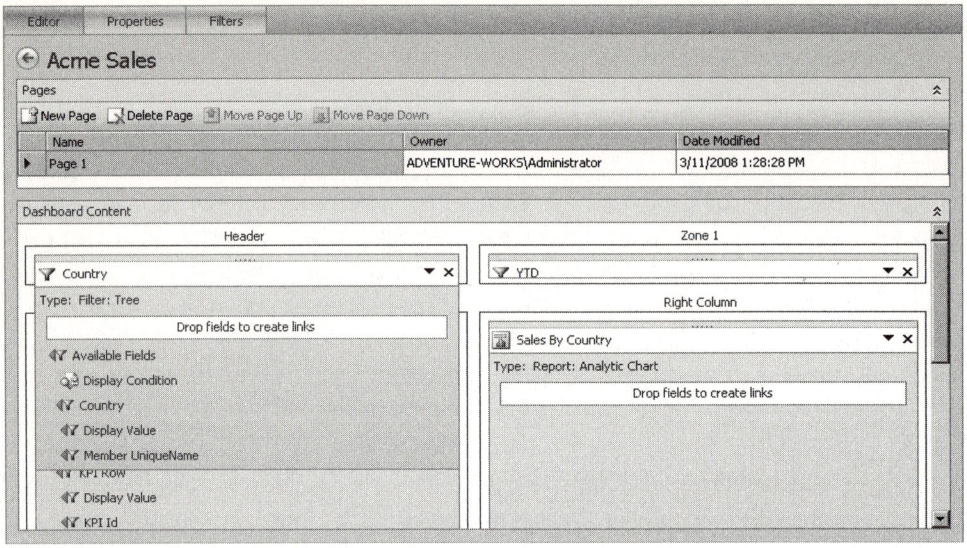

Figure 7-36 Dimension-based filter options

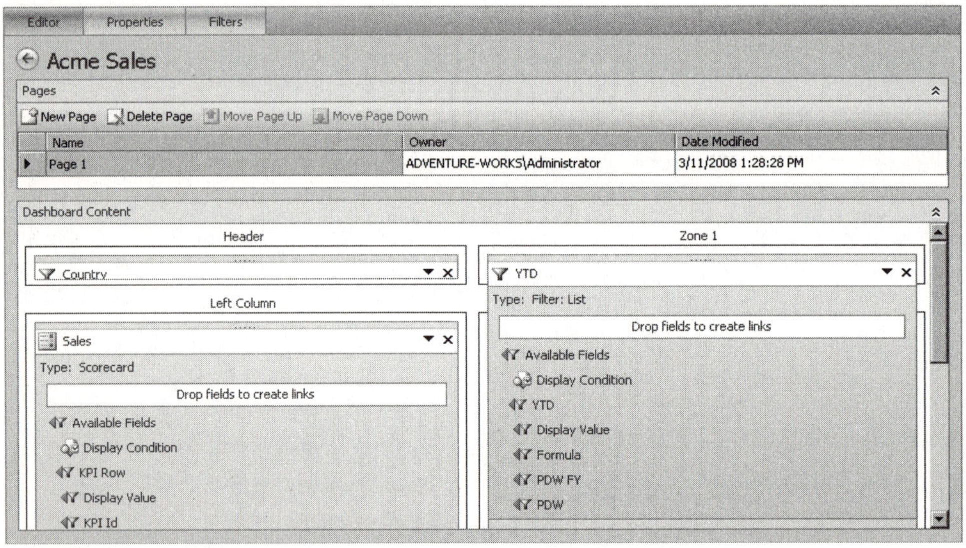

Figure 7-37 Time Intelligence filter options include data sources.

Having multiple data sources allows you to specify which data source you want to use on the filter. Notice also that MemberUniqueName does not appear as an option on the Time Intelligence filter, and that you can set a formula for the filter by using the Formula option. Selecting this option calls the Formula Editor, which you learned about earlier in this chapter.

Using the Display Condition Option

Using the Display Condition filter option allows you to show alternating scorecard and report views with a filter. Using conditional display is an excellent way of saving real estate on the screen. Dashboards can very easily become cluttered with many reports that may end up confusing the user. Conditional display allows the user to see only the reports or scorecards that are pertinent to a particular KPI or filter value. In the example shown in Figure 7-38, USA is set as a display condition on the Sales scorecard. On the SharePoint site, this means that the Sales scorecard will appear only when the user selects USA.

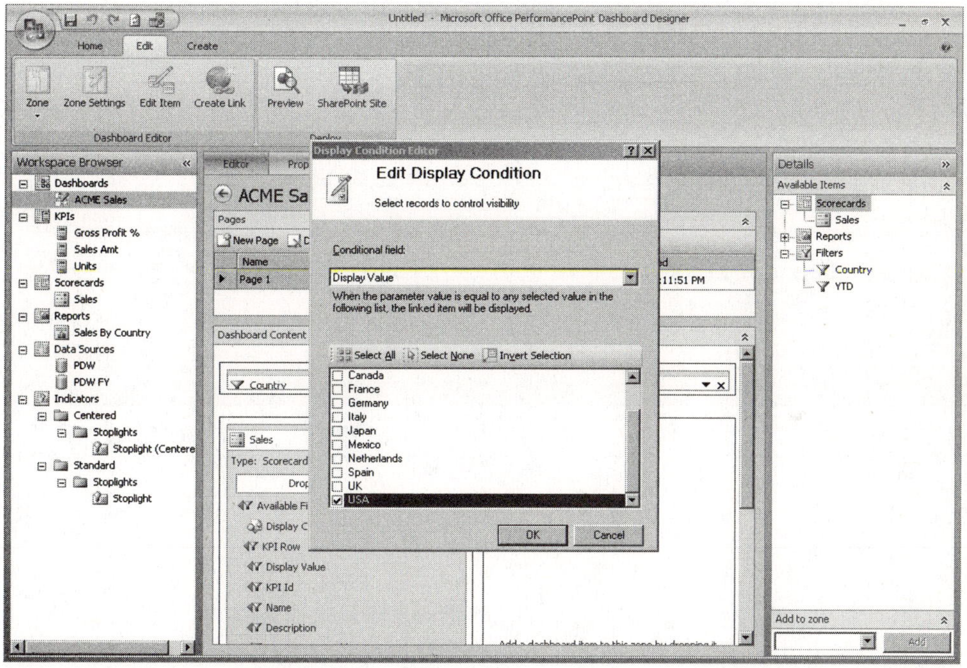

Figure 7-38 Display Condition settings drive multiple views from a single filter.

You can also specify a display condition from a scorecard in a report by dragging the filter from the scorecard to the report. For example, you can use this to display a report only when the user selects a field in the scorecard. In the example shown in Figure 7-39, the display condition is set to Sales Amt. This condition is set on the Country dimension filter that has been dragged from the scorecard to the report.

When the dashboard appears on the SharePoint site, the user sees only the Sales scorecard and not the report, as shown in Figure 7-40.

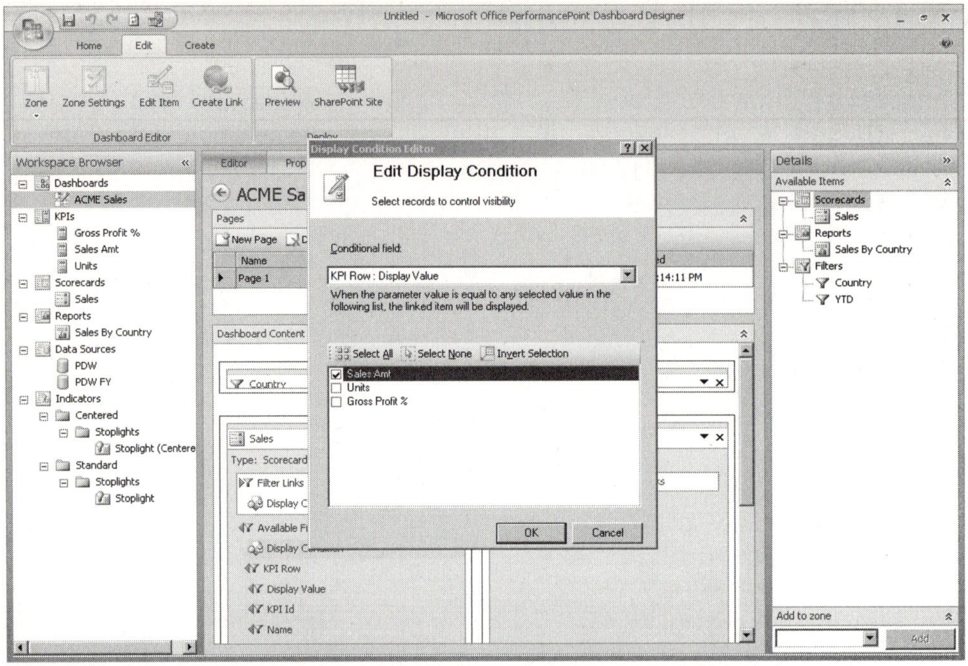

Figure 7-39 Specify a display condition from a scorecard in a report.

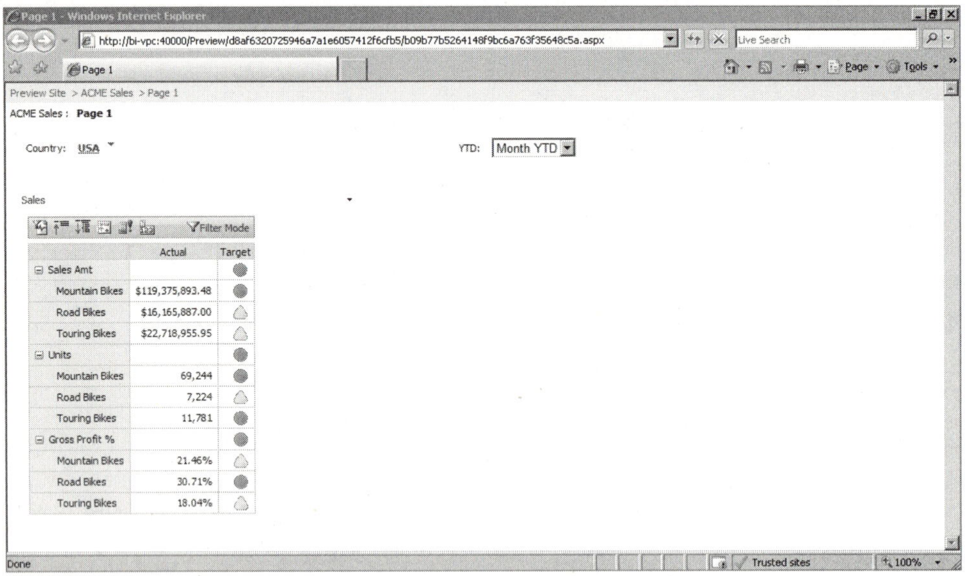

Figure 7-40 Only the Sales scorecard appears on the dashboard.

But when the user clicks Sales Amt on the scorecard, the view changes and the report appears on the dashboard along with the scorecard (see Figure 7-41).

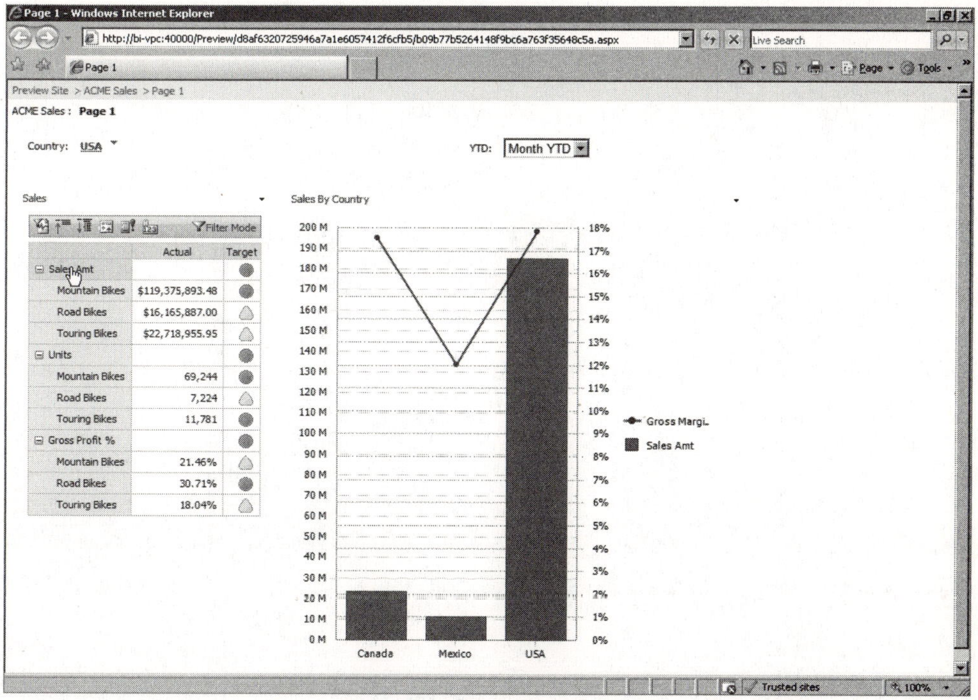

Figure 7-41 Selecting Sales Amt causes the report to appear on the dashboard.

Connecting Scorecard KPIs to Report Views

Connecting scorecard KPIs to report views causes linked report views to display information specific to the KPI selected by the user, providing another way of displaying highly targeted information on the dashboard.

When a scorecard KPI is linked to a report view, the scorecard determines the content displayed in the report by passing a unique member. The unique member is identified by a unique name recognized by the receiving report (see Figure 7-42).

For example, drag KPI Row from the scorecard to the report, and then set the parameter in the Edit Filter Link dialog box. Options for parameters include KPI data, individual cell data, and member data.

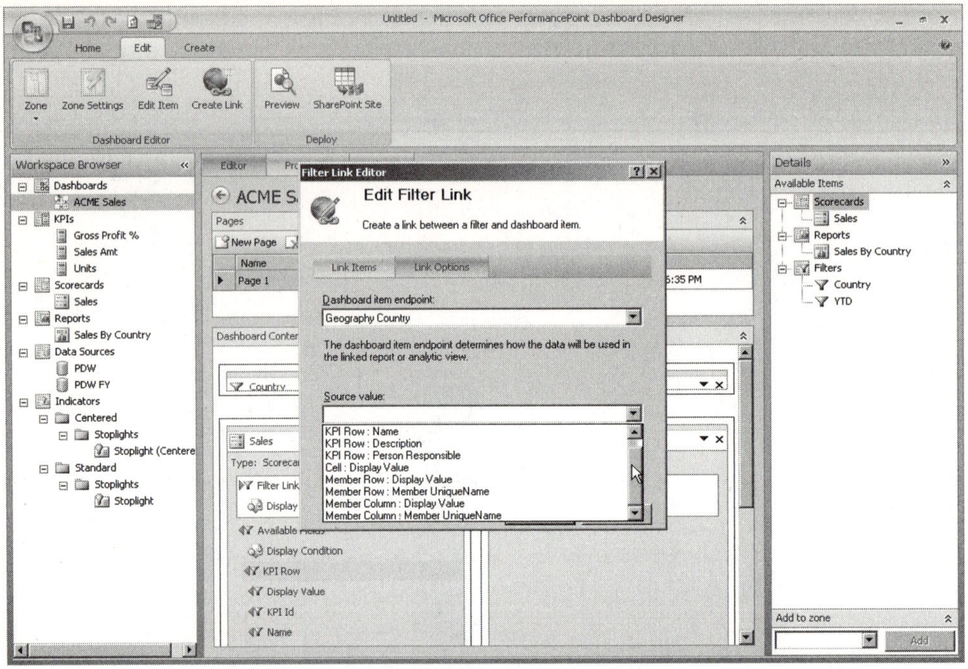

Figure 7-42 Select parameters from KPI data, individual cell data, or member data.

Centralizing Dashboard Elements

Centralizing dashboard elements on PerformancePoint Monitoring Server facilitates the sharing of data and resources across multiple dashboards and scorecards, thus promoting consistency throughout an organization. A business analyst or designer creating a dashboard simply needs to point to an existing scorecard, report, or data source with its security settings already defined. Using centralized resources minimizes the risk of pointing to the wrong data, and ensures consistent and appropriate security settings for valuable business information. As shown in Figure 7-43, the Server tab lists the resources available on the server — in this case, KPIs.

By double-clicking an available resource, business analysts or designers can select a resource for use in the local Workspace tab where the actual design work occurs. In effect, the resource becomes a reusable component in the design framework. As shown in Figure 7-44, the Workspace tab lists the resources available on the local workspace — in this case, KPIs.

Centralizing resources is similar to implementing content and style rules for a Web site. When organizations first started setting up Web sites, there was little consistency or unity. It was not uncommon to see a wide range of functionality and styles across departments in the same organization, from exploding poodles to blinking text. Now, master pages and style sheets have allowed organizations to implement a consistent look and feel to their Web sites. Centralized resources share the same intent. The Workspace tab is like an artist's palette where an analyst or designer can build individualized scorecards or other elements, while the Server tab with the defined resources ensures that the design will be based on the organization's informational structure and design guidelines.

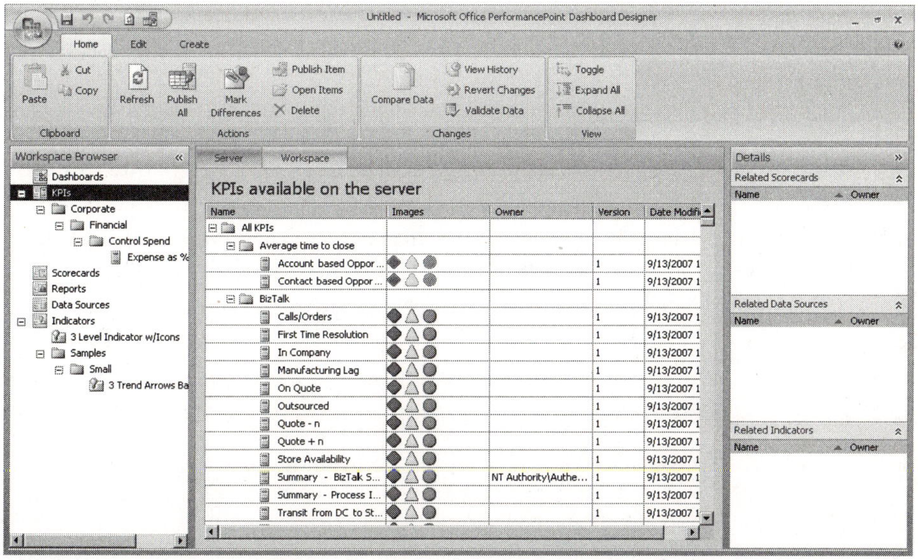

Figure 7-43 The Server tab lists resources available on the server.

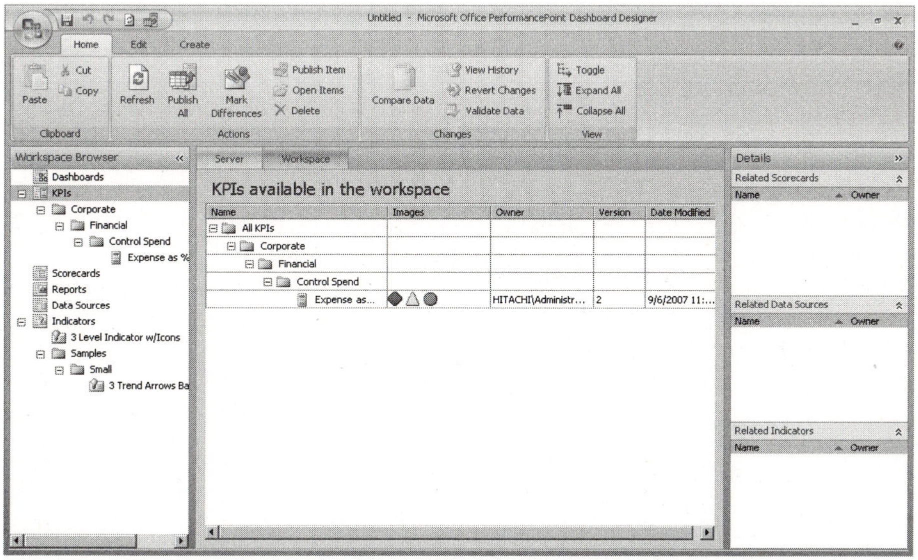

Figure 7-44 The Workspace tab lists resources available on the local workspace.

This promotes consistency in information sharing and reduces the risk of errors with regard to data and security. When a designer or analyst selects a KPI from the list of KPIs available on the server, the KPI along with its supporting information, including data source settings, is brought into the local workspace. Using the KPI from the Server tab ensures that the design will be based on the organization's informational structure and performance measures.

Summary

This chapter described the dashboard design capabilities of PerformancePoint Server, including designing and sizing pages, adding reports, and creating filters. It also provided some prescriptive guidance on dashboard design and maintenance. This general overview will allow you to begin working with Dashboard Designer to create compelling, useful performance dashboards for your organization.

CHAPTER

8

Supplementing Dashboards with Reports

Reports are dynamic displays of business information for monitoring and analyzing business performance and strategy. Examples of reports you can use in PerformancePoint include strategy maps created with Microsoft Visio 2007, spreadsheets, charts, pivot tables, and SQL Server reports that are based on dashboard data. This chapter provides information about supplementing dashboards with these kinds of reports to create targeted views of business information.

The first section introduces a framework for reports in PerformancePoint Monitoring and Analytics by outlining the kinds of questions reports are typically used to answer.

The next section, ''Strategy Maps,'' explains the concept of strategy maps and includes information about designing and creating effective strategy maps.

The subsequent sections cover other types of reports you can add to dashboards, including Excel Services and Reporting Services reports as well as trend charts. You'll learn about when it's appropriate to use these types of reports and about the process of creating and adding reports to dashboards to enhance the overall effectiveness of your performance management solution.

A final section summarizes best practices for reports.

Reports Answer the "What?" Question

PerformancePoint reports provide organizations with the ability to deliver tailored views to users, offering them the personalized experience they need to make decisions within their scope and for their specific objectives (see

Figure 8-1). Reports are efficient tools for providing answers to the following types of questions:

- What was last quarter's revenue compared to this quarter's revenue?
- What is the highest selling product for each region?
- What segment contributed the most revenue last year?
- What is our customer satisfaction rating by region?

"What?" questions are at the heart of reporting and form the basis for the "Why?" questions at the heart of analysis.

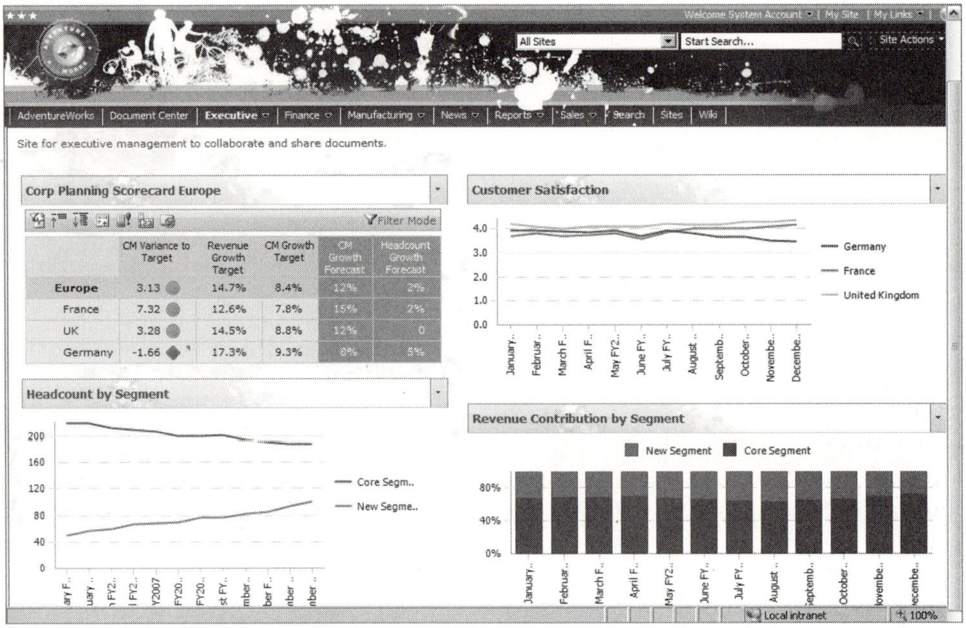

Figure 8-1 Successful dashboard reports facilitate analysis and action.

Reports should not overwhelm employees with irrelevant information but should instead provide targeted and relevant information that facilitates analysis and action. Providing employees with relevant information is different from merely providing access to information. To improve results, allow the employee's experience with information to be as relevant and as actionable as possible.[1]

For example, a business analyst should be able to see from the KPI on the scorecard that sales are down in Europe. What are the sales numbers for each region? Going to the Sales report on the dashboard, she sees that sales are up in all regions except Germany. Drilling down into this report, she further sees that sales in the Cologne store are not doing well. What are the sales by product for this store? A second report that provides product information tells her that this store has not been selling the newest line of products very well. With this information, she's ready to ask, "Why isn't our newest line selling very well in Cologne?" She's also ready to ask, "What action do we need to take to fix this problem?"

Strategy Maps

Strategy maps illustrate in one consolidated diagram the relationship between the four key balanced scorecard areas at the core of the Balanced Scorecard methodology (see Figure 8-2). Chapter 5 covered the Balanced Scorecard methodology and its application within a PerformancePoint monitoring solution. You may remember from this chapter that the Balanced Scorecard is a scorecard based on the performance management methodology developed by Robert Kaplan and David Norton. Kaplan and Norton's comprehensive approach analyzes an organization's performance in four areas collectively called the FOSH metrics:

- Financial performance
- Customer satisfaction
- Operational excellence
- People commitment

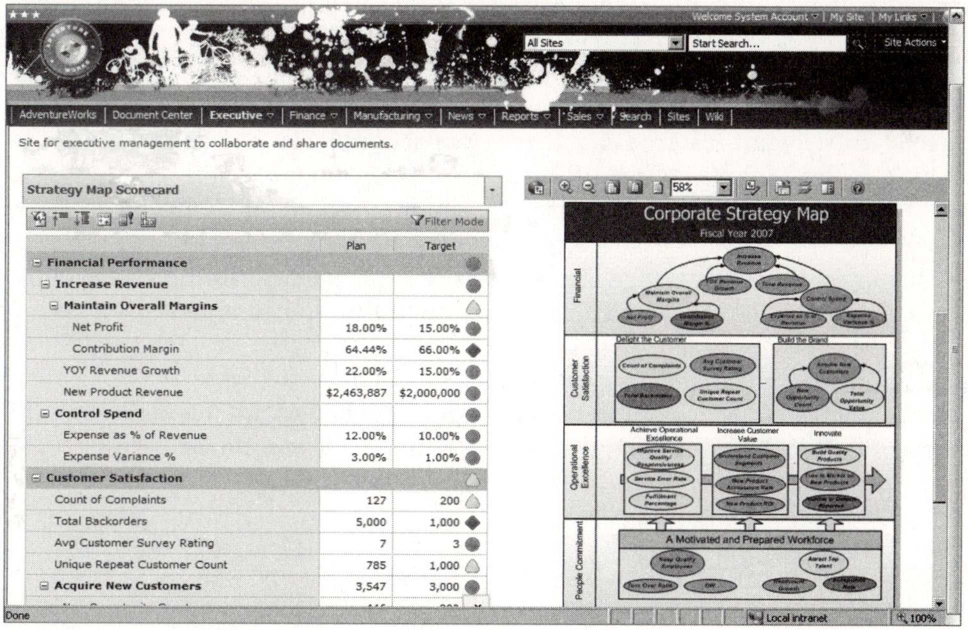

Figure 8-2 Scorecard with a strategy map

Strategy maps connect stated business objectives with four overall business objectives from the Balanced Scorecard methodology into a visual representation that shows cause-and-effect relationships between the objectives.

> *The objectives in the four perspectives are linked together by cause-and-effect relationships. . . . This architecture of cause and effect, linking the four perspectives, is the structure around which a strategy map is developed. Building a strategy map forces an organization to clarify the logic of how it will create value and for whom.*
>
> Robert S. Kaplan and David P. Norton, *Strategy Maps*

The strategy map in Figure 8-2 illustrates each area of the FOSH metrics. The map contains four layers, each with colors and shapes that reflect the KPI performance indicators in the Balanced Scorecard. Arrows connect and define cause-and-effect relationships between the objectives identified in each layer. Notice how the KPI colored indicators are reflected in the colored shapes of the strategy map for objectives as well as KPIs.

Looking at the Financial Performance layer, the top-level objective is green just like the KPI in the scorecard. The second layer objective Maintain Overall Margins has a yellow indicator, which is also reflected in the color of the shape on the map. Of the KPIs that roll up to this objective, Net Profit is green and Contribution Margins is red. The status of these indicators also appears in the colored shapes on the map. This visualization of the colors and the connecting arrows between objectives and KPIs show at a glance the cause-and-effect relationship between the status of the lower-level KPIs and the higher-level objectives.

How does this strategy map fulfill the goal of reports to go from a metric directly to relevant information that supports analysis and action? Without looking at detailed numbers in the scorecard, a business analyst can tell from the map that this area requires further attention. And from a bird's-eye view, executives looking at the strategy map can see that the areas of Customer Satisfaction and Operational Excellence may not be contributing as well as they could be to the overall strategic direction of the organization.

NOTE The strategy map concept is based on the Balanced Scorecard methodology, but an organization is not required to implement this methodology in PerformancePoint scorecards to use the strategy map report type.

Designing Effective Strategy Maps

Clear logic and clear layout make good strategy maps. When designing a strategy map, make sure the shapes and their arrangement accurately reflect the objectives and KPIs in the scorecard as well as the cause-and-effect relationships between the KPIs and objectives.

Visio 2007 is the primary tool you will use to design strategy maps (see Figure 8-3). Visio 2007 provides many different shapes for creating attractive and highly readable maps. You can use most of the available shapes, and you can create interesting designs for the map by using some of the industry-specific Visio shapes.

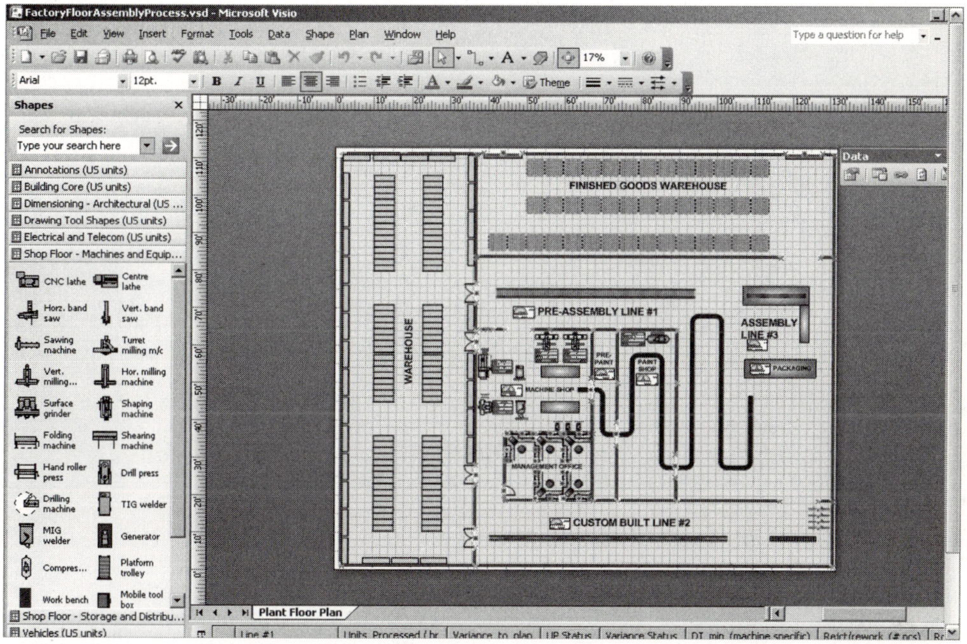

Figure 8-3 Visio 2007 is the primary design tool for strategy map layouts.

For example, a manufacturing plant may want to have a map that displays a blueprint of the factory floor with KPIs connected to specific areas on the floor or to specific machines in the factory. Visio provides blueprint and machine shapes that you can use to create a layout of the factory floor with machines in place. You can then tie KPI data to the floor area or to specific machines. This creates more than a pretty picture. It actually provides highly targeted and actionable information. A manager reviewing this strategy map will know exactly where to go if there is an issue, whereas by looking at a scorecard only it might take longer to identify the actual machine and its location.

TIP **Use 3-D shapes sparingly in strategy maps. 3-D shapes may not appear correctly in the dashboard. Also, although 3-D shapes may look attractive, they can sometimes detract from the information they are meant to convey.**

It is also possible to add meta data such as Date/Time or KPI data such as Person Responsible to shapes on a strategy map. This makes the map easier to read and provides additional actionable information (see Figure 8-4).

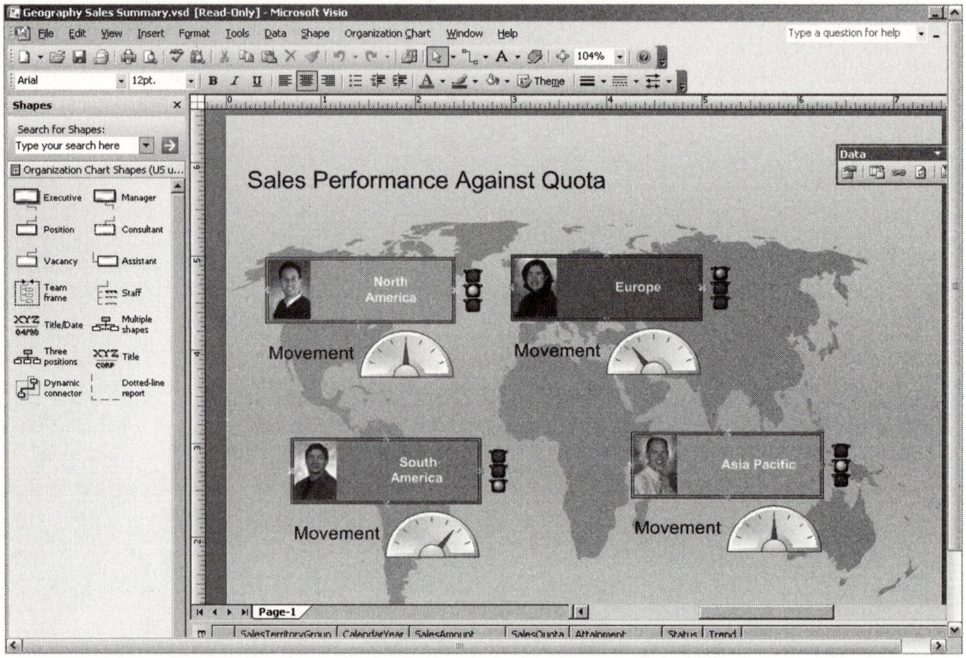

Figure 8-4 Clarity, not clutter, should drive design.

It is possible to create attractive strategy maps that include images and shapes tied to KPIs, but don't get carried away. Make sure that every shape and every image contributes clarity and not clutter to the visualization. Figure 8-4 illustrates an example of an attractive strategy map that contributes useful geographical and personnel information to performance measures.

Creating Strategy Maps

To create strategy maps, you will use Dashboard Designer with Microsoft Office Visio 2007 templates and data-driven shapes linked directly to scorecard KPI values and targets. You must use Visio 2007 for this feature since prior versions of Visio do not support building strategy maps with PerformancePoint. As mentioned in Chapter 4, you will need a license for Microsoft Office Visio 2007 to build strategy maps with Dashboard Designer. Licenses may not be required for all the business users in your organization who may need to view the maps.

Dashboard Designer provides a Strategy Map template to help you through the process of creating a strategy map (see Figure 8-5). During this process, you will use the Strategy Map Editor to add or modify shapes for the map and to connect the shapes to KPIs. The steps for creating a strategy map are described next.

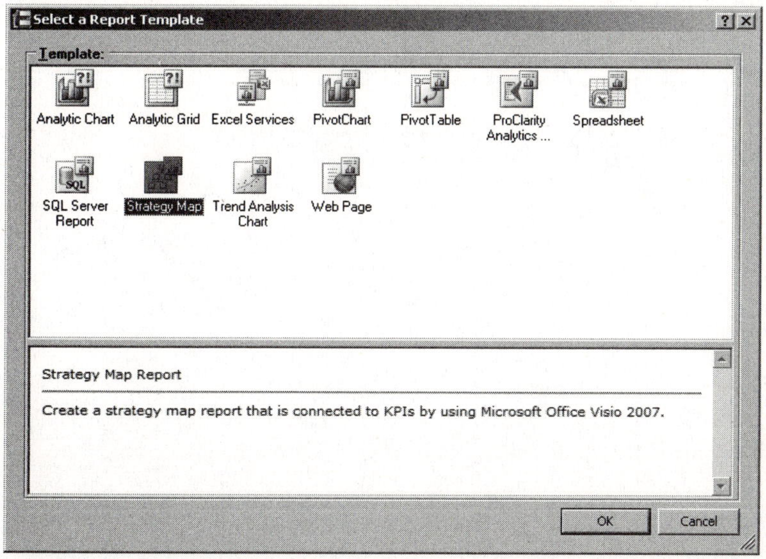

Figure 8-5 PerformancePoint provides a Strategy Map template.

Step 1: Create the Map Layout in Visio

Use Visio 2007 to create and save the shapes and layout of your map. Make sure that the layout of the map accurately displays the relationships between objectives and KPIs in the scorecard. You can use most of the available Visio shapes. Save the file as a regular .vsd Visio file in a location you specify.

Step 2: Create and Name the Strategy Map

In Dashboard Designer, select to create a new report using the Strategy Map template, and then simply name the strategy map and specify a location for the default display folder. Specifying a location for the default display folder is optional.

Step 3: Select the Scorecard

Select the scorecard for which you want to make a strategy map. The template will list the scorecards available on the server. Remember that you can choose to create a strategy map from any available scorecard, even from a scorecard that is *not* a Balanced Scorecard.

Step 4: Create the Strategy Map

After confirming your choices, open the Strategy Map Editor from the Edit tab on the Dashboard Designer Ribbon (see Figure 8-6). Use the Strategy Map Editor to open the Visio file with the Strategy Map layout and to edit, connect, and configure shapes for the map. Shapes also are available here if you want to continue adding shapes or otherwise modify the map layout.

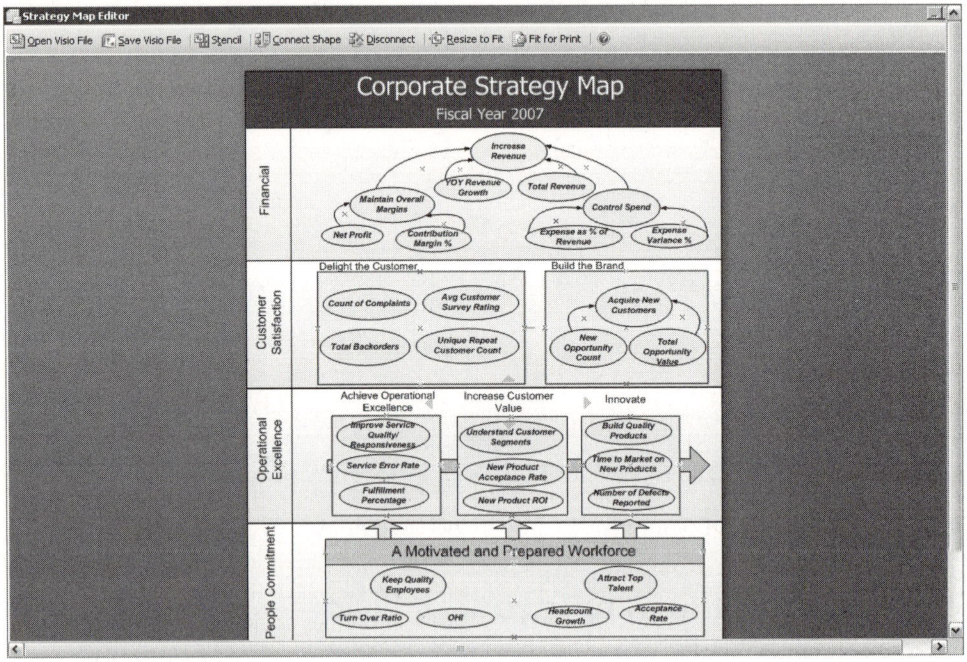

Figure 8-6 Strategy Map Editor

Step 5: Connect and Configure the KPIs

Once you've created the map, use the Connect Shape option to attach KPIs to each shape (see Figure 8-7). You'll be able to choose any of the KPIs from the scorecard you selected to link to the strategy map. Make sure that you connect the KPIs to the shapes so that the visualization accurately shows the relationships between objectives and KPIs in the scorecard.

Adding the KPI name to the shape is optional, but doing so provides additional information to the business user viewing the map and can make the map easier to read, as shown in the example in Figure 8-8.

There are other field types that you can add as meta data to the shape to make the map easier to read and to provide actionable information. For example, add Date/Time information or KPI data such as Person Responsible to the shape.

Use Apply to render the strategy map in the Strategy Map Editor. Use this option to check the design and functionality as you work.

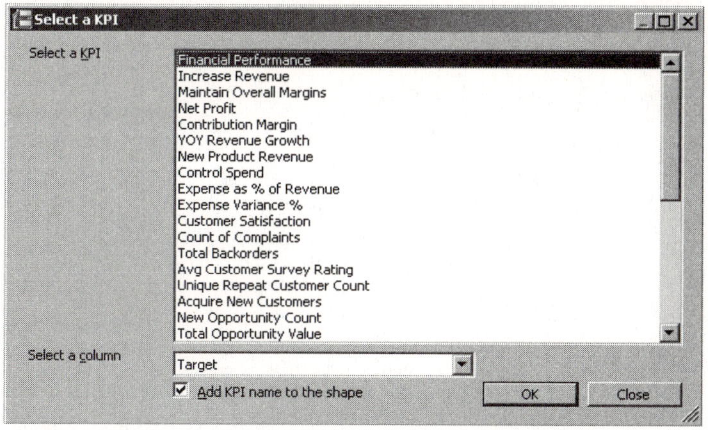

Figure 8-7 Attach KPIs to shapes in the Strategy Map Editor.

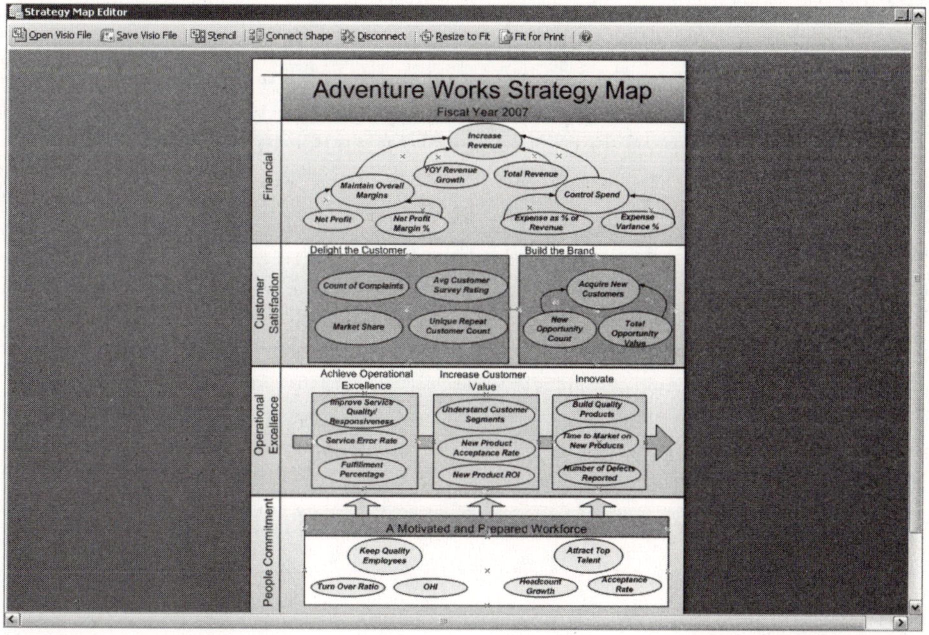

Figure 8-8 For clarity, add the KPI name to the shape.

Step 6: Publish the Strategy Map

After creating the strategy map, publish the map to the PerformancePoint Monitoring Server with the single-click Publish option. When you publish the strategy map from the local workspace to the server, the map is made available to all users who have access to the server and appropriate permissions for viewing reports on the server. The strategy map will appear in the Reports list in the Details pane of Dashboard Designer.

Step 7: Add the Strategy Map to the Dashboard

Finally, drag and drop the strategy map report from the Reports list in the Details pane to its place on the dashboard. Remember that you can configure reports with filters before deploying the dashboard. Connecting filters to reports is another way of providing highly targeted and relevant information on the dashboard.

Excel Services

With PerformancePoint and Excel Services, you can include references to existing spreadsheet reports on your deployed dashboard. Excel Services is part of Microsoft Office SharePoint Server 2007 and is used to extend the capabilities of Microsoft Office Excel 2007 by allowing broad sharing of spreadsheets. This is a good option to use if your community of business users has already been using spreadsheets to monitor and analyze performance and if they are experienced with Excel as a reporting and analysis tool. You can leverage existing spreadsheets and user experience into a monitoring and analytics solution that centralizes information and enhances business value by placing the spreadsheets in the context of dashboards with additional and targeted business information.

With Dashboard Designer, you create a data source using Excel Services, which then allows you to publish Excel spreadsheets to dashboards on a SharePoint site. Excel Services must be enabled on the SharePoint instance in order to use this feature for reports. The image in Figure 8-9 shows a Document Library with Excel spreadsheets ready for use as reports in dashboards deployed on the SharePoint site.

Step 1: Publish Excel Spreadsheets to SharePoint

To start, identify and collect the spreadsheets you will need as reports and publish the spreadsheets to the Document Library on the SharePoint site, where they will be displayed as reports in dashboards.

Step 2: Create a New Report

In Dashboard Designer, select to create a new report using the Excel Services template. Specify a name for the Excel Services Report and a location for the default display folder. The location information is optional.

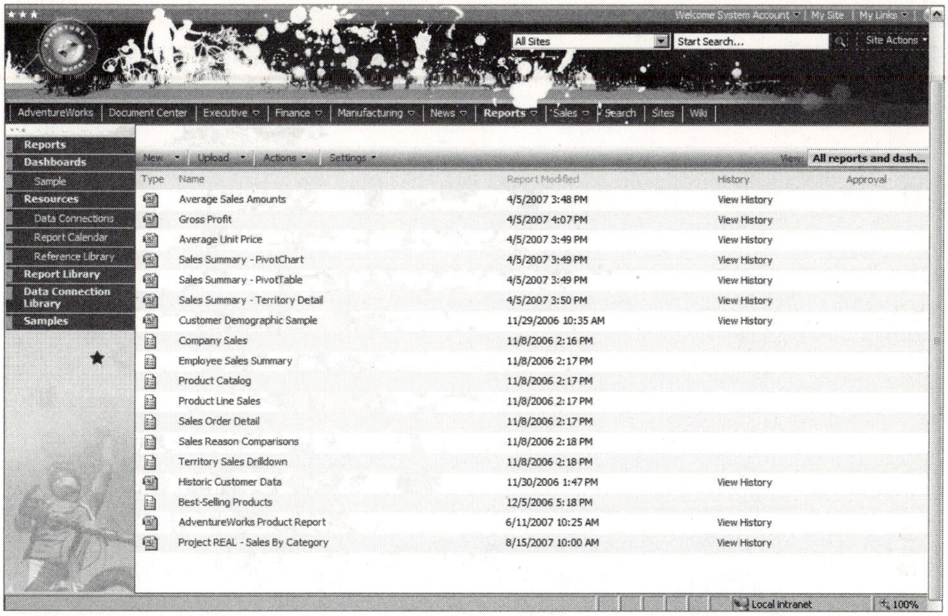

Figure 8-9 Spreadsheets in the Document Library can be displayed as reports on the dashboard.

Step 3: Link to the SharePoint Site

In the Report Settings, link to the SharePoint site by pointing the URL to the appropriate location, and then select the Document Library and Excel Workbook you want to display on the finished dashboard (see Figure 8-10). At this point, you can use View to preview the report.

Step 4: Publish the Report

Using the single-click option, publish the report. The spreadsheet will appear as a report in the Workspace list of items available for use in the dashboard.

Step 5: Add the Report to the Dashboard

Place the spreadsheet report on the dashboard where you want it to appear when the dashboard is deployed. In the example shown in Figure 8-11, the spreadsheet appears at the top right.

Notice that the spreadsheet report is interactive, and users may drill down into the report for detailed information. Spreadsheet reports can also display pie charts and other chart types if these are included in the original spreadsheet (see Figure 8-12).

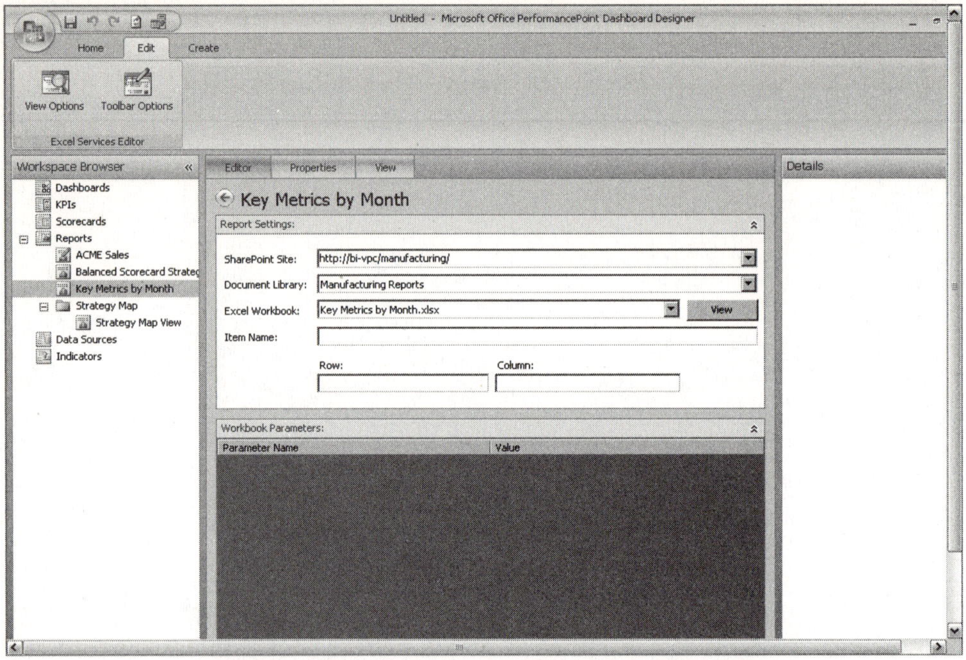

Figure 8-10 Link to the SharePoint site and select the workbook for the dashboard.

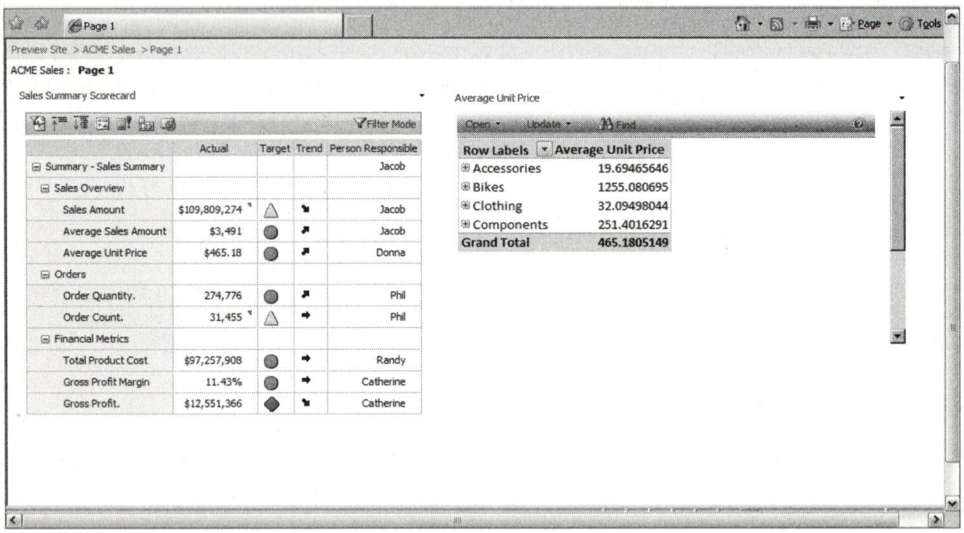

Figure 8-11 Excel Services report in Sales dashboard

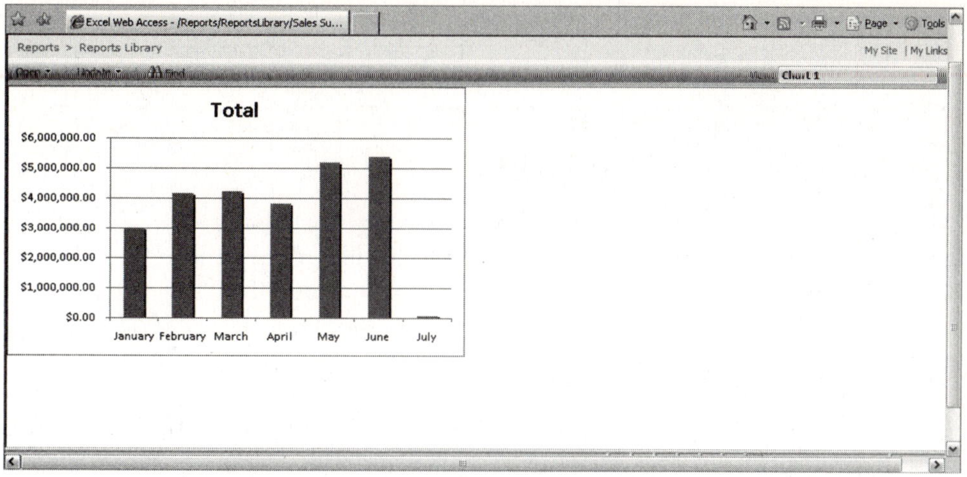

Figure 8-12 Excel Services reports can display charts as well as spreadsheet data.

Reporting Services

With PerformancePoint, you can include references to existing SQL Server 2005 Reporting Services reports on your deployed dashboard. This is a good option to use if you have an existing library of Reporting Services reports already in use by your business community. As with Excel spreadsheets, you can leverage existing reports and user experience into a monitoring and analytics solution that centralizes information and enhances business value by placing the reports in the context of dashboards with additional and targeted business information.

Reporting Services reports can be created with a Reporting Services tool such as Visual Studio. The RDL, or Report Definition Language, files are then published to a SharePoint site where they can be integrated into deployed dashboards.

To use this report option, Reporting Services must be installed in the background. SharePoint acts as the repository, while Reporting Services is the engine operating behind the scenes that determines what data to render and how to render that data. The following steps outline the process of integrating Reporting Services reports into a dashboard.

Step 1: Publish RDL Files to SharePoint

To start, identify and collect the Reporting Service reports you will need. You can choose to run the reports directly from Reporting Services or from the

Document Library on the SharePoint site. If you will be running the reports from the Document Library, publish the RDL files to the Document Library on the SharePoint site, where they will be displayed as reports in dashboards.

Step 2: Create a New Report

In Dashboard Designer, select to create a new report using the SQL Server Report template. Specify a name for the SQL Server report and a location for the default display folder. The location information is optional.

Step 3: Link to the SharePoint Site

In the Report Settings, link to the SharePoint site by pointing the URL to the appropriate location. Configure the Server mode, which allows two ways of managing and deploying reports. Use SharePoint Integrated server mode if the reports are stored in the SharePoint Document Library. Use Report Center if the reports will remain in Reporting Services. Point to the appropriate location of the Reporting Services instance, and to the location and name of the report.

Step 4: Publish the Report

Using the single-click option, publish the report. The Reporting Services report will appear as a report in the Workspace list of items available for use in the dashboard.

Step 5: Add the Report to the Dashboard

Place the Reporting Services report on the dashboard where you want it to appear when the dashboard is deployed. In the example shown in Figure 8-13, the Reporting Service report appears on top.

The Reporting Services report deployed to the dashboard is also interactive, and users may drill down into the report for detailed information.

Trend Charts

With trend charts, you can look forward and backward to examine future growth or past performance. These types of reports are useful for answering questions such as:

- How many units did we sell last quarter?
- How many units can we expect to sell next quarter?

- How much revenue did we generate in the past 3 years?
- How much revenue can we expect to generate in the next 3 years?

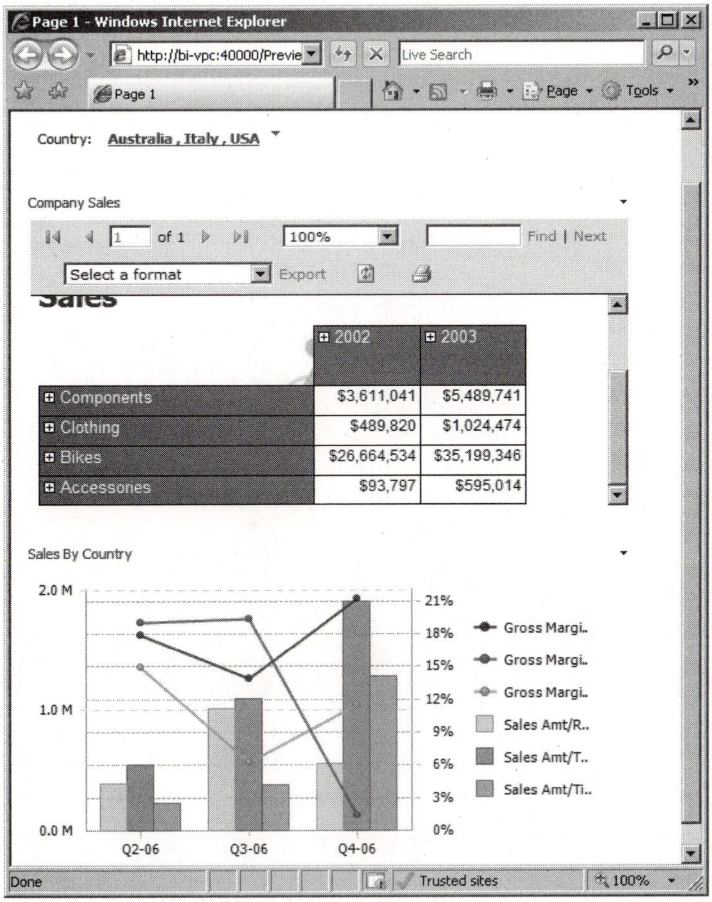

Figure 8-13 Reporting Services report integrated into a dashboard

With trend charts, you can predict future growth based on the key performance indicators you are tracking in your scorecard. For example, a sales organization might create a scorecard to track unit sales by quarter and then create a trend chart to predict unit sales for Q3 2009 based on unit sales for the prior two quarters. The organization may also create a trend chart to view past performance and see how unit sales have performed over time from Q1 2007 to Q4 2007.

Whether they look forward or backward, trend charts make use of scorecard KPIs (see Figure 8-14). In fact, in Dashboard Designer you must connect the scorecard to the trend chart to create trend lines. If you are creating a trend chart to measure past performance, the scorecard KPIs provide historical data to the Time Series Data Mining algorithm in SQL Server Analysis Services 2005, which then creates predictions and forecasts based on the data. Since trend charts use this algorithm, a SQL Server 2005 Analysis Services (SSAS) Server must be available, and this must be the Enterprise Edition version.

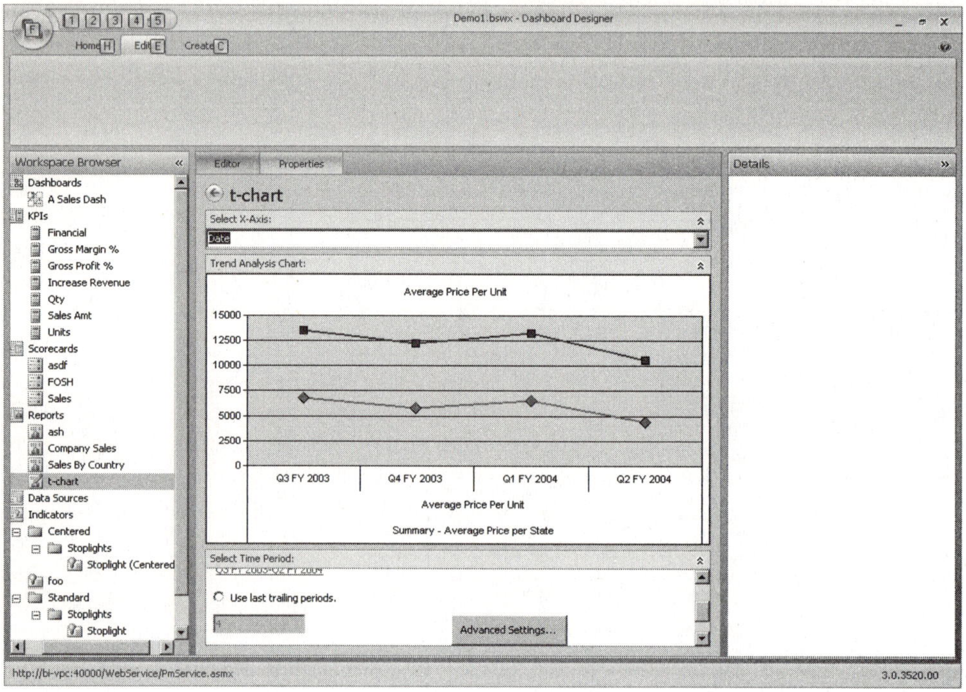

Figure 8-14 Trend charts can display past or future performance.

Step 1: Enable DataMining in Analysis Services

Begin in Analysis Services by enabling the AllowSessionMiningModels property on DataMining. By default this value is set to false so you simply need to set it to true. Enabling the AllowSessionMiningModels property allows external applications to invoke the Data Mining Model.

Step 2: Configure Server Options in Dashboard Designer

In Dashboard Designer, configure the Server options to specify the name of the Analysis Services instance with AllowSessionMiningModels enabled. Use the Connect option in Dashboard Designer to the specify host name.

Step 3: Create New Report

In Dashboard Designer, select the option to create a new report using the Trend Analysis Chart template. Specify a name for the trend analysis chart and a location for the default display folder. The location information is optional.

Step 4: Select a Scorecard and KPI

Select the Scorecard you want to use as a basis for the trend chart, then select the KPI from the scorecard. This is the KPI that the trend chart will produce and display trends for.

Step 5: Set Report Properties

The report appears in Dashboard Designer, where you can set properties (see Figure 8-15). Trend lines appear for every target specified on the KPI.

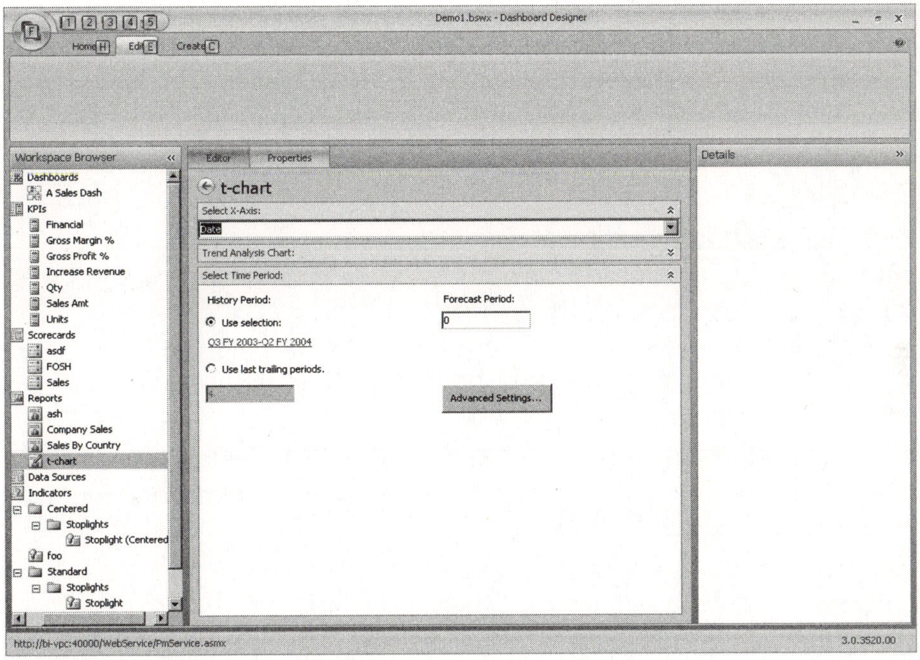

Figure 8-15 Set properties for the trend chart.

Specify the time period, including the History Period and the Forecast Period. Use the default selection or include additional trailing periods. Note that the Forecast Period is based on the time period in the report. If the report is a quarterly report with 2 as the Forecast Period, the report will forecast the next two quarters.

Step 6: Publish the Report

Using the single-click option, publish the trend chart report. The trend chart report will appear as a report in the Workspace list of items available for use in the dashboard.

Step 7: Add the Report to the Dashboard

Place the trend chart report on the dashboard where you want it to appear when the dashboard is deployed.

Best Practices for Reports

- **Keep reports simple.** Don't force business users to wade through reams of irrelevant information.
- **Launch reports from a metric online.** Users should have the ability to generate ad hoc reports from a given metric they are viewing online so that if a metric looks interesting, they can run the report on the spot.
- **Use filters.** Create targeted relevant reports that complement the information on the scorecard.
- **Leverage existing reports.** If you're just starting on monitoring and analytics, find out what reports your users are currently using and build on these existing resources. If you find existing Excel spreadsheet reports or Reporting Services reports, leverage the business value of these existing reports by placing them in dashboards with scorecards and other reports.
- **Remember the goal of reports.** Reports should allow business users to go from metrics on the scorecard directly to relevant information that supports analysis and action.

Summary

This chapter explored the use of reports in PerformancePoint and provided examples of different types of reports that can be added to dashboards, including strategy maps, Excel Services and Reporting Services reports and trend charts.

The chapter provided a general overview of the types of questions that reports are typically used to answer as well as practical information and best practices for designing and creating effective reports.

With this general overview and best practice information, you should now be ready to begin creating and adding reports to your dashboards to enhance the overall effectiveness of your performance management solution.

Notes

1. Bruno Azziza and Joey Fitts, *Drive Business Performance: Enabling a Culture of Intelligent Execution* (Wiley, 2008).

CHAPTER

9

Implementing Security Controls

PerformancePoint Monitoring Server supports four levels of content security: data source, SharePoint Server, application level, and item level. Security surrounding SharePoint content or the data itself is managed within each specific application. For example, if you wanted to secure a portion of your cube data to select users, you would restrict access using Analysis Services 2005 itself. If you wanted to restrict access to the Document Library where dashboards reside, you would configure that security in SharePoint Server. Application-level and item-level security are managed within Monitoring Server itself, which is the focus of this chapter.

NOTE **This chapter focuses on authorization, or what permission a user has to view specific content. Monitoring Server authentication methods are discussed in Chapter 3. Authentication methods determine how users connect to Monitoring Server and individual data sources, for example by using the current user or a computer account.**

Application-Level Security

PerformancePoint Monitoring Server allows you to assign Windows Active Directory users or groups to roles, granting them specific application-level permissions within Monitoring Server. Monitoring Server supports four roles:

- **Admin.** Users assigned this role have full control over Monitoring Server, including create, edit, publish, and delete permissions for all types of content. Users assigned this role can grant both application and item permissions to other users. And members of the local administrator group on the server hosting a Monitoring Server instance are automatically assigned to this role. (Note that these users do not appear in the Dashboard Designer permissions dialog box.)

- **Creator.** Users assigned this role have permissions to create, edit, and publish all content except data sources. The author of a new item is automatically assigned to the item-level Editor role.
- **Data Source Manager.** Users assigned this role have permissions to create, edit, and publish data sources only. The author of a new item is automatically assigned to the item-level Editor role.
- **Power Reader.** Users assigned this role can view all items in the Monitoring Server database. Generally, service accounts or services that need full access to the system should be the only users assigned this role.

NOTE An item can be deleted only if the user is a member of either the Admin role or a member of both the Creator role and the Editor role for that item.

To assign users to roles, first you connect to Monitoring Server from the Server Options dialog box. Open this dialog box by clicking the Application button in the upper-left corner of Dashboard Designer and selecting Options (see Figure 9-1).

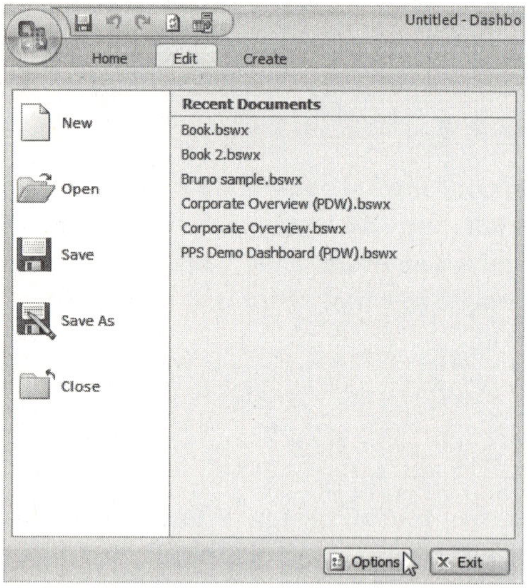

Figure 9-1 Opening the Server Options dialog box

On the Server tab of the Options dialog box, click the Connect button, as shown in Figure 9-2. (The Server name must be properly formatted, using the syntax shown in Figure 9-2.) This will allow you to manage server options, such as caching timeouts, comments, and permissions.

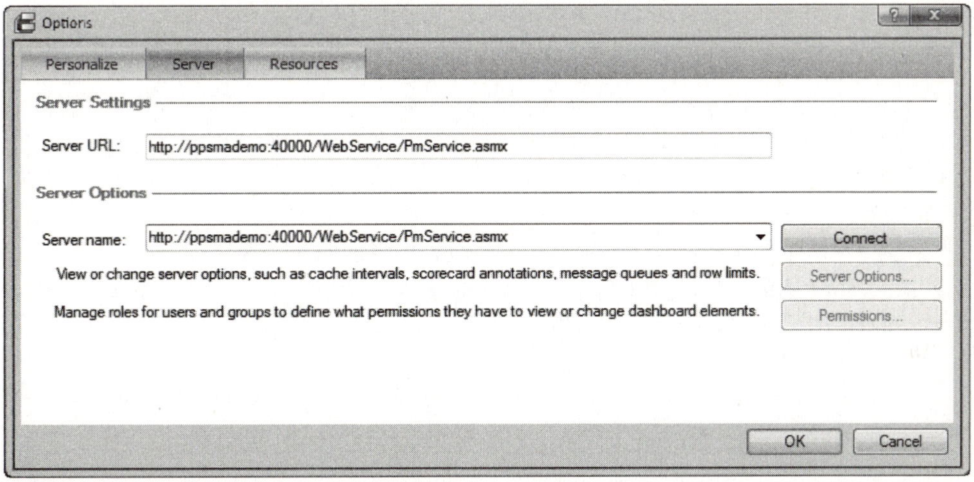

Figure 9-2 Connecting to Monitoring Server

On the Permissions dialog box, add users to roles by clicking the Add button and providing a valid Active Directory user or group. Then, click the drop-down box to assign the identified user to an application role. Figure 9-3 shows a group of users assigned roles for Monitoring Server.

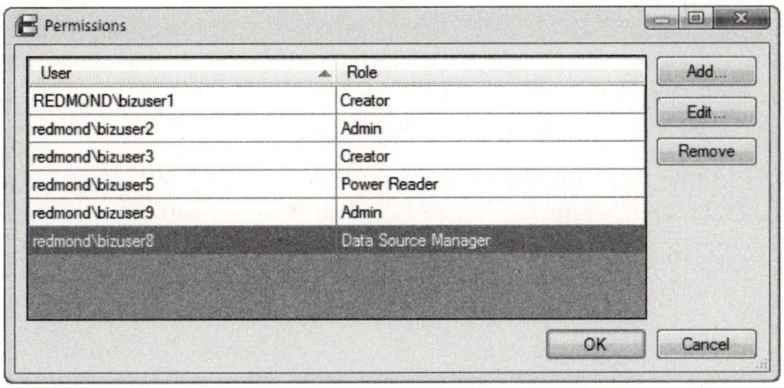

Figure 9-3 Users assigned roles for Monitoring Server

Item-Level Security

Item-level security is applied to the individual items within Dashboard Designer, including dashboards, reports, scorecards, KPIs, indicators, and data sources. This level of security supports two roles:

- **Editor.** Users assigned this role can view, edit, publish, and delete the item. The user creating the item is automatically assigned the Editor role, assuming that they are also a member of the application-level Admin, Creator, or Data Source Manager role for Monitoring Server.
- **Reader.** Users assigned this role can view the item.

NOTE Be cautious when assigning users to the Editor role for a data source. Editors have the ability to change the connection string, which could open access to other network resources.

To assign users item-level roles, display the item in the Dashboard Designer workspace and click the Properties tab, as shown in Figure 9-4.

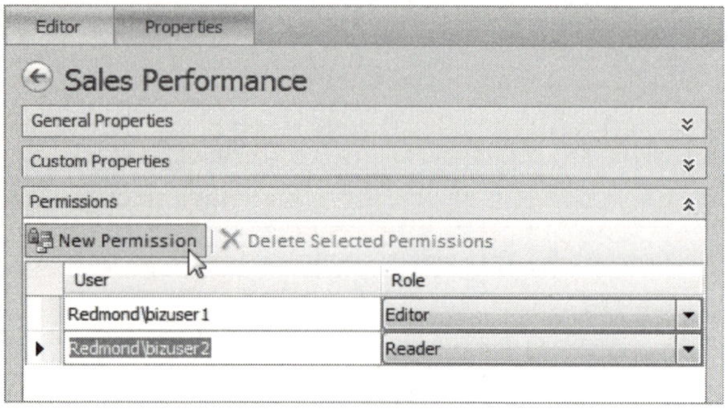

Figure 9-4 The Properties tab of a scorecard

Under Permissions, click New Permission and then type a user or group using the Domain\User Name format. Then, click the drop-down box to the right of the name to assign Editor or Reader permission, as shown in Figure 9-5.

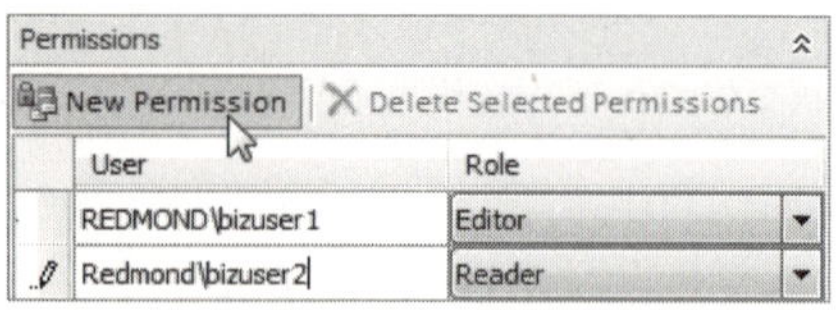

Figure 9-5 Assigning Editor and Reader permissions

Publish the item to Monitoring Server for the permissions to take effect.

NOTE **If non-Admin users aren't assigned either Editor or Reader permission to a particular item, they won't see the item in Dashboard Designer. If non-Admin users are assigned Reader permission only, they will be able to make local changes to the item. However, they will not be able to publish the item back to Monitoring Server.**

As you assign permissions to items, it is important to note that users must have Reader or Editor permission for all items that compose the final dashboard. If a user is not an Editor or Reader for all the items in a dashboard, he or she will not be able to see the complete dashboard in SharePoint Server. The items that need to be secured include any data sources, indicators, KPIs, scorecards, reports, and even the dashboard itself.

Depending on the item type, you may see different behavior if you do not have permissions to it. For example, if you don't have permissions for the data source, you will receive an error when you open the published dashboard. If you don't have permissions for a KPI, the scorecard will be displayed in the published dashboard, but only the KPI name will be shown. No data values, indicators, or scores for the KPI will display. If you don't have permission for the dashboard, you will receive an error message indicating that the dashboard is unavailable.

NOTE **Item-level permissions are only one possible cause of error conditions in published dashboards. You may receive similar errors if you don't have access at the data source or SharePoint Server level as well.**

As you configure application-level and item-level security, consider the following:

- Application-level security generally applies to system administrators and content creators who work in Dashboard Designer. Item-level security generally applies to content creators and dashboard consumers.
- Users do not need to be a member of any application-level role in order to modify and consume content. Users who have been automatically or explicitly granted permissions using item-level security will have Editor or Reader access to those items.
- Only users who are either administrators or members of both the Creator and item-level Editor roles of a specific item can delete it.
- Security applied in SharePoint or on any dependent data source can affect the visibility of data in Monitoring Server. Make sure that you do not overlook these settings in favor of checking the application- or item-specific security.

- With the navigation capabilities available in analytic reports, users may have access to all data in the cube, not just the data available in the original report. Ensure that you have appropriate cube security if this is a concern in your organization.

Summary

This chapter outlined the security options available in PerformancePoint Server at the application level and the item level. It explained the roles at each level and the permissions granted those roles. As you work with PerformancePoint Server security, it is important to note that this chapter captured only a small part of the larger security infrastructure involved in server deployments. These concepts should be incorporated into the overall security strategy and technologies for your organization and systems.

Part

III

PerformancePoint Planning

A critical component of performance management is the ability to properly model and act upon the data of the business being managed. The management activities may be the reporting of actual results such as monthly management reporting, weekly operational flash reporting, or financial results consolidation, or the activities may focus on future performance such as strategic planning, operational budgeting, or sales forecasting. The next several chapters describe the broad feature set of PerformancePoint Server 2007's Planning functionality and how it is applied to the critical business components of performance management. First, though, it's important to outline the key concepts and terminology.

Business Planning

Business planning is the activity of preparing a view into the future. Typically, there are two major objectives in establishing a plan. The first is to outline controls and constraints on what activities are to occur. This is typically the purpose of budgeting. For example, an annual travel budget is established to constrain the money to be spent on travel expenses for an entire year. Within the limits that are set, activities occur, accumulate, and are measured against the amount that was approved to be spent. The second major objective of planning is to best approximate expected occurrences. For example, a sales forecast is designed to provide insight into future revenue. This could be used for purposes such as to provide marketing input on possible promotions or to provide manufacturing input on future product demand. A more recent planning activity that many companies are now engaging in is strategic planning. The objective of a strategic plan is to organize efforts around major activities or investments that are broad in nature and have long-term outcomes. For example, a strategic plan around manufacturing defect reduction may involve activities focused on supplier quality, employee training, and investment in new equipment. Over years, these activities ideally deliver results from the strategic initiatives. In any business, the key to establishing great plans is to understand the fundamental drivers for results and the behaviors that influence them. PerformancePoint Server 2007 is an ideal application solution for modeling these drivers, evaluating behavioral impact, and producing effective plans.

Reporting

Reporting is the activity of presenting data and information to consumers who likely need this information to make decisions, perform actions, or communicate to others. On the surface, reporting would seem like a straightforward task: present the information to users. However, in practice this can prove an extraordinarily difficult task. Data may not be easily accessible, and even when it is, it may have come from different places, making it difficult to put together in a meaningful way. System data and information may not be organized in the way that business users want to think about the data. For example, customer information stored in a system may not be identified by the sales account manager, which might be necessary for a sales opportunity report. Even after information is gathered and defined in a way that makes sense for its business purpose, end users have particular usage requirements. They might want visualizations that make key indicators easily visible or the ability to flag anomalies in an intuitive manner. They might also want to be able to "slice and dice" the information to prepare specific variations on the views that were initially presented. Often, business data ends up in Microsoft Excel for manipulation and presentation. Many of the features of PerformancePoint Planning Server were designed specifically to enable the desired business scenarios of reporting and data visualization.

Consolidation

Consolidation is the activity of putting data together. There are three primary types of consolidation that fit well within the solution objectives of PerformancePoint Server 2007 Planning. The first type of consolidation is the simple aggregation or summarization of data. Imagine 200 departments planning operating expenses for the coming year. That data is summarized into 20 business units, which are summarized into 5 major divisions. Finally, they are added up to a company-wide, consolidated total. The second consolidation type is a management consolidation. This could be used for budgets but may also applied to actual results. In a management consolidation, additional financial operations are performed to present a complete view to management, typically in the form of balance sheets, income statements, cash flow statements, and the like. In these types of consolidations, the process might address things such as multiple reporting currencies, the allocation of overhead costs to operating units, and the elimination of internal transactions between operating units. The final type of consolidation targets legal and statutory reporting. This type of consolidation extends the concepts used in management consolidation but is constrained and guided by regulations such as U.S. Generally Accepted Accounting Principles (GAAP) and International Financial Reporting Standards (IFRS). One section of these regulations specifies how legal entities are to report income and earnings from subsidiaries that are not wholly owned. Many of the regulations vary by geography, and local consolidation requirements may differ from corporate consolidation requirements. PerformancePoint Server 2007 includes a powerful consolidation engine and configurable algorithms with which corporations can define and perform any type of consolidation, based on how they organize, manage, and report their business.

Value Proposition

Planning, reporting, and consolidation are the high-level solution categories where PerformancePoint Planning Server can play a key role. Before drilling into the core capabilities that allow corporations to develop and deliver solutions with PerformancePoint Server, it is helpful to outline some of the advantages it provides that will become evident through the customer solution–focused features discussed later.

Flexibility within a Framework

Microsoft Excel is the most commonly used business data tool today. For example, two-thirds of budgeting is performed in Microsoft Excel,[1] and a large portion of work that is prepared in other tools ends up in Excel and PowerPoint for reporting and visualization. While this is a testament to the flexibility and power of Excel as a tool, many companies struggle to maintain consistency and reliability in their processes. From a business perspective, information workers operating in Excel are putting knowledge and analysis into their spreadsheets, but that does not easily get shared with others. Take, for example, a business unit's multi-year revenue forecast. Generally, this document includes a number of years of historical data that is extracted and prepared, often by a single individual, in a way that aligns with revenue channels expected in the future. Excel is a powerful tool to copy, paste, and move data around so that the forecast template looks proper for the multi-year forecast. However, that activity usually cannot be repeated by other individuals and is very error-prone. What PerformancePoint Planning Server brings to companies is the ability to continue to have a business user perform this type of translation activity but do it with a tool that captures the definitions on a central server. Not only will this make processes more repeatable and eliminate errors, but it also adds key information infrastructure components for auditing, security, and definition sharing.

Microsoft Office and Excel User Environment

Recognizing the ubiquity of Microsoft Excel in the corporate business environment, PerformancePoint Planning Server maintains this environment as the end-user experience for its application solution. This keeps users in a familiar environment where they already understand how to do many operations such as copying and pasting, and creating formulas to link cells together. From a PerformancePoint perspective, end-user training will involve only the added layer it places on top of Excel. PerformancePoint Server 2007 extends the corporate user investment in Microsoft Excel and Microsoft Office

Microsoft BI Solution Platform

PerformancePoint Server is built on top of the Microsoft Business Intelligence (BI) platform. First and foremost, it is a huge advantage to have a consistent core platform. Second, the platform has an established record of proven scalability, reliability, and competitive price performance. Finally, the underlying platform is critical to extension and integration scenarios. The Microsoft BI platform has a well-established infrastructure to support, for example, scenarios like multi-platform data integration and enterprise-wide reporting.

This section outlines high-level business scenarios to which PerformancePoint Server is targeted and provides an overview of the key values of the offering. The scenarios should be familiar, as they've remained largely unsolved or inadequately solved for the past 20 years. In the next section, PerformancePoint Planning Server features will be described in detail in terms of functionality and its application towards addressing critical business problems.

CHAPTER

10

Planning Overview

PerformancePoint Server 2007's Planning component has a couple of key top-level concepts that should be evaluated early in the solution design phase. Over time, changes can be made to evolve an application; however, the upfront considerations are still important. This chapter introduces the Planning components of PerformancePoint Server 2007. In order to provide a proper understanding of the target users of components of the applications, the roles of the intended users are outlined. The overall application flow is then defined, followed by more detail on each component of the application: clients and server. A summary description of items such as applications, model sites, and the Calendar is provided at the end of the chapter.

Product Overview

PerformancePoint Server 2007 is a Web Service–based, three-tier application. The application is built upon well-proven Microsoft technologies, including Microsoft SQL Server, the .NET Framework, SharePoint, and Excel. Before getting into the specifics of the components for the server, service layer, and clients, we will go through an overview of the personas of expected users of various aspects of the system.

Personas

The best way to discuss the roles of the major players involved in Performance-Point Planning Server solution development and operation is to describe the key personas. These personas are generalized representations of the individuals commonly found in organizations and descriptions of the roles they play in performance management activities.

The Business Analyst

The first and most critical persona to profile is the business analyst. This is the role that most deeply understands the function of the business and is tasked with the activities that occur around performance management. When the vice president of sales sees a forecast report that shows that umbrella sales in Seattle will not meet target levels, it is this analyst whom she contacts to understand whether it is due to production supply problems, distribution challenges, competition, or an unusually dry weather forecast for the region. The expectation is that the analyst is in tune with the operational aspects of the business and either has the answer or knows how to find the cause and evaluate whether any action can be taken. The analyst is in tune with the key drivers of the business.

The Input Contributor

The primary end user of a PerformancePoint Planning Server application solution will be the input contributor. This persona encompasses the operational user who is either submitting data to or reading data from the application. This user typically performs the tasks within a combination of Microsoft Office and job-related transactional systems. For example, a salesperson will likely be working in some type of customer relationship management (CRM) system where he will track customers and opportunities. Opportunity data will usually be exported, copied, or keyed over to an Excel spreadsheet where he will build out his next quarter forecast. Once that spreadsheet model is completed, the salesperson will email that spreadsheet to the regional sales manager, who may adjust it and forward it to higher-level management for consolidation with other regions to produce a groupwide total that makes up a portion of the corporate sales forecast.

The Dangerously Technical and Business Savvy

There is a persona that is commonly found but often doesn't have an explicitly defined role or job requirements. This persona is a hybrid who combines both business understanding and technical skills. Sometimes, this is a business analyst with built-up Information Technology (IT) skills. Other times, this will be someone with an IT background who has spent significant time working with and learning the business functions he or she supports. Whatever the route to acquire them, the skills these individuals have are highly valuable and, today, essential to functional success of planning, budgeting, and reporting projects.

The IT Administrator

The Information Technology (IT) Administrator is a role focused on infrastructure maintenance, security, and supportability. The primary objective of the IT Administrator is to support an operational system for the end customers, who are the business user. The IT Administrators' core skills are very technical, for example knowing how to properly backup a Microsoft SQL Server database, and often do not include a very deep understanding of the business they support or the data they maintain.

Application Cycle

These personas encapsulate the primary roles involved with a PerformancePoint Planning application. The manner and timing in which they participate will be driven by the specifics of the business process being facilitated. For purposes of introduction to the components of the application, take the following as just one example of these personas interacting with a system.

Tracing through the process outlined in Figure 10-1, the business analyst begins with defining the dimensional structures and how they participate in models. This activity is perhaps the most critical (and is described concretely in Chapter 11) as the models that are defined will serve as both the enabler and constrainer of application function at execution time. The definitions specified by the business modeler are stored in SQL Server in PerformancePoint Server's meta data format. Consistency is maintained along these steps by logic contained in the business type library. Chapter 11 will cover the business type library in depth; for now, it can be described as a set of rules that business models adhere to in order to ensure proper handling of everything from data summarization to conversion of foreign currencies.

Once the models have been defined, PerformancePoint server deploys them in the environment. This step translates the definition that was created into a physical structure in Analysis Services with each model becoming a cube (see Figure 10-1).

After deployment has occurred and the models exist as cubes, the PerformancePoint Add-In for Excel is utilized to design both reports and data entry forms for the models. Because the models are translated into cubes, any Unified Dimensional Model (UDM)–compliant client can now access that cube structure, assuming that the client user has read permission. PerformancePoint Monitoring and Analytics and Excel pivot tables are common examples of UDM clients that are effectively used with these models.

The final two steps in this abbreviated overview of the application cycle manage the data flow into and out of the application. PerformancePoint Server provides capabilities for defining and managing system processes for loading data into an application in either a one-time or, more commonly, a recurrent process. Finally, in planning applications where new budget or forecast data is being captured, it is often a requirement that this new data be moved into other line-of-business systems to manage the tracking of the actual against the plan. This is accomplished through export functionality, which is all covered under the subject of data integration in Chapter 13.

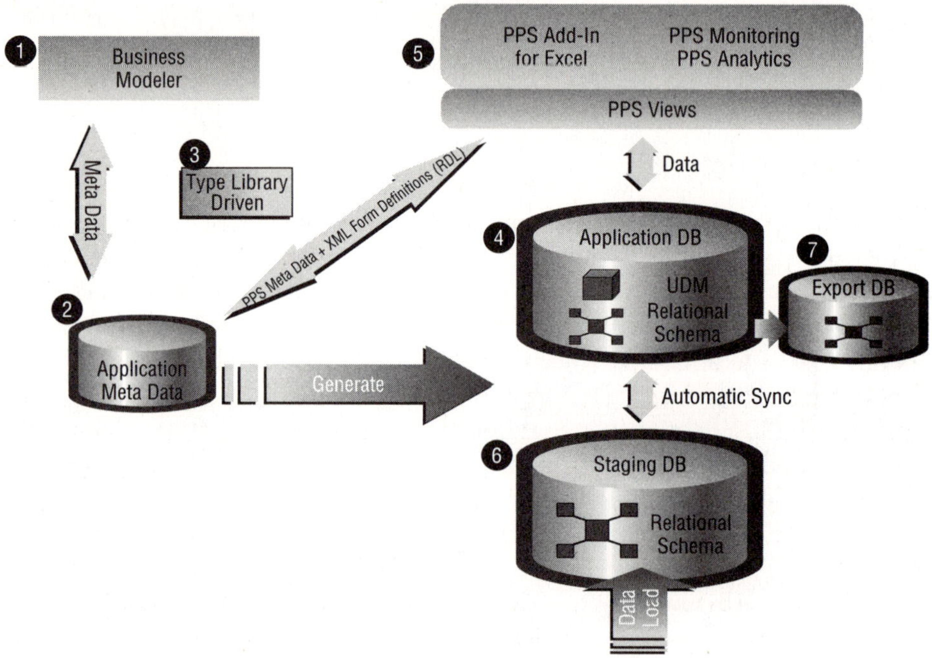

Figure 10-1 PerformancePoint Server Planning application process flow

System Architecture

PerformancePoint Planning Server is a three-tier, Web Service–based architecture. There are client components targeted at different user personas interacting with an application. Those clients communicate via Web Services to a front-end server that handles the majority of logic execution and behavior. A back-end server works with the SQL Server data platform to manage and process an application's data.

Clients

PerformancePoint Server Planning contains three client interfaces to the application, targeted at the user personas who interact with different parts of the application. All three clients are built on top of a set of common client services to enable consistency and ease maintenance of the product. On top of these services, three distinct interfaces are provided to the specific usage requirements of the different applications users. For the end business user, the input contributor, the client is a Microsoft Excel Add-In. For the business analyst who creates and manages the solution, the Business Modeler provides a standalone client interface. Finally, for the IT Administrator there is a Web-based interface to set and change system configuration (see Figure 10-2).

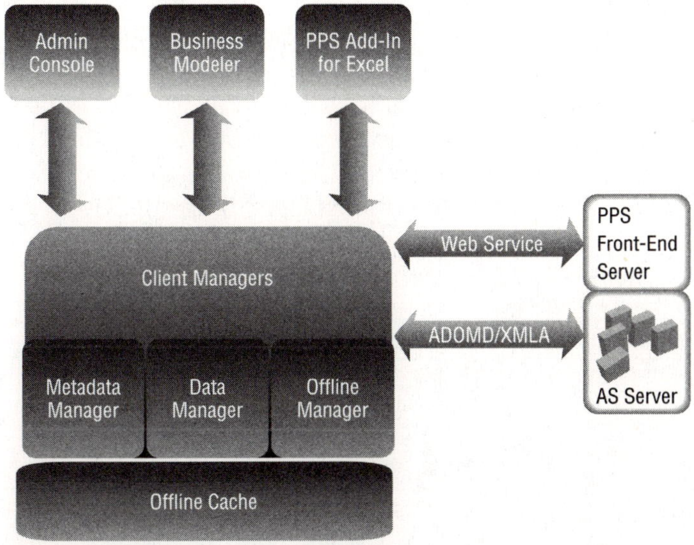

Figure 10-2 Component architecture

These are three different clients, but they all use the same client manager infrastructure and, therefore, they use the same set of server programming interfaces to communicate.

Web Services

PerformancePoint Server provides its client-to-server communications over the Microsoft .NET Framework's Web Services. Web Services provide a Web-based transfer protocol for data and instructions to be transmitted back and forth between the client and the server.

Server

PerformancePoint Server Planning consists of two distinct server components. There is a back-end server, which handles most of the "heavy work" done by the application. A front-end server handles the network interface to clients via the Web Services architecture. These two components work together to provide the complete application functionality. Both the front-end server and the back-end server may be scaled out to support large deployments (see the "Deployment" section in Chapter 17).

Front-End Server

The front-end component of the PerformancePoint Planning Server is an Internet server–based application that handles all communication with the client components. It translates incoming messages and invokes the proper internal procedures to translate the data and perform the necessary action. Security is verified at all incoming stages and, in addition to validating user security, the front-end manager validates user actions. For example, an end user may be able to read data but not execute jobs. This execution permission check is handled in the front-end server components (see Figure 10-3).

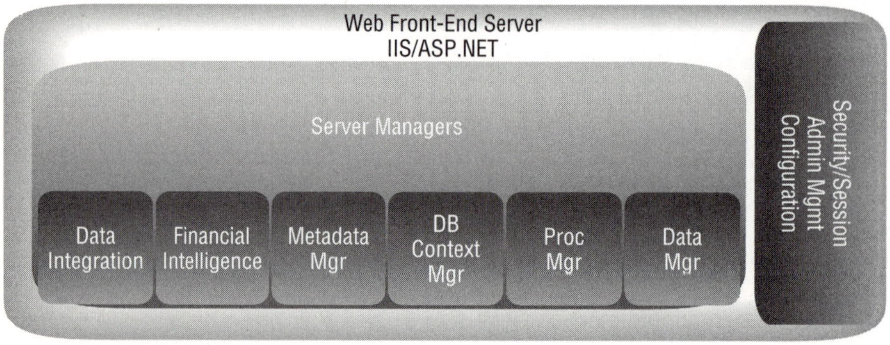

Figure 10-3 Front-end server architecture

Back-End Server

The back-end server provides the core service functionality that performs most of the actions in the application. It's logically divided into several key areas that encapsulate similar behavior. The two major roles are data management and process management. Additional functionality is provided to support other operations such as security and calculations.

Data Manager

The Data Manager handles things related to processing of data within an application. There are two primary data generation functions that it encapsulates. First is the capture and processing of data entry from a client — for example, when a user enters budget data and submits it to the server. The Data Manager takes each individual data submission, performs validation and security checks and, if it is valid, posts it to the model. Data validation entails checks to make sure that the correct data was entered. For example, if budget information is being collected, the Data Manager will ensure that only budget data was written. A security check is also performed to ensure that, for example, a user who entered budget data for department "A101" has write permissions to that department. Additionally, the Data Manager handles the capture of textual annotations that may have been submitted along with the numeric data. Finally, the Data Manager is responsible for triggering a cube process at a given interval but does it in an intelligent way by knowing which data has changed and reprocessing only cubes for which the data has been updated.

Process Manager

The Process Manager is responsible for the process flow control within the application. Processing revolves around the two general categories of data submission and calculations or jobs. For data submission cycles, the Process Manager controls the generation and state of actions assigned to individual end users. For example, if a forecast process involving a set of individuals is defined to begin on January 1, the Process Manager will handle the occurrence of this event, set up the end users' tasks, send notification email if requested, and set the system to understand that data writeback may now occur. Similarly, with calculations or jobs, the Process Manager handles any scheduled execution as well as user-triggered execution. The Process Manager works in conjunction with the Security Manager in these activity/execution tasks to ensure that only users with sufficient permissions may perform actions.

Security and Administration

Security and Administration covers many of the underlying configuration of the application behavior in addition to determining the security functions. Security ensures and validates a three-part set of items: user validity, role membership, and data security (a detailed explanation of security is found in Chapter 15). Application configuration settings are managed through the same back-end server interfaces. These settings control application timing behaviors like process intervals (see the definition of "process intervals" that follows), audit and logging settings, and application properties such as database names.

Most of these configurations are set up once by an IT administrator and rarely change throughout the production cycles of an application.

Other Services

Other services include a set of services that support different function parts of the application. These include services for meta data, financial calculations, data management, and server control.

Metadata Manager

The Metadata Manager covers much of the design-time construction and management of application objects and is the primary interaction point for the Business Modeler client. It is responsible for ensuring that the creation and maintenance of all the application's objects are done in a consistent manner and adhere to built-in dependency rules. For example, it will ensure that each dimension item is uniquely defined and identifiable (Chapter 11 describes the objects and behavior for meta data operations). It also ensures that the internal item types are properly applied to drive desired behavior. Nearly all of the definition of an application solution is done through interfaces to the Metadata Manager.

Financial Intelligence

As its name suggests, the Financial Intelligence (FI) Manager performs all tasks specific to the built-in financial behavior of a PerformancePoint Server Planning application (these behaviors are outlined in Chapter 11 and Chapter 12). There is significant interaction with other manager layers, as Financial Intelligence is built on top of meta data, data, and process components.

Data Integration

Similar to the FI Manager, the Data Integration (DI) Manager is a layer on top of other managers that provides the basis for data movement into and out of the application as well as between distinct components within an application (data integration functionality is covered in Chapter 13).

Database Context Manager

The Database (DB) Context Manager simply handles the underlying SQL Server database connectivity within the application. Many of the managers described previously retrieve and submit data to and from the application's SQL Server database, and the DB Context Manager ensures that this is done in a consistent manner that maintains integrity across the application components at all times (see Figure 10-4).

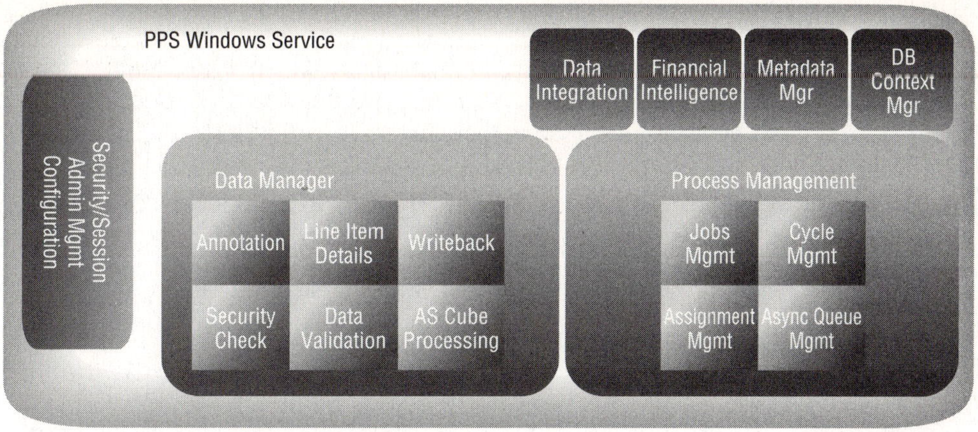

Figure 10-4 Back-end server architecture

Server Processing

Processing in PerformancePoint Server's Planning server is separated into four primary paths, with configuration adjusting the behavior of two of them (process intervals). In order to facilitate some applications that may be high-volume and other applications that may be optimized for reporting of data that won't frequently change, processing is divided between those processes that must execute immediately and those that can be processed on a schedule.

Synchronous and Asynchronous Processing

Many actions requested of the front-end server are executed immediately, synchronously, in the order in which the requests come in. For performance and scaling reasons, however, the back-end server runs off an asynchronous processing queue for better support for activities such as processing high volumes of data and user submissions or long-running jobs. Processing end-user data submissions and executing jobs are actions that could take a significant period of time, depending on the size of the data or complexity of job computations. These processes are always placed into the asynchronous processing queue, and the back-end server's Windows service performs these actions on a schedule. More detailed descriptions are supplied with deployment topologies covered in Chapter 17, but it's important to point out here that the application is designed to enable multiple back-end server asynchronous processors to provide scaling options.

Process Intervals

Process intervals are set and can be changed by IT Administrators. These settings can be configured once or adjusted throughout the lifecycle of an application to achieve desired end-user characteristics within attainable limits of an application, which is driven by things like data volume, usage patterns, and infrastructure hardware. There are two intervals that are used in conjunction to drive overall behavior: Workflow Process and Cube Process.

Workflow Process

The Workflow Process interval controls the frequency at which data change actions are processed by the back-end server. This should also be thought of as the "polling interval" for the asynchronous queue. When the back-end server receives certain types of requests that are predetermined to occur asynchronously, it places requests into the queue to indicate what processing needs to occur. At the Workflow Process interval, the windows service checks to see what, if anything, is in the queue to be processed. It will pick up each item in the order in which it was placed in the queue and execute it. Data submissions and calculation executions are two examples of processes that will be done through the asynchronous queue. Once the processing of the queued tasks is complete, the back-end server will mark the updated models as "dirty" for the Cube Process to execute.

Cube Process

PerformancePoint Planning Server separates processing of the data tasks (Workflow Process) from the reprocessing of the Analysis Services cubes where most client interaction with the data occurs. This second process is called the Cube Process interval. At the designated Cube Process interval, the back-end server will check to see if any Workflow Process has marked any of the models (cubes) as "dirty" and, if so, it will request that Analysis Services reprocess them to update the data. This setting determines how frequently data viewed by end users is updated, which could range from a few seconds to once daily, depending on the application profile and desired end-user behavior.

Data Submission Flow

The Workflow Process and Cube Process intervals are used together to determine the timing of data flowing through an application. The example flow that follows illustrates how this affects an end-user client data submission from the Excel Add-In.

The first step in the data submission process is the entering or changing of data in a data entry form by an end user. When the Excel Add-In opens such a data entry form, it retrieves information from the server about which portion of the data entry form is open for entry as well as what cells the user has write permissions to. The intersection of these two sets of data cells is called the writeable region. When an end user opens a data entry form within the context of an open assignment, the data cells that fall in the writeable region will be shaded to visually indicate what's writeable. As the end user enters data into cells in the data entry form workbook, the Excel Add-In captures each new value in a "changelist," which is stored and managed by the application without the user's knowing it exists. At the time when an end user triggers a save or submit to post updates back to the server, the changelist itself is sent back and stored in the database.

On the back-end server, changes received from clients are not processed immediately; this allows multiple submissions to be entered and processed in batches for performance reasons. At the designated asynchronous processing interval, the back-end server will process the submitted changelist — reverifying that the submitted cells are part of a user's open assignment and that this user has the proper write permissions on the data. Once validation has occurred, the data is placed into the underlying SQL server table for that model (fact table). When the subsequent cube process interval occurs, the updated data will be applied to the Analysis Services cube, which is the source for any queries or reports for the model. Note that there is a period of time, then, between a user's submission action and the time when the cube is updated and the data becomes visible as part of an Excel view or other report. Depending on the setting of the two intervals, this could be a short or very lengthy period. The state of the assignment submission remains "pending" until the entire cycle completes and the cube process occurs to update the data (see Figure 10-5).

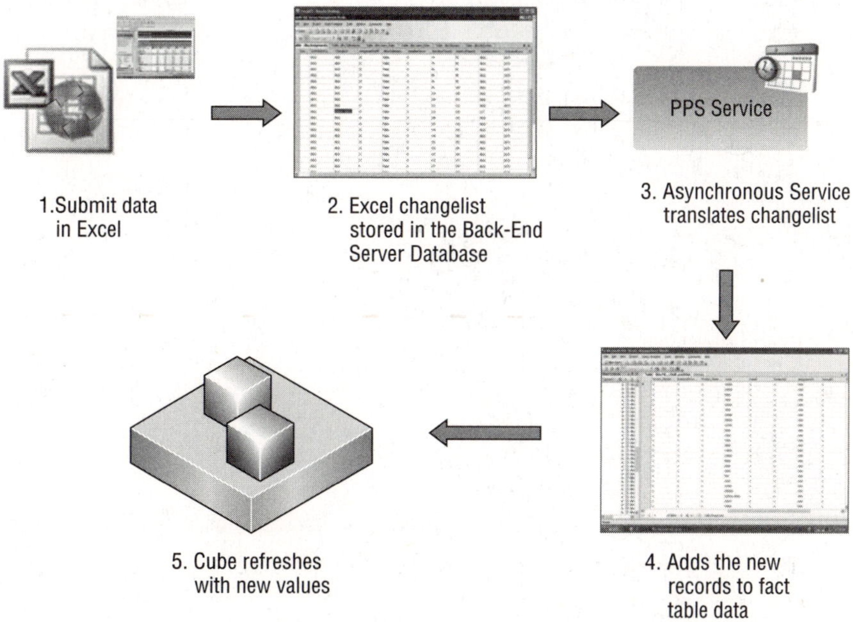

Figure 10-5 Excel data submission process

Due to the potentially long amount of time that may elapse as a change flows through the back-end server processes, it's important to note that the Excel Add-In has logic to support consistency for the user performing the submission. After the submission occurs and the changelist is posted to the back-end server, the client still maintains a copy of that changelist. The client understands the state of the individual assignment and any queries issued to the server will still have the user changelist changes applied to the results. After the entire processing cycle has completed and the server changes the assignment state to either "partial" or "submitted," the client knows that the data changes have been fully applied and will then discard its local copy of the changelist.

Deployment Topology

A PerformancePoint Server Planning application will have many different application deployment topologies, based on several key factors influencing an application profile. Primarily, these factors center around data volumes, user quantity and location, and expected client application behavior. Chapter 17 discusses deployment in more detail, but a basic server deployment topology is shown in Figure 10-6.

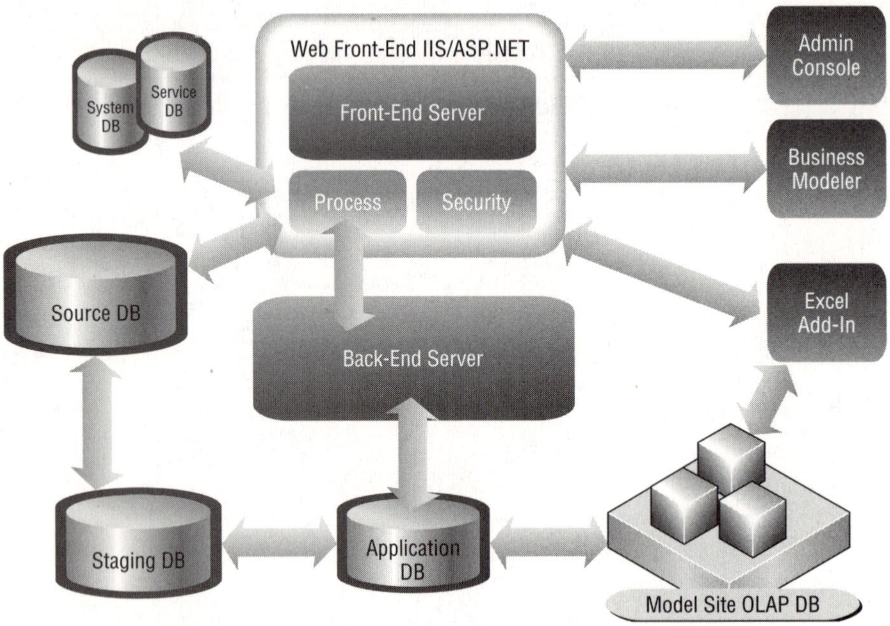

Figure 10-6 PerformancePoint Server Planning deployment topology

Application Concepts

A PerformancePoint Planning Server application is divided into a few high-level sets of objects. Multiple applications are allowed on a server but are distinct and share no meta data. Within a single application, however, the logical grouping of related items, called "sites," segment the pieces of an application. Meta data from sites can be shared within the application to allow for joint use of common definitions. The top-level container for a solution is an application.

Applications

An application could be departmentally focused such as a supply-chain planning application, or it could be company-wide, containing multiple functions such as human resources (HR) planning, supply-chain planning, and financial reporting all within a single application. If a broader application approach is chosen, the functional division can be separated by second-tier objects called model sites. Additional sites can be added to an application over time, allowing it to grow as the usage of the application spreads.

In the example that follows, the application for ACME Corporation is divided into three model sites. There is one site for the overall corporate parts of the application and separate sites for each of its two major divisions: Sales and Services. In the beginning, only Corporate is required to be defined and the Sales and Services divisional subsites can be created at any subsequent time. This allows the application to scale out to more departments or lines of business as it makes sense to do so (see Figure 10-7).

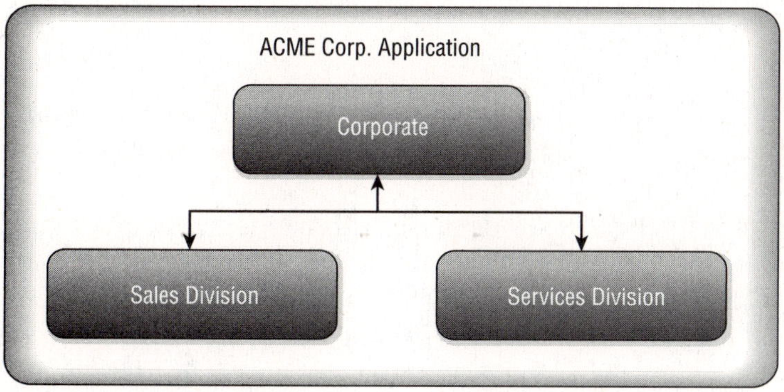

Figure 10-7 Application structure for ACME Corporation

Model Sites

Model sites represent a logical functional grouping of items within a single PerformancePoint Server Planning application. Each model site represents a component of the overall application problem space and contains all the objects necessary for an application. The process and data structures for which the solution is being developed may be contained in a single site and shared with or extended in other subsites.

In Figure 10-8, a definition of the major structural objects (Dimensions and Models) is represented for the Corporate, or top-level model site. At the Corporate site level, the dimensions Account, Entity, Scenario, Time, and Product Family are defined. From those dimensions, Forecast, Pricing, and Consolidated models are built (dimensions and models are described in Chapter 11).

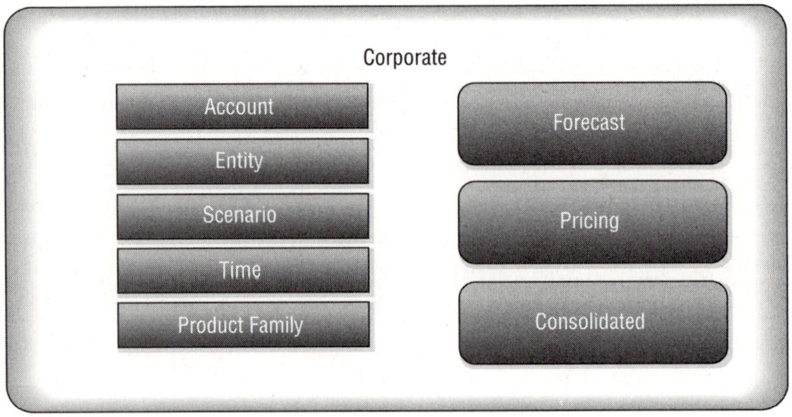

Figure 10-8 Corporate site objects

However, as you saw in the previous diagram, the application contains three model sites, with Sales and Services subsites below Corporate. This is depicted in Figure 10-9.

The business conducted by the Sales and Services divisions is fundamentally different, with the sales division focused on selling products and the services delivering fee-based value to clients. Instead of performing forecasting (as this example focuses on) for these three different businesses with three different applications, each can have its own, distinct model site in which to define its unique structures and business process.

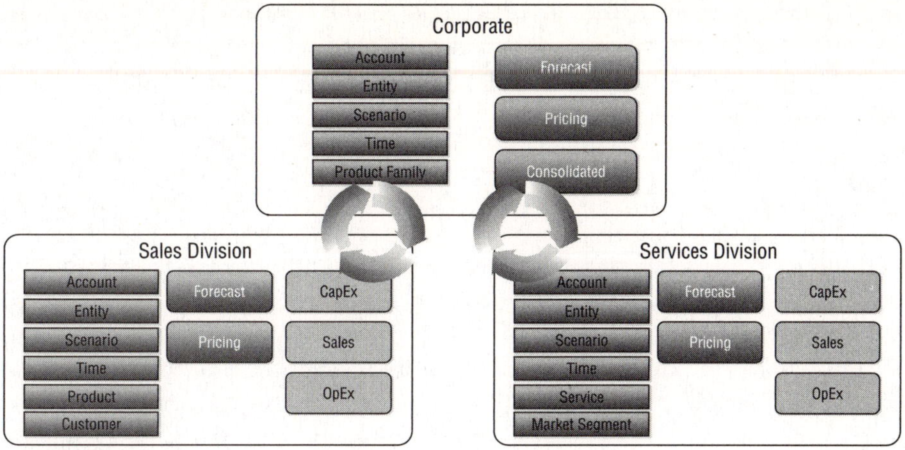

Figure 10-9 Multi-site object structure and flow

Model Site Considerations

Model sites are a mechanism to allow flexibility in an application solution. In the next several chapters, the pieces of a solution (such as dimensions, models, users, cycles, and so on) are covered in more detail. Model sites may share structural objects like dimensions and models, but each model site has its own set of definitions. This allows each site to operate nearly independently with respect to users, data cycles, and reporting. The primary consideration for model sites centers around what the necessary business segmentation is. A common example is HR data. Generally, HR information is highly sensitive, so isolating it in its own model site ensures a different security model than the other sites and tight restrictions can be applied. Additionally, model sites are good for separating distinct business process. A manufacturing division may operate on a very different planning cycle from the sales division. Separate model sites allow easy segmentation of the overall company processes and provide full control to each division to schedule and drive its process on its own schedule. Finally, the underlying infrastructure may be controlled and deployed separately for each model site. This may be employed for geographic distribution or data segmentation to use model sites as a way to distinguish separate data or user regions.

Application Calendar

The application calendar defines the structure for time in the application. This definition is applied once early in the application process and cannot be changed (but can be extended). Because the definition of the calendar is a one-time operation, it should be one of the first steps performed. The application calendar has a couple of key components: the duration it spans and the views of the calendar.

Time Setup

In Performance Point Planning Server, calendar creation is done through a Calendar Wizard. This wizard is surfaced in the Dimensions section of the Business Modeler user interface. The Calendar Wizard provides assistance in making decisions about how to slice time appropriately, from a corporate perspective. Most companies base all their operations on some form of a fiscal calendar. The wizard helps to translate that into terms the application will use for handling data and business processes. There are two primary determining factors for setting up the calendar: the end of the year and the views.

Setting the year's end first determines the starting point from which to build a calendar. Some companies end their year on December 31; others on June 30; still others on September 30. Through the wizard, any day of the year may be set as the end of the calendar year to accommodate existing business definition. Once a year-end is determined, the critical decision is the pattern that the calendar follows. Simple months, matching a Gregorian calendar, are the default. However, many organizations follow one of the built-in fiscal groupings of weeks to months. These patterns are 4-4-5, 5-4-4, and 4-5-4, representing the number of weeks in each month over a 3-month repeating pattern. For example, by choosing a 4-4-5 definition, the calendar will have 4 full weeks in the first and second months, and 5 full weeks in the third month. This pattern repeats to create a full year of 12 months that adhere to the pattern. One additional prebuilt pattern is available: a 13-month calendar where each month is divided into 4 weeks. Once the choice has been made as to how to divide the calendar into appropriate months, the number of years is specified to set the span of the calendar. A calendar will always contain the current year (as defined by the year-end chosen) but may optionally be extended to support historic years and/or future years. For example, if two years of historic data are used in a planning process, the calendar can be defined to go back two years in history to support that data. A planning process looks into the future, so generally one or two future years are required to capture that data. Note that future years may be added to the calendar after its initial creation, but historic years must be set at the beginning and may not be changed.

Calendar Views

A calendar is always based on days. The definition process previously described determines how those days roll up into weeks, months, quarters, and years. However, many business processes are not based on daily data. For example, monthly financial reporting is done using data aggregated at the month level. Calendar views allow multiple definitions of the components of an application calendar that can be used in different modeling activities. For example, a calendar view can be created showing only the month, quarter, and year for the monthly reporting activities. Alongside this process, another calendar view showing the week, month, quarter, and year can be created for a weekly revenue forecast process. Multiple calendar views for a single application provide the agility to have the appropriate time view in the appropriate part of the application. Calendar views are defined in the wizard at creation time, but more views on the calendar may be defined later as well.

Summary

PerformancePoint Server contains several components that work together to provide a complete application solution. Client interfaces targeted towards different user personas, business modeler, and Excel contributor are the primary end-user interaction points. A front-end server handles communication and data traffic with the clients, while the back-end server offloads heavy processing for performance and scalability. An application is the highest-level container of objects and contains a single definition of time through the calendar definition. Each application is divided into model sites, depending on the proper logical grouping of business data and processes for the application. In the next chapter, further detail is provided on the objects defined in the application and model sites.

Notes

1. David A. J. Axson, "Best Practices in Planning and Management Reporting," *Best Practices in Planning and Performance Management: From Data to Decisions (Wiley Best Practices)* (Wiley, 2007).

CHAPTER

11

Application Components

This chapter describes the major objects that, when combined, drive the structure and function of a PerformancePoint Server Planning application solution. The foundation for structures and behavior is the Business Application Type Library. With the Business Application Type Library, structural building blocks called *dimensions* are created. These dimensions range from simple built-in lists to complex, highly structured, and cross-referenced sets of items. On top of dimensions, there are two types of structures called membersets and memberset views. Finally, dimensions are combined into models, where again the Business Application Type Library guides function and behavior. This chapter covers these objects in depth for both system-defined and user-defined elements. First, it's necessary to provide an overview of logical business modeling.

Business Application Type Library

The PerformancePoint Server Planning Business Application Type Library is a patented technology that supports the development and maintenance of application content, the structure and processes needed to provide a business solution. The library consists of core object types, which are exposed as choices to model designers. The application's behavior is determined by the specific type choices. This allows the configuration of the application's behavior simply through the selection of various types.

Many of the type-driven behaviors in a PerformancePoint Server Planning application are designed to support financial-related behaviors. For example, suborganizations, or entities, within a corporation may trade goods and services with each other. For proper accounting of the company's overall performance, these types of intercompany transactions must be eliminated. These elimination rules are included in an application via the Business Application Type Library. It is during the configuration of items in the Entity dimension where type choices, for example "Legal" and "Management," determine whether elimination calculations can be performed for those entities. This is just one of numerous examples where the Business Application Type Library surfaces behavior and configuration through type settings.

Object Types

All objects in a PerformancePoint Server Planning application have system support through the Business Application Type Library. Some of the objects are exposed to users, whereas others remain behind the scenes.

The primary object type that users interact with is the built-in dimensions. These are dimension like Account, Currency, Entity, Scenario, Business Process, and Flow. Each of these dimensions is described later in the chapter. Additionally, Time is exposed as a dimension. The internal application calendar (described in Chapter 10) is a core part of the type system and drives how the Time dimension is built and maintained. For example, a calendar choice of a 4-4-5 pattern is predefined in the type library, and simply by choosing this option, the layout of the Time dimension is created. Again, the day on which the calendar starts is always specified and from there internal system logic based on the type library understands how to build up the application calendar.

In addition to dimension types, another primary user-visible component is the model type. There are just a few model types, but each one has a type library–driven configuration both about structure and rules. Generic type models, for example, require that only Time and Scenario dimensions be used. Any other dimensions are a design choice based on the purpose of the model. Time and Scenario are required because internal validation processes and data entry cycles are defined by Time and Scenario. The type library system ensures that these two dimensions exist in every model in order to facilitate data collection.

The other broadly visible type of object within the application is the business rule. In the case of rules, the type library system drives execution behavior. For example, Allocation is a type of rule available. Multiple allocation rules may be grouped together, but other, incompatible, types cannot be grouped with them. At rule group–execution time, the type-consistency ensures the successful execution of the set of similarly typed rules. This is a prime example of how the type choices drive the runtime behavior of an application solution.

Type Behavior and Interaction

There are numerous examples of how the typing of objects within the Business Application Type Library drives application behavior. Many type choices should be considered as configuration options, as they are used to direct built-in application behavior and avoid any user programming of application functionality. Thus far, the examples covered have been about how the entity type drives intercompany rule behavior, how the application calendar drives Time dimension logic, and how model types specify required dimensions. The following sections cover dimensions and models in greater detail and provide many more examples of how the Business Application Type Library is exposed for configuration and how that drives certain behaviors for each application.

Dimensions

The artful part of a PerformancePoint Planning application solution is the construction of models. Determining the proper structures and relationships can be done in many different ways. These choices drive user experience and performance, so careful consideration is essential.

Dimensional Modeling

This is not traditional data modeling that you might find in an IT application. Rather, it is the logical modeling of a business — the content and relationships by which analysts or other consumers are able to evaluate and interpret data, feeding their decision-making process. Today, this is commonly done in Microsoft Excel. Business or operational analysts add rows, columns, and data to spreadsheets to communicate a message, report a result, and influence decisions. These results are often historical in nature to explain why things have happened, or they may be forward-looking projections to communicate possible future positions, good or bad. All business data is influenced by some set of drivers, and those may or may not be captured in the Excel model. Some drivers may be captured in other models and linked values or formulas may drive the interaction between Excel spreadsheet models.

The critical concept, then, is to mentally transform the rows-and-columns concept that is very familiar in Microsoft Excel into a logical dimensional model. This can be difficult and, because logical models are the keys to application behavior and user interaction, logical modeling is a critical activity and the choices made have lasting effects. Some of the difficulty with logical modeling arises because business users are very familiar with what looks like a two-dimensional model in Excel. Even three or four dimensions can easily be masked as a two-dimensional view.

The left side of Figure 11-11 shows the Excel representation of a model that has products (clothing in this case) in the rows, scenarios (Actual and Budget) in the columns, and time (January through March) as tabbed sheets in a workbook. The fourth dimensional element is the category, Revenue, which is simply specified as a title on top of the data being shown. Within the two-dimensional (rows and columns) space of Excel, a four-dimensional business model is represented. Decomposing this representation, shown on the right side of Figure 11-1, begins to help in visualizing the dimension of time by layering the different pages on top of each other.

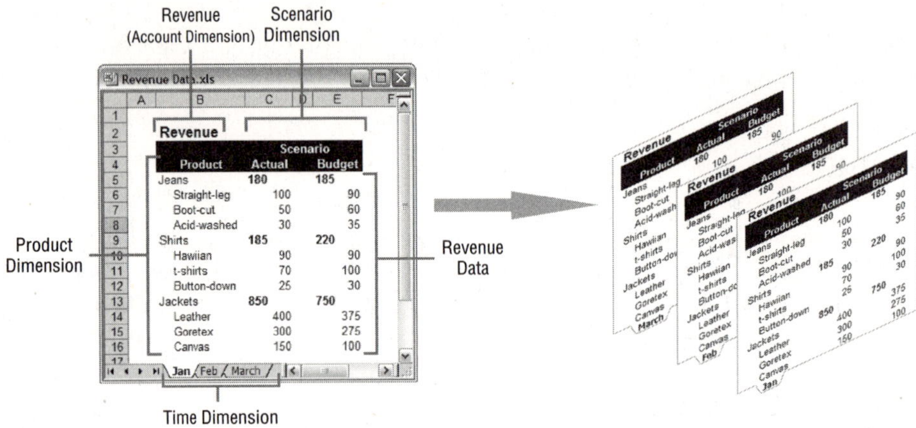

Figure 11-1 Spreadsheet broken down into component dimensions

Figure 11-2, demonstrates how, when the time dimension is layered, a three-dimensional representation appears in the form of a cube.

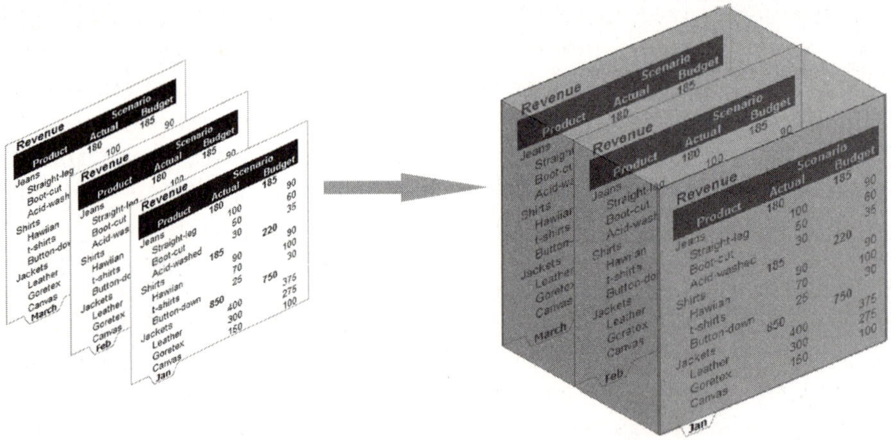

Figure 11-2 Layers the spreadsheets put together into a cube

Finally, in Figure 11-3, time becomes the z-axis represented in the stacking of Excel worksheets, and the x- and y-axes represent the product lines and scenarios, respectively. The Excel spreadsheet concepts have disappeared completely, and the simple logical model is represented in a three-dimensional cube.

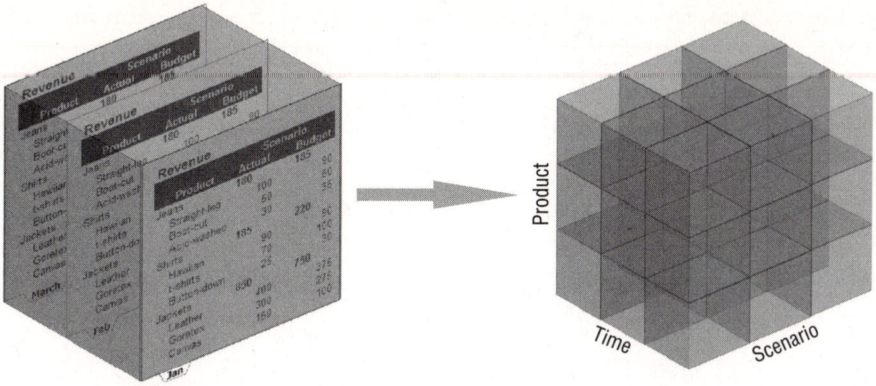

Figure 11-3 Abstraction from the cube into a multidimensional model

In most business models, however, there are more than three dimensions. In the previous simple example, additional dimensions such as customer, sales channel, and geographic region may be added to provide a more actionable logical representation of business operation and structure. Visualizing more than three dimensions becomes difficult, and getting comfortable working with multidimensional design may take time and practice. PerformancePoint Server 2007 Planning makes constructing and using these models easy and straightforward, but it may be necessary to work with some examples early in the design phase to become confident with the logical models created and to ensure they support the proper solution the application aims to provide.

Dimension Overview

As is apparent from the overview of dimensional modeling, dimensions themselves are the key building blocks of a PerformancePoint Server Planning application. Dimensions are the structures that contain the items that will be modeled, displayed, calculated, and secured. A dimension itself can be thought of as a simple list. Each item must have a label and name. The label must be unique within the application and serves as the "key" by which that item will be referenced throughout the application (such as in a calculation). The name need not be unique and can be a friendlier reference to an item. Description is an optional field that can contain a much lengthier textual description of the item. In many cases, there is no need to have a different name and label. However, when you're loading items into a dimension from an external system, these two fields can be very useful. Often, line-of-business systems contain their own key value, which is not a friendly name recognizable by end users. In that case, the label may be the alphanumeric source value and the name can be a more recognizable text representation. Aside from label, name, and description, there may be other attributes assigned to members of a dimension.

Attributes

Attributes are properties that get set for each member or item of a dimension. For system-defined dimensions such as Account or Entity, there are system-defined attributes, which are a requirement of that particular dimension. For any dimension, additional attributes may be added. Attributes can be text, numeric, and Boolean (true/false). Attributes may also be references to members of another dimension. The earlier example where, for the Entity dimension, each member has a property associating it with a base currency is an example where this attribute references members in the Currency dimension.

Membersets

Membersets offer significant functionality on top of dimensions and are the objects that enable true flexibility within a single application. Membersets exist within the context of a dimension and provide both a filter and a hierarchy of parent-child relationships among members. Multiple membersets can be created on each dimension containing completely disjointed sets of members or completely different parent-child relationships. This ensures that among a single set of items, for example Accounts, all parts of the application will be able to access just the items needed and in the proper structure. Take for example Figure 11-4, which shows a very simplified chart of accounts useful for financial reporting or budgeting.

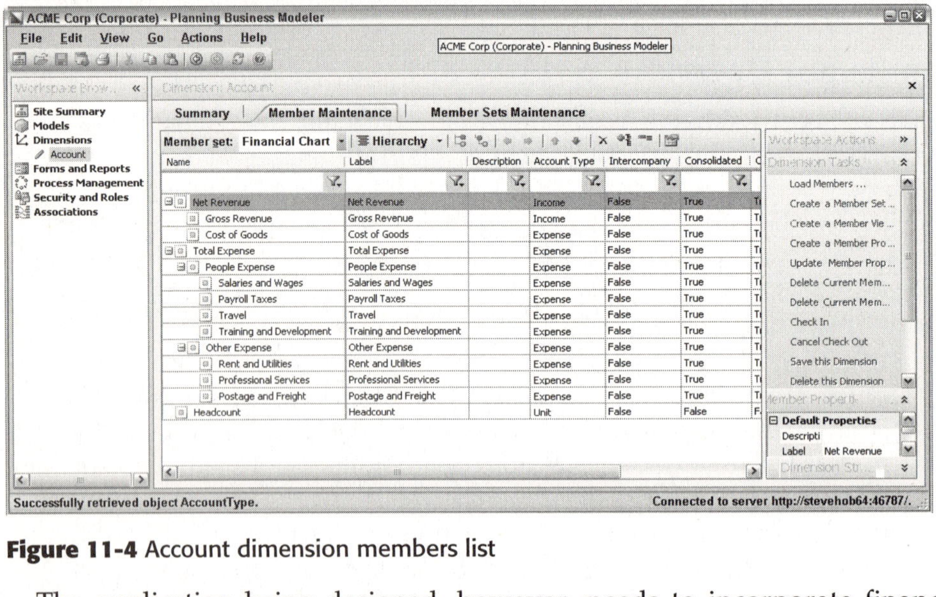

Figure 11-4 Account dimension members list

The application being designed, however, needs to incorporate financial budgeting and sales forecasting. Instead of creating another account dimension with different items and structure, the sales-related items (Units Sold, Unit

Sales Price, and Unit Cost) are simply added to the bottom of the list of members in the Account dimension, as shown in Figure 11-5.

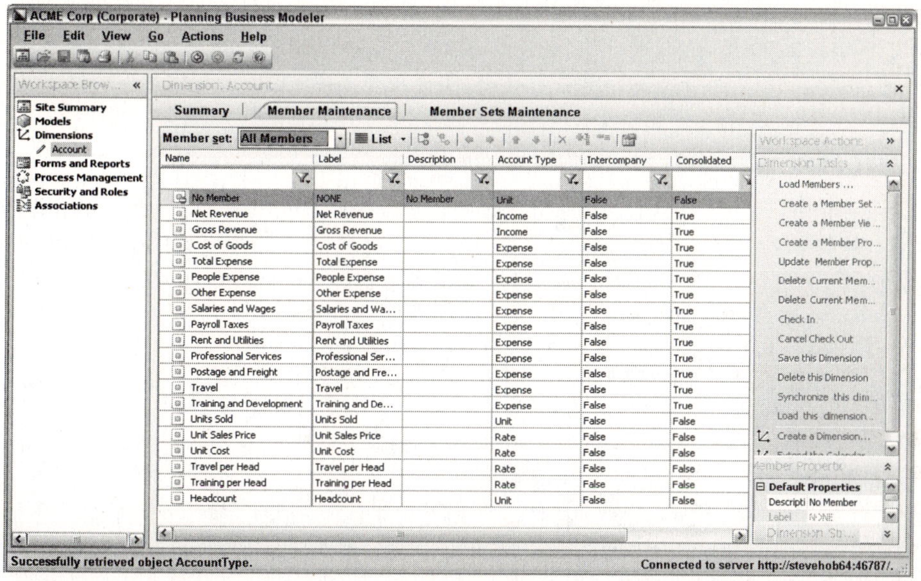

Figure 11-5 Account dimension with sales members included

By the definition of membersets, these Account member items can be filtered and divided into two completely separate membersets, as shown in Figure 11-6, which are usable independently in the appropriate sales and financial models (see the "Model Dimensions" section later in this chapter).

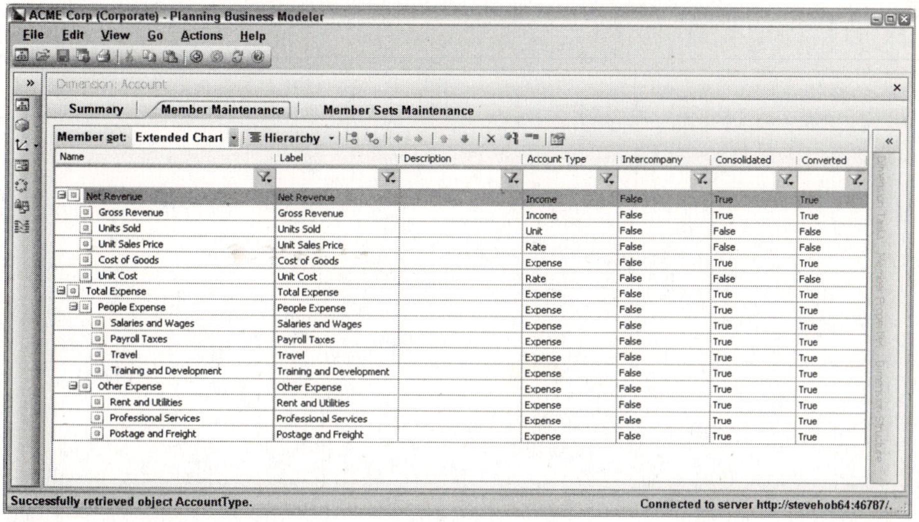

Figure 11-6 Sales and Financial membersets built from the single Account dimension

This example shows the power of membersets to be independently defined and used for distinct purposes, but at the same time they remain within a single application context and share items in common, avoiding the development of any duplication across usages. These membersets are strict parent-child relationships, but for reporting purposes additional rollups might be necessary. For this purpose, memberset views may also be added.

Memberset Views

Attribute-based views are defined on top of dimensions and membersets to support different rollup structures from the strict parent-child membersets. Memberset views are commonly used for cases where several reporting attributes have been defined and a reporting view of those attributes is required. Take, for example, a typical Products dimension, which might have attributes added to denote categorizations like color, weight, size, and so on. Additionally, products within the organization are grouped by Product Family, Product Line, Division, and so on. A memberset view is created by simply specifying in which order the items are grouped. In Figure 11-7, products are grouped by family, line, and division; to provide a useful reporting rollup structure for viewing data differently from a parent-child memberset which has been created.

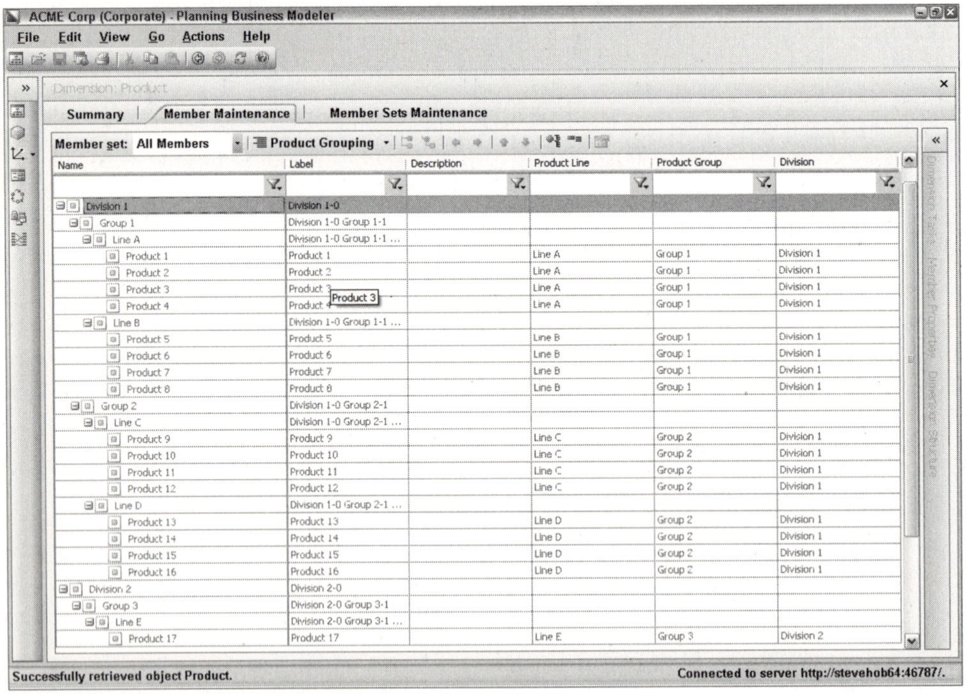

Figure 11-7 Memberset view of a sample Products dimension

Having looked at dimensions in general as well as the attributes, membersets, and memberset views layered on top of them, the following section will look at specific dimensions and their characteristics.

System-Defined Dimensions

There are several built-in dimensions in a PerformancePoint Server Planning application. The two most critical dimensions to understand are the Account and Entity dimensions — particularly if the solution will involve any financially oriented behavior.

Account

The built-in Account dimension is self-evident in a financial solution involving any corporate or subsidiary account ledger. However, it should really be thought of as the "Line Item" dimension and is used in most modeling whether financial or not. The primary reason for this is the built-in aggregation behavior for the Account dimension. This allows such behaviors as having debits and credits both be "positive" numbers, but having the aggregation perform the correct subtraction of debits from credits, as shown in Figure 11-8.

Gross Revenue	(credit)	$ 1,000.00
Cost of Goods	(debit)	$ 650.00
Net Revenue		**$ 350.00**

Figure 11-8 Example of proper Account aggregation

Even in the case of items that are not financially oriented, this behavior is still desirable. For example, unit quantities and ratios should not be aggregated with other values. With the proper Account Type assignment for each item, PerformancePoint Server Planning will correctly determine summary values for all types based on the determined parent-child relationships. The Account Type aggregation behavior is provided for any Financial model type, which may encourage the use of financial models in some non-financial scenarios.

Setting the appropriate Account Type property not only drives correct aggregation behavior but also facilitates proper handling of financial rules (covered in Chapter 12). These are exposed through subtype attributes such as Consolidated, Converted, and Intercompany. For example, an Account Type of LT Asset (long-term asset) is treated differently from Expense when it comes to management and legal consolidated financial reporting. An asset account is treated as a balance sheet account, which means that in a financial model, the proper opening and closing balances will be managed across the flow. Further, built-in logic knows that the year-to-date (YTD) value will be the recent balance.

Currency

The Currency dimension simply contains the list of currencies that will be known inside the application. It is not necessary for an application to use the Currency dimension, but it is required to execute built-in currency conversion logic. The currency display property allows for a specific display string, which can be surfaced in reporting. For example, U.S. dollars may be defined as "USD" with a display property like "US $."

Entity

The Entity dimension contains properties focused around financial scenarios and data integrity. For example, currency conversion scenarios involve capturing data for a "base" currency and then translating that to other currency values based on foreign exchange rates. The Entity dimension is where the currency base is determined and controlled. From that basis, PerformancePoint Server Planning has logic to ensure system integrity — such as preventing users from submitting new data in any currency other than the base currency. For financial consolidation operations, the Entity dimension is treated as the consolidation level. For example, if you are performing intercompany reconciliations, it will be done between Entities participating in a model. The entity type drives a given entity's participation in financial processes through subtypes. For example, a Management entity type will have "Intercompany" set to "True," as this type of entity will participate in intercompany transactions that may be reconciled and eliminated through business rules. Both Legal and Management entities are applied to models that contain partial-ownership scenarios with minority interest computations. A Sales or Corporate entity, on the other hand, will always be assumed to be wholly owned and will not be expected to participate in intercompany transactions.

Scenario

Scenario is a built-in dimension that PerformancePoint Planning Server requires to exist in any model. This dimension is configurable but is designed to contain the data categories common to most data sets such as Actual, Budget, Forecast, Budget Variance, and so on. Categories modeled as scenarios are elements that often, but not always, appear as columns on a report. Scenario is an important dimension to consider in the modeling process, because it is part of the composition of a data entry cycle and must always be included in a model.

Business Process

The Business Process dimension is system-defined and contains both predefined members and a standard memberset providing a hierarchy of the items. These members and their parent-child structure are installed through the Business Application Type Library required for all financial type models and are used to support staged data movement through financial business rules — such as currency conversion or full consolidation. From the structure and member names shown in Figure 11-9, the purpose of these items and this structure is relatively clear. They provide elements to clearly view the components of the financial rule's logic.

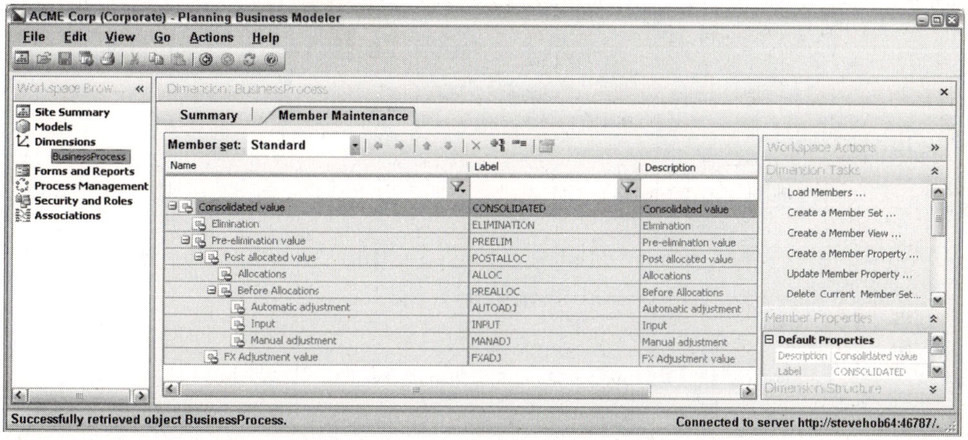

Figure 11-9 Standard memberset of the Business Process dimension

User data in a financial type model is restricted such that input will only ever be accepted for base currencies against INPUT, MANADJ, or ALLOC (generally, entries to the ALLOC element will be done only through Allocation rule types for clean auditing). Additionally, data entries may be made against FXADJ to any currency value for any post-currency–conversion adjustments that might need to be made. AUTOADJ is where intercompany reconciliation values are written, and ELIMINATION is for the consolidation process to store its values. Validation logic on the server will ensure this behavior is always consistent. For this reason, the Business Process dimension does not support additional configuration such as user-defined members or additional membersets.

Flow

The Flow dimension is another set of elements preconfigured by the Business Application Type Library for use in tracking cash flow movements across a balance sheet. As with Business Process, the Flow dimension is required and used in all financial type models, but the Flow dimension does support the addition of items and creation of membersets. When using Flow in a financial model, data is entered or loaded into the CLO (closing) element. From there, financial business rule logic computes MVT (movement) and OPE (opening) balances. FX, FXO, and FXF are where currency conversion differences are stored, as with Business Process, to make these types of adjustments easily viewable.

Consolidation Method

The Consolidation Method dimension is a listing of items that represent options for consolidation rules when using shares or partial ownership methods. Options are available for Equity, Full, Proportional, and so on. These values are computed when preparing shares information via the Shares job (described in Chapter 12). However, the items available in the dimension may be explicitly specified if other than default behavior is desired during consolidation rule execution.

Exchange Rate

The Exchange Rate dimension contains a predefined list of items that represent common types of rates used for conversion. For example, different items such as Average, Opening, and Historical allow the definition of a variety of different rates useful in performing currency conversion.

Special-Case Dimensions

There are three special-case dimensions, which surface as system-defined dimensions but lack some of the standard behavior and flexibility all other dimensions have. These dimensions are: Time, TimeDataView, and Users.

Time

The Time dimension is the result of the application calendar definition covered in Chapter 10. The results of the calendar definition options chosen are surfaced and displayed as a dimension, but there is no ability to edit elements of this dimension.

TimeDataView

The TimeDataView dimension includes a set of member items preinstalled by the Business Application Type Library for displaying running totals like YTD (year-to-date) and ToDate. It also provides some easy comparison values for comparison to the last year and last period. Data entry must always be done against the PERIODIC element of the TimeDataView dimension. In combination with the Time dimension, this facilitates some easy reporting views with rollups and comparisons that are commonly used in reporting scenarios. These items cannot be changed because the type library also installs the calculation logic into financial models to compute the values.

Users

The Users dimension is a list of members that is composed of the user accounts that have been added to the application (see "Security" in Chapter 15). Exposing user accounts through a dimension allows membersets to be constructed and managed that define parent-child relationships of the users. These structures can subsequently be used to manage the data entry review in a business process cycle (see "Data Process" in Chapter 16).

Intercompany

The Intercompany dimension is simply a partial list of the members of the Entity dimension. A copy of each Entity dimension member whose type choice sets the Intercompany flag to True is added to the Intercompany dimension. Using this dimension in a model enables the specification of a buyer and a seller entity for a transaction.

User-Defined Dimensions

PerformancePoint Planning Server supports an unlimited number of dimensions being added by modelers through the Business Modeler user interface. Dimensions should be added to support the creation of proper logical modeling of the business solution needed. For example, in working with sales planning, dimensions to represent products and customers are likely to be necessary. In many cases, the items for dimension are available from an existing data set. If this is the case, dimensions can be "imported" from existing databases or files. Other dimensions such as a dimension to track forecast version (for example, best case/worst case) can be manually created directly by the modeler. A user-defined dimension will initially be created with a simple structure for member name, label, and description. Any number of required additional attributes may be added after initial creation.

Dimensions, whether system-defined or user-defined, are the fundamental building blocks for a PerformancePoint Server Planning application. Items or members of each dimension are filtered and structured into membersets. Not only does each memberset define a filter that determines which items are used, but it also defines the parent-child relationship or hierarchy of those items. Supporting multiple membersets for a dimension means that the same dimension can be used in multiple ways, with each memberset providing variation. This ability to use the items common to dimensions differently for each memberset provides the flexibility for a variety of business models.

Models

A model is constructed of multiple dimensions put together. As described in the previous section, membersets provide different hierarchies for dimensions. When specifying dimensions for use in a particular model, the memberset is selected to determine which view of the dimension is used for that model. Models, then, become the containers for data and business rules within the application. Models become the basis for security and business processes as well. As with dimensions, PerformancePoint Planning Server contains some predefined model types whose behavior is determined through the Business Application Type Library.

Model Types

Model types, like dimension types, include system-defined logic for both initial creation and ongoing maintenance and operation. Model types such as Financial, Generic, and Exchange Rate have the minimum required dimensionality relevant to the specific activities they will be involved in. For example, an Exchange Rate model must include the Currency dimension in order to properly store values as they relate to defined currencies. Beyond the required dimensions for a model, any number of additional dimensions defined for the application can be added to provide the proper modeling structure required for the business purpose of the model. In addition to dimensions, model type choices will include specific system-defined behavior and rules. For example, Financial models include rules and additional rule templates to facilitate both simple and complex financial calculation behavior.

Financial

Financial models offer the most significant structure and behavior predefined by the Business Application Type Library. There are two forms of Financial models: Financial models for "with Shares" calculations and "without Shares" calculations. There are no significant differences between these two types of Financial models, except that "with Shares" supports partial ownership scenarios in financial consolidation logic and provides a Shares Ownership model for specifying the quantities of shares owned by the entities used for the model. In a Financial model "without Shares," all financial scenarios will be treated as wholly owned, and no share model is included.

Financial types of models include the Time and Scenario dimensions automatically, similarly to other model types. In addition to these two dimensions, Financial models include the system-defined dimensions for Account, Entity, Currency, TimeDataView, and Business Process. The system-defined Flow dimension may be included, and if it is, the internal business rules logic will use it appropriately for tracking balance sheet movements. Because the system-defined rules use these additional dimensions, they cannot be removed from the model. For detailed explanations of the included financial business rules and calculations, see Chapter 12.

Generic

A Generic model, as its name suggests, is the most open type of model, which makes it the most general-purpose type. A Generic model only requires the use of the Time dimension and the Scenario dimension in order to support data entry through the data process functionality. Any other dimensions may optionally be added as the business modeler sees fit for that model's purpose. For example, a Sales Forecast model would likely be built as a Generic type of model. User-defined dimensions like Product or Customer can be added relevant to the sales process. System-defined dimensions like Account or Entity are often useful as well. One thing to note about Generic models is that they do not inherit all of the built-in logic from system-defined dimensions. For example, using Account and Entity dimensions in a Financial model allows actions such as intercompany eliminations to be performed through built-in rules. However, those rules are not available in a Generic model, even if the required dimensions, Account and Entity, are included in the Generic model.

Assumption

An Assumption model is a model type used for storage of commonly used but more static driver values that are ''linked'' into other models. As is the case for Generic models, an Assumption model is only required to contain the Time and Scenario dimensions. Additional dimensions required to properly define the business data may be added.

Exchange Rate

An Exchange Rate type of model is a special case of an Assumption model that has added dimensional requirements related to Currency. As could be expected, it requires two representations of the Currency dimension: one for Source Currency and one for Destination Currency to provide an intersection point to contain the proper conversion rate between currency values. Additionally, the Exchange Rate Type dimension is required, which allows the definition of proper rate types for each period (such as Average, Beginning, Ending, and so on).

Model Dimensions

Model dimensions simply represent the concept that there is significant model flexibility provided within a PerformancePoint Planning Server application. Each model has a subset of the available dimensions from which it is constructed. Based on its type, each model has a number of required dimensions. For those dimensions, with the exception of Business Process, it is up to the model designer to choose which memberset of each dimension is used with the particular model. Because any number of membersets can be created on a dimension, there is significant flexibility with the usage even of required dimensions. Once the membersets have been selected on the required dimensions, any number of additional dimensions may be added to a model. These, too, may have multiple membersets available to select from. Dimensions that are not system-defined required dimensions may be added to a model multiple times, each time with a different alias. For example, if a model were being constructed representing automobile configuration choices where, from a single set of colors, there is an interior color distinct from an exterior color, the model dimensions would contain the color dimension twice: once aliased as "Interior Color" and once as "Exterior Color." With the exception of dimensions required for the particular type, model dimensions can be added or removed in the future or the memberset selected for one of the dimensions may be changed. Note that, in these cases, consideration should be made for handling any data that may already be in a model when changes are saved.

Linked Assumption Models

As described previously, Assumption models are designed to store values that are infrequently changing, used as a basis for calculations, and shared across many different Financial or Generic models. This may include things like price lists, budget assumptions, tax rates, and so on. Linking these values from Assumption models to other models provides three key advantages. First, the assumption value cannot be changed in the recipient model, which ensures that the shared values will be used consistently. Second, a central change to the assumption value can, then, be "distributed" to dependent models, and upon recalculation the updates will flow through naturally. Finally, assumptions can be at higher levels of granularity, and the PerformancePoint Planning Server will do the appropriate matching to relate data at the appropriate level.

Driver-based planning, as its name suggest, requires effective and efficient handling of drivers, and Assumption models provide that flexibility. Take, for example, a common people-expense planning scenario. Departmental managers may be budgeting numbers of people to which corporate standard rates for travel, training, and the like are applied. Figure 11-10 represents the budget model with account items for "Headcount" to capture the number of people in each department, and "Travel & Entertainment" and "Training," which will be the number of people multiplied by the standard budgeting value.

Budget Model		
Account:_Budget	Time_Month View	Value
Headcount	Jan 2008	12
Travel & Entertainment	*Jan* 2008	
Training	*Jan* 2008	
Headcount	Feb 2008	15
Travel & Entertainment	*Feb* 2008	
Training	*Feb* 2008	
Headcount	Mar 2008	14
Travel & Entertainment	*Mar* 2008	
Training	*Mar* 2008	

People Budget Assumption Model		
Account:_Budget_Rates	Time_Year View	Value
Travel & Entertainment per Person (rate type)	Year 2008	$ 15,000
Training per Person (rate type)	Year 2008	$ 2,500

Figure 11-10 Budget model with a related Assumption model

When the assumption values are linked into the model, it becomes easy to apply the standard values across all departments. Through the common time dimension, the annual assumption rate can be assigned for each of the proper months for which the budget is being collected. The linking of the values is represented in Figure 11-11.

Budget Model			
Account_Budget	Time_Month View	Value	Rates Value
Headcount	Jan 2008	12	
Travel & Entertainment	Jan 2008		
Training	Jan 2008		
Travel & Entertainment per Person Rate	*Jan* 2008		$ 15,000
Training per Person Rate	*Jan* 2008		$ 2,500
Headcount	Feb 2008	15	
Travel & Entertainment	Feb 2008		
Training	Feb 2008		
Travel & Entertainment per Person Rate	*Feb* 2008		$ 15,000
Training per Person Rate	*Feb* 2008		$ 2,500
Headcount	Mar 2008	14	
Travel & Entertainment	Mar 2008		
Training	Mar 2008		
Travel & Entertainment per Person Rate	*Mar* 2008		$ 15,000
Training per Person Rate	*Mar* 2008		$ 2,500

Figure 11-11 Assumption model values when linked into the Budget model

Finally, Figure 11-12 illustrates how the assumption values are used in calculations to determine budget amounts (for example, Travel = Budgeted People × Travel Rate per Person). If no other dimensions are specified in the assumption model, the rates are spread across all additional dimensions specified in the budget mode. For example, if departments are identified by the entity dimension, all departments will get the same value. If rates vary by

Account_Budget	Budget Model Time_Month View	Value	Rates Value
Headcount	Jan 2008	12	
Travel & Entertainment	Jan 2008	$ 180,000	
Training	Jan 2008	$ 30,000	
Travel & Entertainment per Person Rate	*Jan 2008*		$ 15,000
Training per Person Rate	*Jan 2008*		$ 2,500
Headcount	Feb 2008	15	
Travel & Entertainment	Feb 2008	$ 225,000	
Training	Feb 2008	$ 37,500	
Travel & Entertainment per Person Rate	*Feb 2008*		$ 15,000
Training per Person Rate	*Feb 2008*		$ 2,500
Headcount	Mar 2008	14	
Travel & Entertainment	Mar 2008	$ 210,000	
Training	Mar 2008	$ 35,000	
Travel & Entertainment per Person Rate	*Mar 2008*		$ 15,000
Training per Person Rate	*Mar 2008*		$ 2,500

Figure 11-12 Budget values calculated from Assumption drivers

entity, that dimension could be added to the Assumption model so that a rate could be determined differently per department.

Linked Assumption models are powerful tools with which to spread standard rates and practices easily around a variety of models. These values can only be used, not edited, in the models to ensure that standardized rates continue to be used consistently across the application.

Properties

Every model contains a set of properties. There are two general purposes these properties serve. First, there are properties that determine application behavior for a model. Second, there are properties that contain values that are useful within the model. These value properties are used primarily for calculation rules.

Behavior Properties

Behavior properties are sometimes used for indication purposes only. Model properties such as "Dimension data has changed" are set by the system to manage the internal state of the model. Other model properties such as "Enable annotations" are set at initial model creation time and may not subsequently be changed. These types of properties control things like the availability of model annotations and data submission at summary levels. Other behavior-driving properties such as "Enable offline cube," which specifies whether a model can be taken offline, may be updated at any time to change the behavior.

Value Properties

Model value properties are set to contain values used primarily in calculations. In Financial model types, several value properties are predefined for required input to financial rules. For example "Default currency" is where an item of the currency dimension can be specified so that the currency conversion rule will use it as the default target to convert to. Beyond financially focused properties, model designers may add their own properties. These properties can be text, numeric, or true/false. Alternatively, they can be either a single item from a specified dimension or a set of items from a specified dimension. Outside of properties useful for calculation rules, there is one property that surfaces to end users.

Each model has a Current Period property, which can be set to a member from the Time dimension. This allows a model owner to drive behavior around time. That behavior is surfaced through the Excel client for use in forms and reports (covered in Chapter 14). For example, a monthly rolling 12-month forecast may show the previous 6 months of actual data and capture the next 6 months of forecast data. To avoid redesigning the form each month, it can be defined to span the date ranges of Current Period – 1 to Current Period – 7 for historic actual data and Current Period to Current Period + 6 for forecast data. Within the model, the Current Period property is scheduled to update at the proper system date and time (for example, midnight on the last day of the month). At that point, the property value is changed, so reports and forms automatically pick that up accordingly. Similarly, data entry cycles are driven off this Current Period property (described in Chapter 16).

Business Rules

Business rules are contained within a model and allowed to be configured distinctly in each model, as necessary, to provide proper calculation functionality. Business rules are grouped into rule sets and categorized by type (described in Chapter 12). In Generic models, there are templates included for model designers to use in creating required calculations for the model. In a Financial model, there are predefined rules included in addition to those available through templates. By default, rules to handle the proper Account aggregation based on Account Type and rules to compute the TimeDataView dimension are included. Other rules for currency and consolidation are included but must be executed for those models.

Associations

Model associations are objects that define a relationship, full or partial, between two models. Associations are what enable multiple models to work together to provide a combined business solution. Supporting multiple models provides the flexibility to have necessary specific business logic where desired across different parts of a business process. When it comes time to integrate sales forecast data into the manufacturing forecast, for example, an association defines how the sales model and manufacturing model are related. Data movement can be executed to push or pull data along the paths defined by the association. The more similar the models are in dimensional structure, the simpler the association definition is. However, even in very disjointed-looking models, an appropriate mapping can be defined by an association. Associations may also be defined across model sites where those sites have a parent-child relationship. For example, recall the example ABC Corporation from Chapter 10, which had a Corporate parent site with Sales and Services as child sites. Through an association, a model from Sales can be related to a model from Corporate. Likewise, a model from Services can be related to a model from Corporate. Corporate models may also relate "down" from Corporate to Sales, for example. However, associations cannot go "across" sites, for example from Sales to Services.

Summary

In this chapter, many of the key building blocks of a PerformancePoint Server Planning application were described. At the core of everything sits the Business Application Type Library, which drives the internal type system and establishes behavior from that type structure. Dimensions with any number of membersets defined on top serve as the building blocks from which models are constructed. Through this dimensional modeling, a logical structure representing a business solution space is constructed. Throughout, the Business Application Type Library provides specific types of models with behavior and structural requirements driving system-defined functionality. Within models, properties and business rules provide behavior and configuration for the particular model, whether it is system-defined or user-defined. Finally, associations facilitate forming relationships between models to allow them to work in conjunction on solving an overall business problem.

Now that the basic building blocks of an application have been defined, the next several chapters describe the ways in which to put these blocks together in an application solution.

CHAPTER

12

Business Rules

Closely aligned with modeling and reporting are identifying and designing the calculations that a PerformancePoint Server Planning application will need to execute and what processes, or jobs, will be used to control them. Calculation needs may range from simple variance computations (for example, actual data compared to budget data) to complex allocations that might be used to spread shared infrastructure costs to individual operating units for accurate profitability analysis. Implementation of calculations can become harder or easier, depending on the model design and structure, so it is important to consider both early in the application solution design phase. There are a few key design considerations for efficient calculations.

The chapter begins with an overview of the calculation engine and the business rules logic it provides. Details are then provided about the PerformancePoint Expression Language (PEL), which is the method by which rule logic is specified. General rule topics are explained such as templates, variables, parameters, and jobs. Finally, the chapter ends with coverage of the financial-specific rules included.

Calculation Engine Overview

It should be recognized that some of the calculations that PerformancePoint Server Planning is capable of executing can get very complex. Simple calculations may be authored by a business analyst. For more complex calculations, PerformancePoint provides the ability to manipulate data in Microsoft SQL Server or Analysis Services, which can require expertise to do accurately and efficiently. This may require the help of a database expert or system integration partner to leverage appropriately. In designing the application solution, it's important to understand the types of calculations required and group them appropriately to plan for involving the proper resources in the solution effort.

Calculation templates are designed to provide the common, basic calculations that business analysts may want to include. The template starts analysts with a proper calculation rule, in which they fill in the blanks. In other words, a variance template sets up the calculation, and an analyst then chooses what two scenarios are compared in the variance, such as Actual – Budget. The template also sets the default type and behavior, but more control and refinement of behavior are allowed. Templates enable basic rule definition using the PerformancePoint Expression Language (PEL). PEL, itself, is a complete rule-authoring syntax and can facilitate many more calculations than just those prepared as templates. Business modelers may choose to add rules and leverage the expression power of PEL to author their own rules.

Calculation types drive the behavior of calculation rules in a model. A variance rule is something that is almost always calculated in real time with the data, very much like a spreadsheet calculation in Microsoft Excel. This type of rule is called a *definition rule* and is used to display a result that is never stored. However, a cost allocation rule would be something that is run periodically or on demand by a user, which does create new data values in the model. This type of rule is called a *procedural rule*. Within rule types, you can further control the implementation path of whether the rule is translated and executed at the Microsoft SQL Server relational database management system (RDBMS) level. It could also be translated and executed at the Microsoft SQL Analysis Services Online Analytical Processing (OLAP) level. There are several factors to consider in making the choice, and these should be thought through during the application solution design phase. In addition to the business requirements for when and where to execute a calculation rule, performance will be a key consideration. Model size, structure, and data volume will all be factors to include in this analysis of the proper execution approach. Again, it is important to anticipate and evaluate these potential factors during application solution design and to validate performance and function against representative data during testing. One further mechanism for refining calculations is the use of parameters and variables.

Parameters and variables are very similar, and both provide the ability to qualify or restrict the data scope over which a calculation is executing or to provide additional data values for use in a calculation. The key difference between the two is that the variable value is set in the model, so it does not change at calculation execution time, whereas a parameter is a value that is requested and submitted by a user at execution time. Take, for example, a simple forecast uplift calculation rule that multiplies current forecast revenue by an uplift number. If that number comes from a variable, then a modeler would set its value, let's say 1.05, and all executions of the calculation would multiply current forecast values by 1.05. However, if a parameter is used, then a user is prompted at execution time for a value, and it can be different each time it is run. Parameters and variables, though, are not limited to simple numeric values.

One of the best ways to establish consistency across all calculations used within a model is to employ parameter types that refer to dimensionality within a model. Again going back to the simple forecast uplift calculation, it's not common for such a rule to run over the entire set of forecast data. Generally, ownership of forecast data is divided by region or department. Within this type of model, a single calculation rule can be defined for the forecast uplift with a parameter defined for the department dimension. When a user goes to execute the calculation, he or she will be prompted for the value of the department parameter. The user will be prompted with a dialog that is filtered by the user's security. This enables easy reuse of a single rule definition, but it defines the scoping at execution time based on the value that a user selects from the values for which he or she has security permission. The mechanism through which these calculations are delivered to end users is the job.

Jobs provide the ability to give the calculation execution capability to end users. A job can be defined to execute a single rule or a set of rules together. Rule parameters are displayed and passed from end users to the calculation through the jobs mechanism. Jobs can also be defined and scheduled if more of a batch process is desired to meet the business requirement.

Calculations and jobs provide significant power and functionality to a PerformancePoint Planning Server application solution. The primary concepts of the feature set have been outlined, and the following sections provide additional details on each.

Business Rules Defined

Business rule is a broad term that, in PerformancePoint Planning Server, refers to a range of operations from simple numeric calculation to complex financial logic such as a parent company rollup of partially owned subsidiaries. A business rule begins with a rule definition written in the PerformancePoint Expression Language (PEL) syntax. From this common syntax, choices can be made around execution behavior, which provides the flexibility to allow a proper solution to be developed for any given business problem. Business rules are contained within a model, because each separate model may have different process and purpose requiring distinct business rules. Commonly, a business model will require several related or unrelated calculations for the solution it provides. To aid in the management and execution of these calculations, business rules can be grouped into rule sets.

Rule Sets

A rule set is a container for business rules that either have similar characteristics or are executed in combination to produce an overall result. For example, a process to allocate overhead costs to individual departments may spread several different types of overhead costs and may use different ratios for each type. Rent and utilities costs might be shared based on a percent of headcount, so the department with the most people would get the largest share of rent and utilities. Corporate advertising costs, on the other hand, might be spread to departments based on the percent of sales each department has, in order to distribute the costs according to the return on the advertising investment (making the assumption that advertising translates into sales). Each of these allocation calculations is different, but they have similar purposes and need to be executed together to produce fully allocated views of the business. To enable this, a rule set is created that contains both these allocation rules. Execution can be done on the rule set itself, which will execute each rule in the set in sequential order. For large numbers of rules, where grouping helps in the ease of maintenance, rule sets can be created that contain other rule sets. Extending the earlier example, there may be a rule set containing overhead allocations for shared corporate costs. Another rule set may contain several allocation rules to distribute shared information technology (IT) costs. Another rule set might house allocation rules to move costs from certain manufacturing departments to sales departments. The result of the rules in several rule sets provides a total allocated set of data. A single, parent rule set can contain rules and child rule sets for all these related allocations. Execution of the parent rule set will cause the execution of all the rules in all the contained rule sets. For consistency, rule sets are required to contain rules of equivalent types, which will be covered later in this chapter.

PerformancePoint Expression Language

The PerformancePoint Expression Language (subsequently referred to as PEL) is a language abstraction combining generic rule definition syntax with business-focused capability. This business logic capability works in conjunction with the Business Application Type Library concepts described in Chapter 11. In addition, PEL works as an abstraction layer on top of multiple execution engines to provide flexibility and efficiency of execution from a single definition syntax. Due to its multidimensional behavior and affinity to Microsoft SQL Server, PEL has significant similarity to the SQL Server MDX (multidimensional expression) language syntax. However, it is an extended subset with extensions specifically targeted at statements to deliver business-focused behavior.

Type Behavior

There are two types of options that determine the behavior of a rule: rule type and implementation type. These two options drive how rule logic is calculated and presented to end users of the solution. Having PEL as a common representation of business rules allows easy transfer of behavior among types with little or no change in the definition itself.

Rule Types

Rule type determines the runtime behavior of a business rule. The type of rule selected is driven by the action it performs for the application. There are some specialist types focused on financial consolidation functionality or data loading and some generic types that have broader applications.

Financial Rules

Financial rules are provided to supply the necessary calculations for financial models. These rule types will be available only for financial models. There are three types of financial rules: currency rules, intercompany reconciliation rules, and consolidation rules. As their names suggest, these rule types support necessary functionality such as the conversion of values to different currencies and the reconciliation of transactions performed between two entities within the same company. The full consolidation rule will properly eliminate intercompany results and create the flow of aggregate values, including considerations for partial ownership if supplied, to present a fully consolidated view of data.

Allocation Rules

Allocation rules are used to distribute, or allocate, values within a model. In many scenarios related to profitability or activity-based costing, actual results or budgets are reported to a single location, and this amount needs to be properly spread across individual items. For example, if a retail store is refining profitability models on the products it sells, it will need to allocate rent and utilities paid for the physical store location. Based on some method of defining relative value such as the percent of square footage occupied, the total amounts can be allocated to individual products to identify the expense attributable to each product. An allocation rule is flexible in how the spreading methods are defined, allowing them to be predetermined or calculated at rule execution time.

Assignment Rules

Assignment rules are the broad category of rules that take the form commonly understood for calculations: Select some data, do some calculation, and store a result. A simple example is A + B = C. The result of adding the values A and B together is stored in the value location C. Assignment rules are broad-reaching in a model, as they can span large portions of a model either to get source values or to store new values.

Definition Rules

Definition rules, like assignment rules, compute values based on a source data scope and some calculations. However, a definition rule does not create any data that is stored. The results are always generated, or computed, at request time.

Outbound Rules

Outbound rules offer a mechanism that allows a business rule to position data for output to downstream systems. An outbound rule specifies a scope of data appropriate to "push" to a predetermined database location. From that location, external systems or reports may pick up or query that data, depending on the security access provided at the database level. This facilitates the ability to post final budget data upon completion of the collection and review process, for example, without a database administrator's involvement.

Implementation Types

The *implementation type* of a rule determines how a rule is translated into an underlying execution method. Because PEL allows the rule definition to be separate from the implementation, no language extension is necessary. There are four different implementation choices that a rule author may choose from. There are two types, MDX Script and MDX Query, which operate on the underlying Analysis Services cube. One rule type, SQL, operates against the relational SQL server data underneath a cube. The final type covers financial rules that are executed by PerformancePoint Planning Server's internal engine.

MDX Implementation Types

The choices of MDX implementations execute against the cube that is generated by deployment of a model. MDX rule types are split into Script and Query variations. Script rules become calculations that are deployed by PerformancePoint into the cube. Query rules are executed against the cube, and the results are written to the data, becoming values when the cube is reprocessed (by the Cube Process Interval described in Chapter 11).

MDX Script calculations are performed by Analysis Services as part of any query to return results. Variance calculations are an example of rules that are often deployed as MDX Script types. Variances are results that are part of data retrieval, like reports, which are computed but for which the values aren't necessarily stored. In Figure 12-1, a report displays the difference between Actual and Budget computed as the BudgetVar. The value of the BudgetVar is recomputed with each retrieval request based on the value of Actual and Budget. The advantage of retrieval-time calculation is that the results will always reflect the latest data values. In particular this rule is useful for data entry forms, as it recomputes the results as users change input data values.

Region	Actual	Budget	BudgetVar
East	150	140	10
West	100	110	–10
North	125	120	5
South	110	100	10

Figure 12-1 Variance between Actual and Budget

There are two advantages of expressing this calculation as an MDX Script type of business rule. First, it cannot be changed by end users (as can sometimes be the problem with calculations in Excel). The second is that it spans across the multidimensionality of the model. This means that as different sets of data are retrieved, the commonly defined calculation will be available, providing flexibility to report designers.

MDX Query types, on the other hand, always compute a set of values and store the results. Because MDX Query rule types execute and store values, they are useful for queries that may take time to run and have somewhat deterministic source data changes. They are less dynamic because the data are computed and stored. Any time source data changes, an MDX Query type of rule must be re-executed in order to see the updated results. This execution can be run via a system process or as a user-executed job.

SQL Implementation Types

SQL implementation rule types operate directly on the underlying relational data of a model. This is particularly advantageous for calculations occurring over large data sets. In an MDX type of rule calculating against the Analysis Services cube, each potential cell is already precomputed and the calculation must evaluate it, even if it is empty. In a SQL rule, empty cells and sparse data don't exist, making the rule execution much more efficient. Allocations are an example of rules that are often best executed in SQL.

The disadvantage of SQL rules is that they have limitations executing on aggregate values. In the cube, summary levels of data are preaggregated and can be easily referred to. However, only the lowest-level leaf values exist in the relational table. This manifests as a couple of limitations with SQL implementation types. For example, the average function operates over the data values in a specified scope. When using an MDX rule type, multiple scopes or sections of a cube can be inputs to the average function. However, for the SQL implementation, only a single range can be specified in order for the scope to be properly translated into its equivalent relational table data set. Some other functions, such as TopSum (which returns a specified number of elements from a sorted set) are not supported at all when translated to a SQL implementation. In cases such as this, direct SQL logic through a native SQL rule may provide equivalent functionality.

Specialized Implementation Types

Specialized implementation types of rules are the built-in calculations PerformancePoint Planning Server includes for its financial data computations such as currency conversion, intercompany eliminations, or consolidation. These rules, while still expressed in the PEL language, are executed by the server's own engine and do not have user flexibility in where the execution should occur (as SQL or MDX). Outbound rules are another example of a specialized rule type, which executes in SQL but is driven by internal engine logic and execution steps.

Native Implementation Types

Native variations of MDX Script, MDX Query, and SQL all exist. Native rule types are a bypass mechanism for PEL, which are useful for developers experienced in either the SQL or MDX syntax. A rule of this type will take a text expression in the native SQL query language or MDX query language of Microsoft SQL Server. Those queries will be passed directly to the appropriate underlying engine for execution. This provides flexibility for targeted, specific calculations that aren't addressable through the PEL syntax. Because pass-through language syntax can perform many different actions, additional administrator security is applied for these types of rules and permits a new rule or edited rule to be reviewed before it is made available for execution. At execution time, the rule runs with reduced privileges at the database level to prevent unintended actions (such as dropping tables).

Rule Templates

PerformancePoint Planning Server introduces a new language syntax with PEL. There is some user interface functionality to help build a proper expression, but it has limitations and getting started with rules can be somewhat difficult for users not familiar with expression languages or similar products. To assist with the process of getting initial rules set up for a model, rule templates are included to provide users with a generic form in which they replace placeholders that denote the specifics of their model. An example of the variance template is shown in Figure 12-2.

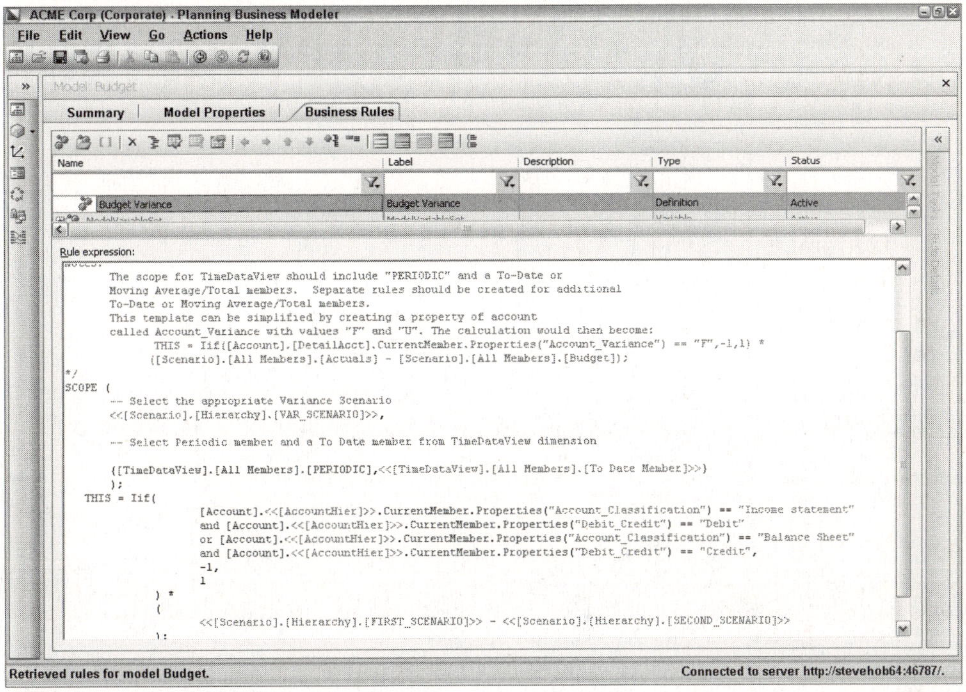

Figure 12-2 Rule template for variance

This shows how the template extends the simple concept of Variance = Actual – Budget to a more intelligent calculation that has the proper model context. Filling out the template might appear difficult, so a wizard helps users to select the required placeholder items (shown in Figure 12-3).

Once the placeholder values from the template have been filled in, a complete and proper rule syntax exists to compute the variance. This simple variance rule demonstrates how the involvement of the account type can add to the functionality of the business rule. In this case, variance is to be shown as favorable for positive income (made more money than planned) and for negative expense (spent less than planned). Figure 12-4 shows the completed variance rule.

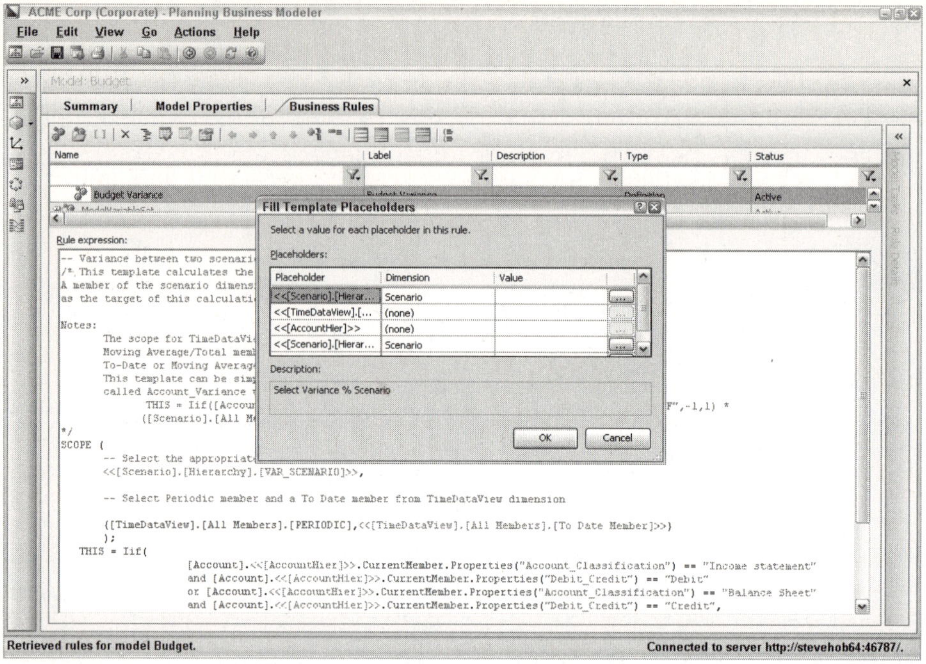

Figure 12-3 Filling out placeholders for a variance template

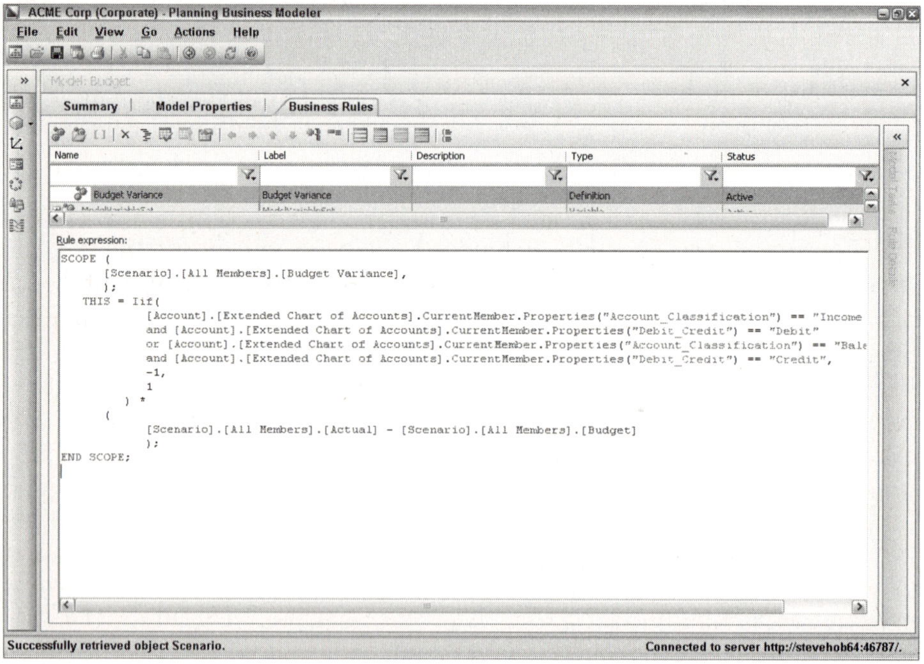

Figure 12-4 Complete and valid variance business rule

Parameters and Variables

Parameters and variables are related concepts that both allow execution-time configuration of rule execution. They are used within a rule to receive a value or values for use in the calculation. For example, take the case of a seeding rule, which computes an average amount from historic actual data and posts that to seed the budget. Once the budget is seeded, users will update some of the initial seeding values. If the seeding rule needs to contain a lifting factor by which to raise the historic average, it could simply be hard-coded into the rule as follows:

```
[historic average] * 1.05
```

However, specifying explicit values is generally a poor practice because, if the value changes, rules must be changed to reflect the update. If several different rules use the same value, the likelihood of missing an update becomes higher and is difficult to detect. Instead, a variable may be defined and used in multiple places as shown below:

```
[historic average] * &lift_factor_variable&
```

Once variables and parameters are established, changes and maintenance become much simpler and consistency is ensured.

The difference between variables and parameters is the point at which their value is set. A variable is defined and its value is set up front. The value can be subsequently changed, but it is set in the Business Modeler interface, so it is more of a static value, always present. A parameter is always determined at execution time. In the lift example, a parameter is specified as follows:

```
[historic average] * $lift_factor_parameter$
```

Upon execution, a prompt will occur for the executor to specify the value to be used. The use of parameters gives users input options to rule execution. As described in the next section, there is a variety of types available for parameters and variables. It should be noted that when parameters are typed for securable objects, such as dimension members, the proper user security is applied to the prompt choice.

Parameter and Variable Types

Parameters and variables may be defined as basic data types such as Boolean (true/false), number (integer or real), and string. This type of value can be used within a calculation (value * variable number) or a condition check (if parameter = true). Additionally, parameters and variables can be defined to items within a model. Assigning a parameter or variable to be a type of member or multiple members from one of the model's membersets enables dynamic definition of a rule's scope. For example, a rule may be defined to have an input parameter or entity that is selected by the user at execution time. In combination with rule security, this produces an ability to define a single rule and to use a parameter to allow proper execution to many different users (see the "Rule Security" section for an example).

Publication as Jobs

Rules or *rule sets* are executable at any time by a business modeler from the client environment. However, many rules are more appropriate to execute either from the Excel client environment by end users or via a system process. The mechanism to enable both of these options is a *job*. Predefined financial jobs are already included, but any rule or rule set can be published as a job. This publication wraps the rule or rule set in a job, which can subsequently be assigned to users for execution privileges or scheduled via the system. Any parameters defined within the rule or rule set will automatically be promoted to a parameter for that job, enabling the prompting of end users to fill in the values at execution time.

Rule Security

One important note about rule security is that the execution of a rule occurs under the context of the PerformancePoint Server. This means that execution is done with an account that has full access to everything. Jobs and parameters are the mechanism by which to filter execution scope to individual users based on their data security. This is an important consideration in rule design for rules that will be executed by end users in particular. Figure 12-5 shows an uplift rule that is applied equally to all departmental entities in the model.

In this example, the rule is generically applied to all departments in the model. If User 1 executes this rule via a job, regardless of his or her department restriction, the rule computes across all departments. This often isn't the desired behavior. The proper way to enable end-user execution is to include the department as an entity parameter to the rule that will expose it as an input prompt for the job execution. Figure 12-6 shows the rule author choice of creating the rule parameter and specifying that its value must be a member of the entity dimension.

Once the input parameter is defined, it is then used in defining the rule. In this case, shown in Figure 12-7, the Entity field is simply replaced in the scope section by the parameter.

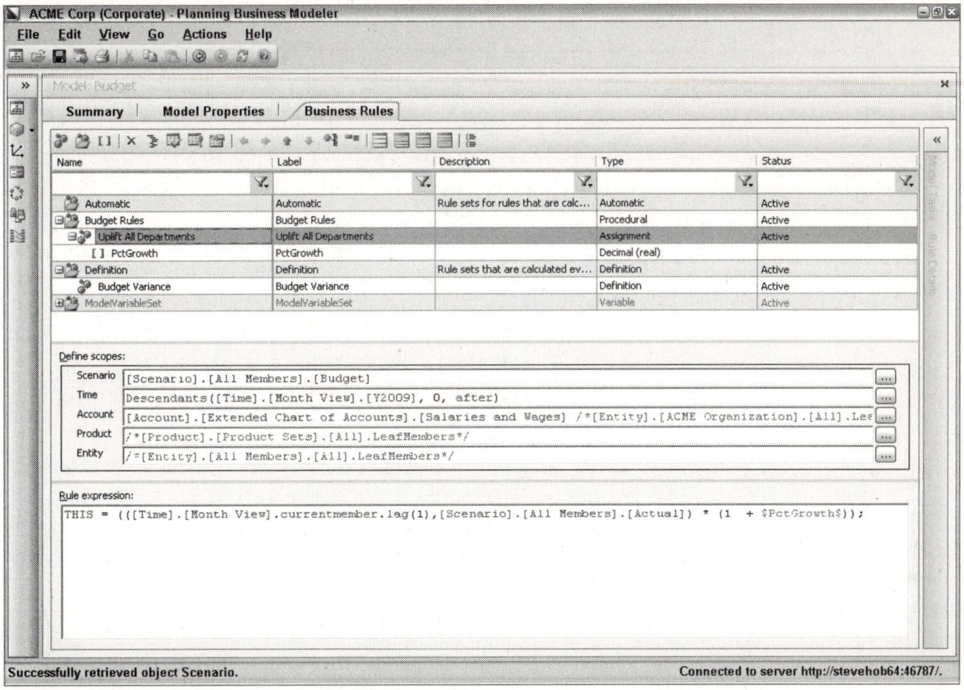

Figure 12-5 Uplift example for all entities

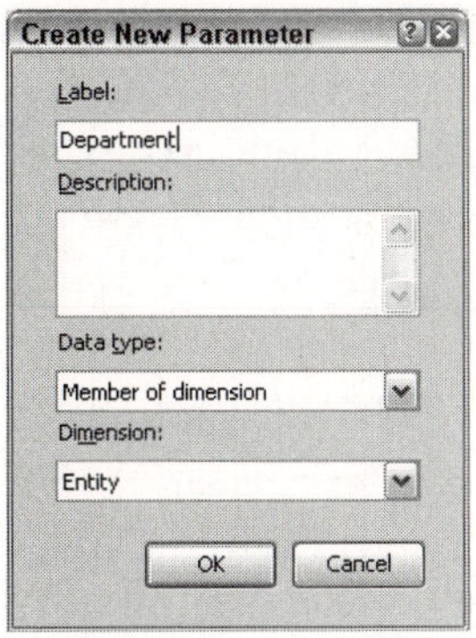

Figure 12-6 Parameter definition

When User 1 executes the rule via a job containing the entity parameter, he or she is prompted to select the department for which to run the rule. The options of departments to choose from are filtered by his or her security at the individual department level.

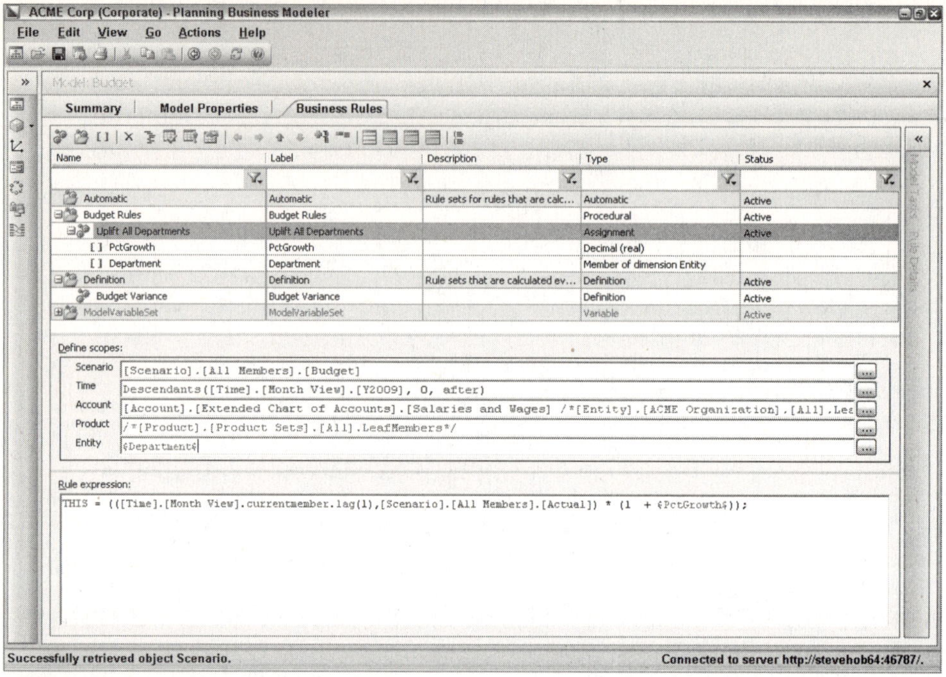

Figure 12-7 Uplift example by entity

From the PerformancePoint Expression language (PEL) defining rules of different types to rule sets grouping similarly typed and related rules, to exposing rules execution as jobs, significant function and flexibility is offered to provide calculation function and expose this behavior to end users as necessary. Built into PerformancePoint Planning Server is a significant amount of predefined calculation logic targeted at financial scenarios.

Financial Intelligence

Financial intelligence functionality is automatically available through the Business Application Type Library in any financial model type. This functionality includes rule types and rules, parameters and variables, and jobs.

Financial Rules

Financial rules are included as built-in templates with any financial type of model. Depending on whether the model is Financial with Shares or Financial without Shares, the rules will already understand if partial ownerships need to be considered in the financial calculations. The financial rules themselves should be considered as providing basic functionality that, when used in conjunction with correct type choices, performs proper and accurate data processing. Any consideration of complex financial behavior such as management or statutory consolidation involves work in understanding the proper configuration of types in addition to the deployment of rules. Depending on the accounting rules followed by any given organization, alterations may be made to the financial rules or financial rules may be augmented with additional rules and jobs. The following sections provide a brief overview of the built-in rule types.

Currency Conversion

Currency conversion rules provide the calculation from base data currency to alternate currency representations. Base data currencies, as discussed in Chapter 11, are determined for each entity, and the currency property for each entity is used by the rules to determine the appropriate source currency. Currency conversion rules rely on an Exchange Rate assumption model being linked into the financial model. The related currency job allows the choice of which type of conversion rate to use for execution in the case that average, opening, closing, or other rate types are appropriate. Within the Exchange Rate model, pairings and conversion rates are established between currencies. Again, via the execution job for currency, the target end currency will be specified. In the case of a currency translation that is not explicitly specified, triangulation through a default system currency is performed. For example, a translation rate from German deutschemarks to South African rands may not be specified. With European common euros as the system default, deutschemarks are converted to euros, and then converted to rands. Currency conversions carry with them intrinsic difficulty with the fact that rates are never computed exactly at the time of a transaction. This problem is particularly acute when eliminating among entities any intercompany transactions, but it applies in many other situations as well. As part of currency conversion calculations, PerformancePoint Planning Server will compute and store necessary currency translation adjustments for balance sheet accounts, provided that the Flow dimension is included in the model. This enables accurate financial reporting to be performed in multiple currencies as required. Finally, currency rules contain default behavior with respect to the rate types to be used. For example, for proper balance sheet accuracy, opening balances are computed with opening rates and movements during a period using the period's average rate. However, this logic is easily changed based on types and their usage within the rule itself if the requirements dictate.

Intercompany Reconciliation

Intercompany reconciliation rules provide calculation logic to check and fix transactions between entities within a company. For example, account types of Intercompany Payable and Intercompany Receivable are allowed to be specified in a reconciliation rule, but not all accounts are required. Multiple rules may be used to compute transactions between different sets of payable and receivable accounts. In addition to these sets of accounts, pairings between groups of entities are specified. From the combination of accounts and entities specified in each rule, it finds all the possible transactions and reconciles the double-sided entries to ensure the balancing of the transactions. This includes factoring for the situation where each side of the transaction may be entered in a different currency. Reconciling entries are posted to the underlying relational data and are uniquely identifiable to that rule's result. Figure 12-3 shows an example of the effect of the reconcile function within PerformancePoint Planning Server. In this example, two transactions have occurred. The Italian subsidiary sold inventory to both the German and French units. Because these organizations are part of one corporation, these transactions were recorded as intercompany transactions. Germany acquired inventory worth €900, and the inventory that France acquired was worth €1000. When the German subsidiary transfer was made, a difference in understanding of the transfer price caused the Italian accounting department to record only the transfer at €850 (instead of the €900 the German accounting department recorded). As the European operations for the company are consolidated, a difference of €50 appears on the books due to this discrepancy in the entries. The reconciliation rule identifies this difference and posts the adjusting entry of €50 to a specified balancing account, making the total of all intercompany transactions balance (shown in Figure 12-8).

	Organization	Intercompany Receivables Debit	Intercompany Payables Credit	Intercompany Difference
Seller	Italy	€ 850.00		
Buyer	Germany		€ 900.00	
Seller	Italy	€ 1,000.00		
Buyer	France		€ 1,000.00	
Total		€ 1,850.00	€ 1,900.00	(50.00)

Figure 12-8 Intercompany reconciliation example

Eliminations

Eliminations are a rule step used in consolidation when transactions between entities within a company must be eliminated from profit and loss as they are aggregated to the overall company level. In a model type of Financial without Shares, this is a straightforward full elimination. However, for models that are Financial with Shares, calculations for percent of ownership and control are used to determine the percent consolidation and the consolidation method to use. PerformancePoint supports Full, Proportional, and Equity methods of consolidation. A modeler may customize the consolidation rules, on a per-model basis, to address behavior regarding the calculation of Retained

Earnings, Minority Interest, and the elimination of equity according to the local Generally Accepted Accounting Principles (GAAP).

Financial Jobs

There are several financial jobs that users with sufficient permission can perform. These jobs correspond to the built-in financial rules and are preconfigured with the necessary parameters required for execution.

Currency Jobs

A currency job is automatically available for any financial model. The currency job allows specification of necessary parameters driving currency rule execution. Through the selection of parameter values (similar to the example shown later for the consolidation job), a user can select the target currency to convert values to as well as specifying what portion of the model to compute and what rates to use. The currency job defaults parameters in a symmetrical manner. For example, converting the "Budget" scenario will default to the "Budget" exchange rates. However, a user may change this at execution time; for example, to convert the budget data at a "Forecast" exchange rate. This can be used in what-if scenarios to see the results of different currency conversions.

Reconciliation Jobs

As with a currency job, built-in job definitions exist to launch eliminations or reconciliations. To launch a reconciliation job, a model and scenario are selected as parameters. From the selected model, any reconciliation rules or rule sets are selected in addition to the time span for the reconciliation. Multiple periods in the time span allow the reconciliation of an individual period, quarter, or full year if desired.

Consolidation Jobs

Full consolidation is performed by launching a *consolidation job*. This job is a shortcut to execute any necessary eliminations and conversions together to achieve a consolidated result. The parameters, shown in Figure 12-9, specify the inputs and targets for the consolidation job. Note that the destination entity is specified and illustrates the ability to consolidate to any level of the organization structure necessary. This can be useful in cases where consolidation results need to be "staged," and at succeeding levels of aggregation, proper audit and adjustments may need to be made.

Shares jobs are related to consolidations and relevant to partial-ownership (or shares) consolidation. An ownership model is loaded to specify the number of shares held of each entity by each entity. The shares job computes the percentages of ownership based on those share numbers. Once the percentages have been computed, a full consolidation with shares job may be executed.

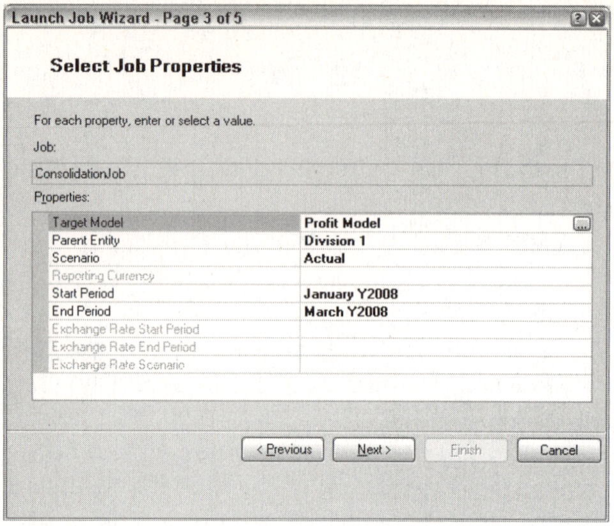

Figure 12-9 Consolidation job parameters

Data Jobs

There are three types of data jobs available within an application. Data Export jobs execute data export rules to push a defined set of a model's data to a predetermined SQL database location. A Data Load job allows user execution of the data integration functionality (described in Chapter 13) to synchronize or load new system data into an application. By enabling this activity through a job, end users may be given a controlled subset of application lifecycle responsibilities. A Data Movement job allows for the execution of data transfer along a defined model association. The association defines a mapping of related structures between two models, and executing the data movement copies the data between the two structures at the database level.

Summary

The key to efficiently utilizing calculation rules in a solution is to understand the requirements and do the proper upfront analysis to deploy them in the manner that delivers the most effective solution. There are many different options for executing calculation logic and rules within an application. Choices such as definition or assignment type produce a computed result but with different execution and data persistence, which results in different performance and user experience. Once calculations are prepared and the proper type is determined, jobs enable additional execution control for end users to help manage an application's data.

CHAPTER

13

Data Integration

One of the primary considerations when putting together a PerformancePoint Planning Server application solution is to understand what data will be required and where it will come from. This varies significantly across organizations and even within operating units of an organization. Many companies today have a good understanding of their financial data, but far fewer are able to easily leverage operational data. As you evaluate data needs for a solution, it's important to consider data source and output destination requirements to design the most effective solution. The tendency of many companies is to build a solution on the data that is currently available and easily acquired. The more effective solution considers the entire application and its requirements to put proper context around the data requirements. While this may seem like a subtle difference, it can often determine the adoption and effectiveness of a solution.

PerformancePoint Planning Server provides data integration functionality designed to work in conjunction with the SQL Server platform to support the data lifecycle of an application. This chapter introduces the data integration components and the processes they are designed to support. From a database perspective, there is a division between application data, staging data, and outbound data to facilitate a structured process management of data flows. For the acquisition of data into an application, the staging database contains validation and synchronization functionality to ensure integrity of the data throughout import and export processes. The chapter closes with a discussion of the key concerns when looking at the data requirements of an application solution.

Data Integration Architecture

The architecture of PerformancePoint Planning Server's data functionality is designed on the principal of isolating and controlling the application data at all times. Many applications include a mix of system data and user data, so strong consideration is placed on providing explicit control over the application data at all times within an application. For this reason, separate databases exist to provide a distinction between application data (in the *application database*) and more dynamic data stored in a *staging database*. For similar isolation of data required by downstream, dependent systems, an *outbound database* may optionally be provisioned for every application. Figure 13-1 shows the database overview.

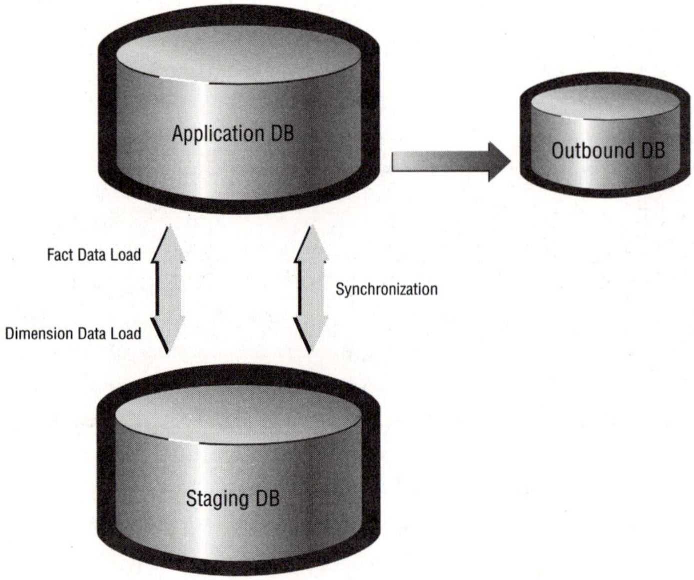

Figure 13-1 Databases for an application

Application Database

The application database is the core database and contains all the data for a running application. For this reason, the application database is tightly controlled by PerformancePoint Planning Server and is not designed for direct database access and manipulation (except for reporting and auditing). The application database contains three key pieces of data of concern in the data integration context.

First, the application database contains table structures for dimensions. A dimension table contains the member elements of the dimension and any property values associated to members of the dimension. Some of these property values will be driven by the internal type system (such as the Account Type property of the Account dimension). Other property values will have broader options because they are for user-defined properties. Related to the dimension table are tables consisting of the parent-child relationships for any membersets (hierarchies) defined for the dimension. Because each memberset may use a different subset of the members, in different parent-child relationships, each memberset will be stored in its own separate table. The final key pieces of data stored are the numbers, or facts, themselves. This data may have been loaded via processes described in this chapter, or they may be created in the application from either user input or the results of business rule execution.

The current system state and valid data are maintained in the application database, and a secondary location may be created for staging data on its way into an application.

Staging Database

The staging database is designed as the container for data on its way into an application. This is generally data coming from line-of-business data systems that is a necessary part of the application solution. This data is often the historic, or ''actual,'' data, and it usually has regular cycles of addition or update to an application's data set. In addition to the actual data, source systems may also be providing dimension and hierarchy information to the application. The staging database contains functionality to facilitate common processes to manage this additional data in the application.

For items that will be managed via outside sources, a synchronization process (described in the next paragraph) creates a mirror of the physical data tables in staging from those that exist in the application. This includes structures to contain dimension data, hierarchy data, and raw fact data. One of the difficulties in dealing with data transformed between the application database and the staging database is that all physical tables contain unique numeric identifiers, or keys, that are assigned by the server. Maintaining these key values is possible but involves a set of database queries. To ease this process, the staging database contains the ability to mirror all data tables with label-based tables. These label tables contain the data with the key translation already done from the numeric value to the proper text value.

The staging database is targeted, primarily, at supporting the import of business data into an application. It may also be used to retrieve user input data back out for ongoing synchronization of new application data. However, this requires proper query of the staging data by custom back-end processes. To support the export of data collected or created in the application, the outbound database is provided as the primary location for application data to be consumed by external systems.

Outbound Database

The outbound database is a location for exporting data that is to be consumed by downstream systems. It supports, in particular, partial data output that enables scenarios where new budget inputs are captured and need to be pushed out into an additional reporting system once the budget is final and approved. The application database will collect the input data and always contain the latest, in-process data. As part of the solution process, the appropriate set of data can be moved into the outbound database at the appropriate time via the appropriate data job.

All three databases — the application database, the staging database, and the outbound database — are managed through data integration process services. These services support many different options for how an application data process is managed.

Data Integration Process

The process by which the objects in the application, staging, and outbound databases work together is facilitated by a set of functions and services provided in PerformancePoint Planning Server. Synchronization allows the creation and management of objects, largely SQL tables, that are used to transfer data. Loading processes bring in new data or update existing data. Finally, refresh processes are necessary to ensure that the application has the proper data values loaded and visible to users.

Synchronization

Synchronization is a key step in integration between an application and its staging database. It's the synchronization process that creates the tables with the appropriate structure in the staging database to mirror what the server has created for the application database. Synchronization is a complete replacement, meaning that if an object already exists in the staging database, synchronization will completely overwrite it with a new object. There is no attempt to merge differences into the staging database. Synchronization always occurs from an application database to a staging database. The synchronization will process the data and structures together.

Loading

Loading is the process of taking prepared data (data preparation is covered in the next section) and loading it into the application. Loading is an executable process that is designed to be triggered at the scheduled time within an application solution's context. Loading can include dimension-related data, member items, hierarchies, and numeric raw data. Loading can also be prepared incrementally so that new items or data can be added to an already existing system. For example, in a monthly reporting system, new source system data and dimension members may be added without any disruption of the prior months' data already in the application. Inversely, deletions may be performed to remove certain pieces of data that are already in the application. Data previously loaded can also be edited to change existing values. These variations of the loading process are controlled by status codes set in the staging database. Once proper codes are set, the data load process is run. It executes validation processes and after success, moves the valid data into the application. Once new items have been loaded into the application database, the final step is to refresh the application.

Data Refresh

With new data loaded into an application database, the data refresh process needs to occur in order for that new data to become visible to application users. There are two phases of refreshing, driven by the types of changes to the application data. The first, and simpler, is the reprocessing of changes to numeric data. This reprocessing refreshes the Analysis Services cubes for each business model where the underlying data was changed. Updating the cube makes the latest data available for user viewing or business rule calculation. This process is similar to that which occurs for data writeback submissions, but it can be controlled per model to reprocess only models for which new data was loaded. The second refresh type is required for any item or structural changes. If changes, additions, or deletions were made to any dimension items or any of their membersets, a redeployment of the structures is necessary to make those changes to the Analysis Services cube. The PerformancePoint Planning Server makes these updates incrementally, so the impact of processing time on the server will be based on the amount of changes made.

Data integration services provide the functionality to manage data passing into and out of an application. These services create the infrastructure around which to build the proper process for data flow in the business solution.

Application Data Lifecycle

The data integration functionality of PerformancePoint Planning Server is designed to facilitate many variations of the data lifecycle necessary for an application. This encompasses bringing data into an application, maintaining and updating that data on an ongoing basis, and pushing data back out from the application to downstream dependent systems or solutions (Chapter 19 describes the application design process in more detail.) One of the more difficult tasks is bringing data into the system in a manner that is expected and consistent. Particularly when data is sourced from multiple systems, there are tasks necessary to ensure that data can be integrated properly. To assist with the development of the process and procedures for this aspect of an application, there are internal functions for data preparation and validation. The process is outlined visually in Figure 13-2.

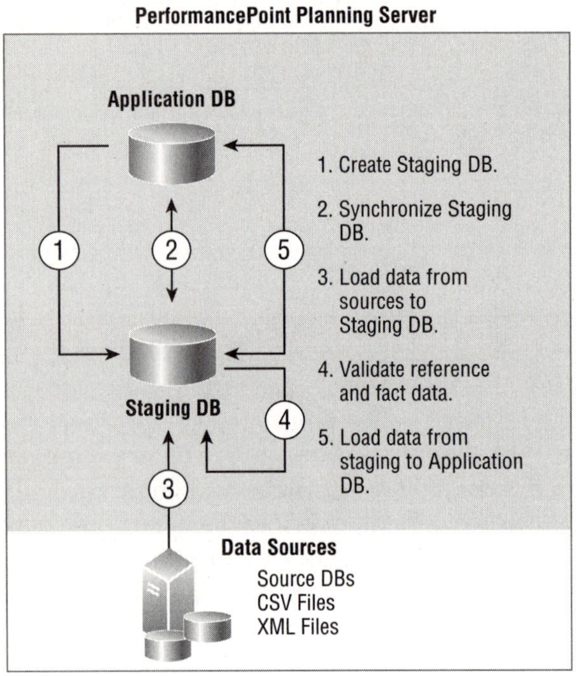

Figure 13-2 Data integration process

The process begins with the creation of a staging database to accompany the application database. Synchronization prepares the structures to contain staged data, but before loading can occur, the data in the staging database must be properly prepared. The preparation of data is facilitated by functions and structures that are used in different combinations, depending on the data coming in from external systems. The PerformancePoint Planning Server capabilities may be used together with other SQL Server functionality to develop a required loading process following the basic steps just described. The next two sections cover the functions for preparation and validation in more detail. Additionally, there are some performance and troubleshooting considerations that should be highlighted to understand how to approach putting together the right data integration processes for an application.

Preparation

Data preparation may be the most variable part of the overall data process. Preparation difficulty (or ease) depends largely on the nature of the source data that is needed for the PerformancePoint Planning Server application. Uniform data from a single system will be easier to prepare for loading than data coming from multiple systems in different formats. PerformancePoint Server itself does not work with data in external systems. Rather, it relies on SQL Server Integration Services (SSIS) for the processing of data into the staging database. SSIS provides the ability not only for loading, but data cleansing and homogenization. Many different routines can be written in SQL or Microsoft .NET C# and included into packages for processing execution. Aside from the PerformancePoint Server functionality, the core SQL Server platform provides all the tools and techniques for getting data into the staging database. It is at this point that specific functionality begins.

The first consideration while working in the staging database is whether or not the previously mentioned label-based tables will be used or if key-based tables will be used directly. In most cases, label-based tables will be easier to work with and should be used. For cases with very large data set sizes, where disk space optimization is a concern, a label-based table may be skipped to avoid making extra copies of the data in the staging database. The advantage of label-based tables is that the uniquely identifying items being specified are still text values (as opposed to generated integer keys). This can mean that data coming from separate systems still may be combined in these label-based tables as long as the source text values are consumable by the single application. Take, for example, loading in customer names for a sales application. If source system A loads data for Customer X and source system B loads data for Customer X, that label will be treated as a single item in the Customer dimension. Thus, these two entries will be recorded to the same customer ID when PerformancePoint Planning Server converts the labels into a unique integer key. It is up to the system architect pulling the data together to understand how the source systems work with data and where common data (referred to as master data) exists and is appropriately managed. The label-based tables exist as an easy route to go from text-based identifiers into the application's integer-based keys. The option to use label-based or integer key tables exists for dimensions, hierarchies, and facts. A mixture of modes may be used, although it's simplest to apply a consistent approach.

Dimensions and Hierarchies

Dimensions and hierarchies are the first objects to consider for loading. Because dimension items become the keys for data values, two elements are critical to properly handling system data. The first is a requirement, across all dimensions, to have unique text as the label identifier. Second, once it's determined how to stage unique values for dimensions, other attribute values must be filled in. For system-defined dimensions with attributes driven by the Business Application Type Library, valid values must be set for required fields. For example, when a new account item is placed into the staging database table for accounts, it needs to have a valid account type property set. For user-defined attributes, values matching the appropriate constraint need to be prepared. In part, this will be enforced by data types in the SQL Server tables so that a text attribute will have a field that contains only text values. Here, though, consideration should still be made to get the appropriate values filled in through the loading process, if possible, to ease maintenance. Many of the attributes have default values set, so if no value is specified in the staged value, the default value will be assigned at load time.

Membersets, or hierarchies, can be loaded if the proper source information exists to tie parent-child relationships together. In many cases, source systems will have parent-child information in a tabular format similar to that shown in Figure 13-3. In this example, products are associated with a parent product line that rolls up under a group and finally a division.

Product	Product Line	Product Group	Division
Product 1	Line A	Group 1	Division 1
Product 2	Line A	Group 1	Division 1
Product 3	Line A	Group 1	Division 1
Product 4	Line A	Group 1	Division 1
Product 5	Line B	Group 1	Division 1
Product 6	Line B	Group 1	Division 1
Product 7	Line B	Group 1	Division 1
Product 8	Line B	Group 1	Division 1
Product 9	Line C	Group 2	Division 1
Product 10	Line C	Group 2	Division 1
Product 11	Line C	Group 2	Division 1
Product 12	Line C	Group 2	Division 1
Product 13	Line D	Group 2	Division 1
Product 14	Line D	Group 2	Division 1
Product 15	Line D	Group 2	Division 1
Product 16	Line D	Group 2	Division 1
Product 17	Line E	Group 3	Division 2
Product 18	Line E	Group 3	Division 2
Product 19	Line F	Group 4	Division 2
Product 20	Line F	Group 4	Division 2

Figure 13-3 Tabular format of parent-child relationships

This table of products and their attributes contains the information necessary to derive proper parent-child relationships. The hierarchical view of this is displayed in Figure 13-4.

Product Memberset A

- Division 1
  - Group 1
    - Line A
      - Product 1
      - Product 2
      - Product 3
      - Product 4
    - Line B
      - Product 5
      - Product 6
      - Product 7
      - Product 8
  - Group 2
    - Line C
      - Product 9
      - Product 10
      - Product 11
      - Product 12
    - Line D
      - Product 13
      - Product 14
      - Product 15
      - Product 16
- Division 2
  - Group 3
    - Line E
      - Product 17
      - Product 18
    - Line F
      - Product 19
      - Product 20

Figure 13-4 Parent-child view of products

There is functionality in the PerformancePoint Planning Server that will generate the desired memberset based on a set of properly defined attributes. This functionality in the staging database greatly simplifies the task of building and managing memberset hierarchies that are fed from external source systems.

Model Data

The preparation of model data is a little different from the preparation of dimension or memberset data. For a model, each data value must have all corresponding dimension items specified. Some of the dimension items will come from the source data, but there may be additional items to specify for dimensions originating within the application itself. For example, the Time and Scenario dimension items are generated from within the application. In order to properly prepare the model data, items for these dimensions will need to be specified. In the case of loading of a month's general ledger data, the proper month label value and scenario label value need to be identified and inserted with each value.

Control over the loading behavior is an integral part of preparation and is accomplished using an internal flag, called the BizSystemFlag. Using this flag, operations like add, update, and delete are triggered in the loading process. This flag exists on all staging tables — both label-based and integer-based — so whatever method is chosen for staging data preparation, the same process logic applies.

Once data process choices are made, proper tables are prepared, and the required data is loaded into the staging database, validation processes ensure that only properly staged data may enter into an application.

Validation

Stored procedures are provided in the staging database to support validation processes. Upon the creation of the staging database, these procedures are in place and ready to use. Validation covers the three primary types of data loaded into a staging database: dimensions, hierarchies, and models.

Dimension validation ensures consistent preparation of member items prior to loading them as new reference data for an application. Because each member item must have a unique label, validation logic checks to ensure that this uniqueness exists within the staged data and that no staged items conflict with any items already in the application. Checks are also performed on any member property fields. For simple property types like text or integer, validation ensures that a value exists of the proper type or that the property is empty. For cases where a property is a reference to another dimension, it will check to see that the specified item exists in the referenced dimension. It is important to note the order of precedence for proper validation. For example, if department Z101 is being loaded into the Entity dimension with a currency property of USD, the USD item must already exist in the application's Currency dimension. If the USD item is being loaded into the staging database at the same time as department Z101, the order of loading events into the application database needs to be properly sequenced. The Currency dimension must be loaded from staging into the application to ensure the USD item exists properly, and then the Entity dimension can be validated and loaded with department Z101. If the sequence isn't properly followed or if items are attempted that don't adhere to the consistency or uniqueness rules, validation will return an error. In the case of errors, each offending item in the staging database will have an entry placed in its BizSystemFlag and BizSystemErrorDetails fields indicating what type of error caused that row item to fail.

Hierarchy validation determines whether proper parent-child relationships are specified in a prepared memberset update in the staging database. Primarily, hierarchy validation checks to ensure that each item specified is a true item that exists for the dimension. Second, it validates consistency in the definition of parents and children. For example, item A could not be a child of both item B and item C. Similarly, if item A is a child of item B, then item A cannot be a parent of item B. These types of validations ensure that a proper structure of parent-child relationships can be generated from the definitions provided in the staged data. As with dimension validation, any hierarchy validation violation is marked in the BizSystemFlag and BizSystemErrorDetails fields with an error code indicating the nature of the problem. Because a dimension may have multiple hierarchies, the validation procedure may be run on a single hierarchy or all hierarchies at once for a specified dimension.

Validating models shares some similarity to validating dimensions and hierarchies, but it also involves data itself. A model definition contains an item from each dimension to identify the proper data intersection as well as the value to be placed at that point. A model has no uniqueness constraint, but each dimension item specified must be a valid item for that dimension. Because a model's dimension is associated to a particular memberset of that dimension, the item must also be part of that memberset in order for the intersection point to be valid in the model. Take the case of a budget model that uses the Acme Organization memberset of the Entity dimension. An item representing department Z101 exists in the Entity dimension, so it is a valid item; however, it has not been included in the Acme Organization memberset. Therefore, a data value for the budget model that has Z101 as its entity element would fail to validate. Further validation checks for similar data integrity for the built-in functionality. For example, by default, model data must be at the lowest, or leaf, level of all dimension hierarchies. Any model with currency must load data to the defined base currency for the given entity. In the case of a model containing the Business Process dimension, the loaded value must be INPUT or MANADJ. All of these are examples of data integrity checks performed against data to ensure that it is valid for loading.

The many validation steps take time to execute and, depending on the data size and server capacity, performance may become a consideration in preparing and loading data into an application.

Performance

Frequently, data volume in a production application necessitates performance consideration, and this remains true in the data integration process. Many of the steps in validation, for example, will analyze rows of data and perform lookups to ensure proper integrity. With a large set of data being validated, this can take a significant amount of time in some cases. Performance tuning for working with data should follow standard tuning procedures for SQL Server databases. For example, data tables created in the staging database do not have any indices at creation time. Depending on the data and the operations that will run against it, adding indices could enable noticeable performance improvements. Additionally, process steps may be sequenced to perform long-running actions at noncritical times. The critical time, generally, is when data is loaded into the application. During this time, an application is usually locked temporarily so as to process the data load in a batch without concern for user transactions interfering. For large data sets, the loading process might run for a significant amount of time because it performs validation by default. This being the case, validation may be run separately ahead of time to ensure completely valid data. If you are confident that validation passed, you can execute the loading process with an option to skip validation, which will reduce the loading time. Performance will vary with the application's purpose and data profile. Different options and process choices provide many approaches to getting the desired behavior for an application's data process. Batching or loading chunks of data using the BizSystemFlag to control batches is one example of options available. The desired behavior and data profile should determine the best option for each circumstance.

Troubleshooting

All actions in the data integration process are audited to allow for investigation and correction of failures. There are three primary classes of errors that may occur in a data-related process. The first is simple server permission or connection issues. Sometimes permissions needed to write data or execute server processes must be granted to users to work properly within the staging database. Or, large volumes of data or slow network connections between downstream systems may cause execution timeouts (the SQL query timeout value may be extended in the Administration Console). These types of errors can occur with any SQL Server data application and can be investigated and corrected in the same manner. The other two classes of issues come from the application data itself and occur during either validation or loading.

Validation errors are the result of one or more failures in the required condition of properly prepared data. For example, attempting to load a dimension item that already exists in the application triggers a duplicate error.

For validation, an error code is placed in the appropriate staging database table for each item in error (BizSystemFlag). Further information about the error is placed in the BizSystemErrorDetails for each item. Going through the failed items, the error code indicates the nature of the problem, and the additional error text provides further information to identify the proper resolution. Basic SQL Server skills are often helpful to write additional data queries to other data tables in order to nail down the problem quickly.

Loading errors may occur when the data is loaded from staging into an application and have more points of failure, which can make them a bit more difficult to troubleshoot. In the default case, loading triggers validation, so the same investigative steps apply. Loading can surface new errors, particularly those related to the update and delete operations. Because update and delete require the data or item to already exist in the application, it can only be checked at load time, so validation may pass, but loading might still fail. The loading process may also run several steps in which any one of the steps might encounter an error. To aid in narrowing down the problem, the server error log will contain a failure entry identifying the loading step that erred. Sometimes the client that is executing the loading will also receive an identifiable error, but often the server error log is the best location in which to find information. This will pinpoint the step and the table with the data problem (instead of having to search through all loaded tables to find which one contains an error code). Again, it can be beneficial to involve a database analyst with good SQL Server skills to perform efficient investigation and resolution of these issues.

Summary

Data integration functionality in PerformancePoint Planning Server is tightly integrated to the SQL Server data platform. This provides a solid base of functionality to build on, as well as facilitating the development of required data processes through standard SQL methodologies. For data integration support, a staging database is provided to mirror the application database. In the staging database, functionality is provided to support data preparation, validation, and loading. These functions are used in different sequences to support the desired data flow process for an application's data lifecycle. Data collected and processed through an application may then be delivered to downstream applications or data stores via an outbound database.

CHAPTER

14

Reports and Forms

The primary interaction for end users of a PerformancePoint Server Planning application is through reports and forms. These are surfaced through the Excel Add-In environment, which is a familiar experience for business users to work with data. Many uses of Microsoft Excel today generate data that is offline or disconnected from any formal system. Additionally, common usage patterns involve email and file sharing as the collaboration environment. Through reports and forms, PerformancePoint Planning Server delivers a connected process to ensure data consistency and integrity while remaining in the familiar environment of Excel. While data submission is limited to the Excel Add-In environment, reporting can utilize PerformancePoint functionality or additional functionality coming from other Microsoft tools such as SQL Server Reporting Services or Microsoft Office SharePoint Server.

This chapter covers the core Excel Add-In functionality of PerformancePoint Server. First, it describes the form and report objects that exist in an application. The behavior of the Excel Add-In environment is covered, both for end users viewing and contributing data to the planning process and for design and maintenance of reports. Finally, the Report Wizard is described and illustrates the guided method for designing common report types for applications.

Excel Client

PerformancePoint Planning Server delivers end-user client functionality through an add-in to Microsoft Excel. The add-in exposes both the design capability and runtime ability for working with data. Forms and reports are the core objects that are designed and used in an application environment. Prior to looking at how to build and work with reports and forms, it's important to get an overview of the client functionality and how it's surfaced to users.

Client Functionality

The Excel Add-In component of PerformancePoint Planning Server provides a familiar experience to end users for designing and viewing reports and forms as well as interacting with the overall application. End users familiar with Microsoft Excel pivot tables should find a very familiar experience when working with PerformancePoint. The example shown in Figure 14-1 shows the Microsoft Excel environment and the PerformancePoint Excel Add-In Report Design pane. The PerformancePoint Action pane, shown on the left side of the screen, looks and behaves similarly to a pivot table designed in Microsoft Excel 2007.

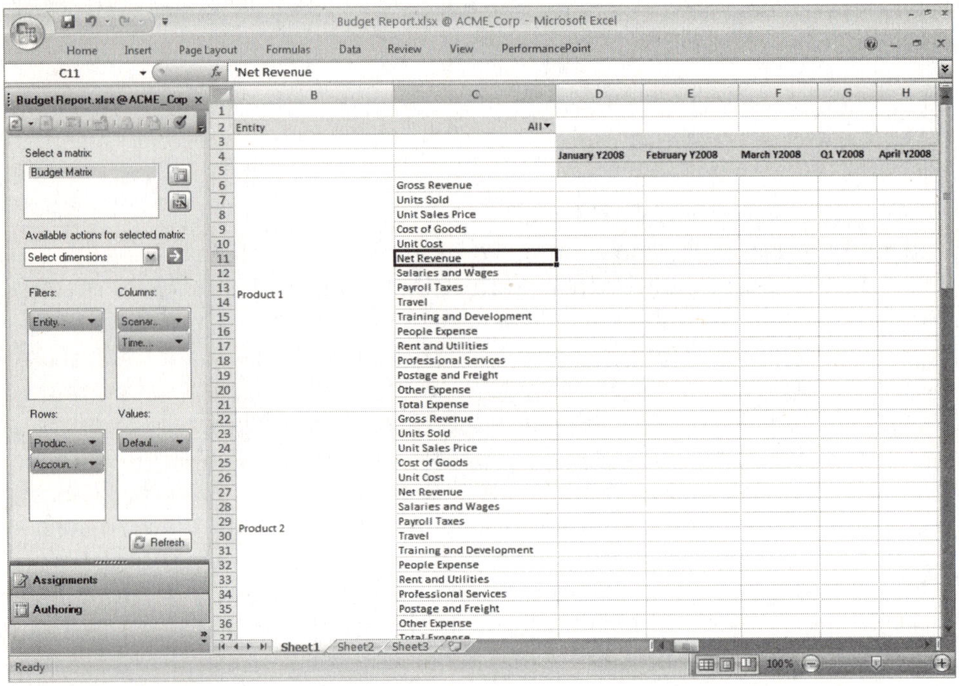

Figure 14-1 Excel Add-In Designer

In addition to a pivot table–like experience, PerformancePoint offers additional design help for many of the commonly required reports for a solution. The Action pane serves as the place for an end user to go to find the current progress of their application tasks. Figure 14-2 shows the Action pane in assignment mode. In this view, information about current data submission tasks is found. Simply selecting an assignment opens the full data entry form in Excel for the user to work with. For each assignment, the Action pane displays additional relevant information, such as the due date, so the end-user contributor has the full context around the assignment he or she is working on. In the example (see Figure 14-2), the user has one current action assigned for budget entry.

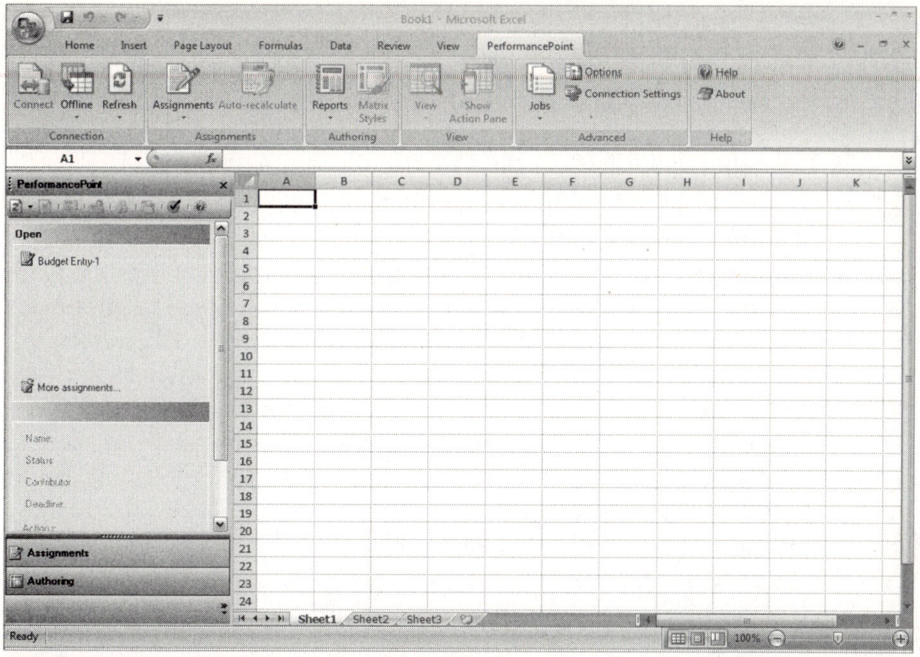

Figure 14-2 PerformancePoint Action pane

The PerformancePoint Add-In Action pane is the primary user interaction point for working with assignments as well as for the design and building of reports (detailed later in the chapter). In addition to the Action pane, further end-user functionality is delivered in a menu bar added to Microsoft Excel. Figure 14-3 shows the ribbon format loaded into Excel 2007. Support exists for Excel 2003 and the menu displayed is consistent with that environment.

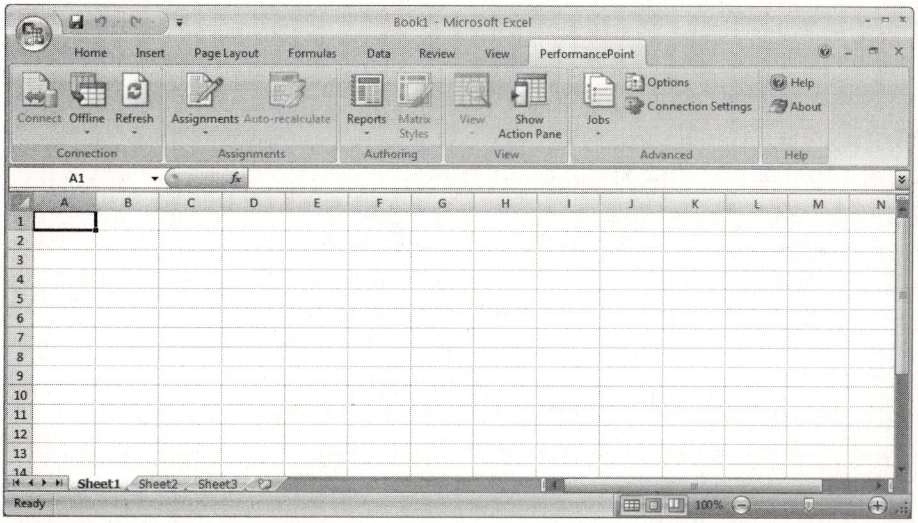

Figure 14-3 Excel Add-In menu

Add-In Menu Options

The PerformancePoint Excel Add-In provides several key menu categories of common end-user activities. The first and most important is Connect. When connecting for the first time, the user will be prompted to specify the location of a PerformancePoint Server. If a user primarily connects to a single server, a default can be set and the user will be automatically connected to this server. A list of "favorite" servers can also be stored. Since end users may have access to multiple different applications, depending on their job function and the structure of the organization's applications and processes, assignments from all applications on the current server will be accessible. Once connected, the Action pane will provide the ability to work with assignments where the current user is a contributor, approver, or reviewer. The Action pane will also allow users to author new reports containing data from the PerformancePoint models to which they have access. The Show Action Pane menu option allows you to hide the Action pane while working in spreadsheets and then recall it when it's needed to modify reports, submit data, or open new assignments. The Assignments menu allows users to search through all their assigned items. This provides the ability to retrieve a prior period's work and see the details from any previous activities they performed. Refresh, as its name suggests, provides the ability to retrieve updated data. This can be issued for assignment information, a single worksheet of data, or an entire workbook. There is also the ability to clear out any changes made within a working assignment. The remaining menu items — Offline, Reports, and Jobs — encompass a broader set of functionality.

Offline is a menu interaction with the system's ability to work on local versions of data and assignments, which provides a disconnected experience for remote or traveling workers. This functionality is part of a multifaceted approach to caching data to enable several work scenarios.

Caching and Offline Behavior

Chapter 10 described the overall system architecture of PerformancePoint Planning Server and illustrated the data storage and retrieval functionality supported through SQL Server Analysis Services. In some circumstances, a planning application will require data input from users who are far remote or completely disconnected from a corporate network while doing their work. For these users, a local cache of data is required to allow them to still function within the context of their assignments. In other cases, very large numbers of users may access data simultaneously, and the frequent server queries may cause an undue burden on a central server. For these users, having a local cache of data allows them to work in isolation and reduce processing load on centralized resources (both server and network). To support these scenarios, PerformancePoint Planning Server supports both explicit and implicit offline behaviors.

The Offline menu item on the Excel Add-In allows users to place their assignment workbooks and data locally into an offline state. A user can choose one or more assignments from any of their active assignments list, regardless of which application the assignment belongs to. The selected list of items determines which Excel forms need to be stored locally as well as what data sets are necessary to work with the forms. The data is retrieved from SQL Analysis Services and stored in local cubes to provide the same multidimensional capability to work with data offline. When data is retrieved, it is still restricted by the individual user's data permissions so that, whether online or offline, the same data security is applied. All files, Excel and data, are stored in the user's secure Windows local storage, which ensures that only that user (or an administrator) can access the files or data locally. Once assignments are taken offline, the user continues to work with them through the Excel Add-In, interacting only with local data. When users come back to a connected environment, they may go ahead and submit data back to the server. If the duration of offline work has been lengthy, a user might want to check to see if updated server data exists, which might impact the submissions he or she prepared offline. From the Action pane, Compare with Server will create a worksheet identifying the differences between the current server data and the user's offline data. This provides the user with an ability to evaluate any changed conditions or updates prior to submitting the offline work he or she did. Using the Offline menu option explicitly supports cases where users are aware they are going to disconnect and work remotely. However, some parts of the offline capability are available to users working online as well.

By default, PerformancePoint Planning Server is set up for the case where a user will work with his or her set of data and not need to query the SQL Analysis Services source data immediately or frequently. This facilitates the case where most of the queried server data will be read for informational purposes, and the user will be entering forecast or budget data. In this default case, when the user opens his or her assignment, the same offline cube is created as when explicit offline downloading is invoked. This local cache of data is timestamped and a user is unaware that subsequent refreshes or filter changes of assignments return data from this local cache. However, because the user remains in an online mode, the system will manage this cache and notify the user if the cache becomes out of date, refreshing it to keep it in sync with the server as necessary. For example, a user can open an assignment and begin work (with data being created behind the scenes). The user may enter some data and submit it back to the server for processing (see Chapter 10 for the data submission process flow). Once the server has processed that user's data, his or her local cache is now outdated and invalid. The next time the user opens the assignment, the Excel Add-In will detect the out-of-date cache and let the user know that it is being updated. A user may influence this cache behavior through the Options menu, where there is an option to disable this automatic local caching of assignments. In some models, there may be important calculations that occur only on the server (via jobs, for example). These server data changes cause the user's cache to become constantly invalid, forcing frequent updates. If this is the case, a model property may be set by the modeler to disallow offline caching. For that model, no offline caching (explicit or implicit) is allowed, which causes every user query to access the server — placing more load on the central server but always providing the latest data results. Disabling the Offline option may also be used in cases of highly sensitive data (such as payroll data), which, even though it's locally secured on a user's machine, is still too risky to store outside a centrally audited server environment.

Reports

The Reports menu provides access to options for both the creation and the retrieval of reports for an application. New reports can be created through either a wizard or a direct editor (described later in this chapter). When you choose a new report, it is always placed into the currently opened workbook. It's often best to create a workbook and name its tabs as desired before creating PerformancePoint reports in the workbook. Reports may be opened from any application to which the user has access. Report definitions themselves are not secured, so any user of the application will have access to its reports. The security is placed on the data, however, so users may open a report definition and will not see any data in that report unless they have read access to the data in the model on which the report was built. New reports are also saved through the Reports menu. Using Excel's standard Save option will not store all the PerformancePoint components of the report — instead, a disconnected static copy of the workbook will be saved. A warning is provided to help users discern which of the save options they should use.

Publish

Once a report has been defined and saved, a user with modeler permissions may publish the report as a form template for use in data entry assignments. This provides the ability for users to create and define their own reports. Subsequently, a modeler can decide which reports are useful in data entry activities and either change them or simply publish them for data process usage. Users may also define reports useful to distribute through broader, production reporting environments. In such cases, a report may be published to Reporting Services. Note that some layouts and query definitions supported by PerformancePoint are not supported in Reporting Services, so there may be some reports that cannot be successfully published. Reports published to reporting services will be set with default formatting. Further adjustments to layout and formatting are achieved outside of the PerformancePoint Add-In for Excel. In both cases of published forms and Reporting Services reports, if changes need to be made, the form or report needs to be re-published to overwrite the prior version.

Export and Import

Reports and forms may also be imported and exported. This functionality is primarily used for supporting a migration between systems — development and testing, for example. A report can be defined, refined, formatted, and reviewed in the development environment. Once it's ready, that report alone may be exported and imported into another system. When a report is exported, a zip file that contains the various elements of a PerformancePoint report is created. When this zip file is imported, a new server or application can be selected for the report. For that system, the model underlying the report should have a similar structure. If it does not, the report will have to be edited in order to query and render the data properly.

Jobs

The Jobs menu provides users with the ability to launch system-defined jobs from the Excel environment when they have appropriate permissions to do so. This keeps the end-user functionality consistently exposed through the Excel interface. The activity to launch a job returns all the application's jobs for which the user has execute permissions. Some jobs may be new and running for the first time. Or, for convenient re-execution, a user can launch an existing job. A job such as currency conversion may be run several times — every time the data changes, the job should be run to process the conversions again. Re-running a job allows for its execution with the same parameter options and makes repeat actions easy. Existing jobs may also be deleted or purged. Once an existing job is re-executed or a new job is created and launched, it goes to the server for processing. Users can track their jobs' progress by using the Job Status option. This menu item simply provides a quick search window to find all launched jobs and returns their execution state, such as "running" or "completed." Once a job is completed and data within the model located on the server has been updated, users can refresh their reports or assignments to see the results of the job.

Forms and Reports

End-user interaction with a PerformancePoint Planning Server application will come, primarily, through forms and reports. Most likely, the target users of the solution are already interacting with similar information in their jobs today, so an understanding of what exists, what is needed, and how it is to be used is crucial to producing a viable business solution. Within an application, data is retrieved and viewed through reports, and data entry is accomplished through forms. Form and report definitions are composed of two pieces of information — layout and data — inside a matrix.

Matrix

A report's definition must first define the scope of data to be retrieved. This definition is done through a matrix. A matrix can be thought of in similar terms to an Excel pivot table. Each matrix is pointed to a single model within an application. From the specified model, the matrix can find which Analysis Services cube contains the model data to retrieve. Once the model is selected, a scope is defined to populate the matrix, which specifies which subset of the data is to be queried from the cube. The matrix, then, contains the returned data and provides the area within an Excel worksheet in which to display that data. As with a pivot table, a matrix can be defined to have filters to allow the display of a key set of data and selection options to change the data view. Figure 14-4 shows an example of a matrix with a filter for Entity.

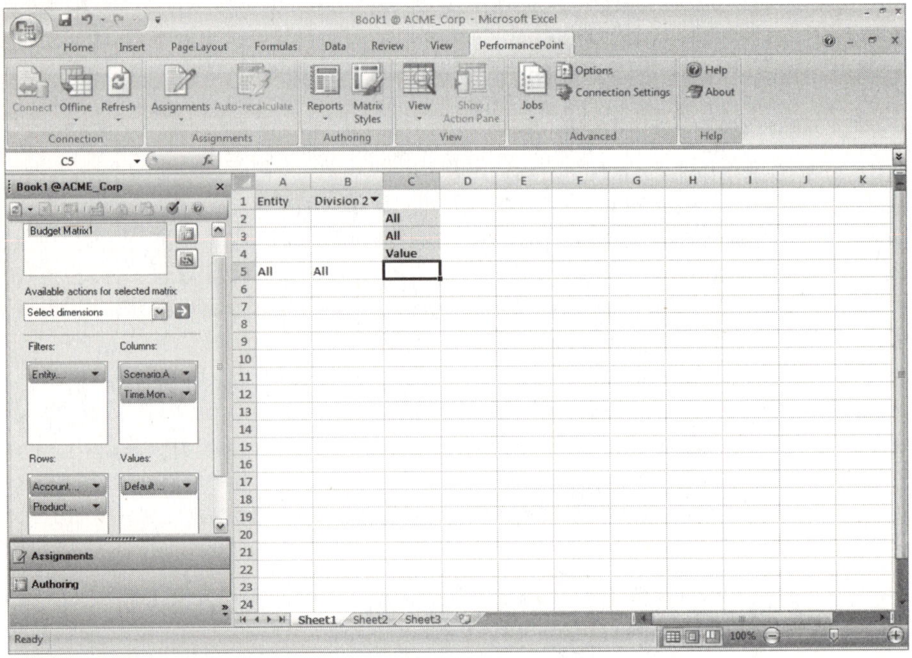

Figure 14-4 Example matrix

Matrix definitions may be changed over time to alter the set of data that is viewed. Each change to a matrix — in its layout, content, or simple filter selection — causes the PerformancePoint Excel Add-In to reissue a query for the data. By default, the data necessary will be cached locally so that filter changes, for example, can reprocess data from a local store. This is also true for any offline assignments that directly form a local cache of potentially required data. It is possible to set a property on a model to not allow local caching.

Report Design

There are several considerations to keep in mind when designing reports.

Ad Hoc Reports

The primary report-design experience is through direct matrix creation. A user must first choose which model to base a matrix on. A workbook or worksheet may contain multiple matrices, but each matrix will be based on a single model. Once the model is selected, its dimension structure is retrieved, and the user selects how to lay its components onto the two-dimensional spreadsheet surface. For each dimension, membersets or memberset views may be shown, which provides multiple layout options. Not all dimensions are required for a report, but it's important to note that a summation exists for any dimension not specified (similarly to how a pivot table functions). It's also critical to note that reports being designed for publishing as forms must specify all dimensions in the layout to facilitate data entry at the individual intersection points. Dimensions can be specified as rows, columns, or filters. Figure 14-5 shows a simple budget-model layout definition.

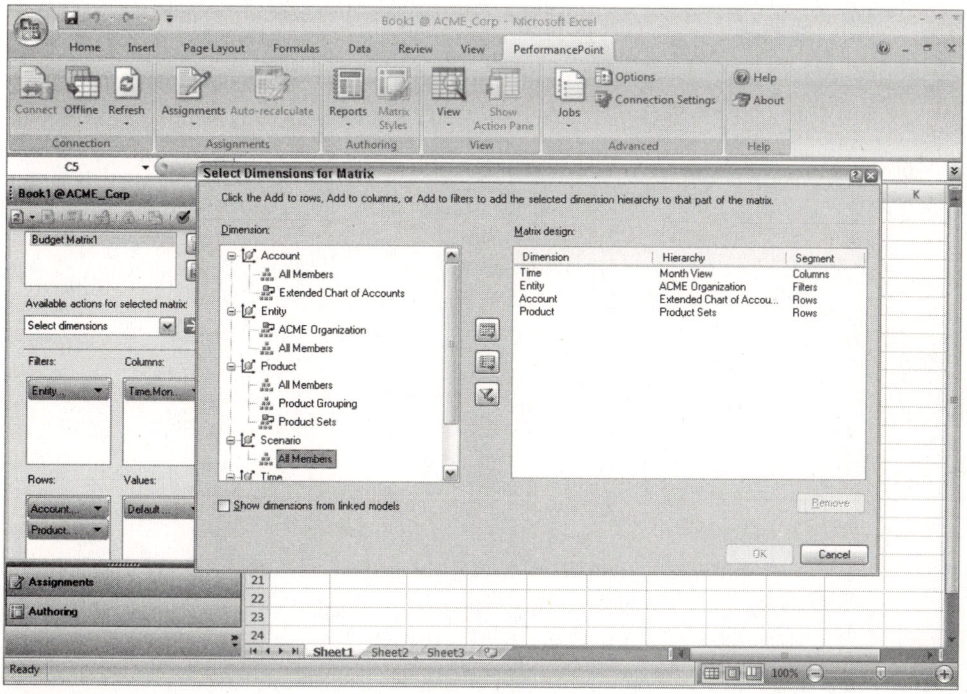

Figure 14-5 Selecting dimensions for a matrix

In Figure 14-5, Account and Product are placed on Rows, Entity on Filters, and Time on Columns. The All Members of scenario (which contains the items Actual and Budget) is highlighted in the dimension list on the left, and simply clicking the Add to Columns button in the middle adds it to the matrix. The resulting layout of the matrix is the basic view shown in Figure 14-4. However, further refinement is necessary to provide the desired report layout. The first step is to identify which individual items are to be shown on the report.

Dynamic versus Static

Once the basic structure of a matrix is defined, the individual items to be retrieved for those structures are specified. In Chapter 15, a type of security is discussed where it can be determined for each user which items are available, but in the definition of a report, the general case is defined. For each dimension and memberset selected for the report, the ability exists to select which member items to display as well as which properties to show for those items. By default, only the label property is shown. Figure 14-6 shows the menu options for these selections in the Action pane. In the Action pane, the layout of filters, columns, rows, and values looks very similar to their layout in the PivotTable Designer.

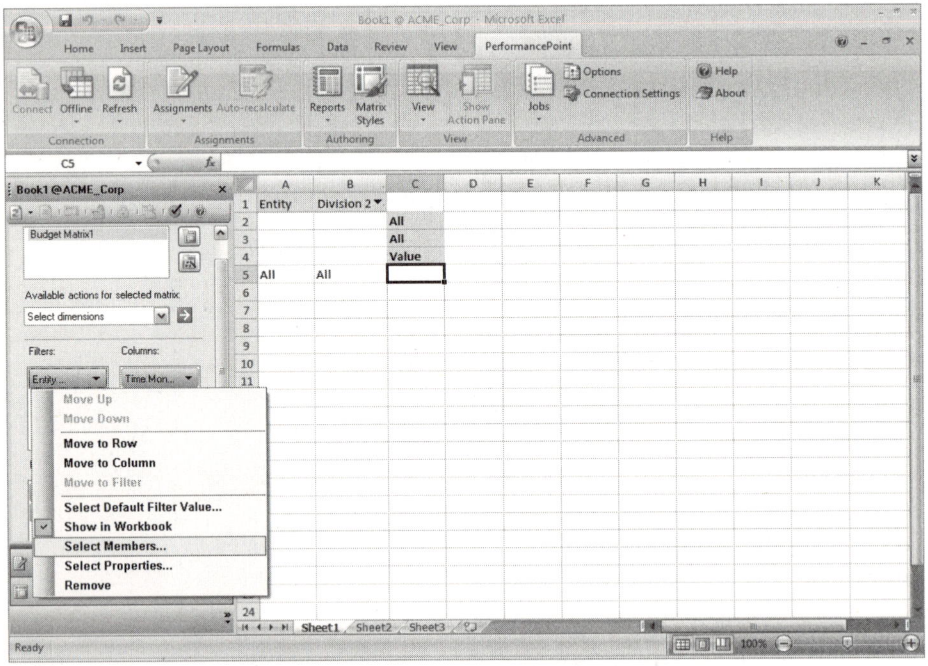

Figure 14-6 Selection of member items and properties to display

Selecting the member items becomes a choice of either static or dynamic presentation. For example, consider an account dimension that has a simple profit-and-loss format of accounts with revenue and expenses. One option to identify items for the report rows is to pick items individually. Each item becomes a static selection in the Selected Members list in the order in which it was selected. In the Selected Members list, the order can be changed to define an exact sequence of items. The list as it appears shows how items will be placed in the report. Because the list is static, any changes to the underlying account items for the model will not appear in the report. For example, a new expense item for Legal Fees that is added under Other Expense will not show up in the report until a report designer places it into the selected list. Reports that are highly structured and do not change often benefit from the consistently defined structure. Specific formatting and layout can be guaranteed because the report itself does not change (rows and columns are always in the same place). For the report to be rendered properly for a user, it is expected that that user has read access for each member item. Figure 14-7 shows the dimension member item selection window with the specific static account list.

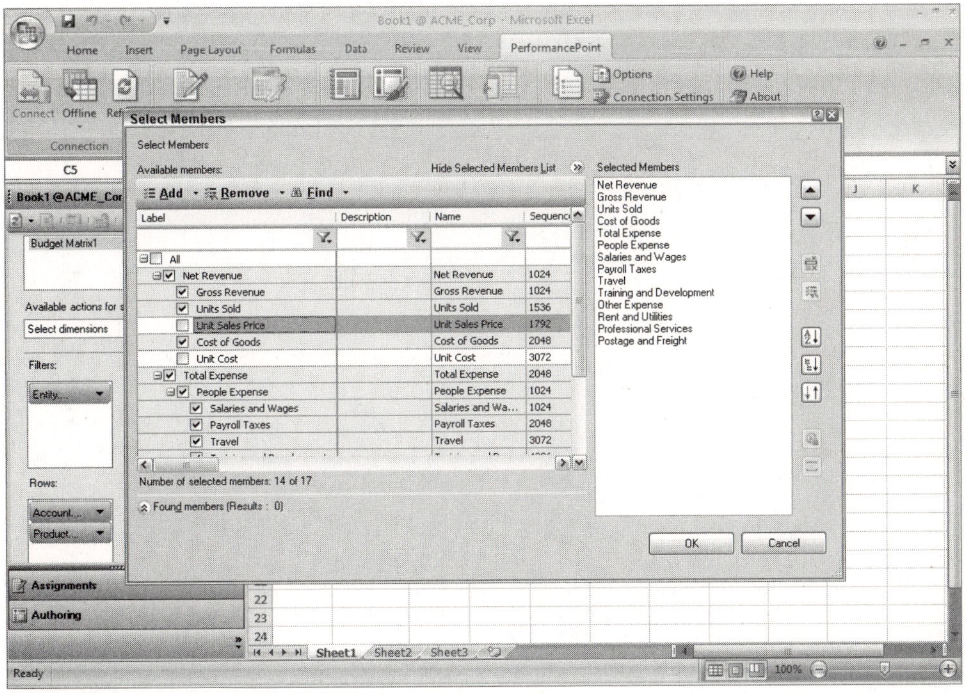

Figure 14-7 Selecting a static set of accounts

For reports built on top of models that have frequently changing item lists (SKUs, for example) or reports that are to be delivered to a broad set of users who have different security access, a dynamic definition is a much better choice. Dynamic definitions are based on some existing item from the structure. It could be the topmost item, All, or it could be something inside the hierarchy of items. Several dynamic functions exist for usage such as Children (all items immediately below the selected item) and Descendents (all items under the selected item, regardless of their level). Figure 14-8 shows the account item selection of everything — descendents of All. This option will display all returned account items at report rendering time in the order in which they appear in the model. If accounts are added or deleted, the rendering adjusts accordingly without notice to the users. Further, if a user opens the report and doesn't have read access to all the account items, the report will render just the items returned by the query (which the user does have access to). This functionality provides a more maintainable environment where the structure or security model may have changes.

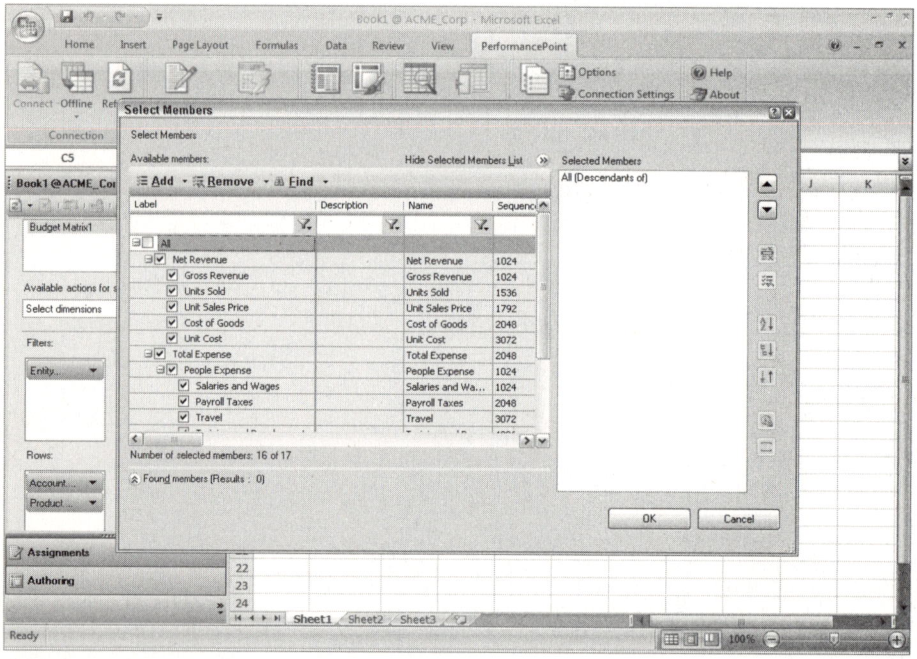

Figure 14-8 Selecting accounts dynamically

The result of selecting member items either statically or dynamically is a report layout that shows the detail items. A modeler user has read access to all items, so in this design, every possible item is returned. Once the layout has been placed into the worksheet, the desired formatting can be specified. If items are dynamically specified, the rows and columns may grow and shrink, as previously discussed, which needs to be factored into formatting decisions. For example, if a total row is underlined when the report is created, there is no guarantee the underline will remain under the row, as different numbers of rows may appear in the report over time or based on different user security permissions. When using Excel 2007, styles may be applied to the matrix, which will change formatting dynamically as the matrix shape changes. The Matrix Styles menu option allows any of the pivot table styles present in the current workbook, including custom styles, to be applied to a matrix. If the style is set to "none," then no automatic formatting will be done. This is beneficial when custom Excel formatting that is overwritten by the matrix style is desired. In addition to selecting a matrix style, formatting options for automatically indenting rows based on the dimension hierarchy and removing blank rows or columns are available. These options can be selected when creating a report, or by using the Report Properties dialog available from the Reports menu. Figure 14-9 shows the report layout that results from selecting account items to show on the rows and time on the columns.

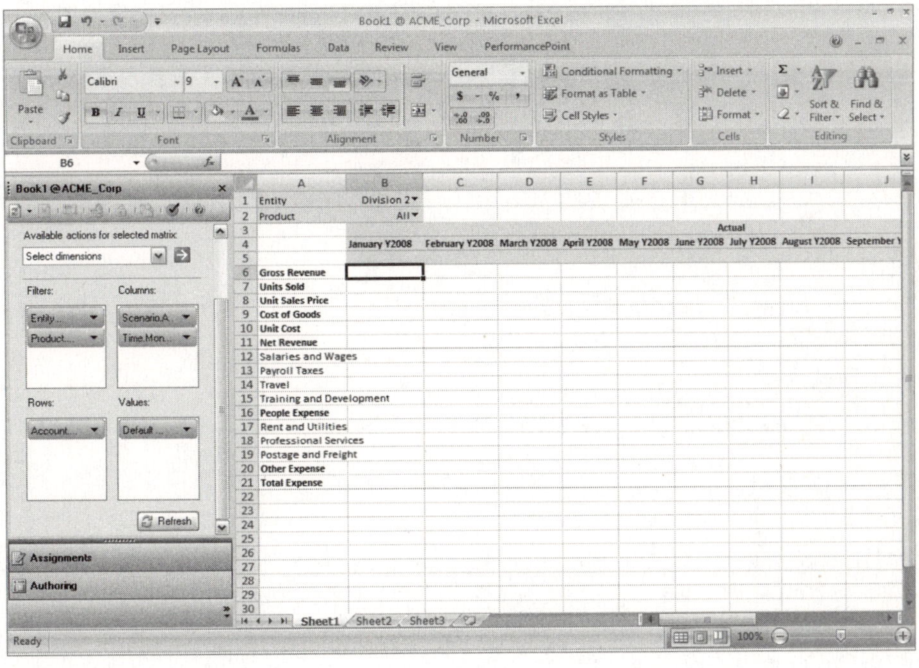

Figure 14-9 Report layout

In addition to defining dimensions and member item layouts for rows and columns, the other primary consideration for a display is how combinations of items are displayed.

Row and Column Intersections

In many cases, a report layout will position multiple dimensions on the same axis. One of the most common examples is to have scenarios like Actual and Budget on columns along with the Time dimension showing months, quarters, or years. In a budgeting report or form, actual results might be displayed for the current year with budget data for the next year. In a rolling 12-month forecast report, the prior 6 months of actual data may be displayed alongside the next 6 months of forecast data. Users familiar with Excel pivot tables will know that most reports generally show all possible combinations, and these types of asymmetric displays can be difficult to construct. The PerformancePoint Excel Add-In allows you to define member intersections for rows and columns so that these common types of layouts can be designed. Figure 14-10 shows a layout of an asymmetric column with the Actual scenario data for the 3 months from October 2008 through December 2008 and the Budget scenario data for the subsequent 3 months from January 2009 through March 2009.

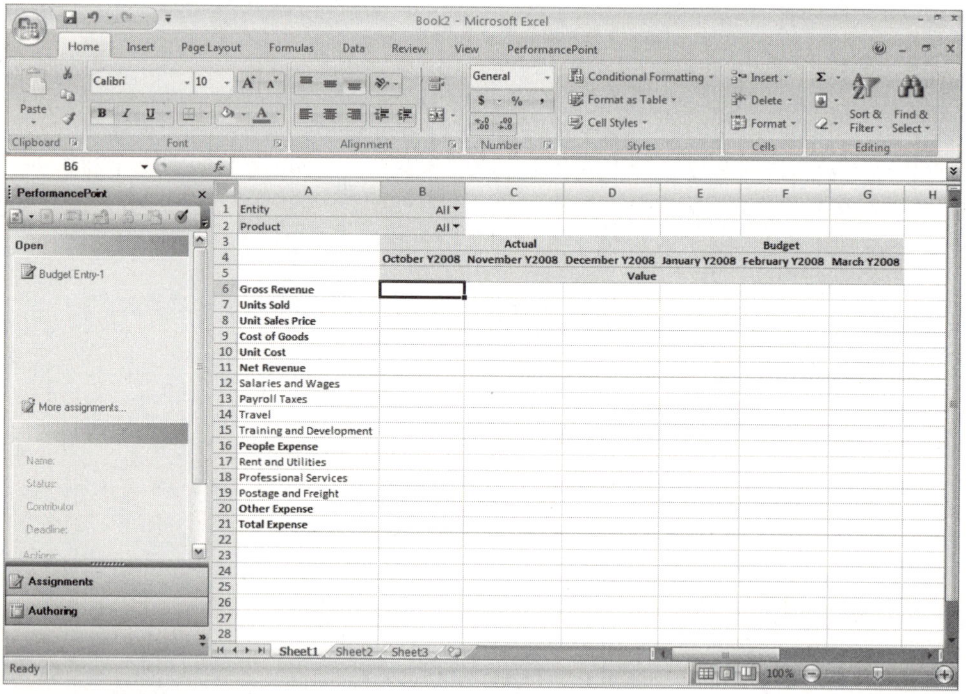

Figure 14-10 Column intersection layout for scenario and time

The definition of column intersections allows the report author to define which member items from one dimension line up with member items from another dimension. Figure 14-11 shows a definition that produces a result like the previous layout. The two intersecting columns are the Month view of the Time dimension and the All Members view of the Scenario dimension. A dynamic selection of Time member items returns the descendents of FY2008, which, in this case, will return all 12 months of 2008. A second selection of Time member items returns all 12 months of 2009, again using the dynamic selection of descendents of FY2009. For the aligned scenarios, a single item static selection is made, first of Actual and second of Budget. In this example, the months of 2008 line up with Actual and the months of 2009 line up with Budget. By default, all intersections are displayed that will be used in the crossing of the two lists, resulting in showing actual data for both 2008 and 2009, followed by budget data for the same years. Some of that data doesn't exist and isn't relevant to this particular report layout, which will produce many empty columns in the final report. When you choose a "Column by column" layout, only the specified intersections are displayed, which results in showing actual data only for 2008 and budget data only for 2009. This is a much more visually appealing report layout, as all columns should contain relevant data with no empty columns. Figure 14-11 shows the definition of the intersection of the scenario and time columns.

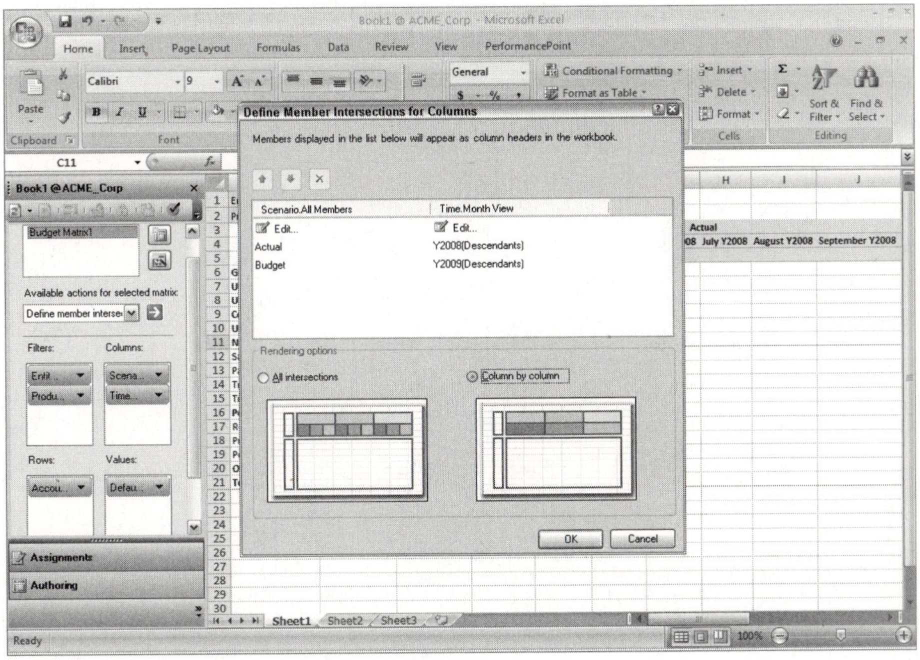

Figure 14-11 Column intersection definition

The layout options of dimensions and selected member items defined dynamically or statically, the intersections of columns or rows appearing in the report, the filtering choices, and the display of properties all provide significant flexibility to design reports and forms necessary to support an application solution.

Report Wizard

When thinking about end-user reporting requirements, one aspect to evaluate is the PerformancePoint Excel Add-In Report Wizard. The wizard provides prepared definitions for the layout of many common reports. These are largely focused on financial scenarios such as cash flow statements, balance sheets, and so on. The wizard defines the standard layout and allows the end user to define how the data from the chosen model fits into the standard definition. The resulting output from the wizard is a matrix that appears similar to an ad hoc defined matrix, but has some added support for layouts that can't be defined through the Matrix Designer.

The Report Wizard begins, as does a standard matrix, with the creation of a new report in an Excel workbook. The first step of the wizard (shown in Figure 14-12) is to define which model will be the source for the report and which template the wizard should begin from. The templates provide a basic structure and layout of common types of financial reports. The example in Figure 14-12 begins with a profitability report template.

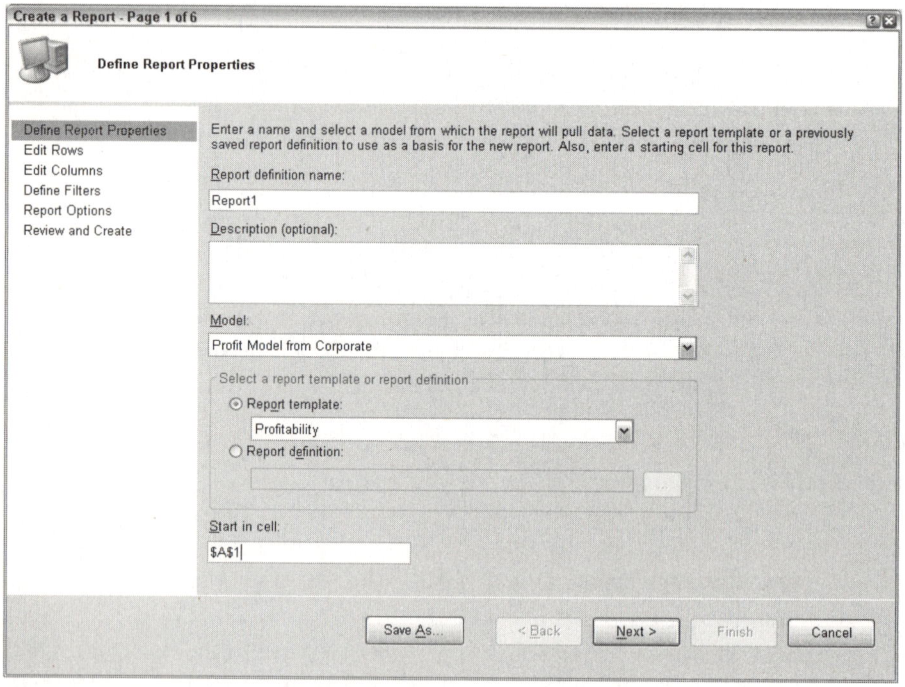

Figure 14-12 Report Wizard properties

Once a model choice is made, the Report Wizard is able to determine from that model what dimensions, member items, properties, and hierarchies are available for the report. The template specifies layouts for the commonly defined model elements. Steps 2, 3, and 4 of the wizard define the layout details for rows, columns, and filters, respectively. The base layouts for rows, columns, and filters are all determined by the report template chosen, but a Report Designer is free to add or remove items as appropriate. In contrast to an ad hoc matrix, though, rows and columns are not just a selection of items — through the Report Wizard, they can be built up with sets of items that function independently. This allows for additional subtotals or the insertion of headers or report-based calculations among the row and column elements. Figure 14-13 shows the row selection step for the profitability report template.

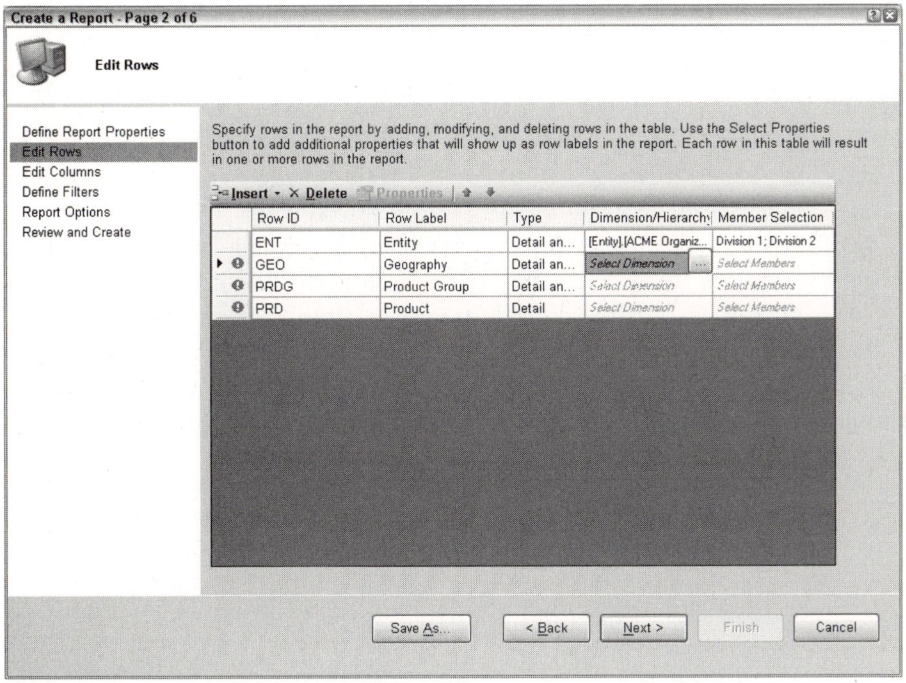

Figure 14-13 Report Wizard row definitions

In the row definition step shown in Figure 14-13, the first row set is defined from the Entity dimension. In this example, the user has specified which hierarchy to use in laying out the report and has selected a subset of the member items for display. As with ad hoc matrix design, member item selection may be dynamic or static. However, since the report template drives the report layout, the formatting can automatically adjust for dynamic definitions. As the Report Designer steps through the wizard, an icon indicates which parts of the definition still need to be defined. In the example from Figure 14-13, the user needs to define three more dimensions. As the user selects a row, he or she can click and make selections via the user interface. If something that is available for the report, like Geography in this example, is not part of the underlying model, the user may simply delete the row item from the template. Similarly, if there are dimension items in the model that should appear on the rows, the user can simply insert a new row item and define it as necessary to achieve the display layout required.

As a Report Wizard definition progresses, the specific selections may be saved in an Extensible Markup Language (XML) format. By saving the partially completed report definition, a user can relaunch the wizard to finish the definition at a later time. Additionally, the partially complete definition can be shared with other users to provide a more customized template-like experience based on the types of models an organization has defined.

Summary

Reports and data entry forms are built on top of the models constructed for an application. In cases where users are accustomed to certain reports and forms, there may be some changes to factor in. Often, it will be best to construct the proper model and then build the report on top. However, there are cases where the reporting is tightly constrained by organizational or regulatory requirements. In the application solution design phase, it is important to jointly design the models, required reports, and desired data entry forms. By doing this, an optimal and appropriately balanced solution will be delivered that matches desired functionality with end-user expectations.

CHAPTER 15

Security and Roles

Security is a critical part of any application. With financially oriented applications in particular, security takes on additional legal considerations from regulations imposed by many governments worldwide. In PerformancePoint Planning Server, security is set for application activities and, most importantly, it is also set for the data contained in an application. This enables application solution designers to set up proper security tasks separately from security concerns related to the data itself. Inversely, with data-level security, you can be certain at any given point what data can be read or written by any individual user.

This chapter covers the configuration and management of both application and data security. It begins by outlining the system roles and what responsibilities they have within an application. User management is key to any application, so how users are added and maintained is covered next. End users will participate in business roles, which are described in the context of an application security model. The means by which data is secured within an application closes out the chapter.

System Security

System security is designed to be managed in an enterprise IT environment. A core responsibility of a technology professional's role is to properly configure and run any application that will be accessible by end users and, as mentioned previously, contains data that may be sensitive either internally or externally. Discussed later in the chapter is the role that a modeler plays in deciding user participation in an application. The critical thing to note is that it always remains a PerformancePoint administrator's role to add and remove users from an application. In many enterprise IT organizations, a single administrator is not given control of all aspects of an application in order to "separate powers" for governance reasons. This separation of administrative functions is accomplished through system roles.

System Roles

PerformancePoint Planning Server defines administrative roles automatically for every application. In order to facilitate end-to-end functionality, at least one user is required for each of the administrative system roles. It's considered best practice to segment these functions to different, appropriate IT personnel, but in some cases, a single user may play multiple system roles in an application. The system roles cover functionality for the global system, modeling, data, and users. The last three — modeling, data, and users — can be scoped to either an entire application or only within a single model site.

Global Administrator

The Global Administrator (GA) role is the only role that starts with one user. The user automatically assigned to this role is the user who installed the PerformancePoint Planning Server. Subsequently, the initial GA user may add other users to the GA role. Users in the GA role can use the Admin Console to adjust system settings such as async queue times, logging settings, and the like. Any GA user may also create and delete applications. Once applications exist, a GA user may assign User Administrators.

User Administrator

The User Administrator (UA) role drives the first step in the overall security process. Users in this role are able to add and remove users to and from an application or a model site within an application. This action is generally performed in the Admin Console, but a UA user has limited access to perform these functions from the Business Modeler. Note that by default, a UA user has no access to meta data or application data. In addition to adding users to an application, a UA user has the ability to place these users into system roles with the exception of the GA role.

Data Administrator

The Data Administrator (DA) role has a slightly different function than its name might imply. The users assigned the DA role have the ability to execute and work with data jobs. These data jobs move data into or out of an application (jobs are described in Chapter 16). The DA role does not assign data security.

This is done via business roles described later in the chapter. The data job functionality is exposed through the Business Modeler interface. It may also be accessed for batch processing through the PPSCmd utility. It is important to note that backend processes that load system data and update system meta data need to be executed under an account that has been added to the DA role.

Modeler

Members of the Modeler role perform the primary design and maintenance activities within an application. Modeler users have access to the necessary functionality within the Business Modeler user interface. As with the other roles, users may be added at the level of an entire application or to a specific site within an application. Users assigned the Modeler role will be able to define business roles and manage the data security for end users participating in an application's process.

Users

As previously stated, users of a PerformancePoint Planning Server application are Windows Active Directory users. These user accounts are added to an entire application or an individual site within an application. Once user accounts are defined in an application, User Administrators can assign them to a system role or Modelers can assign them a data or process role within an application.

Once users are defined and the responsibilities of system roles are granted, the security model can be defined in accordance with the needs of a particular application, or for distinct processes within an application's site.

Application Security

The aspect controlled explicitly by an administrator is inclusion of users in an application. These users must be defined in Windows Active Directory. Windows authentication through Active Directory (AD) is the authentication mechanism for PerformancePoint Server (note that LDAP binding is not supported). When a client request comes to the server, the first step is always to authenticate that user in AD. Once the user is authenticated, there's a second step in the process, which authorizes the user within the application context. This ensures that users within an application can be given different roles, allowing them different abilities to execute application functions. For example, user 1 might just be able to read and write some data as part of a budgeting process, whereas user 2 may be granted the ability to execute certain jobs that change data (such as a currency conversion job). Data security is defined by the application and is specified, again, for the AD user account. This ensures that data security set by PerformancePoint Planning Server can be enforced without the server doing any authorization steps. The advantage is that any data access is now secured, making the data equally usable through PerformancePoint scorecards and dashboards or other data query or visualization tools.

Business roles are the foundation of the PerformancePoint Planning Server security model. Although the security administrator places users into the application, it is by assigning them to a role that the Business Modeler grants the ability to interact with it. It is the business role that is given access to a business model and is assigned read and/or write access to data within that model. That access can be broad, covering all data within a model, or very specific to only a few small data elements within a model. Multiple roles allow different subsets of users to access different portions of data within the same model (or similar access across multiple models).

Business Roles

Business roles are the base definitions for users to interact with portions of an application. A business role is created by a modeler and is defined within the context of a model site. At the time of creation, a default permission choice is made as shown in Figure 15-1. This default sets the initial security to be granted to any user subsequently added to the role. Additionally, at any point, security could be reset to the default level across all users within the role. Once a role is created and defaults are set, specifics for that role can be defined.

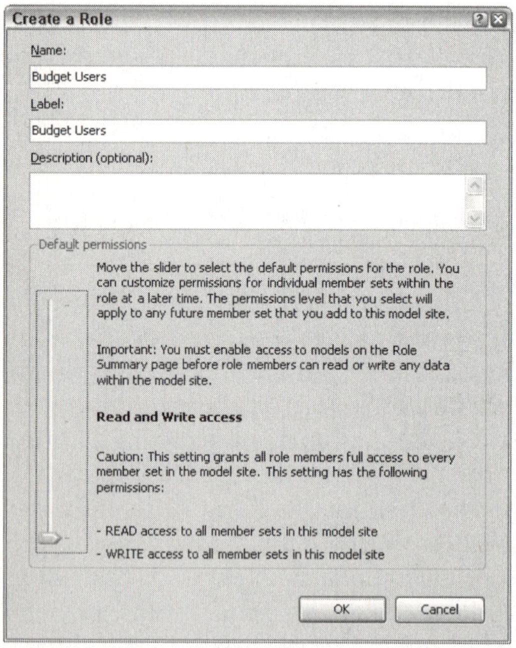

Figure 15-1 Business role creation with the default set to read/write

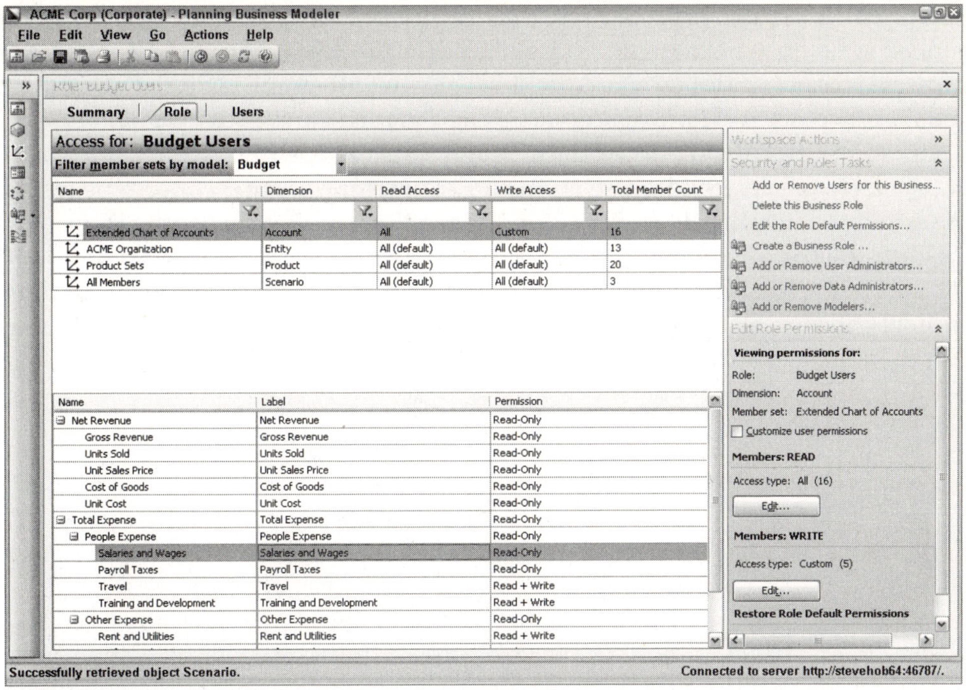

Figure 15-2 Security set on an item in a dimension memberset

Security for business roles can be defined at the most detailed level if necessary. Within a model, the intersection point for all data is the items within the dimensions used in that model. You'll recall from Chapter 11 that when adding a dimension to a model, a memberset is specified. Thus, security definition on a dimension is specified uniquely to a memberset. A key advantage of this ability is that membersets, being completely independent representations of the same dimension items, allow distinct security against the same items. For example, an HR model may include a memberset on the Account dimension that has a salary account. Due to its sensitivity, only a couple of users may have read permission to the salary account when it is used in the HR model. However, in a budget model, the salary account may be visible to each department owner with less security concern because the budget model contains no individual employee information. This is simply accomplished using a different memberset for the budget model and specifying the business role uniquely on that memberset. Security on each item, then, is set to NONE for no access, READ for the ability to see the data, or WRITE for the ability to change the value. READ and WRITE may be specified in combination if appropriate. Figure 15-2 shows a mixture of read and write security set on the Extended Chart of Accounts memberset for the Account dimension. In the budget model, some of the accounts will be used for data entry and others will be calculated or entered from other sources. Once security is defined for the dimension/memberset combinations included in a model, a final access step is necessary.

In order to maintain security in an application with many shared dimensions and membersets, it is not sufficient to assign security just to those membersets. For example, a sales reporting model may use the identical dimensions and membersets as a sales forecasting model. Therefore, a business role needs to be added to each model individually, regardless of any security defined for the dimensions and membersets used in the model. By default a role is off for every model and must be explicitly turned on. Specifying which models are accessible by a business role is shown in Figure 15-3.

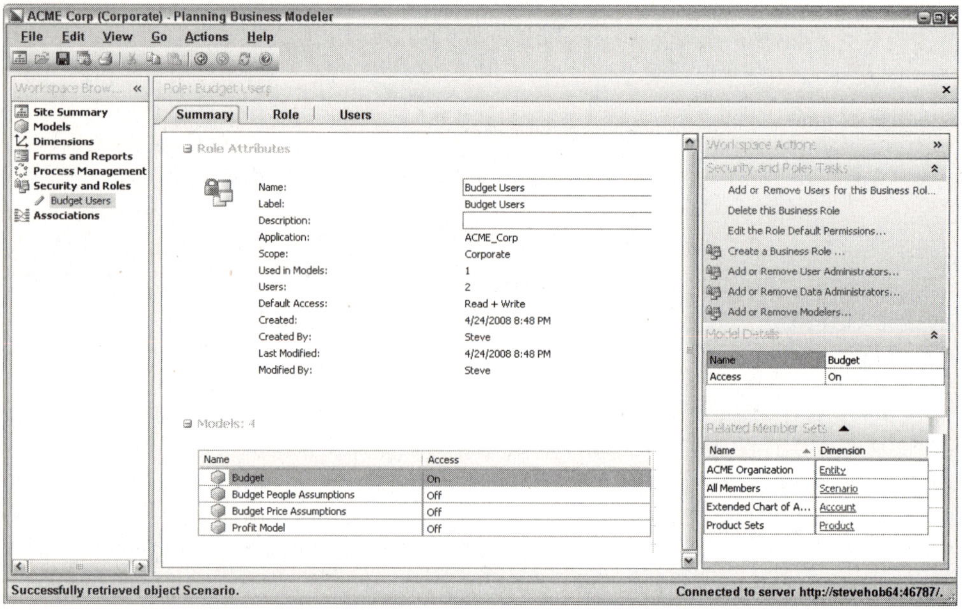

Figure 15-3 Enabling model access for a business role

Users and Roles

Within a business role, users are added. This is similar to adding users to a system role, except that the action can be performed by a modeler. Note that only users already added to the application by the User Administrator are available to be added to a business role. This ensures that a modeler cannot grant new people access to the application. The modeler only defines the participation within an application to which users have already been added. By default, all users within a role get the same security access. There is the ability for a modeler to enable user customization. This customization allows the narrowing of permissions at a user level. For example, all sales team members may have very similar permissions within a model. However, each sales member might only get WRITE permission to his or her particular department (using the Entity dimension). This allows one business role to be defined and then each user to have a unique setting of WRITE permission only along the Entity dimension. Allowing this type of customization should significantly reduce role maintenance.

User Dimension

One special case of users is found in the User dimension. The User dimension appears similar to other dimensions, but it is populated with items corresponding to each user account that has been added to an application. Just as with other dimensions, membersets can be created on the User dimension that allow parent-child relationships to be defined; these membersets are made up of relationships between users in an application. The purpose of creating membersets on the User dimension is that they will be available for specifying review roles within an application's assignment process flow (see Chapter 16). The User dimension plays no role in data security definitions for an application.

Data Security

Data security is a core concern for most PerformancePoint Planning Server applications. In today's environment where there is increasing rigor around audit and control functions, all these aspects can be controlled. By default, no security is granted to any user or role newly added to an application. While it may be tempting to provide a shortcut to allow administrator access to everything, solution designers should carefully consider the security needs of the application and only assign the minimum required security privileges. Not only is this considered proper, safe, and secure, but as an application evolves and expands, it will ensure that unintended user rights are not granted.

Model Access

As mentioned previously, a business role has no access to any models by default. Thus, once a business role is defined, model access must be granted to models where that role is expected to participate. Any models added to an application after the creation of a role will again default to no access to any of the business roles. Note that any structure changes to a model will not affect whether a business role has access to that model.

Configuring Read/Write Security

Initial security for every dimension and memberset combination will be set according to the default for the role. In a highly secured environment, the default security should be set to NONE, which will not allow any access. In an environment less restrictive, a default of READ and WRITE can provide access to everything. From the default, the modeler sets specific permissions on every item. Changes to read permission and changes to write permission are made separately to ensure that there is no confusion about which permission is being altered. Figure 15-4 shows an explicit setting of write security to some members of the Account dimension.

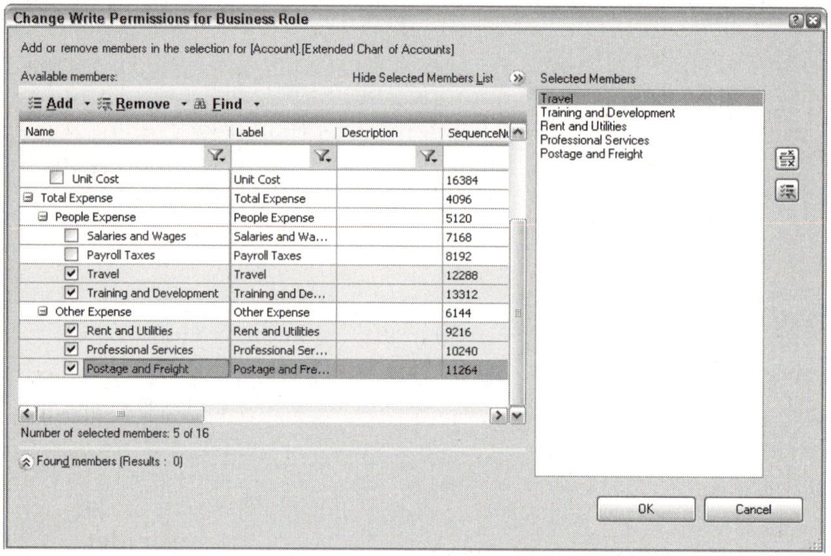

Figure 15-4 Setting write security to some member items

Note that Rent and Utilities, Professional Services, and Postage and Freight are all items under Other Expense. In Figure 15-4, each item was selected for write access individually. This explicit selection means that only these items will be assigned write permission. In the case where more items are added under Other Expense, the security permissions would have to be edited. However, in cases where items change frequently, it may be better to define write security for everything that falls under Other Expense. Figure 15-5 shows how this is done by adding the descendent items to Other Expense.

Setting the security level via a dynamic reference will ease the maintenance for dimensions that receive frequent changes. In the preceding example (see

Figure 15-5), the descendents of reference will assign write permission to any member item that falls under the Other Expense item.

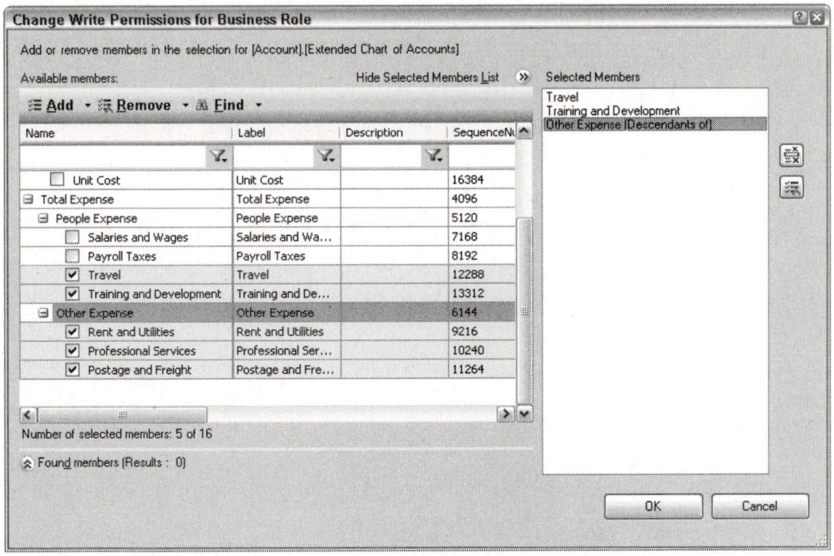

Figure 15-5 Setting write security to descendent member items

Security Deployment

Security definitions via business roles apply directly to the data within an application. Therefore, it's important to note that this is the one type of definition that immediately reflects a running application. As soon as any user or security permission changes are saved, those changes are pushed out and applied to any existing application structures and data. Thus, the security model always reflects what is shown in the Business Modeler definition environment.

The data for a PerformancePoint Planning application is stored within an Analysis Services cube. The security defined via a business role, then, is expressed via user security in Analysis Services roles. In order to allow individual user security specification, roles will be defined specific to each user. This ensures that all data access going through Analysis Services will have proper data-level security applied. The side benefit is that the data cubes themselves are secured. Thus, access to the cube can come through other tools such as PerformancePoint scorecards and dashboards. Any compliant tool that can access Analysis Services may be used, and the users will have the same data restriction they would have directly through PerformancePoint Planning Server.

Summary

Security is a critical component of any data-oriented application. PerformancePoint Planning Server allows significant flexibility and granular control of the user security model to support many different application solution requirements. System roles control the administrative functions within an application and support the segmentation of administrative functionality for governance purposes. Business roles are defined by modelers to define and maintain the data security for users participating in an application. Finally, it's key to note the security deployment model and understand the extended value of deploying security with the data, which enables broader access to application data with high confidence in crucial security adherence.

CHAPTER

16

Data Process

One thing that sets PerformancePoint Planning Server apart is its ability to tie pieces together and implement a business solution. Once application objects are created, business rules are defined, data is loaded, forms are created, and security and roles are configured, the process characteristics of the application solution can be configured. It is necessary to understand the proper data process flow and how end-user contributors will participate in that process. The end-user contributions come through individual assignments contained within broader cycles. Multiple process cycles may be defined in a single application in order to properly segment the activities of a multi-step business process. Appropriate business rules may be incorporated into the process through jobs scheduled within a cycle. All of these pieces work in conjunction with end users to put a standard process around a planning application.

This chapter covers the core process flow objects available in PerformancePoint Planning Server. It begins by outlining definitions and instances that apply to all process object types. Then, it outlines each process flow object individually, describing the configuration and behavior of the objects. Finally, the usage of the objects to formulate an overall process is outlined.

Process Flow Objects

A critical first concept to cover when describing process flow objects is the difference between definitions and instances. Each process flow object described later in the chapter has both design-time definitions and runtime instances. It's necessary to identify the relationship between the two in describing how to build process flow into an application.

Definitions

A definition is the design-time specification of a process flow object. The definition captures properties of that object to identify it — such as name, label, and type — as well as specific configuration properties that vary depending on the type of object. For example, a cycle defines the model to write data into as a property, and a job may have a scheduled date/time property. These definitions can be recurring, allowing a single definition to generate many instances over time. Definitions, themselves, have no execution behavior. For example, nothing may be executed for a job definition. Only under a generated instance may execution occur.

Instances

Instances represent an execution item on which an action may be performed. Instances are generated from a definition. In most cases, definitions will be defined well in advance of the instances themselves as the data process is predetermined for activities like forecasting or budgeting. The instances may be repeating for events that periodically recur, such as a monthly forecast, which are defined once as a recurring event; after that, repeat instances are automatically triggered. Instances are the runtime objects that allow user interaction with the application process.

The critical relationship to understand is that instances are derived from definitions. In other words, at a defined point in time specified within a cycle, instances are generated from it. These instances are dependent on settings from the definition exactly as specified at generation time. For example, a definition of the contributors to an assignment may be defined simply by role. At creation time, the server will generate a unique assignment for each user in the role at the time.

Data Process Flow

Data process flow within an application is largely controlled by process buckets called cycles. Cycles determine what data within a single model are opened up for contribution (input) and for what time period they will be open. The more specific the definition, the tighter audit and control an application will have. In some solutions, such as a long-range forecast, it may be entirely appropriate to have a period of several weeks during which contributors may submit new data or change existing forecast data. However, collecting and consolidating actual data for reporting purposes is generally a process only open for a few days, and submission beyond a certain time point would compromise the integrity of data used for reporting. Figure 16-1 represents the process flow PerformancePoint Planning Server provides to facilitate the collection of data.

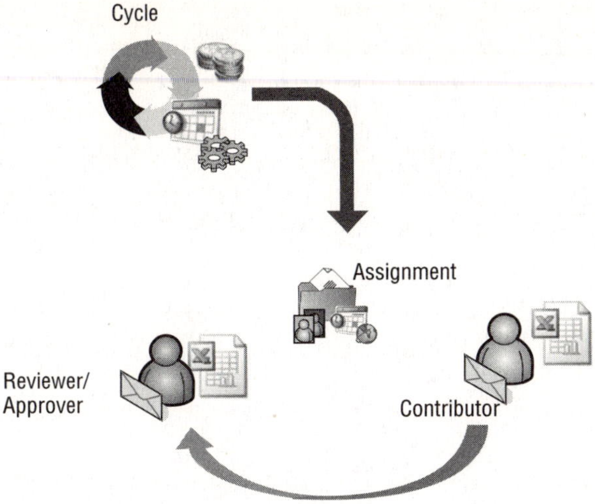

Figure 16-1 Data process flow diagram

Within a cycle, individual contributors are given assignments that personalize their interaction with the application. An assignment is the combination of an Excel data entry form with a user (defined by a business role or a specific user). Any reports that were designed and published as forms are eligible to use in assignments. In defining the proper contributor experience for an application solution, the more comfortable and familiar the end users are with their form, the more efficiently they'll complete the process. Jobs are used within cycles to manage data (calculation, loading, or output) within the specific context of a cycle.

Cycles

Cycles are used to open a section of data for input and manage the contribution process. A cycle in and of itself doesn't grant write access to that data, but it provides the overall scope within which individual users may be given the ability to write data. In addition to being given a name, a cycle is set to a single model choice for submission. This doesn't prohibit the retrieval of data from other models, but it does restrict input to a single model that helps with auditing and data consistency. Once the model is chosen, a cycle has three crucial properties to define what the available write scope is. First, it requires modelers to identify a single member from the scenario dimension. This will commonly be examples like Actual, Budget, or Forecast. Because a cycle is business process–focused, defining one scenario for input constrains each cycle to the proper business context. Within a cycle, you can control which type of data is being collected and ensure that unintended changes aren't allowed (for example, changes to actual data during a budget process). In addition to the scenario, a calendar range is chosen for the time period for submission. Two properties simply specify a beginning and ending range for data entry. For example, an annual budget may capture data beginning January 2009 and ending December 2009. This date range, in combination with the scenario, defines a scope of data that is available for entry. Once the scope available for entry has been defined in a cycle definition, an assignment definition specifies the users and forms used to interact with the data. Figure 16-2 shows a properly defined cycle.

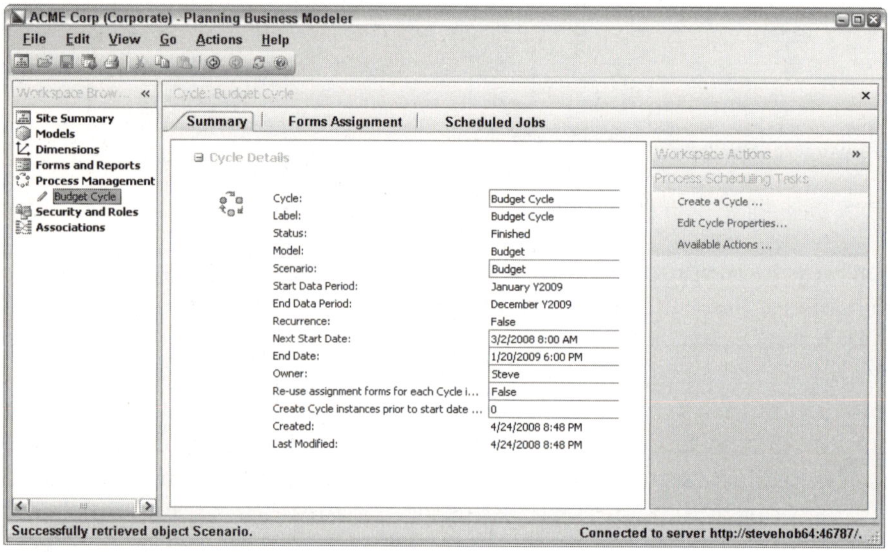

Figure 16-2 Cycle definition

A running cycle instance begins from an already saved definition. Whether the cycle was defined so that it occurs once or as a recurring cycle, it must generate an instance to trigger user activity in assignments or jobs. At the point where the cycle instance is generated, any relative definitions are concretely determined. For example, if a cycle defines its open data entry period to be the CurrentPeriod property value for a model, the exact value (such as May 2008) is retrieved from the property at generation time and remains fixed for that cycle instance. In addition to the cycle instance being created, the instances for assignments and jobs are also created based on the respective definitions for the cycle. Instantiation of a cycle instance is a one-time action that creates the instance objects within that cycle. Once a cycle has been generated, therefore, changes to its definition will not affect the already running instances. A cycle may be regenerated by an administrative owner. Regeneration will delete all the instance objects and replace them with new ones. Any changes to the definition will be reflected in the regenerated objects. A cycle may also be purged from the system completely. Figure 16-3 shows a generated cycle instance with assigned values for its properties.

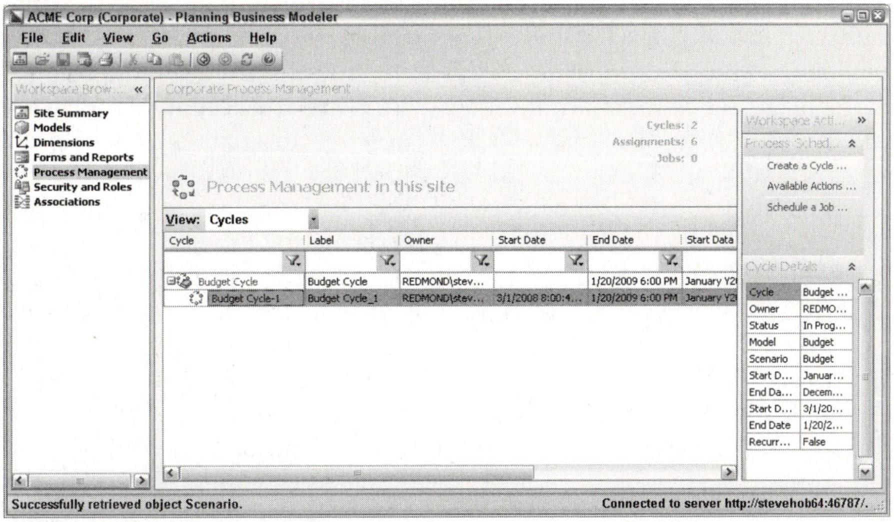

Figure 16-3 Running cycle instance

A cycle is meant to facilitate a business process component of an application. In order to facilitate a dynamic process, some additional administrative control is offered for running cycle instances. First, at any point in time, a cycle may be closed down. Closing a cycle immediately restricts all the data entry permissions that were available through assignments under a cycle. More commonly than completely closing off a cycle, it is necessary at some point of a business process to temporarily suspend data submission or job execution. An administrative owner of a cycle may lock the cycle down at any time. Locking the cycle allows activities such as data loading and data exporting to occur without interruption or the danger of partially processed data causing inconsistency. When a cycle is locked, an optional parameter allows the administrator to determine whether pending submissions are allowed to proceed or fail. For a lock during data loading, pending processing is generally acceptable. However, during a reporting cycle, having any pending submissions failed may be a more appropriate action. After cycles are locked, a modeler or cycle owner simply unlocks them to resume full cycle operations.

Assignments

Assignments are always contained within a cycle and define the presentation of the data within a cycle. Presentation of data depends on three factors. First, an assignment specifies a data entry form to be used. Any report that has published as a data entry form is available for use within an assignment. Note that there is no requirement for the form to display data for the model made available for input through the cycle. Any data shown by a form that is outside the cycle's write scope will simply remain read-only within the assignment. After a form is chosen, contributors to the assignment are chosen from available business users. These users must be part of a business role for the model site. However, in defining an assignment, it's acceptable to select individual users or entire roles. If a business role is chosen as the contributor of the assignment, each individual user within that role will get his or her own assignment when instances are created. The third factor determining data presentation is not explicitly specified. It is the security defined over the users or business roles chosen for the assignment. Because data security is applied, assigning a form to a user will only result in proper data reading or writing if security has been defined for that user or role. It is the responsibility of the modeler to design models, forms, and security in conjunction with the desired cycles and assignments to ensure that the proper display of data for reading and writing occurs to meet the business needs of the solution.

During the timeframe of a cycle, individual assignments allow for the division of tasks during an appropriate portion of the overall time span. For each assignment defined, a specific time window is defined. For ease of definition in relation to the overall cycle, the definition can be made relevant to the overall cycle. For example, an assignment may be made to start two days after its parent cycle begins and end three days before the overall cycle closes. Assignments can be placed sequentially within a cycle to provide appropriate segmentation of events. Sales input might be forecast via one assignment during the first week of a cycle followed by a manufacturing assignment over the second week. By fitting assignments into the proper segment of the overall cycle, a multi-step business process can be defined to involve the appropriate users at the appropriate time.

The final configuration for an assignment defines what form of review and approval will occur once a user has submitted the assignment. This is an optional step but one that enables many common process flows for forecasting and budgeting. A reviewer is someone designated to have the ability to check data submitted by contributor users in their assignments. Reviewers may be responsible for checking the work of several contributors. They are able to reject an assignment and send it back to the contributor or accept it and send it further along the process. Approvers are the final step — they perform similar tasks as reviewers, but an acceptance by the approver officially completes an assignment process. Approvers may review the results from individual contributors or results that others have already reviewed. Both reviewers and approvers may optionally be given the ability to modify data from the original submission. Data changes will be audited so that it is clear what data the reviewer or approver changed. Figure 16-4 shows two assignment definitions together under a single cycle definition.

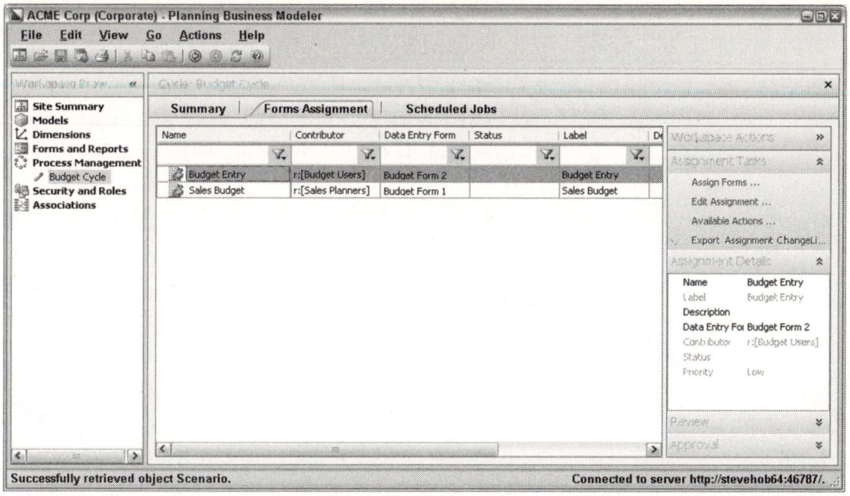

Figure 16-4 Assignment definition

Assignment instances must always fall within the context of a cycle instance. These follow the definitions described in the previous section. At the time of instantiation, a uniquely identified assignment instance is created for each contributor user. When user definitions are based on business roles, each user in the role gets his or her own assignment at generation time. The assignment, then, becomes that user's interaction point with the application for submitting data to a model. Figure 16-5 shows generated assignment instances within a running cycle. In this example budget cycle, there were two assignment definitions, one for sales budgeting and one for general budget entry. Each assignment definition was generated for two contributors, resulting in four distinct assignment instances.

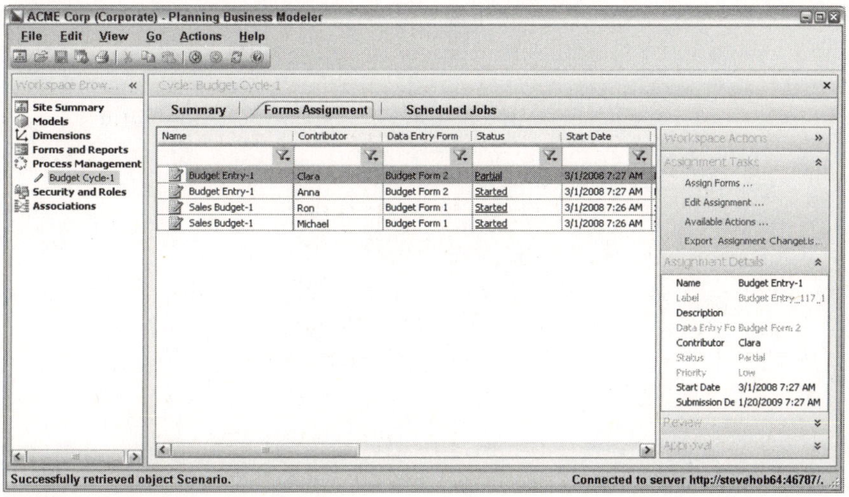

Figure 16-5 Assignment instances

With their individual assignments, users have a couple of different choices for saving their changes. The first option for users is Save Privately. The private option for saving data will store a user's specific changes back on the PerformancePoint Planning Server. These changes are stored separately from the data and are applied for that user over the other data that exists on the server. The other options Submit Draft and Submit, have similar behavior. Both of these forms of submission post data back into the server's processing queue (described in Chapter 10). Any user with sufficient read permissions will be able to see the submitted data once the server has completed its validation and processing. The draft form of submission simply posts the data back, leaving the assignment open in a partial state, which will allow the contributor to return and make another submission (while the assignment instance remains open). A final submission will post data and mark the assignment instance as submitted. This closes off the ability for the user to submit via the assignment and triggers any of the defined process flows, review or approval, which were specified for the assignment.

Review and Approval

The review and approval process follows a straightforward flow of action that is commonly found in planning and budgeting processes. During the definition phase, an option is specified determining whether or not reviewers or approvers may change the submitted data. In some processes, management corrections may be made directly to the data. When a reviewer or approver makes a data change, the server processing is done similarly to the assignment submission itself. Generally, a reviewer or approver has responsibility for multiple individual assignments. Reviewers have the option of looking at changes combined over a set of data that multiple users have submitted or they can look at each user's assignment submission separately. When an adjustment is made by the reviewer or approver, the change is associated with the individual assignment submission that was being reviewed. In addition to viewing and changing data, reviewers and approvers move an assignment back and forth through an overall submission process. Either a reviewer or an approver may reject an assignment. Rejection sends that assignment back to the contributor in a rejected state, which will allow that user to again perform a submission. To advance an assignment, a reviewer marks an assignment as reviewed and an approver marks an assignment as approved. In the case of a review, the reviewed state may be the ending point or, if approvers were defined for the assignment, it will be pushed up to the final approver.

Jobs

Jobs are definitions used to execute an already defined rule or set of rules. With the creation of a job, rule execution can be given a specific name and, just as with a cycle, a date and time window during which the job is valid. The job could be scheduled or set to execute on demand by a user with proper permissions to the job. A job can be defined by itself or it may be defined within the context of a cycle. When a job is defined in a cycle, it can participate in processes through that cycle (such as assignments). Placing a job in a cycle allows contributor end users for that cycle to have permission to execute the job while the cycle is open. This provides a mechanism for allowing end users to execute system processes. There are several built-in job types to choose from. Data integration jobs allow the execution of data loading or data exporting jobs, which can move data around into, out of, and within an application. Financial jobs allow the execution of predefined financial logic such as currency conversion or consolidations. Calculation jobs provide the ability to execute any other defined business rule.

Jobs defined within the context of a cycle will have a job instance created for that cycle. Through security in the definition, these job instances may be executed by end users via the Launch Jobs option on the Jobs menu found in the PerformancePoint Excel Add-In. Jobs can be executed on demand or scheduled by a user. Each instance remains distinct and, like assignments, may be re-run many different times. Job parameters will be saved with the instance, so re-execution of a job instance enables the reuse of the previous set of parameters (although they can be changed with each execution). When scheduling a job, a time is specified. Whether scheduled or executed on demand, jobs are executed asynchronously, so the effects of a job may not be immediately visible. A Job Status menu option is available to check the execution of a job.

Summary

Data process flow in PerformancePoint Planning Server is targeted at common planning and budgeting requirements. A key concept to understand is the difference between definitions and instances. Definitions allow for the specification of recurring processes and the use of placeholder values, which are concretely determined at instance generation time. This allows for flexible definition of significant workflow processes that will be common and repeated throughout an application's lifecycle. End users, then, interact via cycles, assignments, and jobs that are assigned to them.

CHAPTER

17

Deployment and Migration

PerformancePoint Planning Server evolves the application development process from an IT development project to one that more closely partners with business owners. There are still core practices that must be followed and incorporated into the new application solution. One of these is the practice of having cycles that cover development, testing, and production deployments. An application will allow more dynamic maintenance and user interaction, but it will still be crucial to make sure that critical changes are tested in advance of a production release for mission-critical application solutions. PerformancePoint Planning Server includes migration functionality to facilitate this process, but it should be considered in conjunction with the planning for deployment and long-term maintenance of the application solution being delivered.

This chapter covers the deployment of PerformancePoint Planning Server applications. It describes options for development and production application deployments. Facilitating the work within a deployment environment is scriptable, command-line functionality available in PPSCmd. These functions enable migration of environments necessary to support deployments. Finally, the interaction of product data with a deployed environment is described.

Deployment and Scaling

Chapter 10 covered the components of PerformancePoint Planning Server and how they fit into an application. Figure 10-6 showed how those components fit together as part of the overall solution. In Figure 17-1, the components are broken into the client and server layers covered in this chapter.

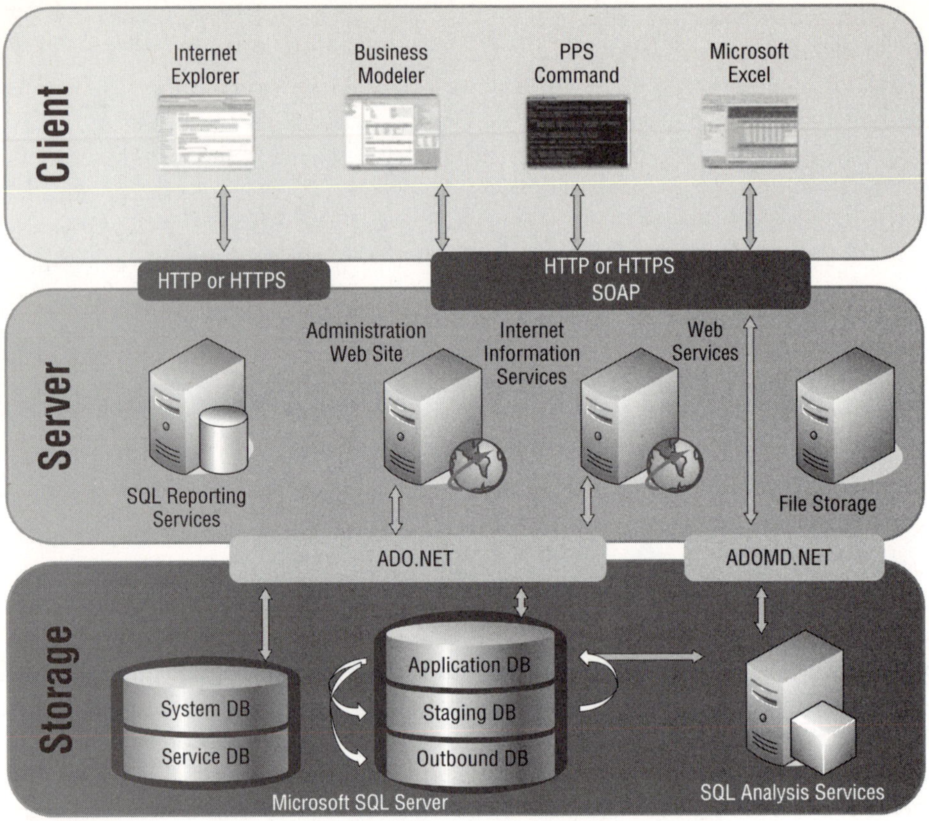

Figure 17-1 PerformancePoint Server Planning deployment guide

The SQL Server components provide storage and management of all the physical data, both the relational databases and the OLAP cubes in Analysis Services. There are many different methods and considerations for data volume deployment and scaling with Microsoft SQL Server. A few items will be covered briefly, but other resources should be referred to for data platform best practices. Files are managed either through SharePoint or other file server technology. File storage is not a primary concern in most deployments and will not be covered in detail here. The two PerformancePoint components of primary consideration in a deployment topology are the two server components: process services and Web Services. These do much of the work while an application is running, and these services have several effects on scaling, which depend on the overall profile of an application.

Deployment

The deployment of an application consists of two steps: installation and configuration. In order to facilitate the distribution of components to different types of server computer hardware, setup allows you to choose which components to install (see Chapter 3 for details on setup). In a proof-of-concept environment, all components may be installed on a single server, including clients. The evaluation edition of the software is designed for this configuration. In other environments, it is generally recommended that you put different components on physically separate machines. Doing so allows for proper load-balancing to support scalability and for segmentation to facilitate security, maintenance, and troubleshooting. Each component area has a few unique considerations to factor into deployment decisions.

Web Services

The Web Services of the front-end server are .NET 2.0 components hosted by Microsoft IIS 6.0. Microsoft Internet Information Services (IIS) provides the Web technologies which PerformancePoint layers on top of. Critical to deployment and scaling considerations is that IIS provides a server farm, which is a common method of supporting Network Load Balancing (NLB). Physical hardware load balancing may be employed as well to gain similar capacity support. Because the Web Services handle all communication and workload transfer with the clients (Business Modeler, Admin Console, and Excel), applications with many users require the ability to balance that workload across servers. NLB support through IIS allows multiple PerformancePoint Web Services to work together as a single interface for an application. They work together through a shared back-end database, which provides a single container for data and a single control point for service operation.

One or more Web Service, front-end servers may be installed as part of the application deployment. The first installed server will create and configure two databases to coordinate the server's behavior: a service database and a system database. These two databases allow subsequent server installations to be directed to the information necessary to allow them to participate as part of a combined, single server. Similar to the Web Service servers, multiple process servers may also used in conjunction to scale up the processing power.

Process Services

The process services are Windows services, which execute much of the processing functionality of a PerformancePoint Planning Server application. The process services execute back-end server functions such as processing calculations and submitted data. Unlike the Web Services, which act together through NLB, each process service runs and executes independently. When a process service is installed, it is directed to a front-end Web Service, which it connects with. The front-end Web server handles the distribution of tasks, synchronous or asynchronous, to process services as required for system actions that need to be performed. The system and service databases that were installed with the first front-end server handle the queue of activities that the process services perform. As new process servers are brought online, they join in and begin processing tasks queued up for action.

Clients

Client deployment is straightforward for PerformancePoint Server. Both the Business Modeler client and the Excel Add-In client are standalone, installable components. They operate independently, so a user may install one or both without any consequences. The deployment consideration to note with clients is that they need to be properly synchronized with the server version to be accessed. This means that as a server infrastructure is installed or upgraded, the clients of that application need to be appropriately installed or upgraded.

Data Platform

The Microsoft SQL Server data platform provides the layer onto which PerformancePoint Server 2007 is deployed. The relational databases for PerformancePoint Server can exist on a single SQL Server instance. Deploying to a single SQL Server simplifies the requirements for the database server. However, different servers can be used for system databases and application databases. For scaling and availability, standard SQL Server methods, such as clustering, may be used. The services running for PerformancePoint will need access to the SQL Server, but not as a full database administrator (DBA). This means that PerformancePoint may securely exist in parallel with other SQL Server applications using different databases on the same server. For SQL Analysis Services, each model site may deployed to a separate server. As with the relational databases, PerformancePoint will operate its own Analysis Services databases, which means that they can be isolated from other applications the server is used for. However, because of performance considerations for Analysis Services, you might not want to host multiple applications on the same server.

Having the full Microsoft SharePoint platform is not a requirement for a PerformancePoint Planning Server application. Either a SharePoint document library or a network file share is required for storage of reports and forms. A report library is necessary to publish reports to reporting services. However, the core functionality works equally well with either type of file system.

Many of the considerations related to the deployment topology of an application are driven by the production profile of the application. Considerations like data volume, end-user query performance, and data processing capabilities are factors that drive deployment choices, based on the performance and scalability needs of an application.

NOTE The Deployment Guide for PerformancePoint Server 2007 contains further details on installing and configuring the components in an application environment. This guide is available from `http://technet.microsoft.com/en-us/library/bb794631.aspx`.

Performance and Scaling

Performance and scaling considerations are partly a function of PerformancePoint Planning Server functionality and partly a function of the Microsoft data platform it is built upon. Data volume capabilities are largely a function of the Microsoft SQL Server platform, but there are some factors in components such as forms and calculations that can significantly impact end-user capability when dealing with large data sets. Finally, in most enterprise-wide applications, users exist in a variety of locations with different network access capacity. This is another factor that must be considered when looking at the overall performance of an application.

Data Volumes

As with any data-intensive application, the volume of data will often dictate performance characteristics of an application. In a PerformancePoint Planning Server application, data volume impacts performance in a variety of ways, and all these must be considered during design and testing. The volume of data in a model can affect query time, making end-user performance slower. Additionally, large volumes of data can make cube-based calculations much slower, necessitating a change to relational or Excel-based calculations for efficiency. At times when a model becomes so large that performance is negatively impacted, optimization or increasing capacity in SQL Analysis Services may deliver improvement. However, it may also be considered that the model structure is not properly focused on key areas to make each model small enough to support the targeted business processes. On the client side, data volumes may impact local cache performance, which is also impacted by network capability. There are other client data volume concerns to evaluate, however.

Many PerformancePoint Planning Server applications are developed with the express purpose of capturing data. While most user data entered will represent small percentages of the overall data that a system contains, data submission transaction processing is a scaling consideration. Because data processing for submissions is done asynchronously, a high volume of submissions is not likely to be a problem. However, the turnaround time for processing new data may be. Multiple processing servers may assist in handling volume. In general, testing environments should attempt to replicate the real data volume experience, as adjustments and model refactoring may be required to meet the performance expectations of end users. This type of change can be made during development and testing but is difficult to achieve gracefully after a production rollout.

Users

Users of an application may vary from a few to several thousand in large organizations. Considering the profile of users is important to take into account for proper deployment. Like the volume of data, the number of users working with that volume of data will determine much of an application's performance profile. Simultaneous user queries over common data sets can greatly impact performance for all users. Available server memory is often a gating factor to simultaneous query access. Of course, data volumes and calculation performance will also impact how user queries behave.

Users of an application have the ability to select how their client caching behaves within the constraints defined by modelers. A modeler can determine whether or not a user may have a local cache of an assignment, including its data. When a local cache is created, data is copied locally into an Analysis Services local cube. This can greatly improve query performance, as the query is accessing data stored locally. The downside, however, is that server calculations or data updates are not visible to the user until his or her local cache is refreshed. For applications that require significant data processing on the server or frequent data updates, disabling caching may be more efficient, as a local cache would almost always be out of date and be forced to query the server anyway — invalidating any local cache.

Location

The location of users and their separation from servers can impact application performance. Network bandwidth will be a significant factor, particularly as data volumes grow. The geographical distribution of users may mean that some users get a sufficient response but others don't. One approach to combat this problem is to make use of the ability to have different model sites on different SQL Analysis Services servers and have the model sites reflect the geographic distribution of users, deploying servers locally accessible to their network environment. Other options such as NLB using the IIS environment or the compression of the network traffic may be provide improvements as well.

NOTE **A performance whitepaper for PerformancePoint Server 2007 provides additional information to help design and test a performance application. This whitepaper is available for download from** `http://technet.microsoft.com/en-us/library/bb794631.aspx`.

Application Migration

Application migration for PerformancePoint Planning Server is designed for moving, or migrating, an entire application from one system (source) to another system (target). In the case where the target system does not already contain the application, migration creates an entire replica on the target system. In the case where the target system already contains the application, incremental migration is performed. The migration functionality itself determines the target system's state, so no configuration of these options is necessary. Using common source and target systems facilitates the process of moving through the application's lifecycle, as it moves through the stages from development to testing and into production.

Development

The development environment is generally a low-end deployment configuration. While in development, an application is generally not loaded with full data volumes, and great performance loads will not be placed on the system in that environment. The development environment is set up for modelers to build the structural components of an application. There may be several attempts, so pieces might be created, deleted, and recreated. This makes the development environment an unstable place to work with data, and the data present is generally used to facilitate experimentation with models and calculations as they are created. Once all the models, calculations, forms, and data processes are created in the development environment, they are migrated to the testing environment.

Testing

The testing environment is designed to simulate production to facilitate the testing of an application prior to its broader release. Generally, the testing environment will mirror the planned production environment so that the results of testing can be used to accurately predict production behavior. This means that a testing deployment will have hardware and a configuration similar to those used in production. A testing environment generally should have an accurate and complete data set to provide a valid user experience, so the data platform must also have capabilities equivalent to those used in the planned production system. Once testing has validated an application, it is migrated to production. That migration might be a full transfer the first time, but subsequent changes in development may be incrementally migrated to production as those changes pass testing.

Production

The production environment is the fully secured and audited application supporting the required business solution. A production deployment environment is usually monitored to address any problems quickly, as well as backed up so that it can be restored in case of emergency. Production deployment servers may be more single-purpose than servers found in development or testing. The production environment is also the place where security control is complete and business processes are fully defined. For example, a forecast data entry cycle with assignments to 50 users allows those 50 people to add data to the system. The complete set of proper users will exist in production as will the correct data capture process and window. This likely won't be true in development or testing where only a limited set of test users will interact with those systems.

Migration

The purpose of the migration process is to move application components between systems. When a migration is performed, application meta data and reference data are transferred from a source system to a target system. Meta data contains such things as models, business rules, and business role definitions. Users, cycles, and assignments are not moved, as they are specific to running processes in the source (past or present) and are expected to be created anew in the target system. For example, a business role may have a couple of users in the test system, but in a production system may have more than 100. Likewise, factual data values are not moved. This is due to the fact that data in development or testing applications is not expected to be used in the production application. Therefore, data for the production application is loaded separately through a data-loading process.

Migration must be performed by someone who has both Global Administrator permissions and Modeler permissions due to the nature of functions being executed by the migration steps. There are two types of migration for an application. First is a full migration, which moves an entire application from its current source to a target system where that application does not exist in any form. Second is an incremental migration, which moves incremental changes from the source system application to the target system.

Full Migration

A full migration is executed using a series of steps, many involving the PPSCmd command-line tool. To ensure that nothing is left in an inconsistent state, the target application should be taken offline from the Admin Console.

This prevents any user actions or system changes while the migration process is occurring. From the source system, a PPSCmd function for migrate/export is performed and generates files containing all the proper application meta data and reference data. On the target system, an empty application is created using the same name and label identifying the source application. Once the shell application is created, a PPSCmd function is again called to perform migrate/import. Following the importing of the application, the application will be placed into a locked state and an administrator can bring it online for normal system functions. Once the migration has occurred, required data processes may be executed to load the data into the created application. Finally, users, security, and data processes can be set up or initialized to put the application into a fully functioning state.

Incremental Migration

Incremental migration follows the same process as that used for the full migration. In the case of incremental migration, though, the target application already exists. The preparation process from the source application remains the same. The existing application in the target system is placed back into the locked state in preparation to receive the changes. When importing the application via PPSCmd, the server recognizes the existence of the application and will update or add the items to the target system that are either not in or are different from those on the source system.

NOTE The Operations Guide for PerformancePoint Server 2007 contains detailed explanations of the functions of PPSCmd and the steps for migration. This guide is available from `http://technet.microsoft.com/en-us/library/bb838772.aspx`.

Data Lifecycle

A PerformancePoint Planning Server application is generally not implemented as a single-point solution. What this means is that it will be used for recurring processes such as monthly reporting, quarterly forecasting, and annual planning. In designing a solution that has a cyclical pattern of operation, one of the considerations will be how data flows into and out of the application solution. Frequently, this will involve IT personnel who own and work with source and target data systems. The three primary factors will be what data is available, where it comes from, and how and when it can be incorporated into a PerformancePoint Planning Server application solution.

The primary task will be to determine what data is required for the solution. The answer should be driven by the business requirements. Similarly to model design, where identifying the driving business factors is key, building a solution with the necessary data will ensure that business needs are met effectively. The first tendency might be to build an application with the data that is already easily available. Often, an application solution is based on data that is already in use and, therefore, easily acquired. However, by not starting from available data, new data requirements might be identified that are crucial to the proper solution. After identifying the data required for the solution, the effort can be made to determine where to source it from.

PerformancePoint Planning Server is not designed to be a transactional system. Some of the data for a performance management application solution will come from an underlying transactional system such as a general ledger, customer relationship management (CRM) system, or other line-of-business system. These systems capture volumes of data that occur in the organization and generally supply the historic Actual data or key drivers for the PerformancePoint Server solution. Once the location the data must come from has been identified, an Extract-Transform-Load (ETL) process can stage the data for proper use by the PerformancePoint Plannning Server application solution. The final step to consider, then, is the timing and process.

There are two steps to move data into and out of an application. The first step is the ETL process that stages the data for the application to use. This should be considered with standard company IT administration and data processes — which commonly have well-defined processes, security, and controls. The second step occurs within PerformancePoint itself and controls how and when the application solution consumes, processes, and publishes its own data.

The data processes and flow control are functions common to most applications, and PerformancePoint Planning Server provides functionality to be used in tandem with Microsoft SQL Server Integration Services to deliver an effective solution. The key steps are to evaluate the data needs and process the flow of that data within PerformancePoint. Once that is done, common data infrastructure practices should be used to create a maintainable and secure data lifecycle process around the application solution.

Summary

Developing, testing, and getting an application into production requires several steps in the overall deployment process. The first step is to consider the proper hardware infrastructure and configuration of the software. Depending on the size and scope of the application, you may choose to have three servers, or five servers, or more. The physical infrastructure needs will be driven largely by the performance requirements of the application. Some key factors like data volume, number of users, and network distribution are considered when looking at performance profiling of the needs of the application. Once the deployment topology is established, PerformancePoint Planning Server offers functionality for migration, which facilitates the movement of application content from system to system; assisting with development, testing, and production cycles.

Part IV

Successfully Engaging Users in Monitoring, Analytics, and Planning

Although understanding the concepts and techniques behind monitoring, analytics, and planning in PerformancePoint is the first step to successfully implementing performance management in your organization, knowing how to execute these concepts effectively within your organization is an equally important step. The following three chapters provide guidance — based on real-world implementations — on how to achieve the results you want with your implementation. They highlight the processes and approaches that have been most successful with customers and make recommendations on how to apply these processes to your own environment.

Chapter 18 uses an extended business example to show how to integrate monitoring, analytics, and planning. Each section progressively explores the Business Planning Modeler, the underlying data for the model in Analysis Services, and how this data appears for use in Dashboard Designer. You learn how a deep understanding of the data allows you to build and deploy secure and targeted dashboards based on data from the planning model.

Chapter 19 focuses on dashboards and how to ensure your users have the content they need to make decisions based on facts, not assumptions. This chapter revisits the concepts of alignment, agility, relevance, and efficiency, providing strategies and recommendations in each area that can be applied to any implementation. It also highlights the most common challenges in enterprise deployments, such as taking on too large a project initially and not securing an executive sponsor. The chapter concludes with suggestions on how to continually improve your dashboards and dashboard content to ensure greater user satisfaction over time.

Chapter 20 focuses on how partnerships between business and information technology (IT) teams work together on performance management (PM) applications. PerformancePoint Planning Server challenges some of the traditional assumptions and implementation patterns of business intelligence (BI) projects. The chapter ends by describing some of the key things to do and considerations to factor into your application development project.

CHAPTER

18

Bringing Monitoring, Analytics, and Planning Together

This chapter makes use of an extended business example to show how to integrate monitoring, analytics, and planning. The first section discusses the value of bringing monitoring, analytics, and planning together. The following sections explore the nuts and bolts of accomplishing this integration. With each section you will progressively explore the Business Planning Modeler, the underlying data for the model in Analysis Services, and how this data appears for use in Dashboard Designer. You will learn how a deep understanding of the data allows you to build and deploy secure and targeted dashboards based on data from the Planning Model.

This chapter makes use of the Business Intelligence 5.1 Virtual PC available for downloading from Microsoft. If you are able, we encourage you to download the Business Intelligence Virtual PC so that you gain hands-on experience as you read through the chapter.

MAP

Circling back to Bill Baker's introduction, we'd like to remind you that "PPS allows companies to manage the three key activities in performance management: plan the business, monitor the execution of the plan and analyze variances to the plan. We call this Monitor, Analyze and Plan, or MAP." (See Figure 18-1.) This integrated Performance Management process is the ultimate vision of Business Intelligence. Using the different capabilities associated with business intelligence (BI), and tying them all together to be fully integrated, allows the project management (PM) cycle to be repeated as often as the business demands. In practice, generating a dashboard based on the Planning Model becomes a competitive advantage through optimization of operational efficiency. By building a dashboard for monitoring and analyzing on the Planning Model, you are able to build performance management into the Planning Model itself to achieve continuous business improvement at the planning level.

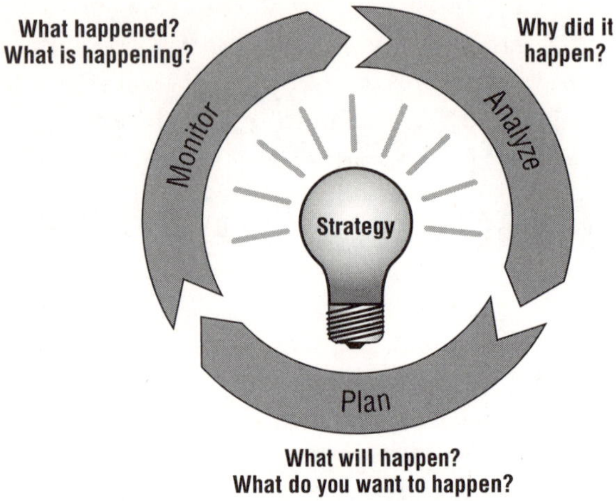

Figure 18-1 MAP supports and enables strategy.

Most organizations already have some form of planning mechanism in their organization, whether it's Excel or a third-party tool. By creating a dashboard and scorecard in the Planning Model, organizations can monitor how well their plan is working, analyze unexpected trends or spikes, and then use the Planning Model in a measure-based reiterative cycle to help refine their plan.

Understand Your Data

Understanding your data is key to successfully accomplishing this integration and gaining this competitive business advantage. This is so important that organizations may want to consider appointing a dedicated person whose primary responsibility is to cultivate a deep knowledge of the data used to plan, monitor, and analyze. Keeping a close and dedicated eye on the inner workings and moving pieces of your business information will help your organization be much more effective during the first years of performance management implementation.

Concepts of performance management and performance management systems have been discussed for years in the academic world. These concepts have only recently become part of the corporate world with the availability of applications and tools suited to the corporate environment. This availability, along with sophisticated data storage mechanisms that allow companies to make decisions from data transformed into information, has driven performance management into the mainstream.

Planning Server as well as Monitoring and Analytics use SQL Server as the centralized database repository, giving organizations the ability to manage business processes from one version of the truth. This is made possible by the fact that data is feeding in from one location, and monitoring and analyzing can be done from the same single location as well. This is significantly different from past approaches, which have generally used ad hoc systems dependent on data from multiple and varied systems.

Putting It Together: The How To

As a first step, you must understand the structure of the model that you will be building as well as the security component associated with the model. It's important to remember that when you deploy a Planning Model, the structure of the cube is slightly different from typical cubes with measure groups and multiple members. Understanding and becoming familiar with the structure of the Planning Model cube is important because scorecard KPIs are based on measures and dimensions of a cube. Generally, a Planning Model has only one cube, although you may associate other models to display more than one cube. In this example, we will use the most typical and simplest standard example where there is only one cube in the model.

Viewing the Planning Models and Dimensions

Let's start by looking at the preexisting PDW application in the Planning Business Modeler, which you learned about in previous chapters on planning. From the Start menu, open the Planning Business Modeler and select the PDW application, which has a single model site, also called PDW, as shown in Figure 18-2.

The application opens to a summary page about the PDW (PDW) model site shown in Figure 18-3.

From the Workspace Browser pane, click Models to see that the site includes two prebuilt models called PDW_Detail and PDW_WI, which are shown in Figure 18-4.

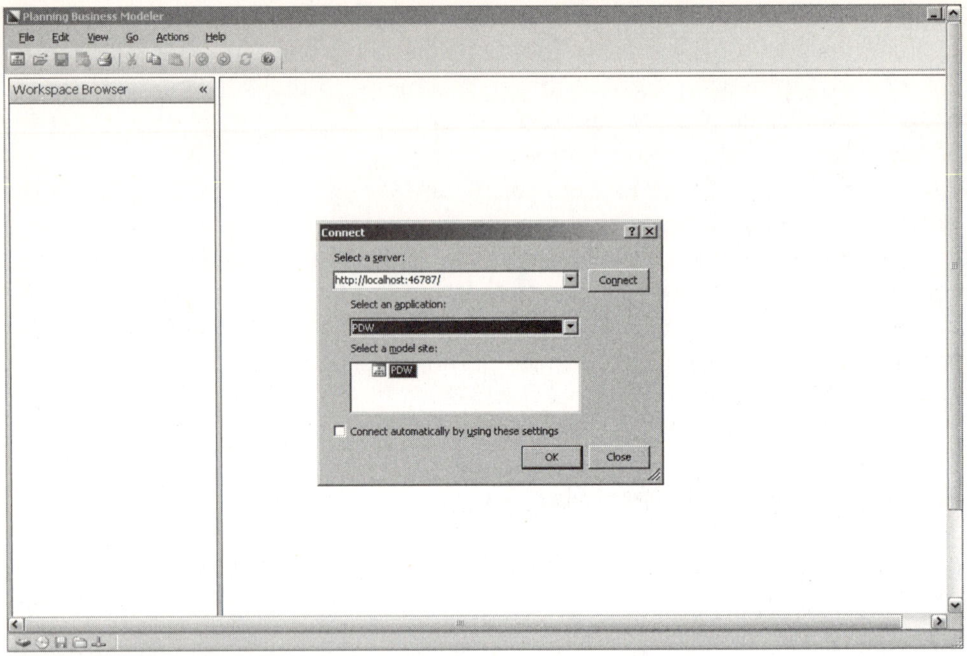

Figure 18-2 Connect to the PDW application with the PDW site.

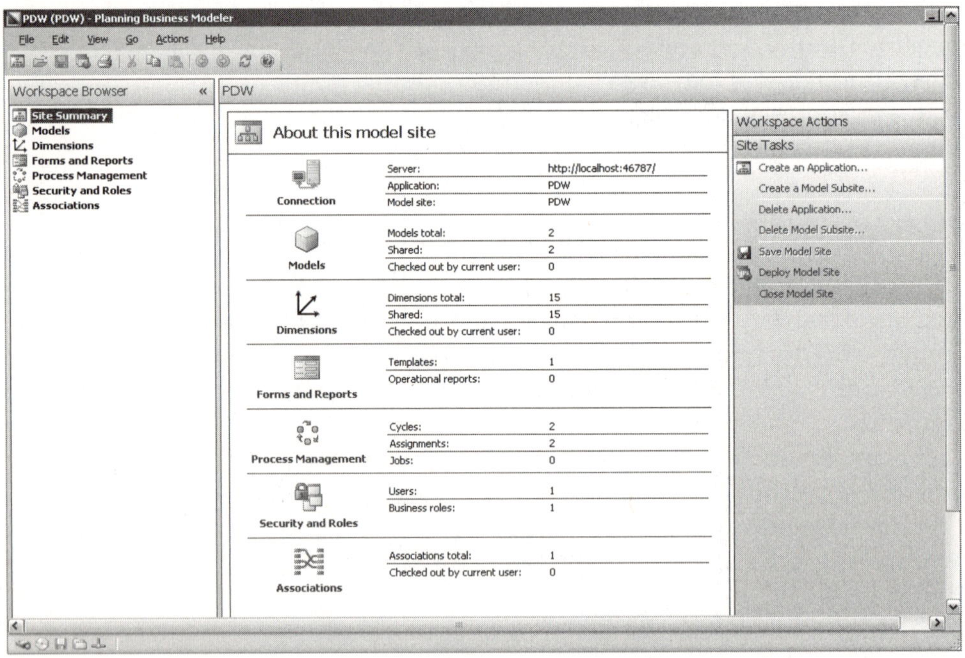

Figure 18-3 Summary page for the PDW (PDW) model site

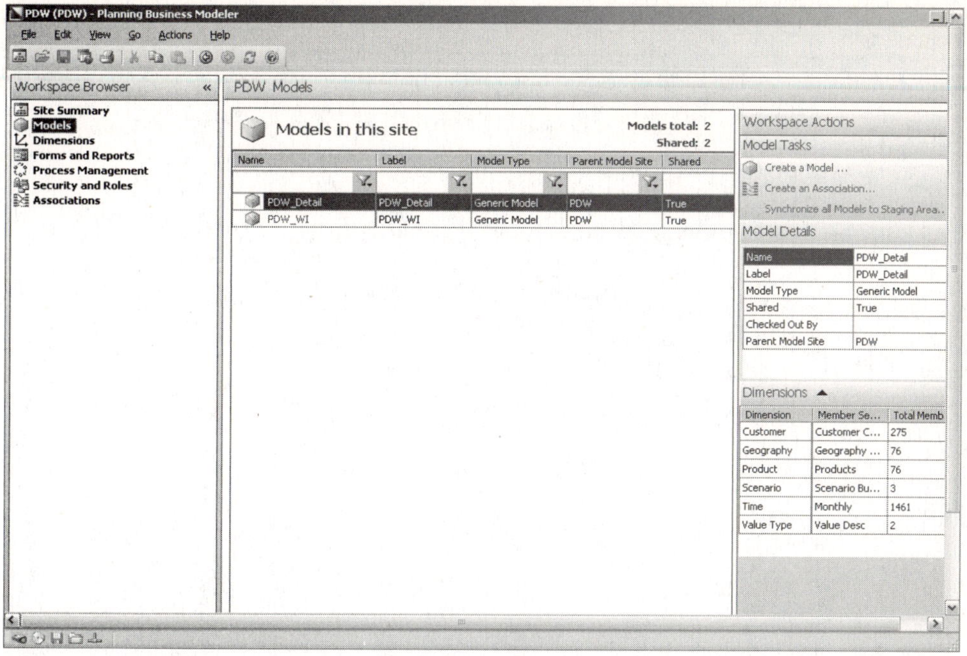

Figure 18-4 This site includes two prebuilt models.

Click Dimensions to examine the supporting dimensions in this site. These dimensions include the standard dimensions that ship with PPS as well as specific dimensions and customized standard, dimensions such as Geography, Product, and Value Type as shown in Figure 18-5.

For now, focus on the Scenario dimension, which is critical to getting the underlying data from Dashboard Designer. In this example, the Scenario dimension includes Actual and Budget dimensions, as shown in Figure 18-6.

Right now, you're simply familiarizing yourself with the data model, examining dimensions and related membersets. At this point, it's useful to look at the dimensions for each model in the site. Looking at the PDW_WI model, you will see that this model has four dimensions associated with it, as shown in Figure 18-7.

The second model, PDW_Detail, is more complex, with additional Customer and Geography dimensions (see Figure 18-8).

In this example, we will use the PDW_Detail model and the dimensions associated with it.

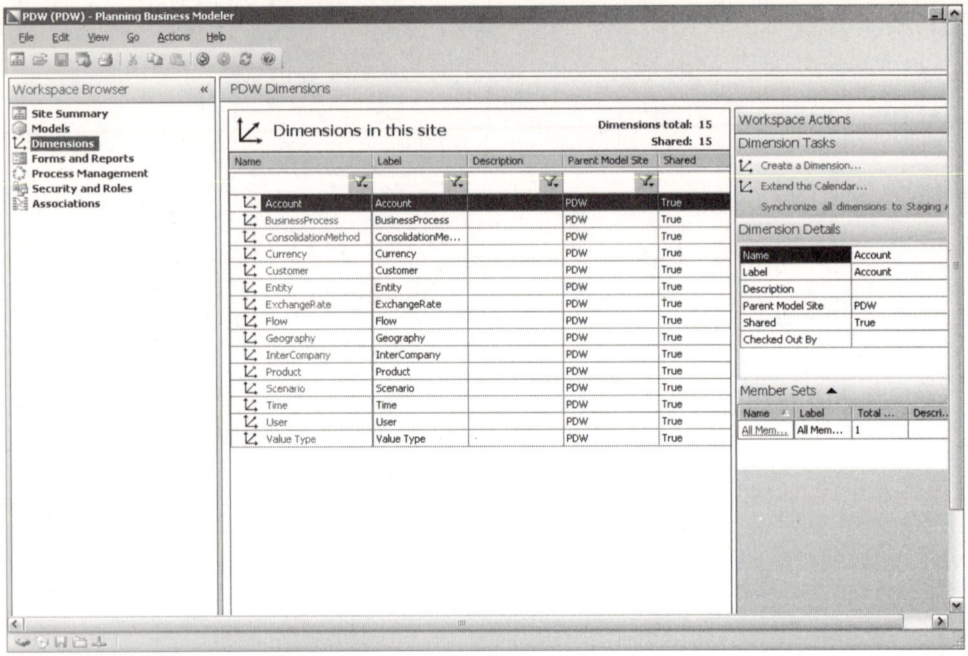

Figure 18-5 Dimensions in this site

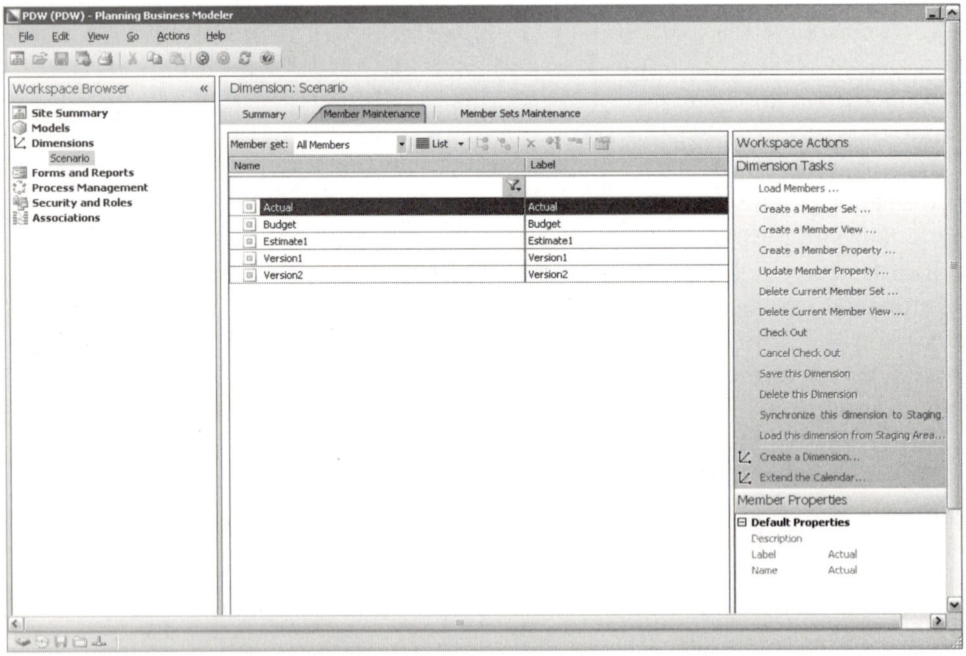

Figure 18-6 Scenario dimension

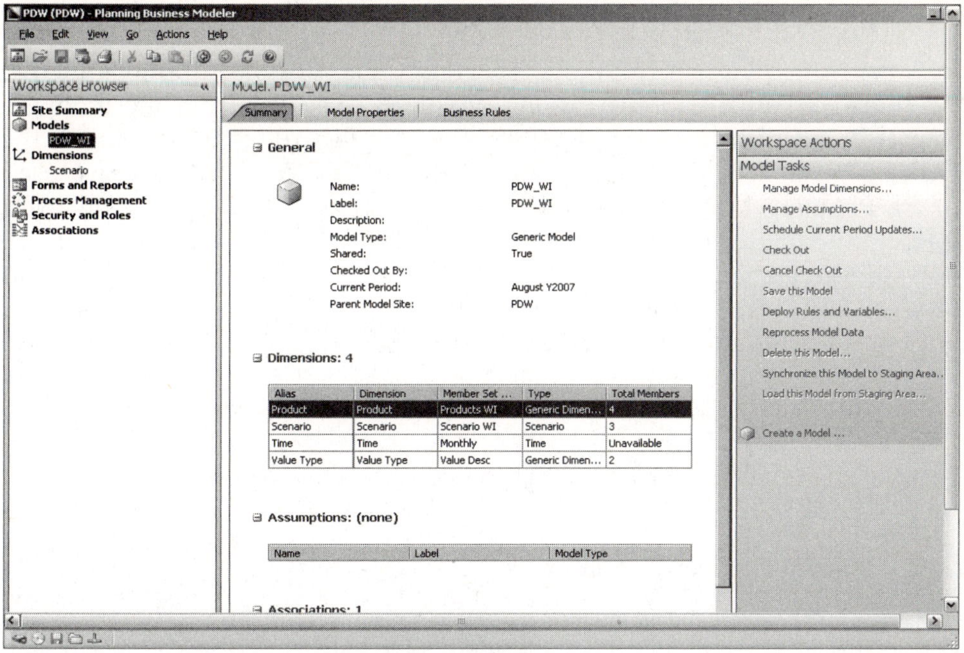

Figure 18-7 Dimensions for the PDW_WI model

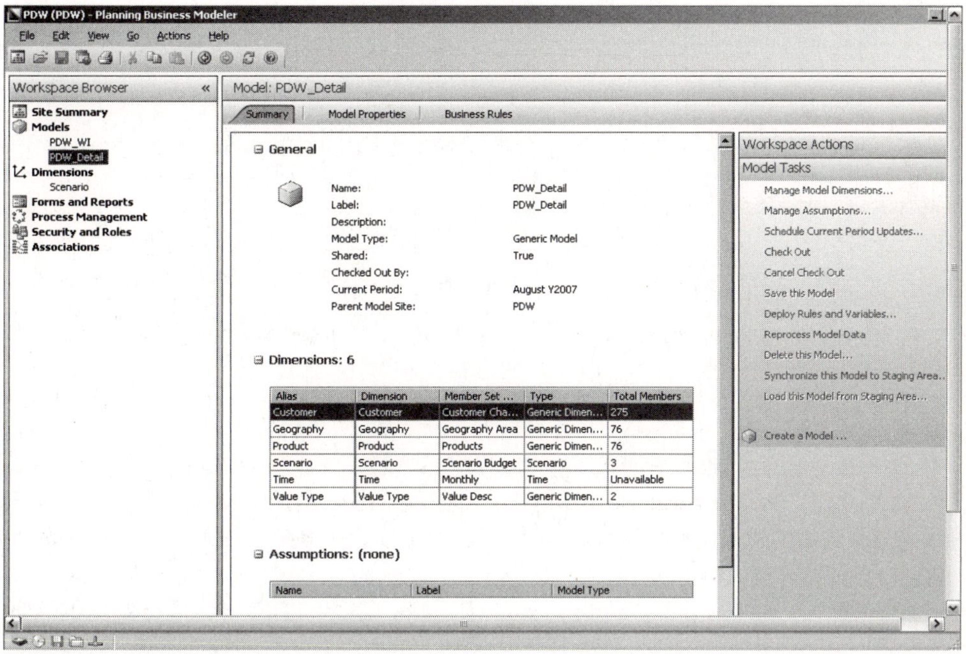

Figure 18-8 Dimensions for the PDW_Detail model

Viewing the Data for the Model

From previous Planning chapters, you know that once you build a model, you must deploy it and that upon deployment, a cube from the model is generated in SQL Server Analysis Services (see Figure 18-9). Looking at the Analysis Services in Databases, you will see the PDW_PDW database used for the Planning Model. (This database is different from the PDW database used in the Monitoring and Analytics examples in previous chapters.) In the PDW_PDW database name, the first PDW refers to the application name and the second PDW refers to the site name. Drilling down into the database, you will see two cubes that correspond to the two models and to the model names.

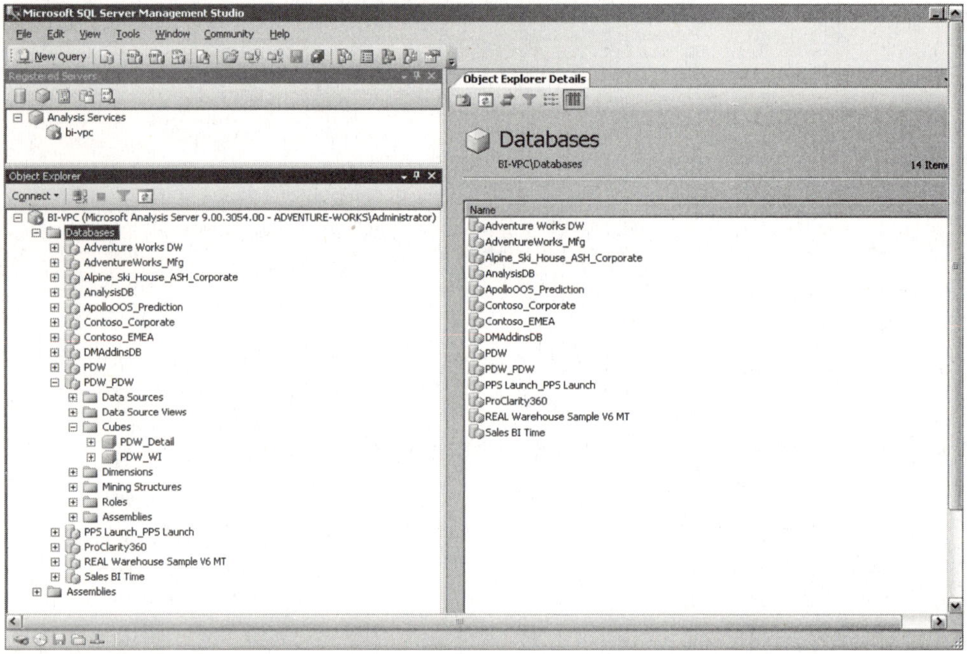

Figure 18-9 During deployment of the model, a cube is created in Analysis Services.

Before going to Dashboard Designer, take a moment to examine PDW_Apps and the tables in the database used by the Planning Model.

In particular, look at the fact tables whose names begin with MG_ (underscore). This prefix identifies fact tables that contain a Value column referred to later in Dashboard Designer (see Figure 18-10). You've now examined the structure of the cube in the model and are ready to open Dashboard Designer to view how the data appears in this application where you can use the data to build and deploy dashboards.

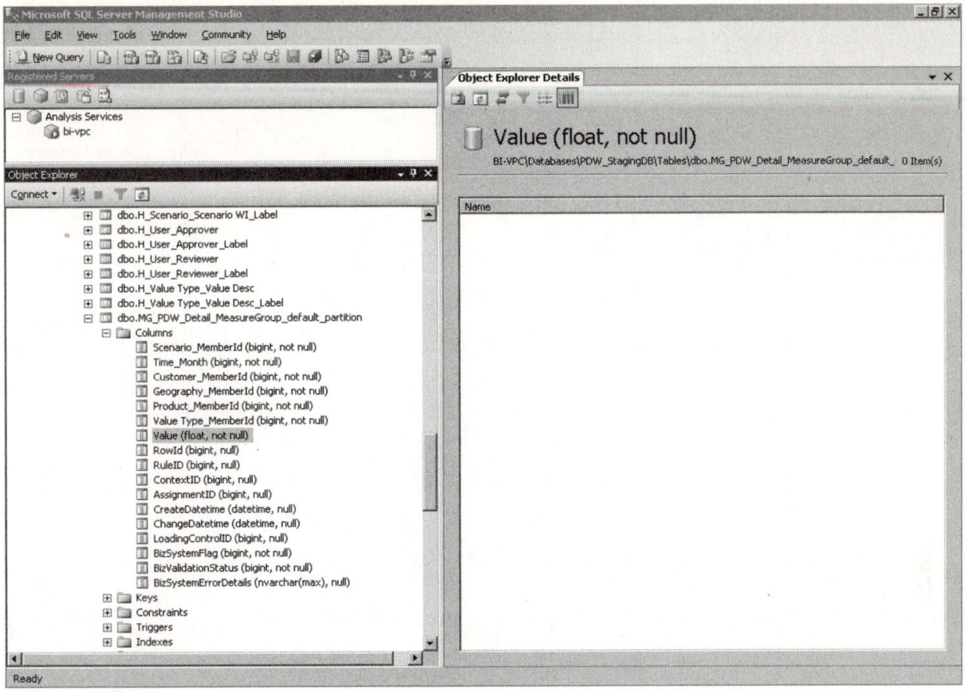

Figure 18-10 Dashboard Designer refers to the Value column in the fact table.

Using the Data Source in Dashboard Designer

From previous chapters, you know that the first step in dashboard design is creating a data source. In this example, select to create a new data source using the Multidimensional Analysis Services Data Source template (see Figure 18-11).

Once the template is selected and you've entered the key point information, you're ready to establish the connection settings. In the Server box, enter **BI-VPC**. Notice that when you click on the Database drop-down list, you see a subset of the databases listed in Analysis Services (see Figure 18-12). What if the PDW database appears but the PDW_PDW planning database does not?

If the PDW_PDW database does not appear, there are two possible reasons for this. Either the database does not exist or Dashboard Designer does not have permission to access the database. We know that the database exists because we've seen it in Analysis Services, so the answer is security. The next section reviews how to set security roles that align across the applications used to build dashboards from the Planning Model.

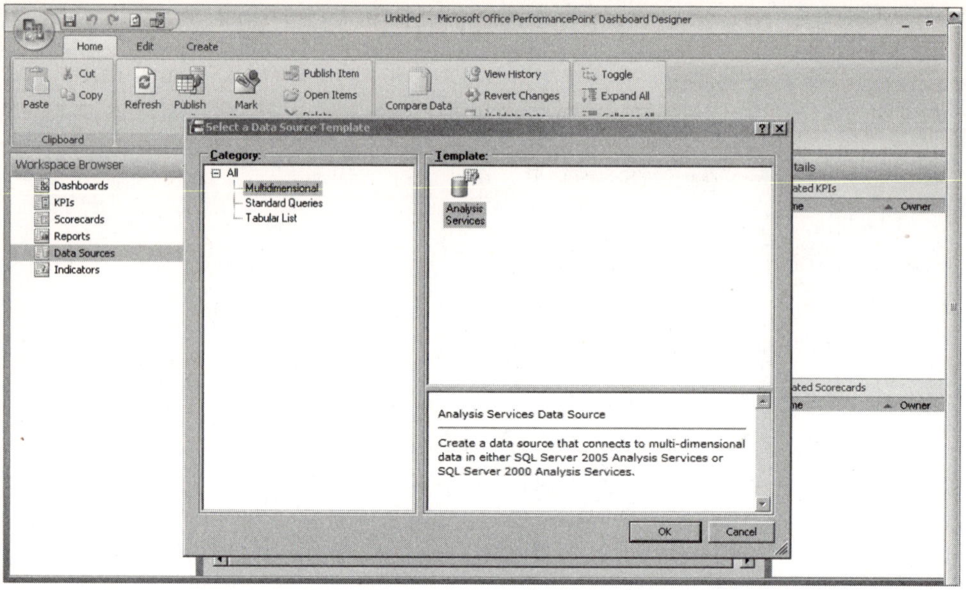

Figure 18-11 Use the Analysis Services Data Source template.

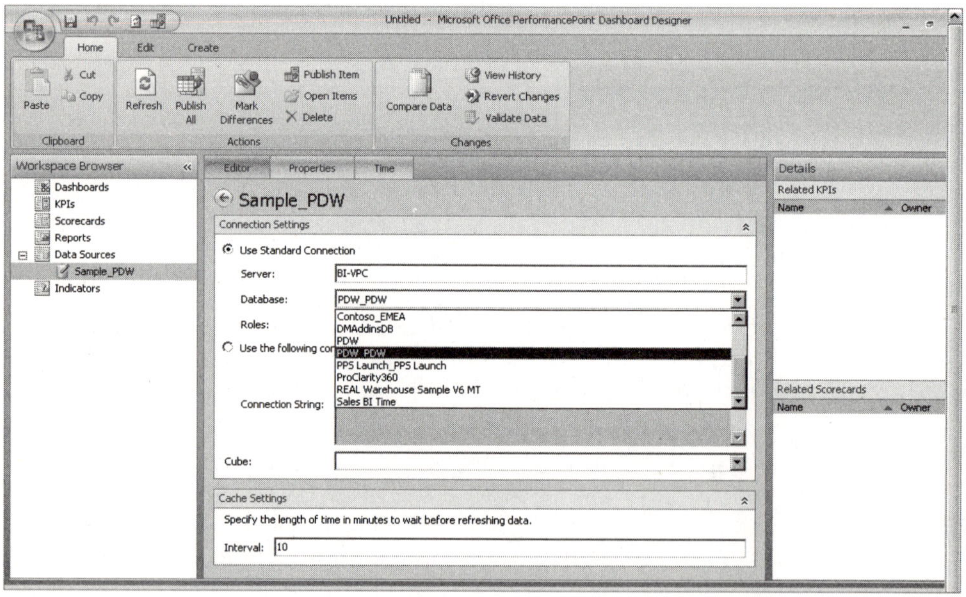

Figure 18-12 A subset of the databases from Analysis Services appears in the Database list.

Setting Security Roles for Dashboard Designer

When building models in the Planning environment, security and roles must be specified for the site. When the Planning Model is deployed, the specified owner is then associated with a role. In this case, the Administrator is specified as the owner (see Figure 18-13).

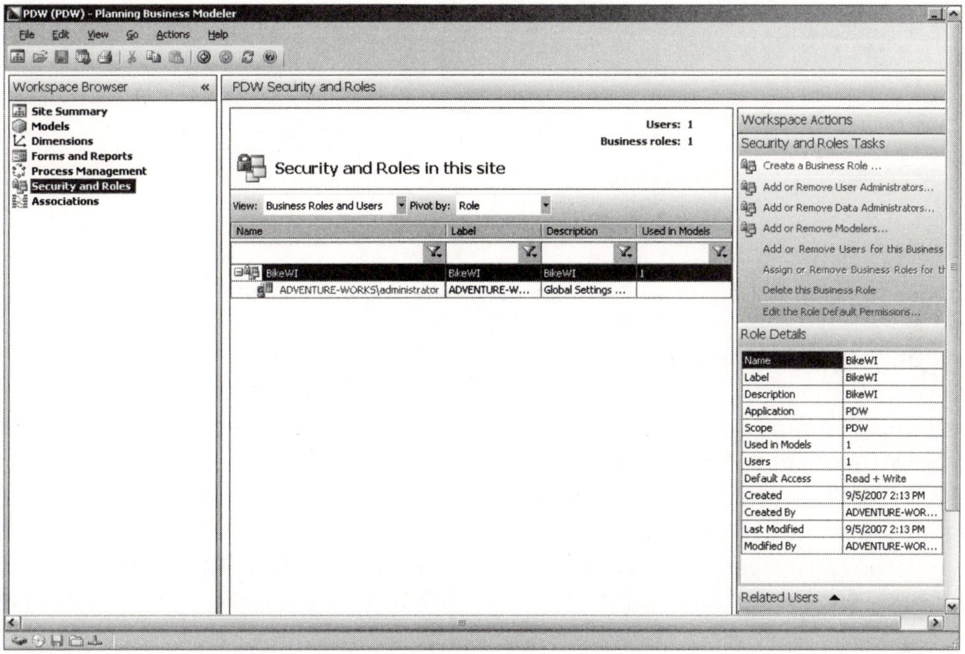

Figure 18-13 The administrator is specified as the owner.

When the cube is deployed, it is associated with a security role. If a role has not been set up for the PPSMonitoringWebService application pool, which includes Dashboard Designer, the cube will not appear in Dashboard Designer. It's very important to know that you must set up a role for the PPSMonitoring-WebService application pool in Analysis Services (see Figure 18-14). You must set up a role if you decide to use the default shared application account, and you must set a role for each user or group if you are using the PerUserConnection security setting. By drilling into Roles in Analysis Services, you can view and modify roles to ensure that accounts connecting to the roles align to roles in Analysis Services as well as to roles and models in the PPSMonitoring-WebService application pool. The SharePoint application pool also must have a security role that will align with the role on the cube.

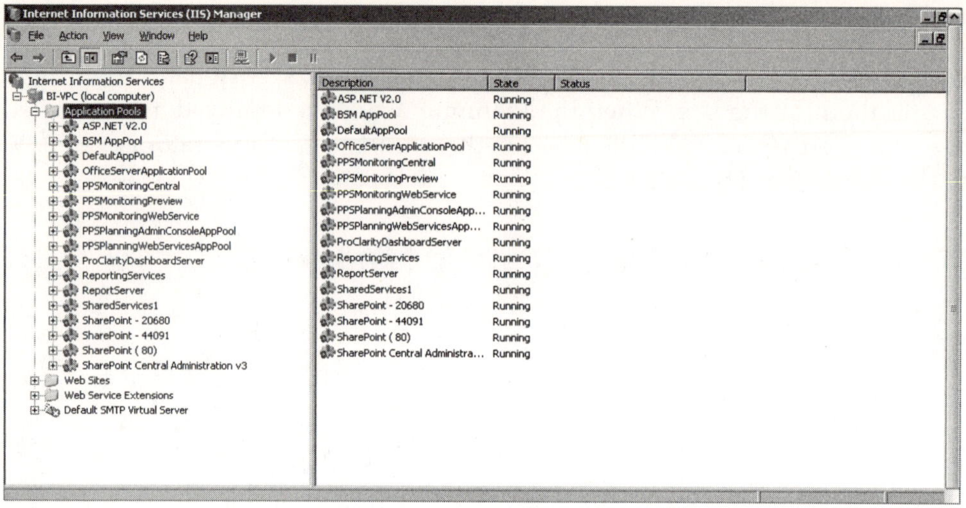

Figure 18-14 Set roles for the PPSMonitoringWebService and SharePoint application pools.

The assignment of roles may seem unnecessarily complex, but the intent is to protect the data by ensuring that applications do not bypass security built into the Planning Model. If your organization intends to deploy and use data from PerformancePoint Planning with Monitoring and Analytics, the Planning Administrator and the Monitoring and Analytics Administrator must agree on appropriate security accounts to use.

For the purposes of this example, we'll create a new role with full permissions for both Administrator and NETWORK SERVICE with users and groups added to each role (see Figure 18-15).

The security role now has a membership that will be understood by both Dashboard Designer and the Planning database (see Figure 18-16). The result is that the PDW_PDW database appears in the list of available databases as does the PDW_Detail cube, and both are available for connection.

Once you publish the data source based on the Planning Model database, you're ready to build a scorecard with the confidence that the different applications accessing the Planning Model database are all following a common and appropriate set of security requirements.

Building a Planning Scorecard

After the data source is set from the Planning Model database, the process of building a scorecard can begin. In this example, create a new scorecard using the Analysis Services template. Select the Sample_PDW data source created from the Planning Model database as the data source to use for the scorecard, and then select the option to create KPIs from SQL Server Analysis Services (see Figure 18-17).

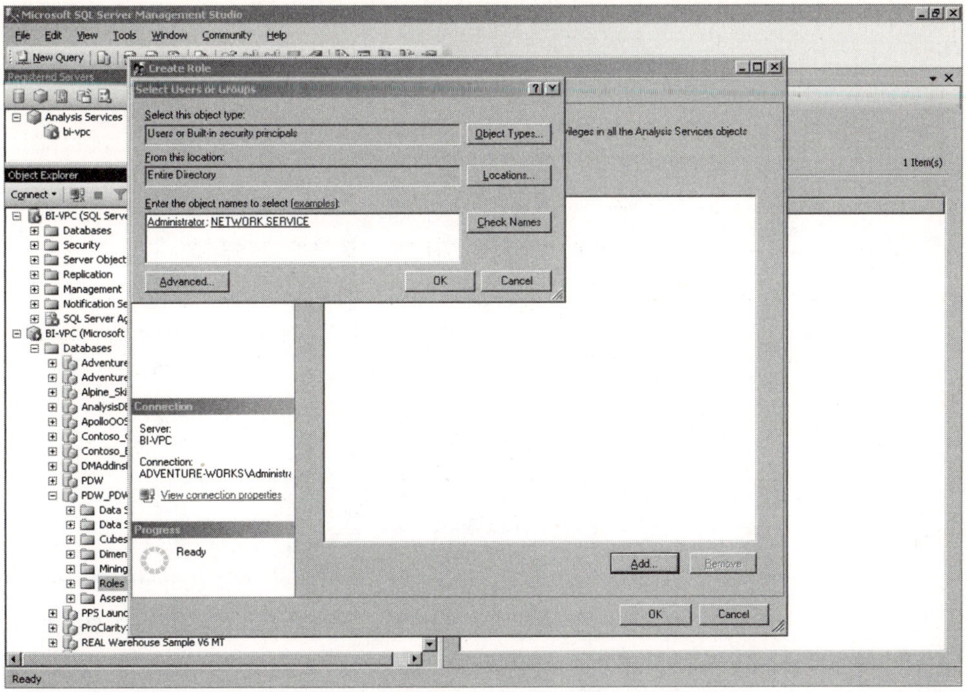

Figure 18-15 Administrator and NETWORK SERVICE roles

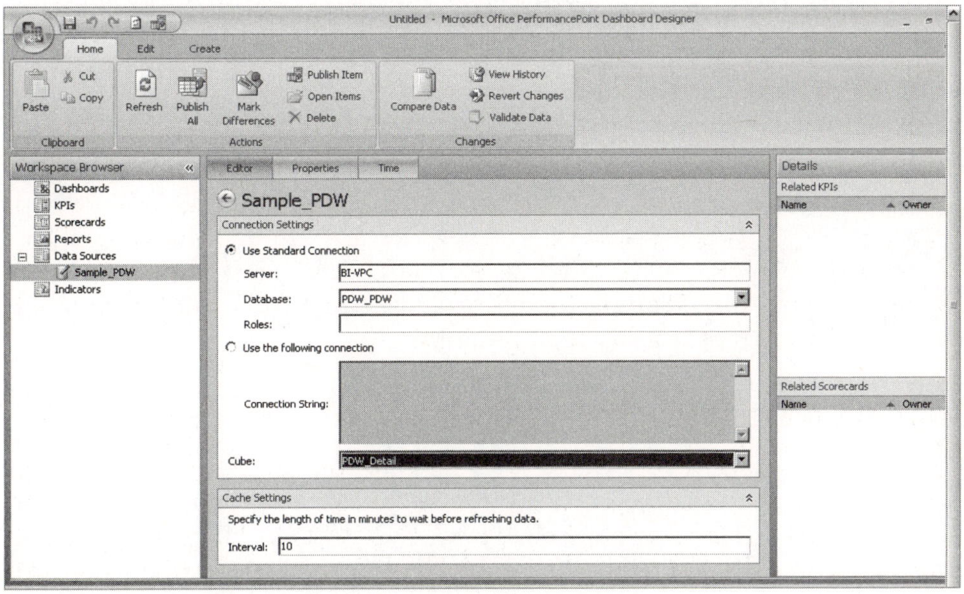

Figure 18-16 Security settings determine database access.

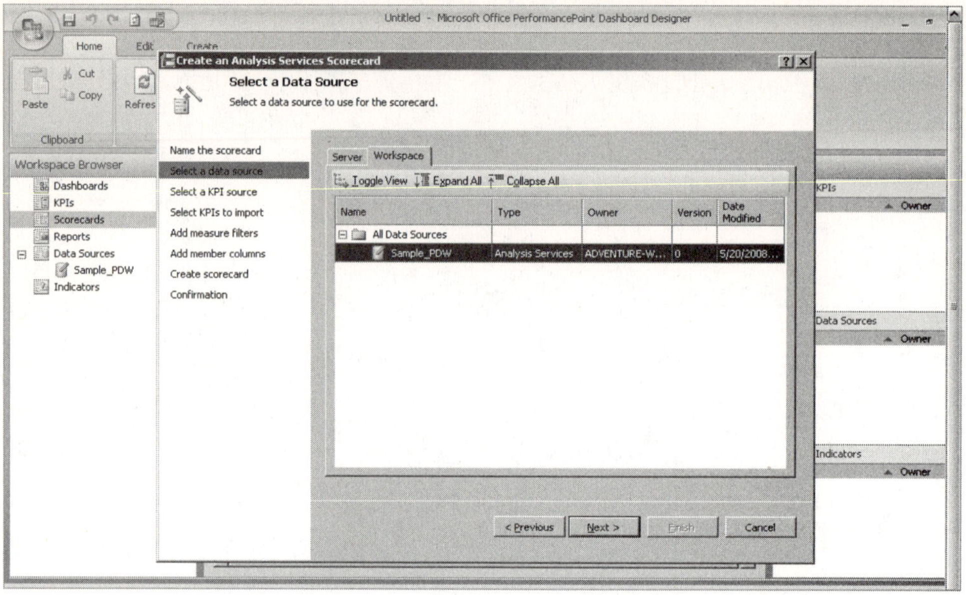

Figure 18-17 Select the new data source based on the Planning Model database to use for the scorecard.

After selecting the data source, click the Add KPIs button. As shown in Figure 18-18, this adds a KPI called Value.

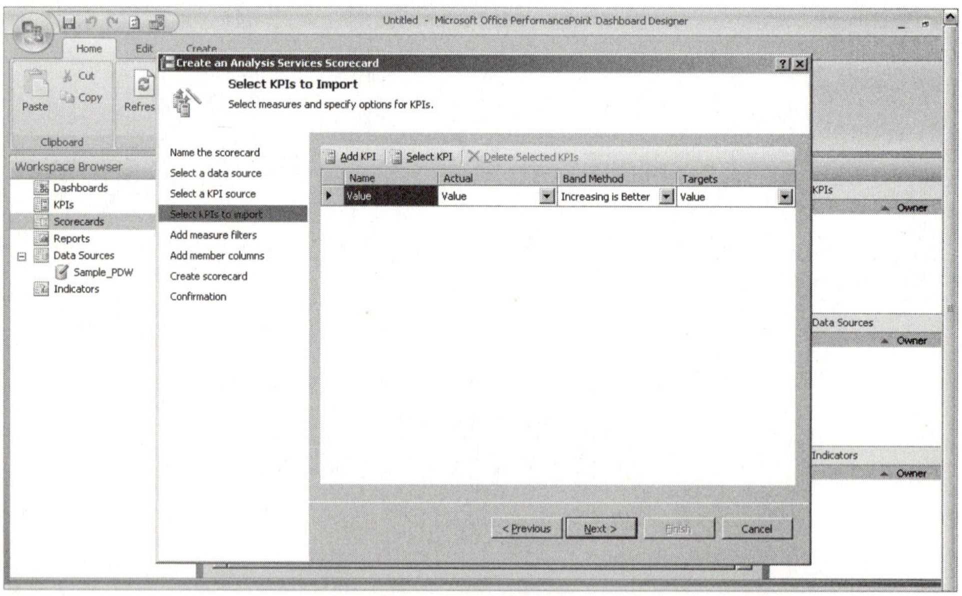

Figure 18-18 Click Add KPI to add a KPI called Value.

Figure 18-19 provides an example of the scorecard created from the KPI default settings. Notice that the Actual and Target values are identical. You'll learn how to change this later in this section. Notice also that expanding the Dimensions in the Available Items of the Details pane on the right displays a long list of Dimensions that exceeds the six dimensions seen in the Planning Model view shown in Figure 18-20.

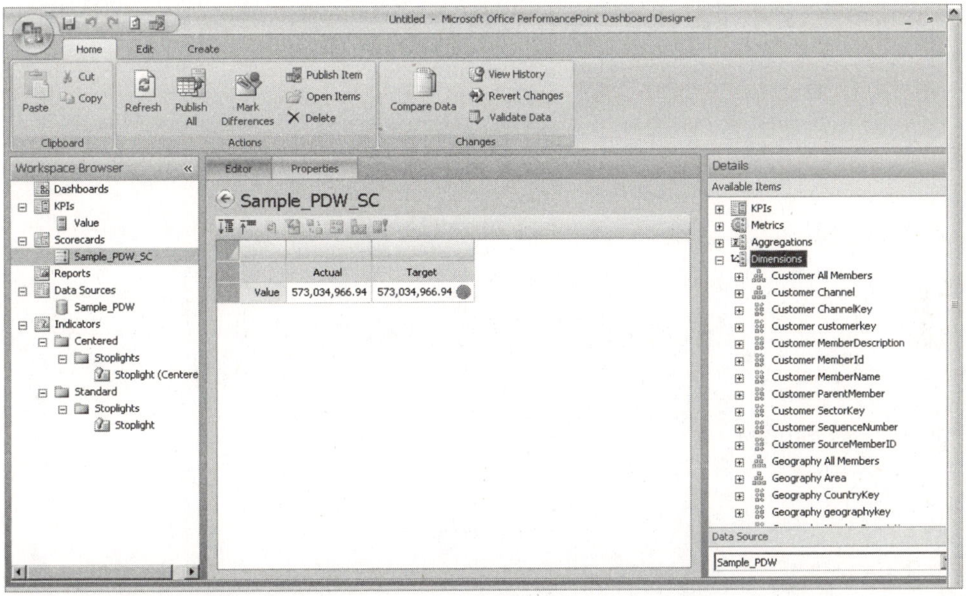

Figure 18-19 Example of a scorecard with default KPI settings

Looking more closely at Figure 18-20, notice that the model includes one association, which accounts for the additional items added to the Dimensions list seen in Dashboard Designer.

Dashboard Designer can make use of these additional dimensions to create a more targeted and personalized scorecard. For example, drag and drop the Geography dimension into the scorecard to create a scorecard that now separates Actual and Target data into four regions, providing targeted business information by region instead of an overall total (see Figure 18-21).

The addition of the Geography dimension has not affected a change in the Target and Actual values, and these values are still the same for each region (see Figure 18-21). This is explained by the fact that the data mappings for the Actual and Target values use default values that point to the same data source, as shown in Figure 18-22.

This can be changed by selecting a different dimension from the Planning Model. For example, using the value from the Scenario.AllMembers dimension is a good choice in this case (see Figure 18-23).

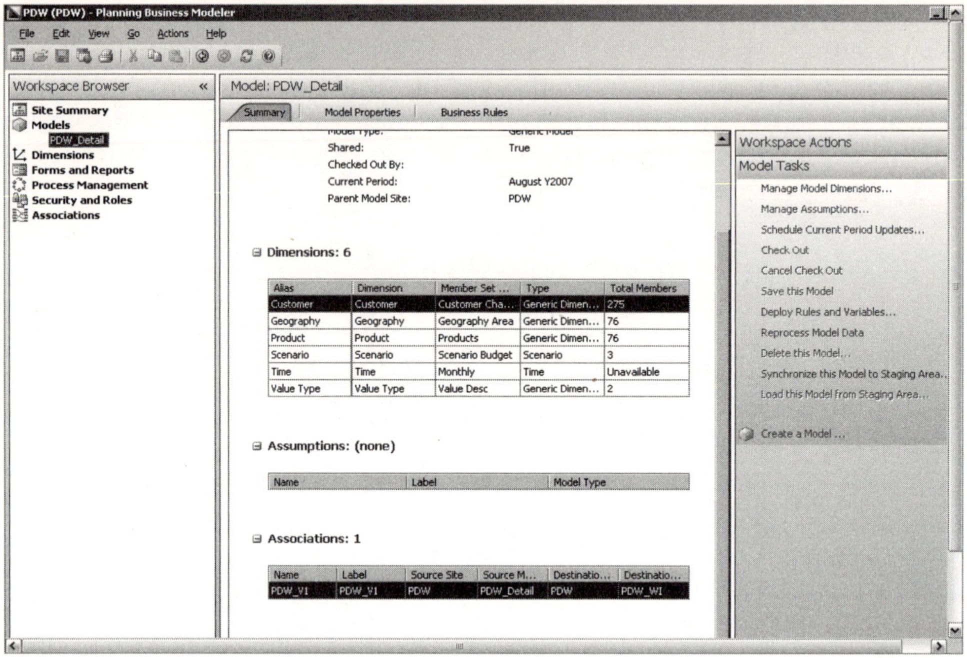

Figure 18-20 Information on dimensions from the Planning Model

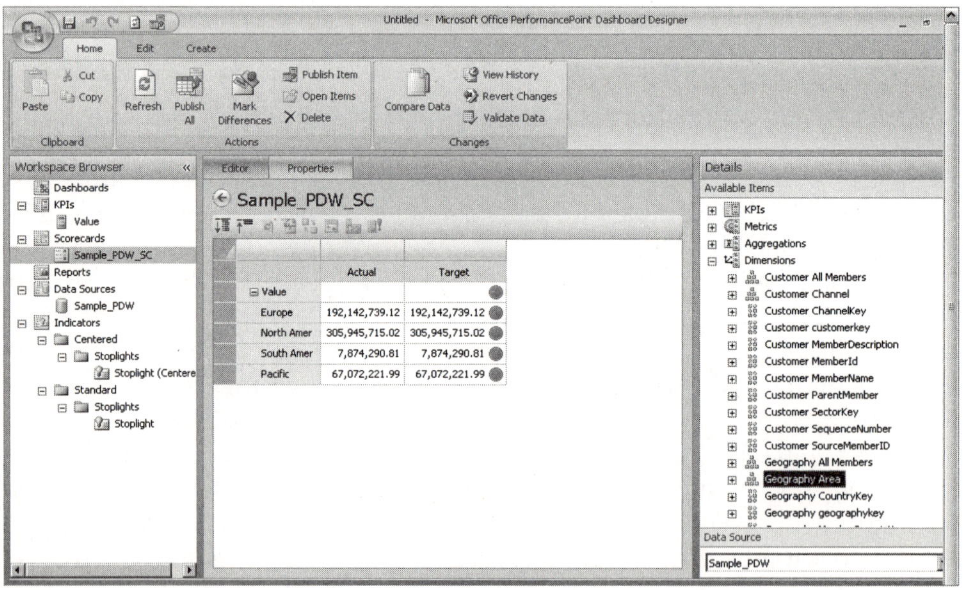

Figure 18-21 Use additional dimensions for targeted and personalized scorecards.

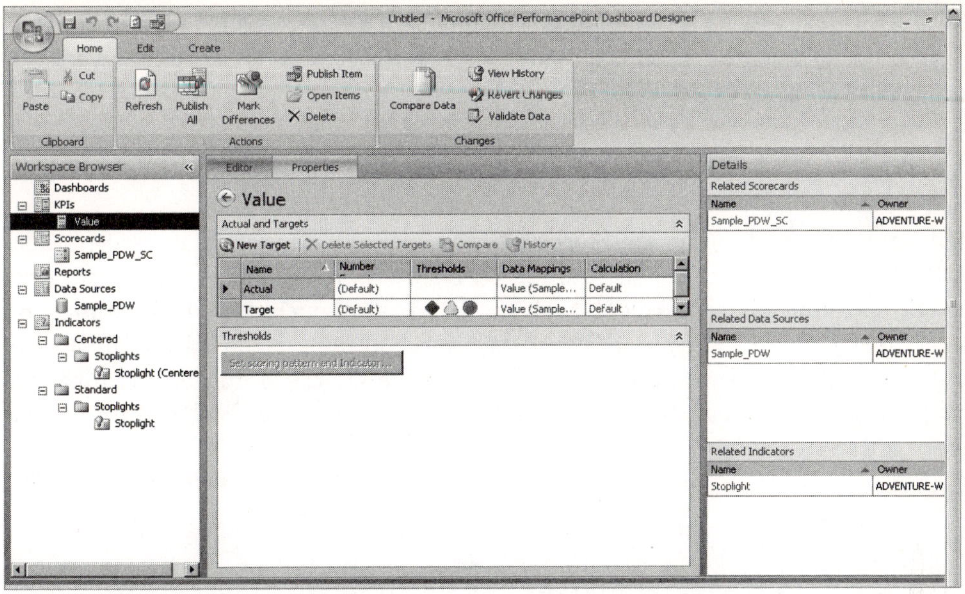

Figure 18-22 Actual and target values point to the same data source.

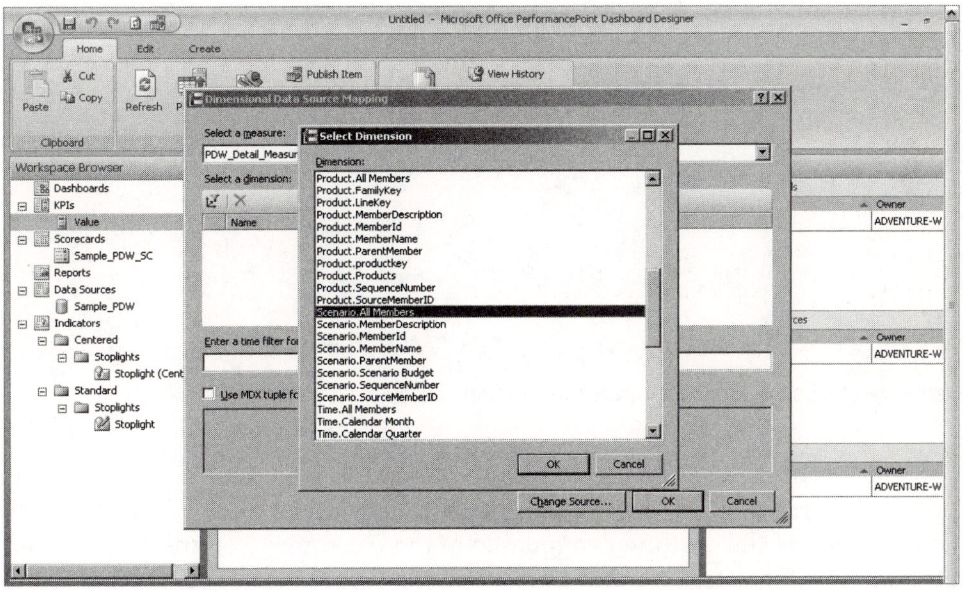

Figure 18-23 Select a different dimension for the Target value data mapping.

NOTE **Selecting a dimension that does not contain data will result in an empty data set, so make sure that you know the overall structure of your data *before* you begin building scorecards.**

Building New KPIs

This section covers building a second scorecard using an alternative approach. In this example, create a Customer KPI based on the Blank KPI template. By default the data source is set to Fixed Value; change this setting by selecting the new Sample_PDW data source built on the Planning Model database. After selecting the data source, customize the Actual Value measure by selecting a member during the Dimensional Data Source Mapping process (see Figure 18-24).

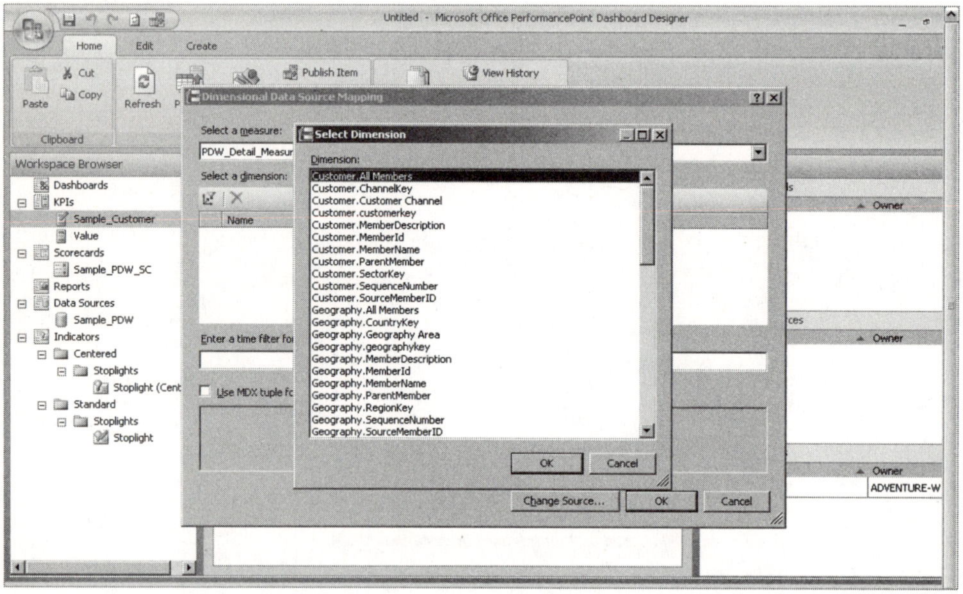

Figure 18-24 Select a dimension for the Actual value.

In this example, select Customer.AllMembers, but remember that it is possible to drill down and select detail customer members to create separate KPIs for each of the customers available in the Customer Members list. When setting new KPIs, keep in mind that the more you filter and customize at the KPI level, the more specific the KPI becomes and the less flexible it is later in the design process.

Now that you've changed the Actual value, you can also change the Target value in the same way. For the Target value, add multiple dimensions by selecting Customer.AllMembers as well as the Scenario.AllMembers dimension with an Actual member.

NOTE **It is also possible to enter a time filter formula or an MDX formula for the KPI when setting the Dimensional Data Source Mapping options.**

After creating the KPI, create a second new scorecard called Sample_Customer_SC, using the Blank Scorecard template (see Figure 18-25). With the blank scorecard on the screen, drag and drop the new Sample_Customer KPI from the Detail list. The result will be a second scorecard, which provides a second view of the Planning Model business information.

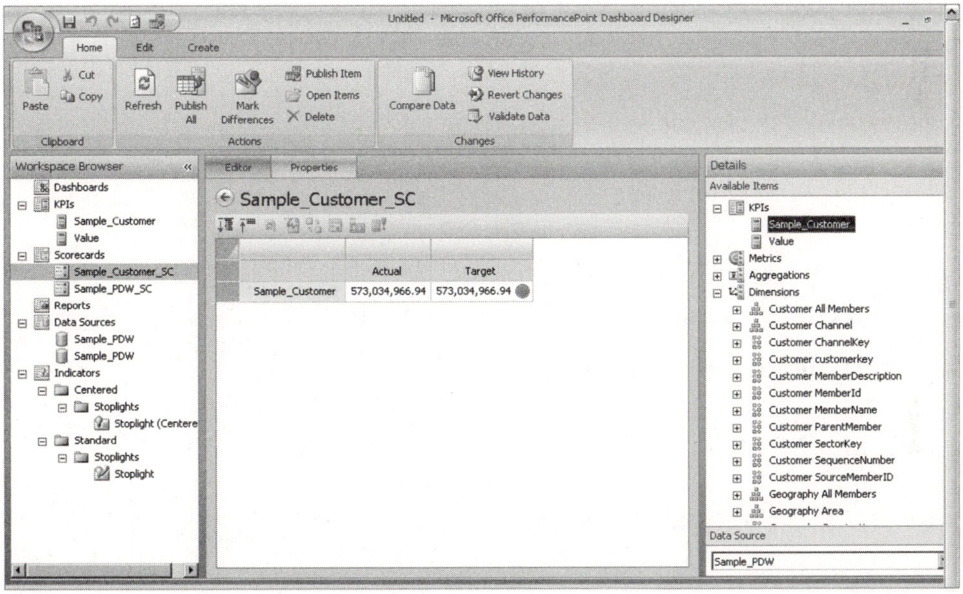

Figure 18-25 Create a second scorecard called Sample_Customer_SC.

At this point, you have created two scorecards, called Sample_PDW_SC and Sample_Customer_SC, which can now be used to create and deploy a dashboard based on the Planning Model database.

NOTE **The approach outlined here for creating scorecards from the Planning Model also applies to creating reports. The importance of knowing the structure of the data and the KPIs applies equally to creating reports for the dashboard.**

Building and Deploying the Dashboard

Use the dashboard template to create a new dashboard based on the Header, 2 Columns template and called SampleCustomerDB. Drag and drop the two scorecards from the Scorecard Available Items list in the Details pane. Figure 18-26 shows how the dashboard will appear in Dashboard Designer.

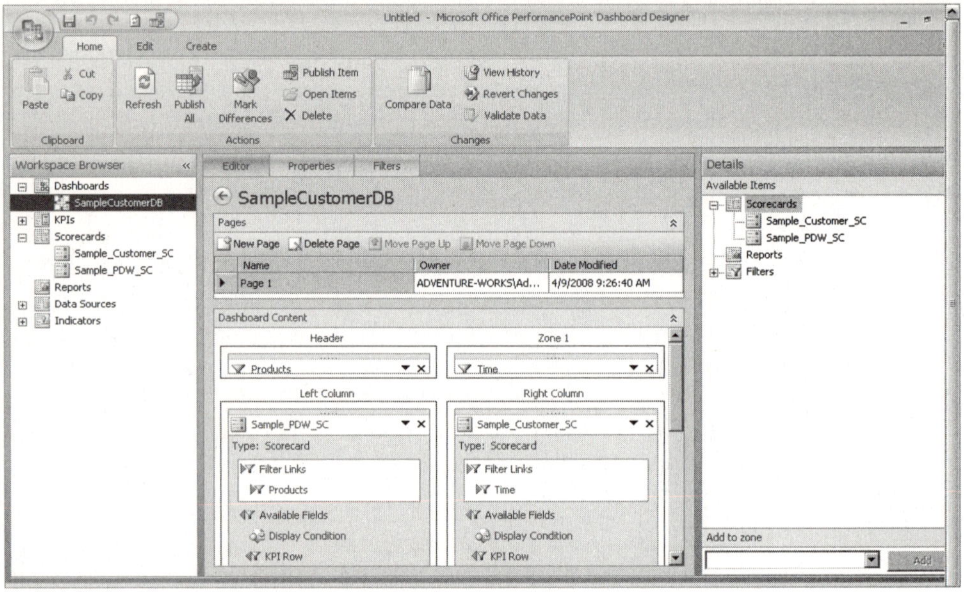

Figure 18-26 The dashboard in Dashboard Designer

Publish and preview to view the dashboard based on the Planning Model (see Figure 18-27).

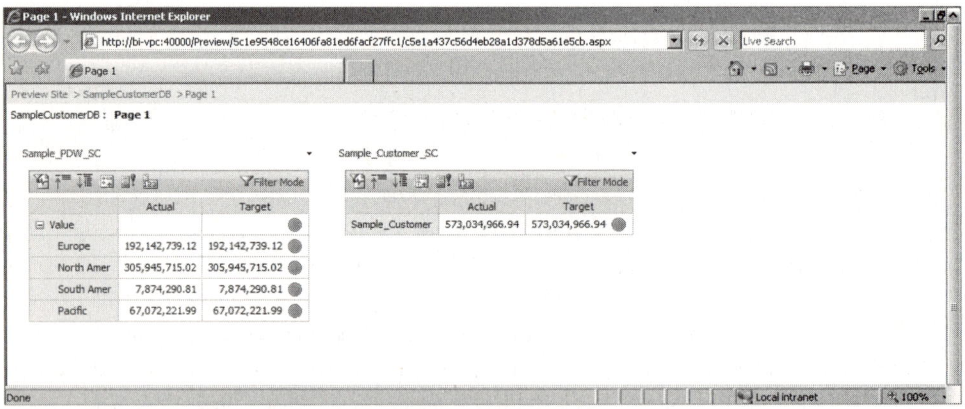

Figure 18-27 The dashboard based on the Planning Model

NOTE **If you are not able to preview the dashboard, make sure that the security settings for PPSMonitoringPreview align with the Planning Model security settings and roles.**

Adding Filters

Adding filters to the dashboard allows for greater customization of information from the Planning Model and provides users with the opportunity to access and view information that is even more targeted and personalized. This section covers how to create filters for the dashboard that has been created from the Planning Model.

To create a product filter for the Sample_PDW_SC scorecard that appears on the left of the dashboard, go to the Filters tab. Select New Filter, and then select the option to use the Member Selection filter template. Use Products as the filter name, and select the option to use the same Sample_PDW data source created previously for the scorecards. Use the Product.Products dimension for the hierarchy, selecting to add all visible members.

When selecting the dimension in Dashboard Designer, it's important to know the Planning Model dimension and the memberset. The membersets are subsets of the dimension and will determine the hierarchy within the filter list, so when selecting the dimension, make sure that the dimension has the right memberset to display the hierarchy required in the filter list.

For Display Method, select the Tree view, then publish the new filter. The new filter appears in the list of Available Items in the Details pane. From the Details list, drag the Products filter to the dashboard header. Now connect the filter to the scorecard using the Member UniqueName with the Column setting (see Figure 18-28).

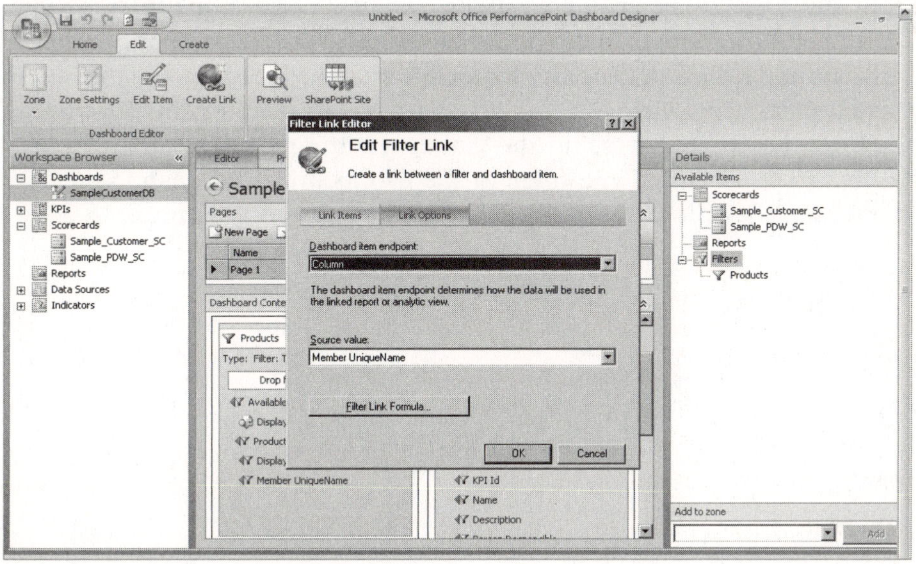

Figure 18-28 Use the Column setting.

Publish and preview the dashboard to see the filter in the dashboard. The dashboard now includes a filter that allows users to select products from the filter list to view targeted data by product. Notice that the filter list shown in Figure 18-29 displays the correct hierarchy.

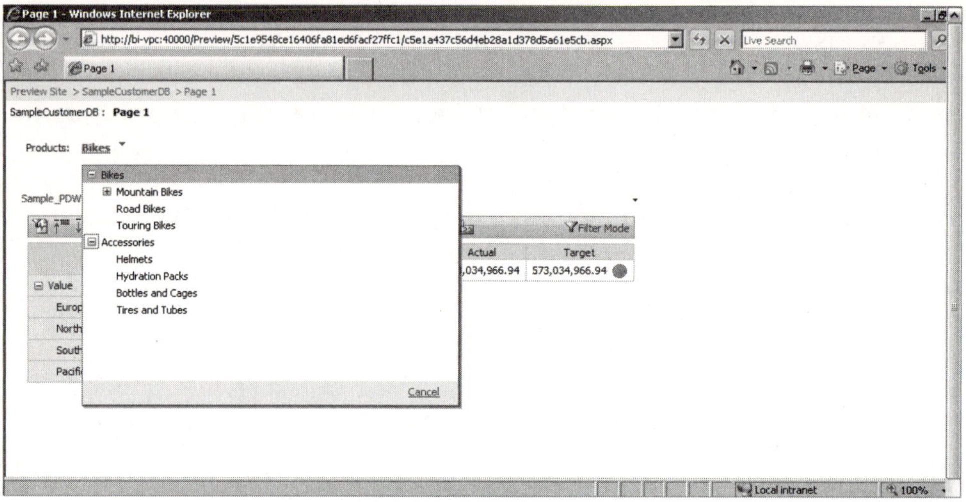

Figure 18-29 The filter list displays the correct hierarchy.

In a second example, create a time-based filter. From the Filters tab, select the option to create a new filter based on the Member Selection template, and name this filter Time. Select the same Sample_PDW data source used for the previous filter and select Time.CalendarQuarter as the dimension. Select all members' Q1, Q2, Q3, and Q4, and choose to display the filter in Tree view. The Time filter now appears in the Available Items in the Details pane. Split the Header Zone and drag and drop the Time filter into the Header from the Filters list in the Details pane. Using Member UniqueName, connect the filter to the scorecard on the right also using the Column setting. Publish and preview the dashboard to see the Time filter in the dashboard. The dashboard now includes a filter that allows users to filter data by quarter (see Figure 18-30).

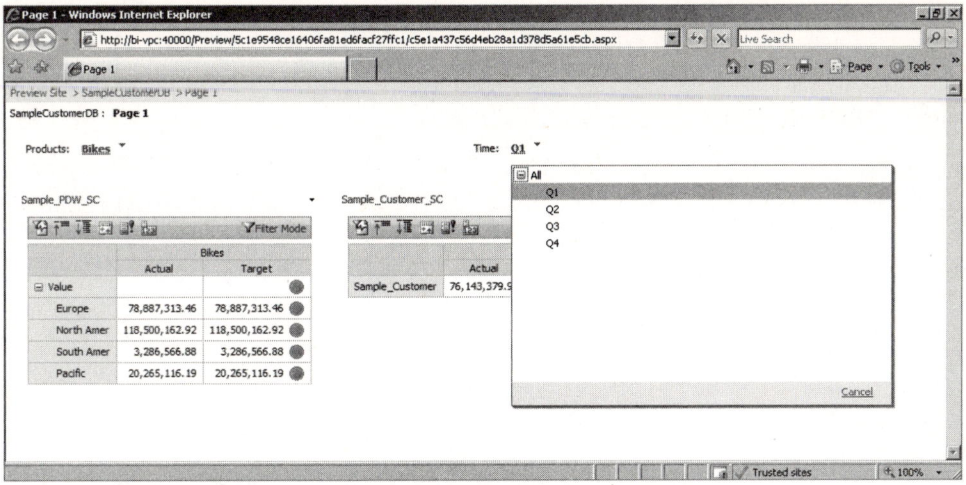

Figure 18-30 With the Time filter, users can view data by quarter.

This dashboard with its scorecard, filter, and KPI elements has been created using the Planning Model database. It's a dashboard that can now be used for monitoring and analyzing on the planning model itself to achieve continuous business improvement at the planning level.

Summary

The chapter began with a discussion about the value of bringing Monitoring, Analytics, and Planning together. By creating a dashboard and scorecard on the Planning Model, organizations can monitor how well their plan is working, analyze trends, and then use the Planning Model in a measure-based reiterative cycle to help refine their plan.

The extended business example explored the nuts and bolts of accomplishing this integration and how data and security flow through the different applications, including the Business Planning Modeler, Analysis Services, and Dashboard Designer. Throughout, the key point is that a deep understanding of the data allows organizations to build and deploy secure and targeted dashboards based on data from the Planning Model.

CHAPTER

19

Planning and Maintaining Successful Dashboards

This chapter provides recommendations on how to succeed with PerformancePoint Server dashboards. It highlights the best practices to employ and common mistakes to avoid, based on successful dashboard deployments.

The last section provides a test that may prove helpful in assessing your organization's capabilities to build effective monitoring and analytics solutions with PerformancePoint Monitoring and Analytics.

Ten Best Practices for Deploying Performance Dashboards

1. **Begin with a process diagram.** Use this to identify key inputs, output, ratios, and cycle times that can be used to determine the health of key business drivers. Use it as a blueprint for your dashboard, scorecard, and analytic views. For examples of process diagrams, see `http://office.microsoft.com/en-us/visio/HP010615721033.aspx`.
2. **Keep it simple.** Simplicity is one of the most powerful techniques used in successful dashboards. Don't overwhelm users with every view or navigation option that might be possible. Focus on what is most meaningful and most useful. A basic line chart may not be flashy or dramatic, but it clearly communicates performance over time. Users will appreciate this simplicity as they are able to quickly uncover relationships without being distracted by items they can't use or apply.

3. **Use simple calculations and dynamic sets.** Business logic can dramatically simplify monitoring and analysis for users. Calculations can ensure standard measurements across the organization, and dynamic sets can easily identify relevant members of a large population. However, if users can't understand how the values or sets are generated, they won't trust the results. Use calculations and sets that can be easily explained to your audience.
4. **Make it personal.** Users will respond much more quickly if the data is personally relevant to them. Scope the data to the level of the individual, whether it is a department, region, or unit. Embed the terminology and metrics he or she currently uses into the dashboard, through naming conventions, formulas, and workflows. Use metrics that relate to a user's daily tasks, commitments, or objectives. And provide users with the ability to display only the items they are responsible for.
5. **Provide context.** Ensure that your users have the right context for the information they see. If they are comparing performance across time, provide not only values for the current day but also values for the past month, quarter, or year. If they are evaluating performance against a plan, include actual values, plan values, and forecast projections. If they are assessing competitive strength, provide information about their product sales and their competitors' sales, or show them their market penetration compared to their competitors.
6. **Select the right visualization method for the monitoring and analysis.** Use the right visualization method for the type of monitoring or analysis your users will perform. Use a line chart for trend analysis or baseline analysis. Use a table or grid for a mix or consolidation analysis. Use a scatter plot to perform a quadrant analysis or to identify outliers. Use a bar chart to compare volume metrics across siblings within a population. And use a decomposition tree to identify root causes. Train your users on these visualizations to help them improve their own monitoring and analysis techniques.
7. **Include a data dictionary.** Prepare a list of terms that is customized to the data your users will be working with and the solution you are deploying. Define dimensions, hierarchies, and measures in their terms and provide examples to help them learn how to use them.
8. **Listen to your users.** As your users work with the data, they may have questions they can't answer with the current data, calculations, or views. These questions can be the starting point for the next iteration of your dashboards. Questions that your users ask define the insight they need to monitor and improve performance. You may not be able to provide

answers to them immediately, but you should consider these questions as you continue to evolve your dashboard library.

9. **Provide guidance.** If a scorecard indicator shows poor performance, provide the user with direction on how to improve that performance. If a budget variance exceeds the threshold, give the user additional information that can expose the problem, such as ledger detail or variance exceptions. Anticipate the questions users will have and provide them with that information.

10. **Establish processes.** As publishers deploy dashboards to users, establish processes to maintain the dashboard lifecycle. Establish how changes will be made and rolled out to users, how changes will be communicated, and what resources will be available to answer questions. Also establish mechanisms to provide feedback and incorporate that feedback in your dashboards.

Common Mistakes to Avoid When Deploying Performance Dashboards

1. **Thinking too big.** Delivering the right content to users is an iterative process. Don't try to build a comprehensive dashboard for every user in your organization — you're doomed before you start. Begin by deploying some basic views and metrics to a small group of users. Gather their feedback and build on their recommendations.

2. **Aiming for perfection.** Creating the perfect dashboard that fully empowers all users to make effective decisions isn't a reasonable goal. Organizations rarely have comprehensive, well-structured cubes with no errors, and they rarely have every key objective mapped to clear and actionable metrics for every individual or team.

   This doesn't mean that delivering incremental views of performance data can't produce significant returns. Even simple dashboards can give users more insight than they had before and engage them in actively improving processes.

3. **Abandoning your users.** Don't assume your users will have the time or desire to learn how to analyze the data in the dashboard without some guidance. Train your users on the content, analysis techniques, and workflow. Then, make sure that your users can practice what they've learned immediately after the training. If they don't use their newly acquired skills and knowledge for several months, they probably won't remember them.

4. **Doing it all yourself.** If you are new to monitoring and analysis, engage an experienced person to help with the design and deployment of your initial dashboard. Tackling the entire process yourself can extend the time it takes to deploy a successful solution. With help, you can deliver quick results and build on the experience of others for future projects.
5. **Underestimating users' interest in the data.** With meaningful views and the ability to navigate, users will be eager to engage with the data. They will explore the content and learn how to apply this information to improve their performance. They will provide feedback on how to improve the views and dashboard, and they will evangelize the benefits to other users in the organization. PerformancePoint Server isn't the only tool needed to improve performance, but it is a tool that empowers individuals to make decisions based on objective and consistent criteria.
6. **Building complex data sources.** Although cubes can contain hundreds of dimensions and measures, some of the most effective cubes are those that are simple and targeted. Collaborate with the users who will be using the data to name hierarchies, dimensions, and measures in the terms they use and understand. Ensure that the structure and measures align with how users understand the organization. Complexity adds noise, making gaining insight more difficult and less likely to happen.
7. **Updating content infrequently.** Users will be more likely to provide feedback if they can see their suggestions incorporated quickly. If they have to wait 12 months for the next release, they will stop providing their feedback, and your content will become stale and less compelling. Make a firm commitment to update content and data sources frequently.
8. **Using the wrong tools.** PerformancePoint Server and Dashboard Designer support navigation and visualization, key components of understanding. They are not designed to produce highly formatted transaction or operational reports. If you need to provide this type of content, invest in a tool specifically designed for this purpose, such as Microsoft Reporting Services.
9. **Losing sight of the objective.** The purpose of performance dashboards is to influence behavior, processes, or thinking. The end goal is not a dashboard; rather, the end goal is changing the way business is conducted. Make sure that you provide your users with the next steps. Outline the actions they can take to use their newly acquired understanding to effect change within the organization.
10. **Missing opportunities to evangelize success.** Even small wins should be recognized and publicized in the organization. As more people hear

about the success of a project or improvements driven by a new perspective on past performance, they will be more willing to start pilot projects in their own departments. They will also be more willing to invest in data quality measures that will enable better analysis over time.

Generate excitement about the potential of performance dashboards with newsletters and the projected timeframe for rollout. Informing users what they will be able to do when they have this tool in their hands is a great way to generate enthusiasm and gain acceptance.

How to Know If You Have the Ability to Build Effective Performance Dashboards

Pervasive performance management means that all decision makers in an organization are aligned, accountable, and empowered and that users have relevant, personalized, and current dashboards available to them at all times. We have discussed the guiding principles to which an organization needs to adhere to monitor and analyze effectively.

To effectively monitor an organization's needs you must maintain:

- **Consistency** of data and information, utilizing both structured and unstructured information, and know how to effectively use KPIs
- **Accountability** through personalized KPIs that are portable across scorecards and dashboards and through the effective use of thresholds to anticipate issues before they become problems
- **Alignment** using methodologies like the Balanced Scorecard and strategy maps to line up individual and team execution with organizational goals[1]

To effectively analyze an organization's needs you must maintain:

- **Agility** to respond quickly to changing market conditions, enabled by allowing more people to leverage analytics via Web-based analytics, and delivering depth when needed, depending on the types of decisions being made.
- **Relevancy** of information enabled by delivering information that is based on the things people care about, while filtering out irrelevant and unnecessary information, and deliver it in a way that makes sense to users by tailoring it for their roles. This makes it intuitive and extremely easy to use.

- **Efficiency** by allowing people to follow their path of inquiry by drilling and cross-drilling to get the answers they need without delay, and making complex sets of information quickly comprehensible through advanced analytics such as performance maps. These techniques enable trends and patterns to be intuitively recognized.[2]

The following test may prove helpful in assessing your organization's capability to build effective monitoring and analytics solutions with PerformancePoint Monitoring and Analytics. Think about the following as a framework around which to organize a conversation on the subject of performance management with your teams across divisions and groups.

Take the Test

Some of the statements here are multifaceted, and you may find you agree with only part of a statement. Answer "True" if you find that the statement is generally true or "False" if you find that the statement is generally false in describing your organization.

1. Our organization has identified business goals and objectives, and communicated these across the organization. Our employees understand how strategic goals relate to operational and tactical goals, and they understand how to translate these goals into actions within their areas of responsibility.
2. Our organization has identified measures for each of these goals and objectives, and everyone has agreed to the measures. These measures have been identified for all areas and levels of decision making in our organization.
3. Our organization is sensitive to the organizational culture and people issues that accompany the deployment of dashboards. Senior management has a history of cultivating a culture of accountability and transparency throughout the organization.
4. For our employees, monitoring and analytics is second nature like email. Our employees are used to tracking and analyzing data. They are used to getting the information they need for themselves to track goals and create analytic materials to support performance in their areas of responsibility.
5. In our organization, information technology (IT) has a good reputation and established relationships with business users at all levels of the organization.
6. In our organization, IT has identified data sources for each of the measures associated with the business goals and objectives. If we don't

have an existing data source, we've got the resources and know-how to build what we need.

7. In our organization, IT has identified the data architecture and data integration infrastructure required for the foundation of our performance management initiative. We're confident that the architecture and infrastructure will be able to ensure that data is secure and consistent and that dashboards can be deployed rapidly and with ease.
8. In our organization, IT has identified the interface and consumer options for users to consume the data. We know how our employees will access the dashboards.
9. In our organization, IT has an established development process that includes a requirement-gathering process suitable for collecting monitoring and analytics business goals, objectives, and metrics. Our organization also has an established governance structure to identify and resolve data quality issues with participation from both business users and IT. The governance structure will be ready and able to resolve data quality issues on deployed dashboards.
10. In our organization, IT has the development and design resources with the training required to build and implement effective dashboards.

Your Score

When reviewing your score, note that the score should not be viewed as an outcome, "How did we do?," but rather as a starting point, "Where are we starting from?" The purpose of the test is not just to give you a number, but to provide a framework for driving performance excellence.

Add up the number of "True" answers you provided. If you answered all of the preceding questions with "True," the people in your organization are equipped with the ability to monitor and analyze, and management has its finger on the pulse of the organization. Otherwise, refer to the following:

0–2 True answers = Limited monitoring and analyzing strength; your score is 1.

3–5 True answers = Moderate monitoring and analyzing strength; your score is 2.

6–8 True answers = Major monitoring and analyzing strength; your score is 3.

9–10 True answers = Superior monitoring and analyzing strength; your score is 4.

Further guidance on how to improve your monitoring and analyzing capabilities is provided in the next section.

Improve Your Results

If you answered "False" to any of the questions in the preceding section, note the number of the question and review the corresponding suggested remedy in the following list to help move toward a "True" answer and, more importantly, provide your organization with a competitive advantage.

1. If your organization has not identified business goals and objectives, and communicated these across the organization, you need to start your performance monitoring and analytics solution right here. At this point, it doesn't matter if IT is ready to implement dashboards. The organization must be ready. Meetings and forums, sponsored by senior management, must be held at all levels of the organization to understand goals, objectives, and measures for each of the key areas in the organization.
2. Ask questions. Find out how employees measure success at all levels of your organization. How does the sales department in your regional office measure a successful quarter? How does human resources measure success? How does IT measure success? Do these measures relate to the organization's strategic goals? If not, provide employees with the knowledge to reassess their measures based on an understanding of strategic goals.
3. Even the most effective and beautifully designed dashboard will not be able to overcome resistance to information sharing and bringing information and decision making out into the open. Get buy-in from the very beginning of the development phase. Involve business users at all levels in the development of dashboards and metrics. Get feedback on a regular basis during development and after deployment.
4. Begin now to put more information into the hands of employees to foster autonomy. Go to business users now to find out what information they would like to have in hand. Find out what decisions they are making daily, weekly, monthly, quarterly, and annually. Work with them to identify the information they need to make these decisions, and where possible, publish this information now. You'll be fostering cooperation and gathering valuable information toward the implementation of a full performance management solution.
5. If IT does not have a good reputation and established relationships with business users at all levels of the organization, start building bridges and mending fences now. Building and deploying successful dashboards is a collaborative endeavor that requires cooperation between all departments at all levels in your organization. Send out your best

IT ambassadors to speak with employees in all departments at all levels. Try to identify issues with quick fixes that will make a difference to business users and that will start to build your reputation as an engaged problem-solving partner in the business community.

6. Begin identifying all sources of data in your organization, from data cubes on the server to the critical spreadsheet on the employee's desk in the shipping department. Build a map of your data that includes information about its source, type, and function.
7. Do a thorough review of your data architecture and data integration infrastructure. Be sure to identify sensitive data and any real or potential security vulnerabilities. Develop a plan to fix any issues you may find.
8. Find out how employees are currently accessing the information they need. Do they regularly access reports from custom applications? Do they use desktop tools to build their own spreadsheets and databases? Is there already a central source of data for employees? Can this central source support dashboards?
9. If IT in your organization does not have a requirements-gathering process, consider establishing one. If you don't want to establish a formal process, make sure to build this activity into your development plan. Decide on a suitable way to collect, document, and review monitoring and analytics business goals, objectives, and metrics with business users. Make sure that stakeholders and business users sign off on these requirements before you begin development. If your organization does not have a formal governance structure to identify and resolve data quality issues, consider establishing one. If you don't want to establish a formal structure, make sure that your development plan includes regularly scheduled data quality reviews for dashboard data. Begin the data quality reviews during the development phase and continue to review data quality during the testing phase and immediately after deployment to production. In your plan, identify the business users and IT resources responsible for resolving data quality issues on dashboards deployed to production. Involve business users in this activity.
10. Install PerformancePoint Monitoring and Analytics as a standalone topology on a single computer so that your development and design employees can familiarize themselves with the application and its capabilities. Point employees to the Microsoft PerformancePoint site, `www.microsoft.com/performancepoint`, where they will find a wealth of information, resources, and examples of effective and well-designed monitoring and analytics dashboards. Consider engaging an experienced person to help with the design and deployment of your initial project.

Summary

In this chapter, we've provided you with lists of best practices to employ and common mistakes to avoid when deploying dashboards. If you've taken the test to help assess your ability to build effective dashboards, you should have a good idea of where you're starting from and how ready your organization is to design, build, and implement monitoring and analytics solutions with PerformancePoint Monitoring and Analytics. From the test results, you should now have a list of topics to help initiate and organize a conversation on the subject of performance management with teams across divisions and groups within your organization.

Notes

1. Bruno Aziza and Joey Fitts, *Drive Business Performance: Enabling a Culture of Intelligent Execution* (Wiley, 2008).
2. Ibid.

CHAPTER

20

Planning Application Development

PerformancePoint Planning Server provides an application solution to business problems. An application solution developed using PerformancePoint will be made most effective if you understand the proper solution requirements, follow good solution development practices, and apply your knowledge and experiences to deliver the best design. This chapter begins by outlining how partnerships between business and information technology (IT) teams work together on performance management applications. PerformancePoint Planning Server challenges some of the traditional assumptions and implementation patterns of business intelligence (BI) projects. Solutions integration partners can play a key role in delivering on the value of a strategic approach to performance management. The chapter closes out by describing some of the key things to do and considerations to factor into an application development project.

Implementation Best Practices — How to Get the Job Done

In this section, we discuss some ways to implement solutions based on the way in which PerformancePoint Planning Server facilitates business solution processes. There are some recommended best practices that are specific to the use of PerformancePoint, and others that apply more broadly to complex business solutions. One of the first situations to evaluate is the organization requiring a solution and the key stakeholders in the outcome.

The Roles of Business and IT Stakeholders

A critical success factor for performance management solutions is the partnership between the business organization that requires, operates, and relies on the solution, and the IT counterparts who deliver and maintain that solution. PerformancePoint Server introduces an evolutionary step in the solution delivery process that improves the effectiveness of the organizations involved. However, as with most changes, it may take some new understanding and approaches to be successful. To make the transition, it is critical to understand the key stakeholders involved in a performance management solution, discuss the larger organizational behaviors influencing them, and identify how PerformancePoint Planning Server components can advance their capacity to deliver effective solutions to business challenges.

Organizational Objectives

Chapter 10 began by outlining the key personas who participate in PerformancePoint Planning Server application solutions. The personas of business analyst, contributor, hybrid, and IT analyst all operate within organizations with their own objectives, which influence their activities. There are two primary organizational structures that can be used as a framework for discussing these objectives and how they factor into the application development process. The first is a structure in which both the operational business unit and its supporting IT organization have common management — for example, where the departmental managers report to the business unit vice president. The second is found in many large companies where the IT infrastructure is consolidated into one central service organization with its own leadership and company-wide charter. It's important to understand how these types of organizations behave because this is a critical factor in the successful implementation of performance management solutions.

Business and IT Together

The model in which business functions and information technology (IT) functions both exist within an operating unit is often found in organizations with strong decentralized models that desire maximum flexibility. The core advantage of this type of structure for a PerformancePoint Planning Server application solution is that everyone involved in designing, creating, and operating the solution shares the same business objective, reinforced by their shared management structure. Often, this can help reduce the resistance to change. There can be fewer excuses not to do something when everyone is clear on what the boss wants. Where the goals of the business and IT functional teams are well aligned, organizations can take advantage of this partnership to create a development model where PerformancePoint Server empowers the business analysts to create the application solution corresponding to their view of the business, with IT providing critical infrastructure support and data expertise. The partnership between IT and business roles establishes the right personnel playing its optimal role in the application development and operational process. IT can focus on core competencies such as data management and integration with external systems, and business users focus on their knowledge of the business functions being modeled and the processes surrounding them.

IT and Operational Units Organizationally Separate

Many large corporations have centralized much of their information technology (IT) functions. This provides commonality and consistency across an organization where multiple operating units can generally share the use of standardized technology resources to reduce costs. In cases of separate organizations, the critical challenge occurs in relation to the goals and objectives of the business. The needs of the business will be foremost considerations in a PerformancePoint Server application solution design and development project, but at the same time, processes and procedures a central organization applies to all supported applications need to be incorporated. Organizational boundaries may force adaptation in existing procedures to allow the PerformancePoint methodology where business users are empowered through application capabilities. A central IT organization may be less familiar with a particular business problem and may need help from the business in properly clarifying their requirements. Components such as the Business Modeler enable business users to play a more direct role in translating requirements into application structure and behavior. However, a central IT organization may have existing methodologies that cause resistance at first, but once adapted will be much more able to share and develop one or more applications that span organizations or reach across the entire company.

No matter which type of organizational structure your company has, central or distributed, PerformancePoint Planning Server brings a shift to some application development paradigms. This is a positive shift but must be understood and factored into deployment methodologies within any organization.

PerformancePoint Server 2007 Planning — Changing the Paradigm

Performance management application development projects generally follow a traditional development methodology. Business teams collect input from key stakeholders and prepare a requirements document. A good requirements document will outline the end-user capabilities, process flow, and data required for and from an application. It can be very hard, though, to get an effective application from even a well-written requirements document. In most cases, some knowledge of the business process and data is necessary to interpret the requirements document correctly. The worst-case outcome is one where a development team takes a requirements document and, after months of work, comes back with an application that does not satisfy the needs of the business. More commonly, there are long iterative cycles between the development team and the business stakeholder community, which are exercises necessary to translate requirements into terms that developers can understand and implement. PerformancePoint Planning Server offers a new approach to business-focused projects.

With PerformancePoint Server, business users have a powerful application that offers them design and build capabilities to produce effective business solutions. This is not to say that IT disappears from the process, and it's essential to clarify that many core roles are not significantly changed from previous approaches. In fact, more focus can be placed on the areas of strength to increase the performance and capability of both business and IT. Using PerformancePoint, a business analyst is able to transfer what is often done in Microsoft Excel into a server-based application without losing the agility tools such as those that Excel provides. Business analysts create the data structure, business rules, end-user forms, and control process all from within an application designed for them. The application presents objects and tasks in terms they understand and abstracts complex coding or data modeling functions. What the application generates at the server layer is database schema and logic that IT developers can easily relate to. In effect, business requirements can be expressed by business users through complete application construction and IT developers can "productionize" the server components and create the necessary interfaces with other corporate systems. No longer will effort be invested in translating business requirements language; now the discussion between business and IT can be more constructive, discussing the operational behavior desired. All parties involved in application solution creation operate in an environment designed for them, where they describe their understanding of a problem's solution and transfer knowledge through meta data definitions they all can understand. By placing more responsibility for structure and design on business users, an application becomes less focused on available data and more focused on the required data.

Some limitations of existing approaches to application development come from starting a solution from existing data. Actual data available, such as data sourced from transactional enterprise resource planning (ERP) systems, is a logical starting point for budgeting a forward-looking version of what is being currently measured. However, it fails to put focus, and can even cloud, analysis of key business drivers. Reports of actual data may show items like total sales, total costs, and total expenses. Those totals may be granular, perhaps specific to a department or operating unit, but they are still the result of drivers in action. Total sales may be the result of the quantity sold less the quantity returned, multiplied by the sale price. These are truer drivers of the sales amount. If a budgeting solution mirrors actual data and asks end users to contribute expected total amounts, it is effectively forcing them to all go off and develop their own offline models outside the budgeting solution. Few, if any, sales planners know an expected total number that they could just enter, so they would build their own logic, usually in a Microsoft Excel spreadsheet, to derive the total sales value to submit. Now the budgeting solution is effective at capturing and aggregating data, but it provides little end-user or business value because it has not solved any critical problems. It does not model the true drivers and influences with which the business is managed, and it requires contributors to do their own work. It's likely to produce inconsistent results due to the fact that amounts derived in offline models will have different business logic across the organization, with no visibility into the inconsistencies of the user models. Perhaps, in some regions, total sales are captured as described here, but maybe other groups ignore the quantity returned and simply compute the total sales as the quantity times the price. Now you can see the exposure this approach opens up. Neither computation for total sales is wrong, but because they are inconsistent, wrong choices may be made. Furthermore, these total amounts are static in the process. If, near the end of the budgeting cycle, it is decided that pricing expectations for a given product need to be adjusted for unforeseen competition, all end users must recompute their numbers and resubmit them. In a driver-based budgeting model, pricing assumptions could simply be adjusted in one location and totals recomputed by business rules defined in the application. Contributors may be asked to evaluate the new model and change some quantity expectations based on their own local market characteristics. Throughout the process, though, the attention is focused on the core elements or drivers. There are clear definitions behind what total numbers appear in budget review reports, and consistency is delivered across the organization.

When preparing a planning application solution, the key message should be to model the business as granularly as possible, targeted at the drivers used for measurement and control, to ensure accountability. Certainly, starting from actual data and reporting views of it that are used to manage the business is the first step, but taking the time to model the primary influencers of those results provides a more effective solution. Particular focus on the influencers that people in the organization can control and can be measured on creates actionable models. A few simple drivers will result in simple calculations and an easy model. A complex business will have many drivers with complicated interactions. The advantage of PerformancePoint Planning Server is that those interactions can be centrally defined once and reused throughout an application. This is far superior to the alternative of either ignoring key drivers or interactions or leaving it up to each individual contributor to determine the computations and submitting a total result. When budget preparers are submitting values for drivers that they can influence, their performance against managing these drivers can be measured and they can be held accountable for items within their control. Building the planning application solution with key drivers and control actions in mind will lead to a far more effective component of an organization's performance management process.

Solution Implementations

PerformancePoint Planning Server is a complex application solution platform created for some hard-to-solve business problems. Deployments are typically phased and ideally align with broader strategic or process change efforts. In this section, some of the considerations to be evaluated in implementing a solution are detailed. The evaluation process itself is described, including proofs-of-concept, as well as some specific design considerations for PerformancePoint Planning Server application solutions. First, though, two critical success factors that apply broadly to any new application solution effort must be understood.

Management support is often sought in new project or solution initiatives. Support from the executive level is often required for funding and resources to be dedicated to a project of significant size or duration. However, as a recommended practice, a different kind of management support should be sought: sponsorship. Performance management application solutions are large, long-term company investments. The return on that investment is difficult to quantify up front. It's hard to articulate how much more revenue a company can capture by driving up customer satisfaction, for example. Few people would argue that positive return would not be seen from increased customer satisfaction, it's just that many performance management efforts don't fit a simple investment portfolio model that easily illustrates return on investment (ROI). Therefore, seeking out executives who believe in the positive transformation of an organization or operational unit's process and measurement can be critical. Change is often resisted, so if senior management communicates the vision and positive future that is driving change, an implementation will face far less difficulty and obtain far more cooperation. Sponsorship will also help guide an implementation team towards effective delivery.

Performance management solutions, by nature, have broad possibilities and applications. If an executive can constrain the phases of solution delivery to key leadership needs, a project team can use that prioritization to determine highly valuable and deliverable components. If a team must go into a 2- or 3-year development cycle before anything is delivered, the likelihood of success is very small for many reasons. However, if valuable solutions to targeted problems can be delivered in 6- to 9-month intervals, success is much more likely. PerformancePoint Server is an ideal platform for the phased, incremental approach because of its flexible application solution architecture. Solution phases can be delivered, each built to extend the prior phase, avoiding the problem of each phase being an independent effort that will be difficult to maintain and likely diverge over time.

Most PerformancePoint Server projects will be undertaken by organizations that have some type of tool they use currently. Whether it is an Excel spreadsheet–based tool or another type, people in the organization will be familiar with the tool and the business process that has formed around it. A business requirements document will often reflect the portion of the current solution that is liked and attempt to articulate the proper way to do the things it presently cannot. While existing solutions should inform a new effort, caution should be exercised not to influence it too strongly. One of the most common tendencies to exemplify this is the end-user budget data entry form. Many times, implementations attempt to replicate the same user experience that contributors are accustomed to. This replication is understandable, as the adoption of a new solution gets easier the more similar it is to the previous one. The problem is that rather than having the proper model of the business drive the architecture and process, the current end-user experience does. In some cases this is acceptable; however, in most cases this leads to less-optimal modeling of the business that results in higher maintenance costs and less flexibility in the new solution. Secondarily, the current solution has likely been in place for at least a couple of years. In many of today's industries, that is a long time, and key business drivers have changed over that time. By not allowing the current solution to have too much influence over the new one, some updated thinking and future anticipation can be incorporated into the solution development process. End-user adoption of the new system is essential, but over time, an effective and accurate solution will be recognized for its benefits far more than the attributes that were similar to the old solution.

Targeted Proof of Concept—Right Scope, Right People

Few companies, large or small, begin a performance management solution effort with a complete picture of where they want to end up over the long term. Of the few that may claim they do, the eventual outcome of the solution effort doesn't always produce the same result they had in mind. In part, this is because managing performance is a multifaceted problem, so its solution also has a variety of components. Performance management is also an ongoing, evolutionary process. This year, a company's strategic goal may be to gain market share, so management focuses on activities related to marketing, promotions, and distribution expansion. However, a couple of years later (having been successful at growth), the company may shift to managing profitability and high satisfaction for all the customers acquired. The key message here is to take a staged approach to beginning any performance management solution effort. PerformancePoint Server facilitates this approach and allows organizations to be able to reuse efforts as they expand a solution broadly to all employees. To get started, the critical first step is to identify and execute a targeted proof-of-concept effort to ensure the core issues are understood prior to beginning a full solution development effort.

Thorogood Associates is a business intelligence and performance management implementation partner with over 20 years of experience as a company delivering highly effective solutions to their clients. Learning from their many engagements over the years, they understand the proper way to gather requirements, project structure, and how to achieve a successful outcome in solution development projects. First and foremost is that successful projects are likely to begin with a proof of concept.

A proof of concept confirms that a specific technology can deliver the requirements. It also provides a rational basis for choosing between competing or alternative technologies. Survey evidence (OLAP/BI Survey 2001/2006, `http://www.bi-survey.com/`) shows a strong correlation between preliminary tool evaluations and successful project outcomes.

Choosing the appropriate technology solution is especially important in large organizations. Planning applications are typically shared applications with many users distributed widely across the organization. A large organization may have several tools already deployed that are potentially suitable for the new application. Each of these tools may have its own constituency of supporters — individuals who have a strong preference for a particular technology because of their experience and skills in it. Each constituency can be expected to lobby for their favorite tool to be selected for the new application. Vendors often seek to encourage these constituencies to make a case for the product and can be very influential. These competing perspectives will need to be brought to a consensus with an objective and rational process of selection.

Although few companies have a corporate standard for planning or business intelligence technologies, it is often the case that the business sponsor for an application will want to be sure to choose a technology that has the potential to be a corporate standard. They will want objective evidence that this is the case. Sometimes consultants are employed to give advice on tool selection and may carry out an exercise that compares the candidate technologies on a range of attributes. These exercises assemble a large amount of information on the products involved, but this rarely helps to build a consensus. The reports of independent analysis firms will always be examined, and they may be informative upon careful inspection. Analyst coverage is comprehensive in examining all aspects of the technology and the vendors' capabilities. Many analysts produce rankings of products and of product vendors and are careful to explain the basis for their rankings. They are also careful to point out that, because of the generalized criteria they are using for their ranking analysis, their overall ranking will not be directly relevant to an individual customer's product-selection decision.

Products and technologies evolve. In particular, fierce competition has driven the software vendors of planning and business intelligence products to offer very similar features and functionality. If a particular feature is missing from a particular release of a particular product, it will probably be in the next release, and if not, it can probably be worked around, or the product can at least have the extensibility to allow the functionality to be provided by the implementation partner. This means that the mere existence of out-of-the-box features and functionality is not likely to be a good basis for discriminating between products. However, such features and functionality can be the basis for including a product within a set of products to be evaluated using a proof of concept, as will the information in independent analysts' reports. Information on product and vendor characteristics is useful for drawing up the long or short list for consideration. However, the proof of concept takes the examination of suitability to a different level.

The proof of concept establishes selection criteria by combining examinations of functionality with measures of performance, scalability, and ease of use. It is important to document requirements that will establish not only the required functionality, categorized by importance, but also the associated criteria for performance, scalability, and ease of use. The most important of these is often performance, but all factors must be considered in a final decision.

Performance is the criterion most closely associated with successful implementations. The performance of particular functions — queries, allocations, and consolidations — will be critical to establishing the users' preferences. Critical functions will need to be fast and easy to use at all levels of scale. Performance is something that will be experienced by all users every time that they use the application, so performance has a dramatic effect on the perceptions and use of the application. Planning processes are typically run to tight deadlines, and slow performance frustrates users. They also generally have high expectations of performance from their experience of Internet search applications, which return queries within fractions of a second.

User requirements for a planning application can be particularly specific. Business users will have been using planning processes and a variety of tools to assist in those processes for many years. Existing applications will have established user roles and expectations. The planning timetable will establish the time limits for each process. This means that the requirements can define both the criticality of functionality and the acceptable performance limits. Some of these functions will be particularly critical, and achieving the functionality and the associated performance standard is mandatory. These requirements can eliminate some vendors' products from the evaluation at an early stage.

Additional vendor products may also be excluded if they fail to achieve a high percentage of coverage of the noncritical functionality. However, most areas of functionality will be achievable by all the candidates, and the discriminators will be performance and ease of use.

The skill of the implementation partner will affect the results of the proof of concept, so it is important that the work to develop competing proofs of concepts be carried out separately and competitively by different implementation partners representing the vendors or by the vendors themselves. Most products offer the flexibility to extend the functionality of the product, and a skilled implementation partner who is committed to the product helps to ensure that each product receives appropriate attention and that the performance results are the best that are achievable. For each requirement, the implementation partner will demonstrate the functionality and the methodology, and measure the performance. Users should repeat the method and confirm the ease of use and the performance claimed by the implementation partner. A matrix should be prepared to show the results for each of the candidate products against each element of the prioritized functionality so that products can be compared objectively on their relative performance. As a result, the proof of concept can result in a clear ranking of the candidate technologies, and a basis for a consensus will have been established.

At this point, commercial considerations can be brought into play. Cost is important because it will affect how widely a successful implementation will be exploited within a company. High software-license costs are often the primary reason that implementations are not rolled out more widely. There is also the prospect for the successful vendor that their product, having demonstrated performance, scalability, and ease of use in a demanding proof of concept, will be seen as a potential strategic product choice, should the customer seek to standardize across the enterprise.

Once the proof of concept has been completed, and the selection made, the code developed for the proof-of-concept exercises should be thrown away and a fresh start made on the implementation. Adapting code created for the proof of concept is not efficient because it was targeted and focused on short-term objectives. Once chosen, the implementation partner should be asked to reformulate a development plan for the full solution. If the implementation partner worked on delivering the proof of concept, the knowledge gained in that exercise will give them a significant head start, but choosing the proper partner should be its own process.

Partnering Effectively with Systems Integrators

Crucial to the success or failure of any performance management application solution are the knowledge and skills of the people designing and implementing it. In the performance management space, the necessary expertise is often not available within an organization or, more likely, a few key individuals do have the expertise but are scattered throughout different parts of the organization. There are two major forms of expertise necessary: business and technical. Business expertise can inform decisions such as on which key drivers the business plans should be based. Technical expertise, then, can answer the questions about how to model those drivers most effectively and deliver a solution to end users. If an organization lacks expertise in either of the two areas, a consulting partner can fill the gaps. In the case of powerful and complex application solutions like PerformancePoint Server, a system-integration partner can be highly valuable in delivering the right solution in the short term and providing a foundation for future expansion. If a partner is being chosen, there are a few critical questions to answer and proper expectations must be set from the client's perspective.

The objective of any planning process is to get an optimal plan, one that produces the best results from the resources available. Such plans will incorporate many different views and perspectives, reconciling the aspirations for performance of the top management with the views of front-line managers. There may be repeated plan iterations and plan revisions as managers optimize the allocation of resources. The efficiency of planning iterations limits how many can be completed, and this can affect the quality of the plan. Plans are prepared with uncertainty about the future conditions under which they will be implemented. Accordingly, managers will want to test how robust the plans are under different sets of assumptions or scenarios, so they will need models built to help them. Managers are also aware that any plans that are made will need to be adapted in due course, not the least because of competitor counteractions. As the famous Prussian Field Marshal Helmuth von Moltke once said, "No plan survives contact with the enemy"; or as the boxer Joe Louis put it, "Everyone has a plan until they get hit." So managers also need the ability to adapt their plans quickly. The more quickly they can adapt, the more effective their response to events will be and the better they will perform. Planning requires that key information is distinguished from very large amounts of relevant but less important information. It is about distinguishing key business drivers, key strategic priorities, and key performance indicators from a mass of detail. Managers need the planning system to help them do this.

People at all levels of the organization are involved in the planning process and will rely on the system. Top management's credibility with the investment community depends on their ability to plan for performance and deliver performance to plan. Operating managers throughout the organization know that their trust relationships with colleagues depend on delivering their commitments under the plan. Everyone benefits from the quality of the work of the analysts who, often working under pressure, collate the information, build the models, and crunch the numbers. All the users will have demanding requirements for functionality with performance, ease of use, and flexibility. Quantifying the key business drivers will require complex calculations and collation of data from multiple data sources internal and external to the firm. Many managers and analysts will be involved in analyzing and reviewing information. The way information is presented to executives will be critical to their confidence in the work that has been done by their subordinates and in the recommendations that they make.

Priorities for such systems will be specific to an individual firm, reflecting the sector, structure, and strategy of the business and the unique dynamics of leaders and their teams. The implementation partner needs the capacity to recognize and respond to all of the requirements. Understanding these requirements is communication-intensive and requires a high level of communication skills. The performance and flexibility of the application will be critical and will require a high level of design skills.

The technical possibilities and the business goals will have to be elucidated in parallel and matched before it will be possible to produce a functional specification and design a data model. The design will have to allow the users flexibility to explore the data in the way that they choose. The design and development process is unlike that of a transactional system, where users have far fewer degrees of freedom. That means the system has to be business- and user-led, not technically led. Customers work with implementation partners in the belief that this will deliver a more successful project. This belief is often based on hard personal experience, but there is also published evidence. The OLAP/BI Survey 2001–2006 has published evidence from questionnaires to customers showing that projects are more successful when they involve implementation partners. The customer can expect the implementation partner to provide an implementation team that brings together an appropriate and cost-effective mix of skills and experience in the technology, in the business application solution, and in project delivery. Often, implementation partners will have spent many years building the balance of capabilities required. However, and most fundamentally, customers should expect that the implementation partner will be able to maintain their trust. Any implementation project carries a degree of risk, and there will be many problems to overcome. The customer needs to know that, notwithstanding any problems, the implementation partner can be trusted to deliver.

For this reason, customers often prefer to work with suppliers who have earned their trust over many years. If a new supplier is sought, then trustworthy implementation partners should have many longstanding customers willing to provide references, but trust relationships aren't established merely by getting references. Who the right implementation partner is should become obvious during the software-supplier selection process, because that person will display the appropriate behavior. The implementation partner will be looking for what is special and different about the customer's business and its issues, and will try to understand what is particularly important to the customer. The chosen partner will have spent time researching and thinking about the customer's business and will be continuously looking to improve his understanding so that, should problems arise, he will be prepared to suggest proper solutions. He will regard being invited to discuss and explore how he might help with the customer's business issues as a privilege. Throughout the interaction, the implementation partner will display credibility, reliability, and an overriding concern for the client's ability to extract the maximum business benefits from the implementation.

Openness and integrity will mean that the client will have complete clarity as to the risks of the project and the responsibilities of both parties. The project management procedures will be flexible and responsive and will give the client control and discretion over what is delivered, and the ability to manage risk effectively. The consultants involved in the implementation will all be personally committed to delivery and will each represent the shared values of the implementation firm. The implementation partner's commitment to delivering value to the customer means that the customer can expect that the implementation will be driven by the business value proposition and, specifically, will not be technically led. The risks of a technically led implementation are considerable. It can result in overspecified and hard-to-use technology and databases full of irrelevant and redundant data in complex and inaccessible structures. Technically led implementations can incur heavy development, support, and maintenance costs and deliver little business value. In contrast, a business value–led implementation will be driven by the business priorities. In a planning application, it will deliver the KPIs and will model the key business drivers completely and elegantly. It will use appropriate technologies to provide the performance, flexibility, clarity, and ease of use that business users require. It will be delivered by a development team whose members have aptitudes for dealing with people, numbers, and business concepts as well as technology.

How to Choose an Implementation Partner (What to Look For)

The implementation services market is very competitive, and the customers for such services are very sophisticated purchasers. Therefore, the companies that survive and prosper in this market have very competitive value propositions and their rates will represent value for money. Unusually low rates in this market should prompt caution and investigation of the supplier's value proposition, because low rates are usually associated with lower skills or lower productivity. However, many suppliers can now deploy project teams that include a mix of onshore and offshore resources and can pass on the lower costs of offshore resources as attractive average rates. The use of offshore resources for development is now so well established that it is unusual for any development project not to use offshore resources to some extent. The actual extent of offshore involvement will depend upon the individual project's characteristics. There is always an additional communication overhead for offshore involvement, but suppliers will be able to show how this is minimized and how that it is more than offset by the other benefits.

The customer's first choice of supplier, particularly for a planning application, would be a firm that has specialist skills in this type of work. Again successive independent customer surveys have shown that specialists outperform all other implementation options. This seems to be because this type of work demands people and business skills as well as special technical competence. Specialist teams have important advantages — a greater level of shared understanding with a commensurably lower communication-overhead means that they are more productive, with more time available for constructive dialogue with the business users of the application, producing a higher-value solution. The role of the specialist is to translate the vision and requirements of the customer into a practical, real-world system. The specialist needs the ability and experience to enter into a dialogue. Sector experience is valuable because it supports communication and understanding, not because it replaces the expertise of the customer.

However, many firms will have preferred-provider arrangements with large generalist suppliers. The main business of such firms is large-scale, routine transactional systems rather than applications built for responsiveness and flexibility. This focus means that specialist skills receive no special priority or encouragement within generalist firms. However, from the customers' point of view, the economies derived from the preferred supplier's volume-related rates on standard projects may offset the inefficiencies of the specialist work. In such cases, it is important to recognize that a trade-off is being made and that the specialist project is going to suffer for the greater good. Be realistic, reduce the scope where possible, and increase the contingencies for cost and time overruns. Forrester (`http://www.forrester.com`) reports that this kind of trade-off is becoming less common as firms move to multi-sourcing arrangements, where they aim to better match suppliers' capabilities to the project requirements, but many firms will find themselves still in this situation.

Because the market for services is highly competitive, and, therefore, would be described by economists as efficient, it is very unlikely that a customer will be able to beat the market; that is, to get a solution implemented for less than the market rate. If it were possible, everyone would do it and there would be a new market configuration. Nevertheless, when budgets are tight, customers may consider trying to mix and match resources from specialist implementation partners, preferred providers, internal resources, and external contractors to achieve the lowest direct project costs. However, these arrangements inevitably add to the complexity of managing an implementation, and either costs or delivery will suffer. Only very experienced project managers would be able to pull off such a feat and would probably know better than to try.

In general, where budgets are tight, the right solution is to focus the scope of the implementation tightly around the capabilities that maximize business value. It becomes particularly critical that the implementation partner be an experienced specialist, capable of recognizing and delivering business value, and that the client trust and follow the implementation partner's advice. Most specialist firms will offer a range of educational events, seminars, or workshops at which they help to keep their customers up to date with developments. These can be good opportunities for potential customers to see the firm's consultants in action and develop a sense of the firm, its values, and its capabilities. It will also be an opportunity to talk to some of the other attendees at the event, who may be past clients of the firm and/or may be from the same sector as the potential customer.

Once the potential customer has made contact with the firm to explore the potential opportunity, they will be in a position to assess the consultant who is assigned to them by the implementation partner. The contact should be a senior consultant with experience in the customer's sector and with the type of application under discussion, and the customer should be able to expect to deal with that individual throughout the implementation — and that the consultant will be actively engaged in the implementation. If this is not the case, the customer is dealing with a salesperson, not a consultant. In the worst case, there can be no guarantee that the promises made by a salesperson can be delivered by the firm. Alternatively, the customer may have been sold on the firm by an "A team" consultant, only to discover that the implementation work is subsequently being passed over to a "B team" consultant. Dealing from the beginning with the consultant who will deliver the work means that the potential customer will also have an early opportunity to assess the credibility and reliability of the consultant and his or her responsiveness to the customer's need for business value.

In general, it makes more sense to assess a firm on its track record and references than on documentation about processes and methodologies. Specialist firms will have developed effective methodologies and practices and will have acquired extensive certifications in relevant technology.

How to Manage an Effective Project

In a planning implementation, it is often difficult to state ahead of time exactly what is required and defining why it is an important part of the project, but it will be important to be able to state what success looks like. It should be sufficient for a good implementation partner, engaged in a good project management framework, to understand the scope and to provide budget and timescale estimates that are realistic. Implementation partners that have been in business for many years will have well-developed engagement support systems, processes, and standards for their project teams. These will include best practice guidance, project management disciplines and systems, resource planning, and time-recording applications.

Using the framework, the customer will be able to maintain control of all the variables that he or she cares about: the business value of the project, the budget, the timescales, and the quality of the deliverable. In other words, the system meets the needs of users, its appearance and usability are right, bugs are absent, and the system outputs are correct. To achieve this, the customer should have complete visibility of all the key activities that keep the project on track: slippage management, with reasons, cost, and time impacts; planning, with responsibilities, tasks, milestones, dependencies, and bottlenecks; issue management, with identification, resolution and replanning; change control processes, with detailed estimates and authorizations; and quality assurance, with user sign-offs, early deliverables, quality reviews, and test after test after test. An experienced implementation partner will have long experience of the things that can throw a project off track and will manage them all carefully. Key project management documents and processes will keep the project on track.

Experienced development team members will all know what they need to do. They will understand their roles in the project and what is expected of them, the time they have, their deliverables, and the dependencies. When anything is unclear, they will push for information and clarification, they will look beyond the current set of tasks and support their fellow team members, they will have everything they need to perform at a high level, and they will proactively anticipate and resolve issues. They will not get bogged down. They will deal professionally and helpfully with business users, using nontechnical language.

Project communications will involve everyone involved in the project: both internally (the end users, the customer's project manager, the project sponsor, internal IT groups, and source system owners) and externally (the implementation project manager, the designer, the technical lead, the configuration manager, the developers, and the software vendor). While these will go a long way toward ensuring success, it is essential that the customer ultimately own the project management process and that the customer engagement be effective, that the business be actively engaged in work on the requirements, and that IT be engaged in providing the appropriate infrastructure. The customer is ultimately responsible for establishing a positive project management–engagement framework from the beginning in order to keep all the people involved in the project (the internal business experts, IT, and the specialist implementation partner) working in harmony.

Summary

PerformancePoint Planning Server is a complex application that can provide solutions for a wide variety of planning, budgeting, and consolidation scenarios. It transforms what business users commonly do in Microsoft Excel spreadsheets into a highly capable, server-based solution without losing the agility and control spreadsheets offer. Because of the complex mix of business and technical aspects in a solution process, there are a few critical project aspects to keep in mind. First, understanding the key stakeholders, their roles, and the support structure helps to identify the human aspects of a solution process. Second, it is essential to view the effort with a solution focus, which requires the proper gathering and understanding of requirements as well as an evaluation of what longer-term objectives may be. This implies that current process and tools, while still considered, aren't the sole factors determining the proper future solution. Finally, acquiring and properly using people with necessary skill sets will help ensure successful delivery. This often involves system integration partners who have significant background and expertise to leverage. Putting together a proper project evaluation and implementation effort can make a significant difference in the deployment of a performance management application solution.

Index

B

C

E

T